The Concept of Marriages of Convenience in EU Free Movement Law

Immigration and Asylum Law and Policy in Europe

Edited by

Elspeth Guild
Valsamis Mitsilegas

VOLUME 53

The titles published in this series are listed at *brill.com/ialp*

The Concept of Marriages of Convenience in EU Free Movement Law

EU and UK Perspectives

By

Aleksandra Ancite-Jepifánova

BRILL | NIJHOFF

LEIDEN | BOSTON

Library of Congress Cataloging-in-Publication Data

Names: Ancite-Jepifánova, Aleksandra, author.
Title: The concept of marriages of convenience in EU free movement law: EU and UK perspectives / by Aleksandra Ancite-Jepifánova.
Description: Leiden ; Boston: Brill/Nijhoff, 2025. | Series: Immigration and asylum law and policy in Europe ; volume 53 | Includes bibliographical references and index. | Summary: "The European Union, commonly described as the largest and most successful voluntary integration project in the contemporary history of mankind, is experiencing challenging times. The past two decades have witnessed two contradictory developments taking place across the continent. On the one hand, the transformation of the EU from an economic to a political community. On the other, the rise of nationalist and eurosceptic sentiments in several Member States. In the area of the free movement of persons, the former process has most clearly manifested itself in three interrelated ways.
Identifiers: LCCN 2024045362 | ISBN 9789004499256 (hardback) | ISBN 9789004499263 (ebook)
Subjects: LCSH: Family reunification–Law and legislation–European Union countries. | Family reunification–Law and legislation–Great Britain. | Emigration and immigration law–European Union countries. | Emigration and immigration law–Great Britain. | Freedom of movement–European Union countries. | Freedom of movement–Great Britain.
Classification: LCC KJC6044 .A97 2025 | DDC 342.2408/2–dc23/eng/20240926
LC record available at https://lccn.loc.gov/2024045362

Typeface for the Latin, Greek, and Cyrillic scripts: "Brill". See and download: brill.com/brill-typeface.

ISSN 1568-2749
ISBN 978-90-04-49925-6 (hardback)
ISBN 978-90-04-49926-3 (e-book)
DOI 10.1163/9789004499263

This book is printed on acid-free paper and produced in a sustainable manner.

Contents

Acknowledgements IX
Abbreviations XI

Introduction 1
1 Setting the Scene: Marriages of Convenience and EU Citizens' Right to Family Reunion 1
2 Limitations 8
3 Sources 8
4 Terminology 11
5 Chapter Outline 14

PART 1
EU and European Human Rights Law

1 **Right to Family Reunion in EU Free Movement Law** 19
1 Introduction 19
2 From 'Market Citizen' to Union Citizen: Evolution of the Concepts of Free Movement of Persons and EU Citizenship 20
3 Right to Family Reunion under the Citizenship Directive 25
4 Derogations from Free Movement Rights 32
5 Conclusion 39

2 **Right to Family Reunion as a Source of Tension between the CJEU and Member States** 41
1 Introduction 41
2 Treating Nationals Worse Than Foreigners: the Phenomenon of Reverse Discrimination 42
3 The Substance of Marriage 46
4 Returning Member State Nationals 47
5 EU Citizens Forming Families in the Host Member State 53
6 Visas for Non-EU Family Members Travelling to the UK 55
7 Family Reunion Cases outside the Scope of the Citizenship Directive 56
8 Marriages of Convenience as the Only Form of Abuse of Rights? 62
9 Conclusion 64

3 **After *Metock*: Marriages of Convenience as an Apple of Discord between the EU and Member States** 66
1 Introduction 66
2 All You Need Is Love? The Controversial Notion of Marriages of Convenience 67
3 The Judgment in *Metock:* Opening a Pandora's Box 70
4 Exploitation of the Vulnerable? EU-8 Nationals in Focus 75
5 UK and Three Other Member States Demanding Change 82
6 Pre-referendum Settlement: an Unprecedented Concession to the UK 86
7 Conclusion 89

4 **Europeanisation of Relationship Standards? Marriages of Convenience in EU Soft Law** 91
1 Introduction 91
2 EU Soft Law in a Nutshell 92
3 EU Soft Law on Marriages of Convenience 97
4 Conclusion 122

5 **The Concept of Marriages of Convenience and European Human Rights Law** 124
1 Introduction 124
2 Articles 12 and 8 of the ECHR in a Nutshell 125
3 Articles 8 and 12 of the ECHR and Immigration Control 128
4 The Legality of Targeting Marriages of Convenience for Immigration Purposes 131
5 ECtHR Case Law on Marriages of Convenience vs EU Free Movement Law 135
6 Conclusion 137

PART 2
UK Law

6 **Historical Development of Family Reunification Provisions in UK Law** 141
1 Introduction 141
2 1948–1977: the End of Free Movement for Commonwealth Nationals 142

3 The 'Primary Purpose Rule' (1977–1997) 144
4 After the 'Primary Purpose Rule': Focus on Pre-wedding Controls 146
5 Certificate of Approval Scheme: Tarring Everyone with the Same Brush 147
6 The Blame Misplaced: Citizenship Directive as a 'Loophole' 153
7 Conclusion 157

7 Marriage Controls during the Pre-Brexit Period 159
1 Introduction 159
2 Pre-marriage Controls: 'Referral and Investigation Scheme' 159
3 Post-marriage Controls 177
4 Conclusion 195

8 Marriage Controls after Brexit 197
1 Introduction 197
2 Position of EU Citizens in the UK after Brexit 197
3 Family Members of EU Citizens in the UK 201
4 Marriages of Convenience Post-Brexit 206
5 Conclusion 214

9 Assessing the Nature of Marriage: Conduct of Investigation 216
1 Introduction 216
2 'Risk Profiles' and Marriages Perceived as 'Suspicious' 216
3 Interview Questions: Focus on Discrepancies and Cohabitation 224
4 Hostile Interviewing Style 227
5 Cases Involving Pregnancy or Childbirth 228
6 Home Visits 229
7 Conclusion 231

10 Legitimising the Illegitimate: Marriages of Convenience and the UK Judiciary 233
1 Introduction 233
2 Burden of Proof 235
3 Focus on Cohabitation and/or Present State of the Relationship 241
4 Definition of Marriages of Convenience 246
5 Cases Involving Pregnancy or Childbirth 257
6 Conclusion 262

Conclusion 265

Annexes

Annex 1 281
Annex 2 284
Annex 3 288
Bibliography 316
Index 343

Acknowledgements

This book is a revised and updated version of my doctoral dissertation that I defended at Queen Mary University of London in January 2021.

Its origins date back to a sunny afternoon in autumn 2011 when I entered the School of Law building at Queen Mary campus in Mile End. I had arrived in London to meet my then future Ph.D. supervisor, who had expressed an interest in my research proposal. Professor Valsamis Mitsilegas greeted me with an open smile and invited me to take a seat. A few months later, in January 2012, I officially embarked on my Ph.D.

The journey towards completing my thesis, however, has not been easy and has taken much longer than I initially expected. I was doing my Ph.D. in the UK part-time whilst simultaneously working in journalism in Germany. Over the following years, I constantly commuted between Bonn, where I worked for the German international broadcaster Deutsche Welle, and London, where I engaged in my research and teaching responsibilities.

Although my mode of research has enabled me to benefit from a truly multicultural and multidisciplinary environment, I was faced with the complex task of sustaining motivation and commitment to my Ph.D. project whilst working in an unrelated field in another country. At Deutsche Welle, I was covering European and world affairs for DW's Russian Service, with Russian and German as the main working languages. In my Ph.D., I delved into the complex intersection of EU, European human rights, and British domestic law. A further challenge was that before commencing my doctoral studies in the UK, my legal background was rather limited. I started with Latvian master's degrees in European Studies and Legal Linguistics that covered EU law only briefly, which meant that I needed to work twice as hard as someone holding an LLM degree from the UK.

Despite all the challenges, my Ph.D. marathon eventually turned out to be one of the most transformative, enriching, and intellectually stimulating experiences of my life that has profoundly changed the way I look at migration, mobility, and citizenship. It has also taught me resilience and the power of small steps, a strategy that helped me keep going every time I was just about to give up. In January 2021 – exactly nine years after I started – I passed my Ph.D. viva with no corrections, an outcome I did not even dare to dream of. Soon after that, I fully transitioned from journalism to academia where I have since expanded my research into the area of asylum.

I am incredibly thankful to all the people without whom completing this study would have been impossible. First, I would like to express my deepest gratitude to my Ph.D. supervisors, Professor Valsamis Mitsilegas and Professor Elspeth Guild, for their understanding, patience, encouragement, insightful comments, suggestions, and support, as well as their flexibility in accommodating my schedule. My sincere appreciation is extended to my Ph.D. thesis examiners, Professor Daniel Wilsher and Professor Kees Groenendijk, who have provided me with rich and detailed feedback and made my thesis defence a delightful experience. I would also like to offer my warmest thanks to my interviewees, who kindly agreed to share their views on my research subject: Nath Gbikpi, senior associate solicitor at Leigh Day; Priya Solanki, barrister at One Pump Court; David Tang, principal solicitor at David Tang & Co; Carla Clarke, legal director of the charity Public Law Project (PLP); and PLP's research fellow Mia Leslie.

This book is a small tribute to all the families separated by borders, immigration laws, and passports and to all the couples whose relationship does not conform to the authorities' normative perceptions of how a 'genuine' marriage should look like. It is partly dedicated to all those whose ability to be together depends on restrictive family reunification rules that – to paraphrase the famous quote by Indian novelist Arundhati Roy – lay down who should be loved by whom, in what way, and how much.

Finally, I dedicate this book to the memory of my great-grandfather, Maxím Fyódorovich Yepifánov (Максим Федорович Епифанов, 1875–1925), who lived his entire life in a small village in the north-east of European Russia until he suddenly died of a stroke at the age of 50. His five surviving children, including my grandfather, ended up scattered across different parts of the then Soviet Union, some of which later became independent states. I visited his village back in 2018. It is no longer on the map, yet the monumental red brick church where my great-grandparents were married still stands – a silent witness of the tumultuous century-long history of wars, revolutions, movements, and constantly shifting borders and boundaries. This is the place where my roots are, and this is where my story began.

Abbreviations

AG	Advocate General
AIT	Asylum and Immigration Tribunal
CJEU	Court of Justice of the European Union
CoA	Certificate of Approval
COMPAS	University of Oxford's Centre on Migration, Policy and Society
CRC	Convention on the Rights of the Child
DG	Directorate General
DRO	Designated Register Office
DVLA	Driver and Vehicle Licensing Agency
EC	European Community
ECHR	European Convention on Human Rights
ECSC	European Coal and Steel Community
ECtHR	European Court of Human Rights
EEA	European Economic Area
EEC	European Economic Community
EESC	European Economic and Social Committee
EMN	European Migration Network
EU	European Union
EU-8	Czech Republic, Estonia, Hungary, Latvia, Lithuania, Poland, Slovakia, and Slovenia
EU-12	Bulgaria, Cyprus, Czech Republic, Estonia, Hungary, Latvia, Lithuania, Malta, Poland, Romania, Slovakia, and Slovenia.
EU-15	Austria, Belgium, Denmark, Finland, France, Germany, Greece, Ireland, Italy, Luxembourg, Netherlands, Portugal, Spain, Sweden, and the UK.
EUCFR	European Union Charter of Fundamental Rights
EComHR	European Commission of Human Rights
EFTA	European Free Trade Association
EUSS	European Union Settlement Scheme
FOI	Freedom of Information
FREEMO	Commission expert group on the right to free movement of persons
FtT	First-Tier Tribunal
GP	General Practitioner
HEUNI	European Institute for Crime Prevention and Control affiliated with the United Nations
IAC	Immigration and Asylum Chamber
ICCPR	International Covenant on Civil and Political Rights
ICE	Immigration Compliance and Enforcement

ICIBI	Independent Chief Inspector of Borders and Immigration
ILPA	Immigration Law Practitioners' Association
ILR	Indefinite Leave to Remain
IMA	Independent Monitoring Authority
IOM	International Organisation for Migration
IRC	Immigration Removal Centre
ISEC	EU programme 'Prevention of and Fight against Crime'
JHA	Justice and Home Affairs
LIBE	European Parliament Committee on Civil Liberties, Justice and Home Affairs
LLR	Limited Leave to Remain
MRAU	Marriage Referral and Assessment Unit
PLP	Public Law Project
SSHD	Secretary of State for the Home Department
TCN	Third-Country National
TFEU	Treaty on the Functioning of the European Union
THB	Trafficking in Human Beings
UDHR	Universal Declaration of Human Rights
UT	Upper Tribunal
UK	United Kingdom
UKVI	UK Visas and Immigration
UN	United Nations
US	United States

Introduction

> Normally, people cannot remember the exact date they first met. I say to them, "Go home, pretend that you are a movie director, and write a detailed script based on facts. Let's say it was 2 o'clock on the 5th of March, it was rainy, you were at the bus station, and she walked past". I want them to write everything together, read it every day, and then when they go for an interview, they will tell the same things.[1]

1 Setting the Scene: Marriages of Convenience and EU Citizens' Right to Family Reunion

The European Union, commonly described as the largest and most successful voluntary integration project in the contemporary history of mankind,[2] is experiencing challenging times. The past two decades have witnessed two contradictory developments taking place across the continent. On the one hand, the transformation of the EU from an economic to a political community. On the other, the rise of nationalist and eurosceptic sentiments in several Member States.

In the area of the free movement of persons, the former process has most clearly manifested itself in three interrelated ways. First, the extension of the personal scope of Treaty rights to non-economic actors. Second, the introduction of EU citizenship. And third, the creation of a general right to permanent residence for EU citizens[3] and their family members. Moreover, during this period, the Union underwent the most significant expansion in its history. Over the nine years from 2004 to 2013, it was acceded by 13 new,

1 Interview with David Tang, principal solicitor at David Tang & Co (London, 20 February 2019).

2 See for instance, an interview with Federica Mogherini, (now former) High Representative of the Union for Foreign Affairs and Security Policy, in Mark Leonard, 'Shaping Europe's Present and Future' (*European Council of Foreign Relations*, 11.01.2019) <www.ecfr.eu/article/commentary_shaping_europes_present_and_future> accessed 2 April 2024.

3 For the sake of brevity, throughout the study, EU, EEA, and Swiss citizens are referred to collectively as 'EU citizens', unless specified otherwise.

 | DOI:10.1163/9789004499263_002

predominantly Central and Eastern European Member States.[4] This led to a significant increase in intra-European mobility. Within a decade following the 2004 enlargement, five million EU-12 nationals relocated to EU-15 Member States,[5] with the UK becoming their principal destination – not least because it immediately opened its labour market to workers from countries that joined the Union in 2004.[6] Over this period, the number of EU-12 nationals residing in the UK increased more than tenfold, from 113,200 in 2004 to 1.5 million in 2014.[7]

Although the rise in free movement provided a significant contribution to EU-15 economies,[8] the public and political debate in some Western European Member States soon began to increasingly focus on the perceived negative effects. In several receiving states, the significant numbers of EU-12 arrivals within a short period triggered the fear of losing control, particularly in light of the recession that hit the global economy in 2008 and 2009. Certain groups of mobile EU citizens[9] were now regarded as a threat to the security and economic prosperity of the host Member States. This provided a platform for populist and racialised discourses about poor or otherwise undesirable Eastern Europeans who 'take jobs' from locals and are involved in the so-called welfare/benefits tourism or in criminality.[10]

Frequently employed in the nationalist and anti-immigrant rhetoric of the Conservative party and further reinforced by local media outlets, such narratives gained particular prominence in the UK, whose electorate has long been

4 In 2004, the EU was joined by ten countries: the Czech Republic, Estonia, Hungary, Latvia, Lithuania, Poland, Slovakia, Slovenia, Malta, and Cyprus. They were followed by Bulgaria and Romania in 2007 and Croatia in 2013.

5 Agniezska Fihel and others, 'Free Movement of Workers and Transitional Arrangements: Lessons from the 2004 and 2007 Enlargements' (Centre of Migration Research, University of Warsaw 2015) 21.

6 Other Member States fully opened their labour markets to this group only in 2011 (except Sweden and Ireland which followed the UK approach).

7 Fihel and others (n 5) 88.

8 See for instance, Commission, 'Employment and Social Developments in Europe 2011' (DG EMPL 2012) 274–75.

9 By 'mobile', the author refers to EU citizens who have exercised their free movement rights. By contrast, the term 'static' is used in the book to designate Member State nationals who find themselves in purely internal situations. For an overview of the distinction between the two categories in the context of the present study, see Chapter 2.

10 For a general discussion on the implications of such discourses, see among others: Sandra Mantu, 'Alternative Views on EU Citizenship' in Carolus Grütters, Sandra Mantu, and Paul Minderhoud (eds), *Migration on the Move* (Brill 2017) and Jean-Michel Lafleur and Elsa Mescoli, 'Creating Undocumented EU Migrants through Welfare: A Conceptualization of Undeserving and Precarious Citizenship' (2018) 52 *Sociology* 480.

amongst the most eurosceptic in the EU.[11] Over the years preceding Brexit, the UK authorities consistently raised concerns about the perceived abuse of free movement. They made regular attempts to persuade EU institutions and other Member States to massively restrict Treaty rights, ultimately threatening to leave the EU altogether. Although the Union finally succumbed to the British demands,[12] this did not affect the outcome of the 2016 Brexit referendum where the majority cast their vote in favour of leaving the EU.[13] Following a lengthy negotiation process, the UK officially ceased to be a member of the Union on 31 January 2020, effectively becoming the first country in the Union's nearly 70-year history to exit from the bloc.

Along with the narratives of 'poverty migration' and criminality which contributed to the negative perception of free movement among British voters, a further major point of contention between the EU and the UK related to the generous family reunion rights enjoyed by mobile EU citizens under EU law. Since the inception of the EU, the possibility for mobile EU citizens to live in the host Member State with their third-country national (TCN) family members has been considered an essential precondition for intra-European mobility. Yet, over the past two decades, the EU approach started to come into considerable tension with domestic family reunification policies in (predominantly Western European) Member States. Aiming to reduce the number of family migrants who could not be selected based on the same criteria as the foreign labour force, a number of governments made family reunification of their own nationals subject to the fulfilment of conditions which are most commonly associated with economic migration, such as high income thresholds, integration conditions, and language tests.[14] By contrast, applying additional requirements to family members of mobile EU citizens is precluded under Directive 2004/38/EC[15] (further referred to as the 'Citizenship Directive'). This

---

11 See for instance, Deanna Demetriou, 'Discourse on Immigration in the UK: Representations and Evaluations of Romanians and Bulgarians as "Benefit Tourists"' (Dphil Thesis, Canterbury Christ Church University 2018); Noah Carl, James Dennison, and Geoffrey Evans, 'European but not European enough: An Explanation for Brexit' (2019) 20 *European Union Politics* 282.

12 See Chapter 3, Section 6.

13 For a discussion on the nexus between the negative perception of free movement and the Brexit vote, see for instance, Sara B Hobolt, 'The Brexit Vote: A Divided Nation, a Divided Continent' (2016) 23 *Journal of European Public Policy* 1259.

14 For a discussion, see Chapter 2, Section 2.

15 Directive 2004/38/EC of the European Parliament and of the Council of 29 April 2004 on the right of citizens of the Union and their family members to move and reside freely within the territory of the Member States amending Regulation (EEC) No 1612/68 and

directive is the principal instrument codifying EU law on the freedom of movement of Union citizens and their family members, which lies at the heart of the present study.

Due to the growing dichotomy between the two sets of rights, family reunion in EU law began to pose a significant challenge to mainstream theories of European integration, centred on the idea that that the readiness of national governments to comply with EU-set rules largely depends on the perceived or real benefits they receive.[16] For some Member States, the gains from the facilitation of free movement through the right to family reunion were no longer viewed as outweighing the loss of sovereignty in migration matters. The growing number of TCN family members claiming Treaty rights began to be seen as a route enabling unwanted foreigners to sidestep restrictive national immigration provisions and was commonly denounced as an abuse of free movement rights.

At the heart of Member States' anxieties have been the so-called marriages of convenience, allegedly contracted between mobile EU citizens and third-country nationals in order to enable the latter to regularise their status. At the European level, several Member States have repeatedly claimed that such arrangements constitute a serious problem and called for limitations on the right to family reunion under the Citizenship Directive. The UK has traditionally been the most concerned about the issue, not least because of its long-standing fears of losing sovereignty over migration from outside the EU. Whilst immediately opening its labour market to nationals of EU-8 Member States, the UK[17] retained national control over non-EU arrivals by securing opt-outs from most of the EU-level measures adopted in the area of immigration, asylum, and border control. The latter included the Schengen regime and Directive 2003/86/EC[18] (further referred to as the 'Family Reunification Directive') regulating family reunification of lawfully resident third-country nationals.

From the mid-2000s, the topic of marriages of convenience involving mobile EU citizens started to gain significant prominence on the British political and media agenda. At the core of this discourse lay gendered and racialised

repealing Directives 64/221/EEC, 68/360/EEC, 72/194/EEC, 73/148/EEC, 75/34/EEC, 75/35/EEC, 90/364/EEC, 90/365/EEC, and 93/96/EEC [2004] OJ L158/77 (Citizenship Directive).

16 See for instance, Richard Perkins and Eric Neumayer, 'Do Membership Benefits Buy Regulatory Compliance? An Empirical Analysis of EU Directives 1978–99' (2007) 8 *European Union Politics* 180, 185–86.

17 Alongside with Ireland.

18 Council Directive 2003/86/EC of 22 September 2003 on the right to family reunification [2003] OJ L251/12 (Family Reunification Directive).

narratives of female nationals of EU-12 Member States who, often guided by facilitators, marry male migrants from the Indian subcontinent for financial gain. Such anxieties have ultimately found expression in a set of legislative measures adopted in the UK in pre-Brexit years. At the very same time, the pressure exercised by Member States prompted EU institutions to respond to their concerns by developing a position on the issue and *inter alia* adopting two soft law instruments aimed at assisting governments in tackling alleged marriages of convenience.

The significance of these developments cannot be overstated. State-exercised controls aiming to determine the authenticity of marriage may significantly impact the position of EU citizens whose close ones have not been fortunate enough to possess the nationality of one of the Member States. First, such measures may come into tension with the objective of protecting the right to family reunion as an intrinsic component of free movement, which is consistently highlighted in CJEU case law.[19] Second, they may pose a challenge to the protection guaranteed to families under European human rights law, particularly Article 8 of the ECHR,[20] Article 7 of the EUCFR[21] (the right to respect for private and family life), Article 12 of the ECHR, and Article 9 of the EUCFR (the right to marry and to found a family). Last but not least, the concept of marriages of convenience for residence purposes may not be easily compatible with the regulation of marital relationships in family law, an area that falls within the exclusive competence of Member States and incorporates a separate set of rights and obligations.

Despite the importance of the issue, the regulation of marriages of convenience in EU free movement law and its impact on national legal systems has been significantly under-studied. In the academic literature, the notion of marriages of convenience has been addressed from various disciplinary perspectives, such as political science, sociology, anthropology, and gender studies, with most of the authors engaging in criticism of the normative division between acceptable and not acceptable marriages for residence purposes. A major limitation of this scholarship, however, is that it predominantly looks at the issue from a domestic perspective, with the EU-dimension being largely neglected.[22] The same refers to the relevant legal literature, which

19 For an analysis, see Chapter 2.

20 European Convention for the Protection of Human Rights and Fundamental Freedoms, CETS No.005 (04.11.1950) (ECHR).

21 Charter of Fundamental Rights of the European Union [2000] OJ C364/01 (EUCFR).

22 For non-legal literature focusing on the UK, see, Katharine Charsley and Michaela Benson, 'Marriages of Convenience and Inconvenient Marriages: Regulating Spousal Migration to Britain' (2012) 26 *Journal of Immigration, Asylum and Nationality Law* 10; Natasha Carver,

primarily considers the subject within the framework of domestic family reunification provisions.[23] The only studies specifically devoted to the regulation of

---

'Displaying Genuineness: Cultural Translation in the Drafting of Marriage Narratives for Immigration Applications and Appeals' (2014) 3 *Families, Relationships and Societies* 271; Anne-Marie D'Aoust, 'A Moral Economy of Suspicion: Love and Marriage Migration Management Practices in the United Kingdom' (2018) 36 *Environment and Planning D: Society and Space* 40; Georgie Wemyss, Nira Yuval-Davis and Kathryn Cassidy, '"Beauty and the Beast": Everyday Bordering and "Sham Marriage" Discourse' (2018) 66 *Political Geography* 151; Daniel Nehring and Clive Sealey, 'Intimate Citizenship and the Tightening of Migration Controls in the United Kingdom' (2020) 54 *Social Policy & Administration* 427. On Austria, see, Irene Messinger, *Schein oder nicht Schein*: *Konstruktion und Kriminalisierung von 'Scheinehen' in Geschichte und Gegenwart* (Mandelbaum 2012). On Belgium see, Maïté Maskens, 'Bordering Intimacy: The Fight against Marriages of Convenience in Brussels' (2015) 33(2) *The Cambridge Journal of Anthropology* 42; Mieke Vandenbroucke, 'Legal-Discursive Constructions of Genuine Cross-Border Love in Belgian Marriage Fraud Investigations' (2020) 17 *Critical Discourse Studies* 175. On Finland, see, Saara Pellander, '"An Acceptable Marriage": Marriage Migration and Moral Gatekeeping in Finland' (2015) 36 *Journal of Family Issues* 1472; Saara Pellander, 'Buy Me Love: Entanglements of Citizenship, Income and Emotions in Regulating Marriage Migration' (2019) *Journal of Ethnic and Migration Studies*. On France, see, Hélène Neveu Kringelbach, '"Mixed Marriage", Citizenship and the Policing of Intimacy in Contemporary France' (2013) University of Oxford: International Migration Institute Working Paper No 77 <www.migrationinstitute.org/publications/wp-77-13> accessed 2 April 2024. On the Netherlands, see, Saskia Bonjour and Betty de Hart, 'A Proper Wife, a Proper Marriage: Constructions of "Us" and "Them" in Dutch Family Migration Policy' (2013) 20 *European Journal of Women's Studies* 61; Apostolos Andrikopoulos, 'Love, Money and Papers in the Affective Circuits of Cross-Border Marriages: Beyond the "Sham"/"Genuine" Dichotomy' (2019) *Journal of Ethnic and Migration Studies*. On Norway, see, Wencke Mühleisen, Åse Røthing and Stine H Bang Svendsen, 'Norwegian Sexualities: Assimilation and Exclusion in Norwegian Immigration Policy' (2012) 15 *Sexualities* 139; Helga Eggebø, 'A Real Marriage? Applying for Marriage Migration to Norway' (2013) 39 *Journal of Ethnic and Migration Studies* 773. For comparative or non-country specific research, see, Anne-Marie D'Aoust, 'In the Name of Love: Marriage Migration, Governmentality, and Technologies of Love' (2013) 7 *International Political Sociology* 258; Federica Infantino, 'Bordering "Fake" Marriages? The Everyday Practices of Control at the Consulates of Belgium, France and Italy in Casablanca' (2014) 1 *Etnografia e ricerca qualitativa* 27.

23 For legal literature focusing on the UK, see, Helena Wray, 'An Ideal Husband? Marriages of Convenience, Moral Gate-keeping and Immigration to the UK' (2006) 8 *European Journal of Migration and Law* 303; Lisa Pilgram, 'Tackling "Sham Marriages": The Rationale, Impact and Limitations of the Home Office's "Certificate of Approval" Scheme' (2009) 23 *Journal of Immigration, Asylum and Nationality Law* 24; Helena Wray, 'The "Pure" Relationship, Sham Marriages and Immigration Control' in Joanna Miles, Perveez Mody and Rebecca Probert (eds) *Marriage Rites and Rights* (Hart 2015). On Austria, see, Daniela Digruber and Irene Messinger, 'Marriage of Residence in Austria' (2006) 8 *European Journal of Migration and Law* 281; Irene Messinger, 'There is Something about Marrying ... The Case of Human Rights vs. Migration Regimes using the Example of Austria' (2013) 2 *Laws*, 376 <https://ideas.repec.org/a/gam/jlawss/v2y2013i4p376-391d29258.html> accessed 2 April 2024.

marriages of convenience in EU free movement law have been conducted by Betty de Hart[24] and Marcello Di Filippo.[25] Both have attempted to critically examine the applicable legal framework by focusing on the soft law adopted by the European Commission (further referred to as the 'Commission') in recent years. Yet, whilst representing an important contribution to the field, their research is limited in its scope and does not address all the critical issues raised by the relevant legal instruments. Furthermore, their studies fall short of providing a comprehensive and systematic analysis of the development of the concept of marriages of convenience in EU law and its relationship with other relevant provisions in the area of the free movement of persons.

The present study aims to contribute to filling this gap. Situated at the complex intersection between EU free movement, human rights, domestic immigration, residence,[26] and family law, it specifically explores the concept of marriages of convenience in so far as it concerns the exercise of Treaty rights by EU citizens and their non-EU family members. Marriages of convenience are viewed here as a legal and social construct employed by the state as an immigration control technique. Within this framework, this research aims to provide a critical analysis of legal grounds that are used or may be used by the state to attack something as sensitive and private as marriage, notwithstanding the protection guaranteed to families under both international human rights and EU free movement law.

On Belgium, see, Marie-Claire Foblets and Dirk Vanheule, 'Marriages of Convenience in Belgium: The Punitive Approach Gains Ground in Migration Law' (2006) 8 *European Journal of Migration and Law* 263. On Denmark, see, Helena Wray, 'Regulating Spousal Migration in Denmark' (2013) 27 *Journal of Immigration, Asylum and Nationality Law* 139. On the US, see, Kerry Abrams, 'Immigration Law and the Regulation of Marriage' (2007) 91 *Minnesota Law Review* 1625; Kerry Abrams, 'Marriage Fraud' (2012) 100 *California Law Review* 1. The only notable exception to date is an article written by Chiara Berneri who provides an overview of EU and ECHR approaches to marriages of convenience and their impact on UK legislation. Due to its limited scope, however, her analysis is rather brief and lacks deeper elaboration of the topic. See, Chiara Berneri, 'Marriages of Convenience: The Limitations of the UK legislation' (2015) 29 *Journal of Immigration, Asylum and Nationality Law* 372.

24 Betty de Hart, 'The Europeanization of Love. The Marriage of Convenience in European Migration Law' (2017) 19 *European Journal of Migration and Law* 281.

25 Marcello Di Filippo, 'Can EU Free Movement Rights be Abused? Critical Remarks on the "Marriages of Convenience Clause"' in Antonio Marcello Calamia (ed) *L'Abuso del Diritto* (G.Giappichelli Editore, 2017).

26 For the sake of precision, a distinction between 'immigration' and 'residence' law is made in this book to separate the domestic legal instruments covering the position of third-country nationals from those applicable to mobile EU citizens, respectively.

With this view, the study is structured around two main research questions: first, it looks at how the concept of marriages of convenience is addressed in EU free movement and European human rights law, and second, it explores how the issue is regulated in UK law. The selection of this country as the case-study is rooted in the fact that, amongst the EU Member States, the UK had consistently been voicing the strongest concerns about the issue, which ultimately led to significant regulatory changes both at the EU and the domestic level. In this context, it is important to note that EU law provisions addressing the issue of marriages of convenience continue to be applicable in the UK post-Brexit – in particular, with respect to UK-resident EU citizens covered by the EU-UK Withdrawal Agreement.[27] The analysis of the relevant EU and UK-level regulations offered in this book reflects the situation up until 31 January 2024.

2 Limitations

The principal limitation of this study is that it does not intend to offer an exhaustive analysis of the concept of marriages of convenience in EU law and only focuses on the area of free movement of persons. Therefore, other instruments addressing this notion, most notably the Family Reunification Directive, are not discussed in the present book. Likewise, when performing an analysis of UK domestic law, the focus of the study lies on the marriage control instruments targeting couples that consist of a mobile EU citizen and a third-country national. A thorough evaluation of measures directed to other groups is outside the remit of this research; the study touches upon these only where it is necessary to ensure the coherence of the argument or where the two settings overlap.

3 Sources

Aiming to examine the research subject from different angles, this study relies on a variety of legal and non-legal sources. First, to explore the development of the concept of marriages of convenience within the general framework of EU free movement law, it draws heavily on EU primary legislation, as well

27 Agreement on the withdrawal of the United Kingdom of Great Britain and Northern Ireland from the European Union and the European Atomic Energy Community [2019] OJ C384/1 (Withdrawal Agreement). For an analysis of the developments in the UK after Brexit, see Chapter 8.

as Directives, Regulations, and several non-binding instruments specifically addressing the issue, such as Council Resolutions and Commission Guidelines. A significant part of the analysis rests on CJEU case law. The dialogue between the EU institutions and Member States is further reflected in different types of Council documents; Commission communications and reports; Member State letters to the Commission and the Presidency; and in the minutes of the meetings of the Commission expert group on the right to free movement of persons (FREEMO). In addition, several Commission-funded studies and Europol reports offer a more in-depth insight into the prevalent discourses on marriages of convenience in different Member States, particularly where it concerns the perceived link between the phenomenon and organised crime. Furthermore, to add a human rights dimension to this research, the study refers to the main instruments of European human rights law, most notably ECHR and EUCFR, and the relevant Strasbourg jurisprudence.

An analysis of the regulation of the issue in UK law is primarily based on legal instruments belonging to two principal categories: UK immigration legislation and measures implementing EU free movement law (a further category dealt with in this book, albeit to a lesser degree, is family law). The key instruments employed in this context are Acts of Parliament, Regulations, Immigration Rules, and non-binding guidance for Home Office staff. As noted above, some of the instruments cover more than one domain and apply to both static UK nationals and mobile EU citizens.

Next, in order to consider how UK courts approach the concept of marriages of convenience, the author has analysed nearly 200 Upper Tribunal (UT)[28] Immigration and Asylum Chamber decisions. In addition, the author has examined several high-profile cases on the issue, delivered by the former Asylum and Immigration Tribunal,[29] the Court of Appeal, the High Court of England and Wales, and the Supreme Court. Furthermore, this study has consulted a large number of other sources, such as Home Office explanatory memorandums; papers and impact assessments; reports of parliamentary debates; political speeches and statements; ICIBI reports; ILPA documents; statements by politicians; media reports; and government statistics. With regard to the latter, it should be stressed that there is a lack of publicly available data related to the identification of marriages of convenience. Although some numbers have

28 The Upper Tribunal is responsible for hearing appeals against decisions made by the First-tier Tribunal, the court of first instance in the UK.

29 The Tribunal was abolished in 2010 and its functions transferred to the new Asylum and Immigration Chamber of the First-tier Tribunal.

been disclosed following the author's FOI requests to the Home Office,[30] these have not been answered in full.

Furthermore, to provide a concise overview of pre-Brexit referendum negotiations between the UK and the EU and the subsequent developments, this study has mainly looked at documents concerning a new settlement for the UK within the EU, which ultimately never entered into force due to Brexit, as well as the EU-UK Withdrawal Agreement, UK Withdrawal Agreement Act,[31] and the EU Settlement Scheme (EUSS).[32] Additionally, where it is relevant, the study also refers to the legislation of European countries other than the UK; a comparative analysis of the respective aspects, however, falls outside the scope of this book.

Furthermore, to develop a better understanding of the operation of marriage controls in practice, the author conducted semi-structured interviews with three London-based immigration practitioners who deal with family reunion cases on a daily basis: Nath Gbikpi, senior associate solicitor at Leigh Day; David Tang, principal solicitor at David Tang & Co; and Priya Solanki, barrister at One Pump Court. In addition, the author interviewed representatives of the Public Law Project (PLP), an independent legal charity which aims to improve access to justice: PLP's legal director Carla Clarke and research fellow Mia Leslie. The meetings took place in person in February 2019 and online via the Zoom platform in November-December 2023, with the list of key questions being sent to the discussants beforehand. The author also held an informal conversation with a Commission representative involved in drafting a Handbook on the issue of marriages of convenience,[33] which took place in March 2017 in Brussels. As opposed to a formal interview, the chosen discussion format allowed the author's interviewee to talk more in-depth about the drafting procedure and share their views on specific provisions of the document. The perspectives of the author's informants are essential for understanding the rationale behind various elements of marriage controls and the practical implications of such measures for the individuals concerned. The information obtained has been used accordingly throughout this study to strengthen its argument.

---

30 Ministerial department of the UK government, responsible for Home Affairs.

31 European Union (Withdrawal) Act 2018 (WA 2018) as amended by European Union (Withdrawal Agreement) Act 2020.

32 See Chapter 8 for more details.

33 Commission, 'Staff Working Document – Handbook on addressing the issue of alleged marriages of convenience between EU citizens and non-EU nationals in the context of EU law on free movement of EU citizens' SWD(2014) 284 final.

Finally, completion of the present analysis would not have been possible without consulting the rich academic literature on various issues closely intertwined with the subject matter. In addition to the above-listed scholarship, which explicitly addresses the concept of marriages of convenience, this research engages with studies on several other interrelated topics, such as: the general development of EU free movement law and citizenship; the right to family reunion and the concept of abuse in EU law; the relevant fundamental rights; family reunification rules in several Member States and the situation in the UK; as well as tensions between the EU and national governments. Given the plethora of literature available in these fields, the choice of sources has been inevitably dictated by their quality, novelty, and relevance to the topic of this study.

4 Terminology

4.1 *'Marriages of Convenience'*

As will be shown in Chapter 3, the concept of marriage contracted in order to secure the right of residence for the foreign spouse has originated in the national domains. It is designated in domestic legal and public discourses by various terms, such as 'marriages of convenience', 'residence marriages', 'sham', 'bogus', 'fake', 'false', 'fictitious', 'fraudulent', 'pro forma' marriages, as well as 'marriage fraud', the term most commonly used in the US and Canada. Whilst the definition(s) of the relevant concept will be discussed in subsequent chapters, the EU-level instruments adopted in the area of free movement law invariably employ the term 'marriages of convenience'. By contrast, the UK legislation on the issue uses both the terms 'marriages of convenience' and 'sham marriages' to refer to the phenomenon in different legal settings.

To avoid unnecessary confusion, this study adopts the terminology used in EU documents and consistently employs the term 'marriages of convenience'; the term 'sham marriage' is only used to highlight the terminological differences between the various pieces of UK domestic law. Another exception is direct quotations where different terms are used interchangeably; in such cases, the exact wording of the source material has been reproduced. It should also be noted that the term 'fraudulent marriages' in EU law has a meaning distinct from 'marriages of convenience' and relates to cases where individuals rely on false documentation to claim Treaty rights.[34] Furthermore,

34 For an analysis, see Chapter 1, Section 4.2.1.

for the purposes of this research, the concept of 'marriages of convenience' shall normally be understood as including the analogous concept of 'registered partnerships of convenience'; this point is specifically addressed in the study where relevant.

4.2 *'Citizen' v 'National'*

Although the terms 'nationality' and 'citizenship' are widely regarded as synonymous, some authors draw a distinction between the two, arguing that the former is a concept of international law and the latter belongs to the municipal law domain. Whilst 'citizenship' is specifically linked with the enjoyment of civil and political rights, 'nationality' is considered to be broader and covers all those who formally belong to the state.[35] Without engaging in this very interesting debate, the present study accordingly employs the term 'nationality' in the meaning of the European Convention on Nationality. The relevant concept is understood there as 'the legal bond between a person and a State', which 'does not indicate the person's ethnic origin'.[36]

The notion of EU citizenship, meanwhile, does not seem to easily fit within this framework, not least due to its conceptual ambiguity.[37] Notwithstanding that, Article 20 (1) TFEU[38] states that 'every person holding the nationality of a Member State shall be a citizen of the Union' and '[c]itizenship of the Union shall be additional to and not replace national citizenship.' Given that Member States enjoy exclusive competence to decide upon who their nationals are,[39] it has been left to the governments to impose their own understanding of nationality onto EU institutions,[40]

---

35 For an overview of the relevant literature, see, Hennie Strydom, 'The Theory of Citizenship: A Reappraisal' (1985) 18 *The Comparative and International Law Journal of Southern Africa* 103.

36 European Convention on Nationality ETS No.166 (06.11.1997), art 2.

37 For a critical discussion on EU citizenship, see among others, Dimitry Kochenov, 'The Essence of EU Citizenship Emerging from the Last Ten Years of Academic Debate: Beyond the Cherry Blossoms and the Moon?' (2013) 62 *International and Comparative Law Quarterly* 97; Jo Shaw, 'EU Citizenship: Still a Fundamental Status? in Rainer Bauböck (ed) *Debating EU Citizenship* (Springer 2019).

38 Consolidated versions of the Treaty on European Union and the Treaty on the Functioning of the European Union [2016] OJ C202/1 (TFEU).

39 Ibid, arts 3 and 4 *a contrario*.

40 In this context, it is peculiar that not all nationals of Member States are recognised as such for the purposes of free movement law. Prior to the UK accession to the then Community in 1973, the Dutch government demanded that the UK adopt a unilateral declaration limiting the scope of its nationals who would be covered by the Treaty. The UK authorities did so, essentially depriving migrants from former British colonies of the right to free

notwithstanding the fact that this would determine the scope of application of EU law.[41]

For the sake of clarity, the present study refers to 'nationals' or 'nationality' to emphasise the individual's formal belonging to a particular state. Meanwhile, the terms 'citizens' or 'citizenship' are used here exclusively in the meaning of 'EU citizens' or 'EU citizenship' as defined under Article 20 (1) TFEU. The designation 'third-country national' is employed in the book to cover any individual who is not considered an EU citizen, including stateless persons. Terms such as 'foreigner', 'foreign national', 'non-EU national', and 'migrant' also refer to this group and should be regarded as synonymous with the term 'third-country national' for the purposes of this research.

4.3 *'Family Reunion' v 'Family Reunification'*

Although the terms 'family reunion' and 'family reunification' describe the same process, the two are employed in separate legal settings. Whilst the concept of 'family reunification' is typically used in domestic contexts, 'family reunion' is the wording most commonly found in the area of EU free movement law. For the purposes of this study, 'family reunion' should hence be understood as entry into or residence in a Member State by the TCN family members of a mobile EU citizen. Conversely, when referring to 'family reunification', the author is referring to entry into or residence in a particular country by family members of its static nationals or residents other than mobile EU citizens, including refugees and persons under international protection.

---

movement. The link between the UK declaration and EU citizenship was later endorsed by the CJEU in Case C-192/99 *Kaur* [2001] ECR I-01237, para 27. For an analysis, see, Dora Kostakopoulou, *Citizenship, Identity and Immigration in the European Union* (Manchester University Press 2001) 43–4; Dimitry Kochenov, 'Ius Tractum of Many Faces: European Citizenship and the Difficult Relationship between Status and Rights' (2009) 15 *Columbia Journal of European Law* 169, 188–90.

41 Although the determination of nationality must be exercised with 'due regard to Community law'. Case C-369/90 *Micheletti and Others* [1992] ECR I-04239, para 10. For general criticism of the 'derivative' nature of EU citizenship, see, Kochenov, 'Ius Tractum of Many Faces' (n 40); Helen Oosterom-Staples, 'The Triangular Relationship Between Nationality, EU Citizenship and Migration in EU Law: A Tale of Competing Competences' (2018) 65 *Netherlands International Law Review* 431.

5 Chapter Outline

The book is structured into two parts, comprising five chapters each. The first part looks at how the concept of marriages of convenience is addressed in EU free movement and European human rights law. The second part examines the regulation of the issue in UK law and its compliance with EU law (or, more recently, the EU-UK Withdrawal Agreement) in so far as it concerns the residence rights of EU citizens and their family members.

Chapter 1 aims to demonstrate what impact a marriage to an EU citizen may have on the TCN spouse's residence status. First, the evolution of EU citizenship and the extent to which it is moving away from market citizenship is briefly explored. Next, the chapter addresses the position of TCN spouses of Union citizens – in particular, in which situations do they fall within the scope of beneficiaries of the Treaty rights. The final sections of the Chapter are devoted to the relevant provisions of the Citizenship Directive, including the concept of abuse of free movement rights. Chapters 2 and 3 examine the extent to which the development of the concept of marriages of convenience in EU law reflects the Member States' concerns about the perceived abuse of free movement rights. Chapter 2 provides an overview of the key CJEU jurisprudence in the field, whereby Chapter 3 explores the Member States' positions on the issue and the EU institutions' responses to their concerns. Chapter 4 contains a critical analysis of the relevant soft law measures adopted by the Commission in recent years. Chapter 5 deals with the concept of marriages of convenience in ECtHR case law, particularly focusing on Articles 8 and 12 of the ECHR.

Chapters 6 to 10 are devoted to the concept of marriages of convenience in UK domestic law in the context of the implementation of the Citizenship Directive and the decision of the UK to leave the EU. In particular, the chapters explore if and how the relevant concept is reflected in UK law applicable to couples consisting of UK-resident EU citizens and third-country nationals. Chapter 6 provides a brief historical overview of the development of UK domestic family reunification provisions with a focus on the perceived abuse of law. The following chapters offer a contemporary perspective on the legislation covering intended and existing marriages between EU citizens and their TCN partners. Chapter 7 examines the situation in the UK during the pre-Brexit years. It begins by exploring how the UK dealt with the limitations of EU law concerning pre-marriage controls. With this aim, the chapter discusses the implications of the 'referral and investigation scheme', introduced as part of the then 'hostile environment' policy in 2014, and shows how it affected the position of EU citizens. The chapter then moves on to post-marriage controls and assessing if and how EU law protected the families of mobile EU citizens from antagonistic policies of the host Member State. To answer this question, the chapter performs an analysis of the implementation of relevant provisions of the Citizenship Directive into UK law. Chapter 8 proceeds to explore the relevant developments in the UK after Brexit, whereby Chapter 9 describes Home Office practices in selecting and investigating suspicious marriages, as well as evaluating their compatibility with EU law. Chapter 10 contains an analysis of the UK jurisprudence on marriages of convenience. By focusing on the relevant UT decisions, it seeks to determine how British courts have approached the relevant national provisions and to what degree their interpretations comply with EU law.

PART 1

EU and European Human Rights Law

CHAPTER 1

Right to Family Reunion in EU Free Movement Law

1 Introduction

Over the decades, the institutions of first the EEC and later the EU have gradually expanded the free movement rights of Member State nationals, ultimately transforming them from purely economic agents into Union citizens. Since the very inception of the then Community, the right of an individual to enjoy family life with their close ones has traditionally been viewed as an intrinsic component of free movement. This approach has been further cemented in the Citizenship Directive.[1]

The purpose of this chapter is to set out the general legislative framework for further analysis by showing how the Directive regulates the position of non-EU family members. The chapter begins by providing a brief overview of the evolution of free movement rights and EU citizenship and the extent to which it is departing from the purely economic paradigm. Following that, it moves on to specifically examine the relevant provisions of the Citizenship Directive. First, by exploring under what conditions EU citizens may benefit from the right to family reunion and what impact a marriage to an EU citizen may have on the non-EU national's residence status. Second, it addresses the question, on what grounds can the right to family reunion be limited? In this context, the chapter focuses on two sets of provisions in the Directive which, as will be seen further, the UK authorities have relied on to tackle perceived marriages of convenience: those related to public policy and abuse of rights.

1 Directive 2004/38/EC of the European Parliament and of the Council of 29 April 2004 on the right of citizens of the Union and their family members to move and reside freely within the territory of the Member States amending Regulation (EEC) No 1612/68 and repealing Directives 64/221/EEC, 68/360/EEC, 72/194/EEC, 73/148/EEC, 75/34/EEC, 75/35/EEC, 90/364/EEC, 90/365/EEC and 93/96/EEC [2004] OJ L158/77 (Citizenship Directive).

 | DOI:10.1163/9789004499263_003

2 From 'Market Citizen' to Union Citizen: Evolution of the Concepts of Free Movement of Persons and EU Citizenship

2.1 *On the Way towards the Citizenship Directive*

The roots of today's European Union date back to the post-war years, commonly associated with economic reconstruction and the emergence of federalist ideas. In 1951, six European countries – France, West Germany, Italy, the Netherlands, Belgium, and Luxembourg – created the European Coal and Steel Community (ECSC), which abolished nationality-based restrictions with regards to the employment of nationals of other Member States.[2] At the time, however, the scope of the labour force admitted was merely confined to qualified workers in the coal and steel industry. Yet, these limitations were soon to be lifted. In 1957, the governments of the six ECSC Member States signed the Treaty establishing the European Economic Community.[3] The document, known as the Treaty of Rome, signalled a shift away from the sector-based approach towards full economic integration, as well as the course taken towards a political union. The Treaty expanded the right to free movement to all Community workers, irrespective of their field of employment. Another crucial principle enshrined in the document was that of non-discrimination on the grounds of nationality, provided that nationals of other Member States were to be treated equally with nationals of the host Member State with regards employment, remuneration and other working conditions.[4]

The subsequent years were crucial in terms of developing secondary legislation which gave substance to, as some commentators call it, an 'incipient form' of the European citizenship.[5] A transitional period, during which there was no full-fledged free movement, was finalised by the adoption of two key documents defining the scope of Treaty-based rights: Regulation 1612/68[6] and

2 Treaty Establishing the European Coal and Steel Community, 261 UNTS 140 (18.04.1951) (ECSC Treaty), art 69.

3 Treaty Establishing the European Economic Community, 298 UNTS 11 (25.03.1957) (EEC Treaty).

4 Ibid, arts 7 and 48(2).

5 See for instance, Richard Plender, 'An Incipient Form of European Citizenship' in Francis G Jacobs (ed.), *EU Law and the Individual* (North Holland 1976) (as cited in Dimitry Kochenov and Richard Plender, 'EU Citizenship: From an Incipient Form to an Incipient Substance? The Discovery of the Treaty Text' (2012) 37 *European Law Review* 369, 372).

6 Regulation (EEC) No 1612/68 of the Council of 15 October 1968 on freedom of movement for workers within the Community [1968] OJ L257/2.

Directive 68/360.[7] From then on, for nearly forty years, both documents served as the main source for the rights of Member State nationals under the free movement provisions. At this stage, however, the measures adopted to facilitate the free movement and residence rights of mobile Member State nationals were strictly confined to those engaged in economic activity. The only exception were workers who had ceased their occupational activities in the host Member State but wished to stay there.[8]

Furthermore, the secondary legal instruments limited the *ratione personae* of free movement to those holding nationality of a Member State.[9] It must be noted that the original EEC Treaty, apparently, did not foresee such an interpretation; indeed, it simply referred to 'workers' in the broadest sense of the word, drawing no distinction between nationals and residents of a Member State. Yet, when enacting the secondary legislation, the Council chose to apply this concept in a way that might not have been intended by the Treaty-makers. As a consequence, a significant part of the European labour force was excluded from participation in the development of the internal market. The restrictive approach was dictated by political reasons, in particular, by anti-immigration discourses, often race and class-based, that were gaining power in the political agendas of Member States during the 1960s.[10] As Dora Kostakopoulou observes, '[s]ince migrant workers were not regarded as equal participants in European societies, they could not be rightful beneficiaries of freedom of movement.'[11]

From the 1970s onwards, it was the CJEU that began to progressively play the most substantial role in transforming the perception of Member State nationals from a mere factor of production to the so-called, 'market citizens'.[12] Having consistently followed the aim of creating an 'ever-closer union among the European peoples' as set out in the Treaty of Rome[13] and subsequent

7 Council Directive 68/360/EEC of 15 October 1968 on the abolition of restrictions on movement and residence within the Community for workers of Member States and their families [1968] OJ L257/13.

8 EEC Treaty, art 48(3)(d).

9 Reg 1612/68, art 1 and Dir 360/70, art 1.

10 Dora Kostakopoulou, *Citizenship, Identity and Immigration in the European Union* (Manchester University Press 2001) 42–43. For more details on Member States' approaches to immigration during this period, see Chapter 2, Section 2.

11 Ibid 43.

12 For an analysis, see, Ferdinand Wollenschläger, 'New Fundamental Freedom Beyond Market Integration: Union Citizenship and its Dynamics for Shifting the Economic Paradigm of European Integration' (2011) 17 *European Law Journal* 1.

13 Preamble to EEC Treaty.

Treaties,[14] the Court favoured a wide and inclusive interpretation of the concept of 'worker'. It stated that any person would fall within the definition, provided that they are pursuing a 'genuine and effective' activity for remuneration and the work is not purely marginal and ancillary.[15] The Court also expanded this concept to persons whose income from employment activities was insufficient and thus had to be supplemented by social benefits paid by the host Member State.[16]

In the 1980s and early 1990s, the Court extended the scope of those eligible for free movement rights to those indirectly contributing to the economic objectives of the Community: students,[17] service recipients,[18] and consumers.[19] The CJEU approach was subsequently codified in three directives which extended the right to free movement to all mobile Member State nationals, both economically active and inactive, provided that the latter satisfy the self-sufficiency condition.[20]

The process of transforming 'market citizens' into members of a political community culminated in the introduction of Union citizenship in the Maastricht Treaty[21] in 1992, a status that provided its beneficiaries with a set of novel, including political, rights. From then on, EU citizenship has been subject to rich and controversial academic debate.[22] Yet, whilst a comprehensive analysis of the developments in the field falls outside the scope of the present research, it is important to note that governments have demonstrated

14 Almost the same wording is found *inter alia* in the Preamble to Consolidated versions of the Treaty on European Union and the Treaty on the Functioning of the European Union [2016] OJ C202/1 (TFEU).

15 Case 53/81 *Levin* [1982] ECR 01035, para 17.

16 *Kempf v Staatssecretaris van Justitie*, Case 139/85.

17 Case 293/83 *Gravier* [1985] ECR 00593.

18 Joined Cases 286/82 and 26/83 *Luisi and Carbone* [1984] ECR 00377; Case 186/87 *Cowan* [1989] ECR 00195.

19 Case C-362/88 *GB-INNO-BM* [1990] ECR I-00667.

20 Council Directive 90/364/EEC of 28 June 1990 on the right of residence [1990] OJ L 180/26; Council Directive 90/365/EEC of 28 June 1990 on the right of residence for employees and self-employed persons who have ceased their occupational activity [1990] OJ L180/28; Council Directive 93/96/EEC of 29 October 1993 on the right of residence for students [1993] OJ L317/59.

21 Treaty on European Union [1992] OJ C191/1 (Treaty of Maastricht).

22 See among others, Dimitry Kochenov, 'Ius Tractum of Many Faces: European Citizenship and the Difficult Relationship between Status and Rights' (2009) 15 *Columbia Journal of European Law* 169; Kochenov and Plender (n 5); Helen Oosterom-Staples, 'The Triangular Relationship Between Nationality, EU Citizenship and Migration in EU Law: A Tale of Competing Competences' (2018) 65 *Netherlands International Law Review* 431.

no political will to extend Treaty rights to long-term residents.[23] On the contrary, upon the introduction of Union citizenship, the nationals-only approach found its way into primary law,[24] a clear indication that the perceived need to protect state sovereignty remained the key factor determining the scope of the new concept.[25]

2.2 *Citizenship Directive*

Introduction of the status of EU citizenship in the Maastricht Treaty paved the way for the consolidation of the piece-meal approach to free movement. This process ultimately manifested itself in the adoption of the Citizenship Directive on 29 April 2004, which coincided with the largest single expansion in the Union's history involving ten new Member States. By integrating all the prior legislation covering the field, the Directive pursues a teleological approach by providing new rights without limiting the existing ones.[26] Whilst giving legislative expression to the right of movement and residence conferred by Articles 20(2)(a) and 21(1) TFEU, the Directive introduced a gradual system governing residence in the host Member States. The stages of residence are differentiated by its duration, as well as the rights attached and the conditions to be fulfilled.

Article 6 of the Directive provides Union citizens and their family members[27] the right to reside in a host Member State for up to three months with the only requirement being the possession of a valid identity card or passport. Article 7(1) of the Directive confers the right of residence in another Member State for a period of longer than three months to three different groups of EU citizens and their respective family members: (a) workers and self-employed persons, (b) those who are not economically active but have sufficient resources for themselves and family members, as well as comprehensive sickness insurance, and (c) students.

Workers and self-employed persons remain the most privileged group of EU citizens with regards to their entitlement to free movement rights. Unlike

23 Several pressure groups invited the 1996 EU Intergovernmental Conference to do so but to no avail. Dora Kostakopoulou, 'Nested "Old" and "New" Citizenships in the European Union: Bringing out the Complexity' (1999) 5 *Columbia Journal of European Law* 389, 406.

24 TFEU, art 20(1).

25 Siofra O'Leary, *European Union Citizenship: Options* for *Reform* (IPPR 1996) 91 (as cited in Kostakopoulou, *Citizenship, Identity and Immigration in the European Union* (n 10) 55).

26 The CJEU explicitly stated that 'Union citizens cannot derive less rights from that directive than from the instruments of secondary legislation which it amends or repeals'. Case C-127/08 *Metock and Others* [2008] ECR I-06241, para 59.

27 The position of family members is specifically explored in Section 3 below.

other groups listed in Article 7, they are exempt from the self-sufficiency and comprehensive sickness insurance requirements. Union citizens who have ceased their economic activity may retain their status of workers or self-employed persons in a number of situations, such as illness or involuntary unemployment.[28] Furthermore, retired workers and self-employed persons, or those who have become permanently incapacitated, can continue to reside in the host Member State, provided that conditions pertaining to their length of work and residence are satisfied.[29]

The third category of individuals who fall within the scope of Article 7(1) is EU citizen students. The right of residence of this group is subject to possession of comprehensive health insurance and the availability of sufficient resources for themselves and their family members.[30] It must be noted that students who are at the same time engaged in an employment activity fall within the definition of 'worker' and therefore are not subject to restrictions reserved to the student category.[31]

Article 14 of the Directive, in conjunction with Recital 16 of its Preamble, sets out the principles Member States should respect when verifying if the conditions for the retention of residence rights are satisfied, as well as regulating the circumstances under which expulsion may follow. First, it is clarified that Member States are prohibited from carrying out systematic checks to verify that the conditions of residence under Article 7 are fulfilled, and instead can only examine 'specific cases where there is a reasonable doubt' about that.[32] Second, the Preamble specifies that beneficiaries of the residence rights should not be expelled, as long as they do not become an unreasonable burden on the social assistance system of the host Member State.[33] Moreover, their recourse to social assistance shall not be automatically followed by expulsion.[34] It is also highlighted that expulsion of workers, self-employed persons, or job-seekers is prohibited in all situations,[35] except for public policy or public security grounds.[36]

---

28 Citizenship Directive, art 7(3).

29 Ibid art 17(1).

30 Ibid art 7(1)(c).

31 Case C-46/12 *L. N.* ECLI:EU:C:2016:674, para.48. Working students also enjoy a more advantageous position with regard to family reunion. See Section 3 below.

32 Citizenship Directive, art 14(2).

33 Ibid recital 16.

34 Ibid art 14(3).

35 As long as job-seekers continue to seek employment and have a genuine chance of being engaged. See ibid art 14(4)(b).

36 Ibid recital 16, art 14(4). For more details, see Section 4.1 below.

One of the most substantial innovations introduced by the Directive is a general right to permanent residence for EU citizens and their family members. Whilst in prior legislation this right was limited to workers and self-employed persons and their family members in several specific situations,[37] the Directive extended it to all its beneficiaries who have continuously resided in the host Member State for five years.[38] Those with a permanent status no longer need to satisfy the conditions set out in Article 7 and must be treated equally with the nationals of a particular Member State in all areas covered by the Treaty, including access to welfare.[39] Further, permanent residents enjoy stronger protection against expulsion.[40] According to Article 16(4), this status may be lost after the consecutive absence from the host Member State for at least two years.

3 Right to Family Reunion under the Citizenship Directive

3.1 *Rights of Family Members as Derivative Rights*

Although the TFEU or the preceding Treaties do not contain a provision on family reunion, the secondary legislation in the area of free movement rights has addressed this issue since the very creation of the Community. The right of workers to live in the host Member State with their family members was already enshrined in the first instruments which were issued during the transitional period.[41] Over the subsequent decades, equivalent rights were granted to family members of service providers,[42] persons who had ceased their economic activity,[43] and those who were not carrying out economic activities, at all.[44]

37 Such as retirement and permanent incapacity to work, subject to certain conditions. See Regulation (EEC) No 1251/70 of the Commission of 29 June 1970 on the right of workers to remain in the territory of a Member State after having been employed in that State [1970] OJ L142/24, arts 2 and 3(1). Equivalent provisions for self-employed persons and their family members were established by arts 2 and 3 of the Council Directive 75/34/EEC of 17 December 1974 concerning the right of nationals of a Member State to remain in the territory of another Member State after having pursued therein an activity in a self-employed capacity [1970] OJ L 14/10.

38 Citizenship Directive, art 16.

39 Ibid arts 16(1) and 24.

40 See Section 4.1 below.

41 Regulation 15/61 [1961] JO 1073/61, art 11; Regulation 38/64 [1964] JO 965/64, art 17.

42 Council Directive 73/148/EEC of 21 May 1973 on the abolition of restrictions on movement and residence within the Community for nationals of Member States with regard to establishment and the provision of services [1973] OJ L172/14, art 1(1)(c) and (d).

43 Reg 1251/70, art 1; Dir 75/34, art 1.

44 Dir 90/364, art 1(2); Dir 90/365, art 1(2); Dir 93/96, art 1.

The decision to grant Member State nationals the right to be joined by their family members seems, at least at the outset, to have been primarily dictated by economic rather than humanitarian considerations. The main focus of the Community institutions in post-war years was on the need to encourage unemployed Italian workers to move to regions with a shortage of labour, such as France or Germany. It was therefore considered that precluding family members from accompanying migrant workers in the host Member State would diminish their incentive to relocate which would consequently seriously impede freedom of movement and the creation of the single market.[45] This logic is clearly reflected *inter alia* in the Preamble of Regulation 1612/68, which states that 'freedom of movement constitutes a fundamental right of workers and their families' and that 'obstacles to the mobility of workers shall be eliminated, in particular as regards the worker's right to be joined by his family and the conditions for the integration of that family into the host country'.

However, in the subsequent stages of its development, the EU chose to depart from a purely economic paradigm and started to view the right to family reunion from a broader social and civic perspective, with the CJEU taking the leading role in transforming the original approach. In a number of judgments, the Court reminded Member States of the need to respect family life protected under EUCFR[46] and ECHR[47] and held that by enabling EU citizens to enjoy family life, the host Member State would facilitate the EU citizen's integration into its society.[48] Notably, the shift was directed not only towards improving the position of mobile EU citizens who wished to enjoy their family life, but also enhancing the protection of their TCN family members who, with the introduction of the Citizenship Directive, were provided with an opportunity to obtain an independent, including permanent, right of residence, subject to certain conditions.

Under the Directive, family members of mobile EU citizens, irrespective of their nationality, are entitled to take up employment or self-employment in the host Member State.[49] Should their planned period of residence exceed

45 For an analysis, see Chiara Berneri, *Family Reunification in the EU* (Hart 2017) 26–28.

46 Charter of Fundamental Rights of the European Union [2000] OJ C364/01 (EUCFR).

47 European Convention for the Protection of Human Rights and Fundamental Freedoms, CETS No.005 (04.11.1950) (ECHR). Case C-60/00 *Carpenter* [2002] ECR I-06279, paras 41–42; Case C-109/01 *Akrich* [2003] ECR I-09607, para 58; Case C-304/14 *CS* ECLI:EU:C:2016:674, para 36.

48 Case 59/85 *Reed* [1986] ECR 01283, para 28.

49 Citizenship Directive, art 23. The rights of family members are also recognised in recital 5 of the Preamble that provides that '[t]he right of all Union citizens to move and reside freely within the territory of the Member States should (…) be also granted to their family members, irrespective of nationality'.

three months, Member States must issue non-EU family members a residence card. In contrast to EU citizens relocating to the host Member State, who only *may* be asked to register with the competent authorities, in the case of TCN family members, such a requirement is mandatory.[50] It is nonetheless clarified that a residence card merely serves to attest the existing rights under EU law and cannot be made a precondition for their exercise.[51]

Up until the acquisition of a permanent residence permit, the rights of family members of EU citizens are derivative in nature. As will be explored below, their existence depends on two key conditions: a family relation to a Member State national and the exercise of free movement rights by the primary beneficiary. There are nonetheless situations when these rights can be transferred into being autonomous: the death or departure of the EU citizen from the host Member State, as well as divorce, annulment of marriage, or termination of a registered partnership, subject to certain conditions. Such measures are introduced by the Directive for the first time and primarily affect the position of non-EU nationals: prior to that the couple had to stay married in order for the TCN spouse to enjoy the right of residence and economic activity, whereby the only option for the latter to obtain an independent right of residence would typically be naturalisation.

Article 12(1) guarantees protection to family members of EU citizens, who are EU citizens themselves, in the event of the death or departure of the principal. According to the Directive, such events do not affect the right of residence of the relevant family members in so far as they satisfy either of the conditions set out in Article 7(1). Article 12(2) expressly refers to the rights of non-EU family members in the event of the death of the EU principal. It states that family members may retain their right of residence in such a situation, provided that they (a) have been residing in the host Member State as family members for at least one year before the Union citizen's death and (b) fulfil the requirements equivalent to those set out in Article 7(1). If these conditions are satisfied, TCN family members 'retain their right of residence exclusively on a personal basis', meaning that the nature of their rights transforms from derivative into autonomous.

Unlike the provisions of Article 12(1) dealing with EU citizen family members, Article 12(2) does not protect the residence rights of non-EU nationals whose principal has left the host Member State. Certain categories of persons can nonetheless retain such rights under other provisions of the Directive.

50 Emphasis added.

51 Citizenship Directive, art 25(1).

Article 12(3), for instance, provides that, in the event of the death or departure of the EU principal, their children in education in the host Member State can continue living there until the completion of their studies. The right to reside is also granted to their other parent who has 'actual custody' of them, irrespective of the parent's nationality.

Another option is to rely on Article 13, which provides for retention of residence in the event of divorce, annulment of marriage, or termination of registered partnership. Similarly to Article 12(1), Article 13(1) stipulates that such events do not affect the right of residence of family members who are EU citizens themselves, given that they satisfy the conditions set out in Article 7(1). By contrast, TCN family members retain this right only in a number of particular scenarios set out in Article 13(2). First, prior to initiation of the divorce, annulment or termination proceedings, the relevant union needs to have lasted at least three years, including one year in the host Member State.[52] It is assumed that the country/countries in which the couple has previously lived are irrelevant. Moreover, the one year of residence in the host Member State does not necessarily have to occur immediately before the start of proceedings.[53] In a second scenario, the TCN spouse should have, by agreement or by court order, custody of or access to the EU citizen's children.[54] Alternatively, the spouse of an EU citizen should have suffered from 'particularly difficult circumstances, such as having been a victim of domestic violence while the marriage or registered partnership was subsisting'.[55] In addition, in all these cases, the non-EU national needs to comply with the conditions equivalent to those listed in Article 7(1).

In the context of the present research, it is important to distinguish two categories of non-EU family members who, most likely, will lose their residence rights upon the EU citizen's departure from the host Member State. The first group, which bears particular relevance to this study, consists of TCN spouses who neither have custody over nor access to the EU citizen's children, nor has their marriage lasted for at least three years. The second group includes childless, unmarried TCN partners who are not covered by Article 13 at all.[56] It, therefore, follows that the right of residence of third-country nationals

52 Ibid art 13(2)(a).

53 See Elspeth Guild, Steve Peers and Jonathan Tomkin, *The EU Citizenship Directive: A Commentary* (2nd edn, Oxford University Press 2019) 179.

54 Citizenship Directive, art 13(2)(b) and (d).

55 Ibid art 13(2)(c).

56 This has been confirmed by the CJEU in Case C-45/12 *Hadj Ahmed* ECLI:EU:C:2013:390, para 36. For categories of persons falling within the definition of 'family members', see Section 3.2.

belonging to these categories is fully dependent on the continuous residence of the EU citizen principal in the host Member State.

Article 16(2) extends the right of permanent residence to TCN family members who have legally resided with the Union citizen in the host Member State for a continuous period of five years. Article 18 additionally provides that non-EU nationals who have benefitted from Articles 12(2) or 13(2) also qualify for this status after five years of residence, provided that the requirements of economic activity or self-sufficiency are still satisfied. The only exception is reserved for the family members of certain groups of EU citizens who stop working in the host Member State: these groups may enjoy permanent residence before the completion of the five-year residence period.[57]

3.2 *Who Is Considered a Family Member?*

Article 2(2) of the Citizenship Directive defines the scope of the so-called 'direct' family members who have the right to join or accompany an EU citizen in the host Member State. These are:

a) Spouse.
b) Registered partner if the legislation of the host Member State treats registered partnerships as equivalent to marriage.
c) Direct descendants who are under the age of 21 or are dependants and those of the spouse or registered partner.
d) Dependent direct relatives in the ascending line and those of the spouse or registered partner.

The list of family members above is not exhaustive. Article 3(2) deals with so-called 'extended' family members who do not fall within the scope of Article 2(2). This category includes, in particular:

a) Any other family members who are dependants or members of the EU citizen's household in the country from which they have come, or require the EU citizen's personal care due to a serious health condition.
b) Unmarried (or unregistered) partner 'with whom the Union citizen has a durable relationship, duly attested'.

The main difference between the two articles is that Member States are obliged to admit the family members listed in Article 2(2), whilst only 'facilitate'

57 Citizenship Directive, art 17.

admission of categories found in Article 3(2), which is subject to a degree of their discretion.[58] It must be noted that non-working students are disadvantaged in comparison to other groups of EU citizens; the former are only entitled to live in the host Member State with their spouses or registered partners and dependent children. Likewise, the scope of the student's 'extended' family members is limited to dependent direct relatives in the ascending line and those of the student's spouse or registered partner.[59]

3.3 *Married Couples as a Privileged Group*

The nature of the legal concept of 'spouses' is of particular relevance to the present study. When interpreting Regulation 1612/68, the CJEU explicitly clarified that it involved solely married couples, whereas unmarried couples could not be regarded as spouses due to 'the absence of any indication of a general social development which would justify a broad construction'.[60] Yet, the proposal for the Citizenship Directive, presented by the Commission in May 2001,[61] opened the opportunity to re-evaluate the concept of family members and depart from the 'spouses only' policy.[62] The first draft proposed to include the category of 'unmarried partners' within the scope of direct family members in Article 2, provided that the legislation of the host Member State treats them equivalent to parties to a marriage.

The Commission justified its initiative by relying on the increasing numbers of alternative family forms, such as unmarried couples, an arrangement that was already legally recognised in a number of Member States.[63] However, the amended Commission proposal of mid-2003 and the common position subsequently adopted by the Council confined the scope of Article 2(2) to registered partners only, requiring Member States to merely facilitate admission of durable partners instead of granting them directly effective rights.[64] At present, the

58 See also, Case C-83/11 *Rahman and Others* [2012] ECLI:EU:C:2012:519, para 26.

59 Citizenship Directive, art 7(4).

60 *Reed* (n 48), para 15.

61 Commission, 'Proposal for a European Parliament and Council Directive on the right of citizens of the Union and their family members to move and reside freely within the territory of the Member States' COM (2001) 257 final (Proposal for Citizenship Directive).

62 For an analysis, see, Helen Toner, *Partnership Rights, Free Movement, and EU Law* (Hart 2014), 60–61; Clare McGlynn, *Families and the European Union* (Cambridge University Press 2006) 127–28.

63 Proposal for Citizenship Directive (n 61) 7–8.

64 Commission, 'Amended proposal for a Directive of the European Parliament and of the Council on the right of citizens of the Union and their family members to move and reside freely within the territory of the Member States' COM (2003) 199 final, 10–11; Council, 'Common Position (EC) No 6/2004 of 5 December 2003 adopted by the Council, acting

Directive explicitly distinguishes the terms 'spouses' and 'registered partners' under Article 2(2) and 'durable partners' under Article 3(2). The EU, hence, has shown reluctance to depart from the traditional, conservative notion of the family as a legally married (or registered) union, using marriage (or registered partnership) as a central organising principle in the determination of a non-EU national's right of residence.

Against this background, one important aspect addressed by the CJEU is the principle of non-discrimination on the grounds of nationality. The key judgement in this context is *Reed*,[65] delivered before the adoption of the Citizenship Directive. The case concerned Ms Reed, a UK national, who relocated to the Netherlands following her unmarried partner, also a UK national, who was employed in the country. Initially hoping to find a job in the Netherlands, one year later Ms Reed was still unemployed and claimed a residence permit on the basis of Regulation 1612/68, as she was living with a then EEC worker. Her application was rejected although the couple was cohabiting and had been in a relationship for five years. Having acknowledged that unmarried partners cannot be regarded as spouses for the purposes of the Regulation, the Court argued that the relevant Dutch policy breached the principle of non-discrimination on the grounds of nationality. Whilst the domestic immigration law allowed Dutch nationals and permanent residents to bring unmarried partners to the country, this right was unlawfully denied to nationals of other Member States.[66] According to the CJEU, Ms Reed was therefore entitled to the right of residence.

It must be stressed that EU citizens would only be entitled to live with unmarried partners if the host Member State reserved that right for its own nationals. Conversely, had there been no such provision in Dutch law, Ms Reed would have no right to remain in the country. Further, it is worth noting that, in comparison to married couples, unmarried partners may find themselves in a disadvantaged position, not only because Member States are not obliged to recognise such relationships, but also because these must be 'duly attested' even where they do so. Whilst the Directive does not foresee systematic checks

in accordance with the procedure referred to in Article 251 of the Treaty establishing the European Community, with a view to adopting a directive of the European Parliament and of the Council on the right of citizens of the Union and their family members to move and reside freely within the territory of the Member States amending Regulation (EEC) No 1612/68 and repealing Directives 64/221/EEC, 68/360/EEC, 72/194/EEC, 73/148/EEC, 75/34/EEC, 75/35/EEC, 90/364/EEC, 90/365/EEC and 93/96/EEC' [2004] OJ C54E/12.

65 *Reed* (n 48).

66 Ibid, paras 29, 30.

or additional requirements with respect to married couples; unmarried partners may be required to comply with extra conditions, as well as undergo a thorough examination to convince the authorities that their relationship is of sufficient quality.

4 Derogations from Free Movement Rights

As observed above, national governments have very limited powers to remove mobile EU citizens and their family members merely because they do not comply with the conditions of economic activity or self-sufficiency. The only remaining grounds for exclusion reserved in the Directive are those of public policy, public security, public health, and the abuse of rights. Two of them – namely, public policy and abuse of rights – are of particular importance to this study. As will be shown in Chapters 7–10, these exceptions have been used by the UK *inter alia* to deny residence rights to nationals of EU Member States and their non-EU spouses whose marriages are considered to be ones of convenience. The following sub-sections explore the relevant provisions in more detail.

4.1 *Public Policy, Public Security and Public Health*

Since the early days of the Community, national governments were provided with the opportunity not to admit nationals of other Member States or to remove them on the grounds of public policy, public security or public health. Initially incorporated into the Treaty of Rome,[67] the respective limitations found their way into the succeeding Treaties and secondary legislation,[68] and ultimately, TFEU[69] and the Citizenship Directive.

The CJEU, on the other hand, has early on held and consistently maintained that the relevant derogations must be interpreted strictly,[70] with its key case law later consolidated in the Citizenship Directive. Restrictions of the right to

67 EEC Treaty, art 48(3).

68 Council Directive 64/221/EEC of 25 February 1964 on the co-ordination of special measures concerning the movement and residence of foreign nationals which are justified on grounds of public policy, public security or public health [1964] OJ 56/850. See also, Preamble to Reg 1612/68; Dir 73/148/EEC, art 8; Dir 90/365/EEC, art 2(2); Dir 90/364/EEC, art 2(2); Dir 93/96, art 2(2).

69 TFEU, arts 21(1), 45(3), 52(1) and 62.

70 See among others, Case 41–74 *Van Duyn* [1974] ECR 01337, para 18; Case 36–75 *Rutili* [1975] ECR 01219, para 28; Case 30–77 *Bouchereau* [1977] ECR 01999, para 35; Case C-50/06 *Commission* v *Netherlands* [2007] ECR I-04383, para 42.

free movement on the grounds of public policy, public security or public health are found in a separate chapter of the document.[71] The public security exception is typically linked with concerns related to national security,[72] whereby the public health ground is limited to serious infectious or contagious diseases and is rarely imposed. Public policy is the grounds most frequently employed by the governments; it is relied on to exclude EU citizens whose character is deemed to be insufficiently good. One such example is the approach of British authorities who consider it legitimate to use the public policy provision to remove EU citizens allegedly involved in perceived marriages of convenience with non-EU nationals.

Whilst the relevant UK practices will be explored in-depth in Chapters 7–10, it must be underlined that Member States are bound by a wide array of restrictions when applying the public policy test. First, neither the TFEU, nor the Citizenship Directive provides a definition of public policy; determination of the concept is left to the Member States. The Directive nonetheless offers EU citizens and their family members extensive guarantees when it comes to their potential exclusion on public policy grounds. First, it introduces a system linking the level of protection against expulsion with the length of the individual's residence in the host Member State. EU citizens holding a permanent resident status, i.e., those who have been living in the country for at least five years, can be expelled only on 'serious grounds' of public policy or public security.[73] The same level of protection is equally guaranteed to their family members, irrespective of nationality. As Chiara Berneri reasonably observes, this can be explained not only by the EU legislator's desire to protect family out of humanitarian considerations, but also to ensure that the effectiveness of EU citizens' right of residence is not jeopardised by the possible removal of their close ones.[74] Notably, EU citizens whose residence lasts for ten years or more, or who are minors, enjoy an even higher level of protection and can be expelled only on 'imperative grounds of public security'.[75]

Second, the Directive sets out a number of principles that Member States need to respect when invoking public policy grounds. First, such measures

71 Citizenship Directive, ch VI.

72 The CJEU has nonetheless held that the 'public security' concept may also be applied to cases involving exceptionally serious crimes. Case C-145/09 *Tsakouridis* [2010] ECR I-11979, para 56; Case C-348/09 *P.I* ECLI:EU:C:2012:300, para 33. For a discussion, see, Dora Kostakopoulou, 'When EU Citizens Become Foreigners' (2014) 20 *European Law Journal* 447, 457–60.

73 Citizenship Directive, art 28(2).

74 Berneri, *Family Reunification in the EU* (n 45) 72.

75 Citizenship Directive, art 28(3).

must comply with the principle of proportionality and be based exclusively on the personal conduct of the individual concerned, whereby the latter 'must represent a genuine, present, and sufficiently serious threat affecting one of the fundamental interests of society'.[76] Previous criminal convictions themselves should not be regarded as a reason for exclusion, nor are considerations of general prevention accepted.[77] Further, before taking an expulsion decision, the host Member State must consider such factors as the length of residence of the individual in its territory, as well as their age; state of health; family and economic situation; social and cultural integration; and the extent of their links with their country of origin.[78]

The CJEU case law further specifies that, when assessing the proportionality of such a decision, fundamental interests of the host Member State must be weighed against the interests of the person in exercising their free movement rights.[79] The assessment may also involve a number of factors, including the nature and gravity of the offending activities, the time that has elapsed since that conduct, the individual's behaviour during that period, and the degree of social danger caused by the presence of the person concerned in the host Member State.[80] Moreover, the 'fundamental threat' test is forward-looking, meaning that the individual concerned shall be likely to repeat their conduct in future.[81] Last, like in every situation falling within the scope of EU law, due regard must be paid to the best interests of the children involved, as laid down in Article 24(2) of the EUCFR.[82]

As to the duration of restrictive measures taken on public policy grounds, the Citizenship Directive provides that the individuals affected may submit a request for lifting the exclusion order not earlier than three years after its adoption. In their application, they must demonstrate that there has been a 'material change in circumstances' which informed the original prohibition. The Member State concerned shall consider their request in six months' time; during this period, the applicants are not allowed to enter its territory.[83]

---

76 Ibid art 27(2).

77 Ibid.

78 Ibid art 28(1).

79 *Tsakouridis* (n 72), para 50; Joined Cases C-331/16 and C-366/16 *K and HF* ECLI:EU:C:2018:296, paras 62, 67.

80 *K and HF* (n 79), para 70.

81 *Bouchereau* (n 70), para 29; *P.I* (n 72), para 30; *K and HF* (n 79), para 56; Case C-193/16 *E* ECLI:EU:C:2017:542, para 23.

82 See among others, *CS* (n 47), para 36.

83 Citizenship Directive, art 32.

4.2 *Abuse of Rights*

Another ground for derogation from the free movement of persons is found in Article 35 of the Citizenship Directive which deals with the concept of abuse of rights or fraud. The relevant provision reads:

> Member States may adopt the necessary measures to refuse, terminate or withdraw any right conferred by this Directive in the case of abuse of rights or fraud, such as marriages of convenience. Any such measure shall be proportionate and subject to the procedural safeguards provided for in Articles 30 and 31.

Recital 28 of the Preamble further adds:

> To guard against abuse of rights or fraud, notably marriages of convenience or any other form of relationships contracted for the sole purpose of enjoying the right of free movement and residence, Member States should have the possibility to adopt the necessary measures.

The Directive is the first legal instrument in the area of free movement of persons introducing this concept; the preceding legislation contained no reference to abuse of rights. The wording of the relevant provisions suggests that these must be interpreted similarly to restrictions based on public policy grounds and public security grounds that can be used to justify the denial of Treaty rights in exceptional cases.[84] Procedural safeguards referred to in Article 35 concern the notification of relevant decisions (Article 30) and access to judicial or administrative redress procedures in the host Member State (Article 31), both equally applicable to public policy or public security cases.

Further, the word 'may' makes it clear that application of Article 35 is not mandatory and Member States enjoy discretion as to the withdrawal of the rights in question in proven cases of abuse or fraud.[85] Although the Directive does not contain a definition of abuse or fraud, the specific focus on marriages of convenience nonetheless implies that the main area of concern is the right to family reunion with non-EU nationals who may obtain residency in the host Member State following marriage to the principal. It does not, however, follow

84 Katja S Ziegler, '"Abuse of Law" in the Context of the Free Movement of Workers' in Rita De la Feria and Stefan Vogenauer (eds), *Prohibition of Abuse of Law: A New General Principle of EU Law?* (Hart 2011) 295–96. This has also been implicitly acknowledged by the CJEU in *Metock and Others* (n 26), paras 74, 75.

85 For this opinion, see, Guild, Peers and Tomkin (n 53) 312.

that this is the only form of abuse; Article 35 and the Preamble apparently leave a possibility for other situations to be equally classified as such, provided that the sole purpose of such conduct is to enjoy free movement rights. Hence, before specifically turning to an analysis of the concept of marriages of convenience, this study will explore the basic principles of application of the concept of abuse in EU law, as well as look at how, and to what extent, it is applicable in family reunion cases in the context of free movement provisions. These issues are accordingly dealt with in Section 4.2.1 below and Chapter 2.

4.2.1 Doctrine of Abuse of Rights in EU Law

At present, the concept of abuse of rights has been subject to extensive CJEU jurisprudence in several areas, particularly company and tax law, giving rise to discussion of whether it constitutes a general principle of EU law.[86] The origins of the abuse of rights doctrine in EU law are found in the CJEU judgment in *Van Binsbergen,* delivered in the 1970s in the area of free movement of services.[87] In its ruling, in essence, the Court granted Member States broad permission to impose anti-abusive measures in so-called 'U-turn' situations where either persons or goods move to another Member State, although their final destination is the home Member State.[88] Such practices are typically a consequence of more restrictive domestic regulations that governments apply to their own nationals or products in purely internal situations, a phenomenon known as reverse discrimination.[89] The main aim of exercising free movement rights in

86 The CJEU has consistently referred to the prohibition of abuse of rights and fraud as a 'general principle' of EU law. See among others, Case C-321/05 *Kofoed* [2007] ECR I-05795, para 38; Case C-359/16 *Altun and Others* ECLI:EU:C:2018:63, para 49; Case C-356/15, *Commission v Belgium* ECLI:EU:C:2018:555, para 99; Case C-557/17 *Y.Z. and Others* ECLI:EU:C:2019:203, para 62. There is nonetheless no unanimity among scholars as to the interpretation of this finding. Whilst some commentators merely see the principle of prohibition of abuse as an interpretative instrument, others regard it as a full-fledged general principle of EU law. For discussion, see, Paul Farmer, 'Prohibition of Abuse of (European) Law: The Creation of a New General Principle of EU Law through Tax: A Response' in De la Feria and Vogenauer (eds), *Prohibition of Abuse of Law* (n 84) 4; Anthony Arnull, 'What is a General Principle of EU Law?' in De la Feria and Vogenauer (eds), *Prohibition of Abuse of Law* (n 84) 22–23; Karsten Engsig Sørensen, 'What is a General Principle of EU Law? A Response' in De la Feria and Vogenauer (eds), *Prohibition of Abuse of Law* (n 84).

87 Case 33–74 *Van Binsbergen* [1974] ECR 01299.

88 For an analysis, see, Rita de la Feria, 'Prohibition of Abuse of (Community) Law: The Creation of a New General Principle of EC Law through Tax' (2008) 45 *Common Market Law Review* 395, 399–400. See also, Anders Kjellgren, 'On the Border of Abuse – The Jurisprudence of the European Court of Justice on Circumvention, Fraud and Other Misuses of Community Law' (2000) 11 *European Business Law Review* 179.

89 This issue will be discussed in detail in Chapter 2.

these cases, therefore, is to avoid application of the national legislation of the home Member State.

Following *Van Binsbergen*, the CJEU continued to apply the same approach in other 'U-turn' cases.[90] The late 1990s, however, were marked by a significant change of the CJEU position on the issue which most notably manifested in the judgment in *Centros*,[91] delivered in the field of company law. Having recalled that Member States are entitled to take measures to prevent abuse,[92] the Court underlined that it must be established on a case-by-case basis and based on objective evidence, whereby an assessment of the relevant conduct must take place 'in the light of the objectives' of the EU law provisions that are sought to be relied upon.[93] The CJEU then proceeded to conclude that the mere fact that a person intends to obtain a certain advantage by placing themselves within the scope of a less restrictive regulatory regime does not, in itself, constitute an abuse of free movement rights.[94]

One of the most important limitations of the judgment in *Centros* was that it did not provide explicit criteria distinguishing use and abuse of EU law. The issue, nonetheless, was soon clarified in *Emsland-Stärke*,[95] delivered in the field of free movement of goods, which equally dealt with a 'U-turn' situation. In its judgment, the CJEU introduced a two-limb abuse test which reads:

> A finding of an abuse requires, first, a combination of objective circumstances in which, despite formal observance of the conditions laid down by the Community rules, the purpose of those rules has not been achieved. It requires, second, a subjective element consisting in the intention to obtain an advantage from the Community rules by creating artificially the conditions laid down for obtaining it. (…) It is for the national court to establish the existence of those two elements, evidence of which must be adduced in accordance with the rules of national law, provided that the effectiveness of Community law is not thereby undermined.[96]

90 See among others, Case C-148/91 *Veronica* [1993] ECR I-00487; Case C-23/93 *TV10* [1994] ECR I-4795.

91 Case C-212/97 *Centros* [1999] ECR I-1459.

92 Ibid para 24.

93 Ibid para 25.

94 Ibid para 27.

95 Case C-110/99 *Emsland-Stärke* [2000] ECR I-11569.

96 Ibid paras 52–54.

The *Emsland-Stärke* case has been subject to an intense scholarly discussion that reveals two main concerns about the application of the test. The first relates to the element of 'intention', for determination of the subjective motives is a difficult task that would typically require interrogation of the persons concerned.[97] In the subsequent tax law case of *Halifax*, the CJEU, however, objectified the subjective element by stating that motives can be inferred from the objective circumstances of the case.[98] Yet, as will be demonstrated in Chapters 9 and 10, reliance on the objective circumstances to determine the purpose of marriage may equally appear problematic.

Further, a distinction has been made between the concepts of 'abuse' and 'fraud'. As noted in the introduction to this book, the former refers to a situation where formal requirements for the exercise of a right have been met, but the purpose of the relevant conduct is considered unacceptable. The notion of fraud, by contrast, appears to be confined to situations where persons or legal entities present false documentation to prove that the conditions for the exercise of the relevant right have been fulfilled.[99] Cases of fraud are, hence, relatively straightforward, as Member States may deny Treaty rights to those concerned without having to prove their motives.[100] The same approach is employed in the context of the Citizenship Directive. Commission guidelines for the application of the Directive define abuse as:

> [A]n artificial conduct entered into solely with the purpose of obtaining the right of free movement and residence under Community law which, albeit formally observing of the conditions laid down by Community rules, does not comply with the purpose of those rules.[101]

---

97 For criticism of this element, see, Dennis Weber, 'Abuse of Law – European Court of Justice, 14 December 2000 – Case C-110/99, *Emsland-Stärke*' (2004) *Legal Issues of Economic Integration* 43, 51–54; Karsten Engsig Sørensen, 'Abuse of Rights in Community Law: A Principle of Substance or Merely Rhetoric?' (2006) 43 *Common Market Law Review* 423, 456–58.

98 Case C-255/02 *Halifax* [2006] ECR I-01609, para 86.

99 See among others, Case C-285/95 *Kol* [1997] ECR I-03069, paras 25, 29; C-63/99 *Gloszczuk* [2001] ECR I-06369, para 75.

100 For a discussion on the concepts of 'fraud' and 'abuse', see, Kjellgren, 'On the Border of Abuse' (n 88) 180–83; Sørensen, 'Abuse of Rights in Community Law' (n 97) 431–32.

101 Commission, 'Communication from the Commission to the European Parliament and the Council on guidance for better transposition and application of Directive 2004/38/EC on the right of citizens of the Union and their family members to move and reside freely within the territory of the Member States', COM (2009) 313 final (2009 Guidelines), 4.1.2. For an analysis of the Guidelines, see Chapter 4.

Fraud, on the other hand, 'is likely to be limited to forgery of documents or false representation of a material fact concerning the conditions attached to the right of residence', such as a false EU passport or certificate of marriage to an EU citizen.[102]

Notwithstanding the development of extensive CJEU jurisprudence on the issue of abuse of rights, it appears that the Court has not applied this concept to all fundamental freedoms in the same way. Whilst acknowledging the growing relevance of the concept of abuse of law in other areas of EU law, academic discussion tends to reject its impact within the area of free movement of persons[103] and EU citizenship.[104] The reason for such an assessment has been the extreme reluctance of the CJEU to find abuse in situations where interests of national governments have come into conflict with those of nationals of other Member States claiming their Treaty rights. Chapter 2 explores if and how the concept of abuse is addressed by the CJEU in family reunion cases revealing such tensions, and whether it covers other situations apart from perceived marriages of convenience explicitly mentioned in the Citizenship Directive.

5 Conclusion

The ability of Union citizens to live in the host Member State with their (non-EU) family members has always been regarded by the EU legislator as a key precondition of intra-European movement. The rights to family reunion, already incorporated in EEC secondary law in the 1960s, have since been expanded in line with the general development and strengthening of the Treaty rights. Currently, the Citizenship Directive provides families involving mobile EU citizens a high level of protection, enabling TCN family members to enjoy virtually the same rights as the principal, with the only condition being that the latter falls within the scope of the Directive. This instrument has further transformed the situation of non-EU family members who may now acquire

102 Ibid, 4.1.1.

103 See Ziegler (n 84) 306–13; Eleanor Spaventa, 'Comments on Abuse of Law and the Free Movement of Workers' in De la Feria and Vogenauer (eds), *Prohibition of Abuse of Law* (n 84).

104 See Cathryn Costello, 'Citizenship of the Union: Above Abuse?' in De la Feria and Vogenauer (eds), *Prohibition of Abuse of Law* (n 84). Michael Dougan, 'Some Comments on the Idea of a General Principle of Union Law Prohibiting Abuses of Law in the Field of Free Movement for Union Citizens' in De la Feria and Vogenauer (eds), *Prohibition of Abuse of Law* (n 84).

an independent status after having lived in the host Member State for at least five years, as well as, in certain situations, before this date.

Regarding the scope of family members defined as such by the Directive, marriages and registered partnerships (provided that the host Member State treats the latter as equivalent to marriage) are privileged over unregistered relationships. Whilst Member States are obliged to admit spouses or registered partners of EU citizens without any additional requirements, the residence of the so-called 'durable partners' continues to be subject to the discretion of national governments.

There are two types of derogations from free movement rights permitted under the Directive that are relied on by Member State authorities to target perceived marriages of convenience. The first one is the public policy provision which is relied on by the UK to remove mobile EU citizens allegedly involved in such arrangements with non-EU nationals. Whilst this point will be specifically discussed in Chapters 7 and 8, it should be stressed that the Directive imposes a very high threshold for the public policy grounds to apply. The second ground for derogation is contained in Article 35, which explicitly allows Member States to exclude individuals in cases of abuse of rights, such as marriages of convenience. Chapter 2 looks at how the CJEU has interpreted this Article in family reunion cases and explores its relationship with the general doctrine of abuse of rights in EU law.

CHAPTER 2

Right to Family Reunion as a Source of Tension between the CJEU and Member States

1 Introduction

Chapter 1 demonstrated that the Union legislator and the CJEU have continuously extended the boundaries of free movement, including the right of mobile EU citizens to live with their family members. EU decision-makers considered that the absence of such a possibility would prevent Member State nationals from relocating and hence impede the creation of the single market, as well as hinder EU citizens' integration into the society of the host Member State. Starting from the 1990s, however, this paradigm began to sharply contrast with the relevant developments in domestic family reunification laws in a number of Member States. Aiming to reduce the number of family migrants who could not be selected in the same way as the foreign labour force, Member States tightened up the rules for the entry and residence of family members of their own nationals. This created a peculiar situation where individuals not covered by Treaty rights can find themselves in a discriminatory position compared to mobile EU citizens enjoying more generous provisions under EU law.

The gap between the two sets of rights has given rise to anxieties among several governments who started to complain about the growing numbers of non-EU nationals allegedly seeking to circumvent restrictive national immigration rules by marrying mobile EU citizens. Such practices are commonly designated by Member States as abuses of EU law and routinely linked with the discourse on marriages of convenience which are viewed by policymakers as a significant problem. The tensions between the EU and Member States became visible in two principal settings. First, in CJEU case law, and second, on the political level when Member States expressly advocated for the restriction of family reunion rights under the Citizenship Directive.[1]

1 Directive 2004/38/EC of the European Parliament and of the Council of 29 April 2004 on the right of citizens of the Union and their family members to move and reside freely within the territory of the Member States amending Regulation (EEC) No 1612/68 and repealing Directives 64/221/EEC, 68/360/EEC, 72/194/EEC, 73/148/EEC, 75/34/EEC, 75/35/EEC, 90/364/EEC, 90/365/EEC and 93/96/EEC [2004] OJ L158/77 (Citizenship Directive).

 | DOI:10.1163/9789004499263_004

This chapter reveals how the tension over family reunion rights has been reflected in CJEU case law. With this aim, it identifies the main points of friction between EU law and Member States addressed by the Court, paying particular attention to the concepts of abuse and marriages of convenience. The chapter commences with a brief overview of the phenomenon of reverse discrimination, where mobile EU citizens residing in a host Member State are treated more favourably than static nationals of the particular state. It then proceeds to examine the relevant CJEU jurisprudence on the substance of marriage, situations concerning EU citizens returning to their own Member State or forming families in the host Member State, as well as family reunion cases outside the scope of the Citizenship Directive.

2 Treating Nationals Worse Than Foreigners: the Phenomenon of Reverse Discrimination

As observed in Chapter 1, the personal scope of family members eligible to accompany or join the EU principal in the host Member State has, from the very outset, included third-country nationals. At the time of adopting the first secondary law provisions on the issue, immigration was not perceived by Member States as a problem. To the contrary, Western European countries actively relied on foreign workers, many of whom came from their former colonies, as a means to rebuild their economy.[2] This type of migration, however, was largely seen as a temporary solution, used in response to labour market needs.[3] Indeed, the open-door policy proved to be short-lived and changed dramatically after the 1973 oil crisis, which seriously hit the coal and heavy industries, leading to rises in unemployment. As a response, the receiving countries tightened up their immigration laws, giving preference only to highly skilled workers, and started to promote voluntary return policies among migrants already present in their territory.[4]

2 For instance, France recruited workers from Algeria; the UK recruited from the Indian subcontinent and the Caribbean; the Netherlands recruited from Indonesia and the Carribean (Surinam and the Netherlands Antilles), as well as from Turkey and Morocco. For an overview of post-war immigration patterns to Western Europe, see among others, Klaus Bade, *Migration in European History* (Blackwell 2003); Chiara Berneri, *Family Reunification in the EU* (Hart 2017) chs 1 and 2.

3 Berneri, *Family Reunification in the EU* (n 2) 30.

4 Ibid 30–34.

Yet contrary to Member States' expectations, many foreign workers did not move back to their countries of origin. This gave rise to anti-immigrant and xenophobic sentiments amongst the local population, particularly those with lower socioeconomic status, which were further fuelled by populist media and political narratives.[5] Over the years, most of the descendants of migrants who decided to stay in their host country acquired its nationality, either by birth or after undergoing a naturalisation procedure. Having reached marriageable age, many began looking for spouses in countries of their parents' birth to bring them over to their state of residence.

Such practices became increasingly problematised by the respective Member States for two principal reasons. First, the governments could not select family migrants based on the same criteria as foreign workers; hence, family reunification was seen as a route enabling unwanted foreigners to enter the country. Second, marriages between migrants and naturalised nationals were viewed as a symptom of failed integration of the latter group. A particular focus was placed on forced and arranged marriages. These were typically seen as a product of a 'backward' culture, closely intertwined with highly gendered and racialised narratives on young, uneducated, and vulnerable Muslim women who would be unable to integrate, and therefore, become a burden on the society of the receiving state.[6] In the UK, on the other hand, the state anxieties centred on male migrants from the Indian subcontinent who allegedly only intended to use marriage to a British-settled woman as means to gain residence rights in the country.[7] As commentators reasonably argue, such discourses, in effect, question the membership of nationals of migrant origin, transforming them into second-class citizens who do not deserve to live with their close ones in their own country.[8]

5 Ibid.

6 On this topic see among others Albert Kraler, 'Civic Stratification, Gender and Family Migration Policies in Europe' (International Centre for Migration and Policy Development 2010); Helena Wray, 'Regulating Spousal Migration in Denmark' (2013) 27 *Journal of Immigration, Asylum and Nationality Law* 139; Saskia Bonjour and Betty de Hart, 'A Proper Wife, a Proper Marriage: Constructions of "Us" and "Them" in Dutch Family Migration Policy' (2013) 20 *European Journal of Women's Studies* 61; Saskia Bonjour and Laura Block, 'Ethnicizing Citizenship, Questioning Membership. Explaining the Decreasing Family Migration Rights of Citizens in Europe' (2016) 20 *Citizenship Studies* 779.

7 For more details on the UK, see Chapters 6 and 7.

8 See among others Kees Groenendijk, 'Reverse Discrimination, Family Reunification and Union Citizens of Immigrant Origin' in Elspeth Guild, Cristina Gortázar Rotaeche and Dora Kostakopoulou (eds) *The Reconceptualization of European Union Citizenship* (Brill 2014) 188; Bonjour and Block (n 6) 791.

Starting from the late 1970s, Western European countries (most notably, the UK, the Netherlands, and Denmark) have attempted to limit the number of family members eligible for joining the principal. With this view, the governments made this right conditional upon the fulfilment of certain requirements, such as high visa and application fees; language and integration tests; age and income thresholds; cohabitation requirements, and probationary periods. Whilst their principal target remained nationals with foreign roots marrying within their ethnic group, such policies equally apply to those of the majority ethnicity. As a consequence, both groups are effectively punished for choosing partners of undesirable origin instead of marrying a national of a particular country, an approach reflecting the generalised fears of the state that marriages with foreigners may undermine the envisioned national community.[9]

Meanwhile, EU citizens exercising their free movement rights are not subjected to any additional requirements when it comes to living with their non-EU family members. Yet, according to the division of competences between the EU and Member States, EU provisions on family reunion do not apply to Member State nationals if their situation is purely internal, a principle that was already confirmed by the CJEU in its early jurisprudence on the issue.[10] This created a peculiar situation where static nationals of a particular Member State are treated less favourably than nationals of other Member States residing in the country.[11] The issue has been extensively criticised by a number of scholars who argue that such reverse discrimination is inconsistent with the logic of EU citizenship and advocate for bringing the rights of static EU citizens in line

9 For a general discussion on contemporary family reunification policies in Western Europe, see among others, Kraler (n 6); Helena Wray, *Regulating Marriage Migration into the UK: A Stranger in the Home* (Ashgate 2011); Bonjour and de Hart (n 6); Wray, 'Regulating Spousal Migration in Denmark' (n 6); Helena Wray, Agnes Agoston and Jocelyn Hutton, 'A Family Resemblance? The Regulation of Marriage Migration in Europe' (2013) 16 *European Journal of Migration and Law* 209; Laura Block, 'Regulating Membership: Explaining Restriction and Stratification of Family Migration in Europe' (2015) 36 *Journal of Family Issues* 1433; Laura Block, *Policy Frames on Spousal Migration in Germany* (Springer 2016); Anne Balke Staver and Helga Eggebø, 'Everything but the Marriage Certificate: Unmarried Partners in Norwegian Immigration Regulation' (2023) 30 *Social Politics: International Studies in Gender, State & Society* 1018; Katharine Charsley and Helena Wray, 'Kept Apart: Routine Family Separation in the UK Family Immigration System as Times of Crises' (2023) 11 *Migration Studies* 380.

10 See among others, Joined Cases 35/82 and 36/82 *Morson and Jhanjan* [1982] ECR 03723, paras 16–18; Joined Cases C-64/96 and C-65/96 *Uecker and Jacquet* [1997] ECR I-03171, paras 16–17.

11 For an overview of discrepancies between EU law and national family reunification provisions, see, Elspeth Guild, 'EU Citizens, Foreign Family Members and European Union Law' (2019) 21 *European Journal of Migration and Law* 358, 369–72.

with those provided by the Citizenship Directive.[12] Such a proposal was indeed put forward by the Commission in 1999 during the negotiations for the Family Reunification Directive[13] but was unable to overcome opposition from the Netherlands, one of the countries with the most restrictive family migration policies.[14]

The CJEU has been equally reluctant to act contrary to the will of resistant Member States. In its landmark ruling in *Metock*, delivered in 2008, it confirmed that any difference of treatment between mobile and static Union citizens with regards to conditions of entry and residence of TCN family members falls outside the scope of EU law.[15] It must nonetheless be noted that levelling up the domestic provisions was not the issue at stake at the relevant proceedings. In fact, the contrary was the case: several national governments essentially demanded the CJEU level down the family reunion rights of certain groups of EU citizens, claiming that a more inclusive interpretation of the Citizenship Directive would result in 'unjustified reverse discrimination' of their own nationals.[16] The Court, however, refused to follow the logic of Member States and impose obstacles, real or potential, to the free movement of EU citizens and their family members.

Metock, which will be extensively discussed in the following subsections, is only one of the numerous cases concerning the residence rights of EU citizens' family members that, over the last three decades, has been referred to

12 For this opinion, see among others, Niamh Nic Shuibhne, 'Free Movement of Persons and the Wholly Internal Rule: Time to Move On?' (2002) 39 *Common Market Law Review* 731; Helen Oosterom-Staples, 'To What Extent Has Reverse Discrimination Been Reversed?' (2012) 14 *European Journal of Migration and Law* 151; Chiara Berneri, 'Protection of Families Composed by EU citizens and Third-Country Nationals: Some Suggestions to Tackle Reverse Discrimination' (2014) 16 *European Journal of Migration and Law* 249.

13 Council Directive 2003/86/EC of 22 September 2003 on the right to family reunification [2003] OJ L251/12 (Family Reunification Directive).

14 Commission, 'Proposal for a Council Directive on the right to family reunification' COM (1999) 638, recital 9 and art 4. For an analysis see Anne Walter, *Reverse Discrimination and Family Reunification* (Wolf Legal Publishers 2008) 41; Groenendijk, 'Reverse Discrimination' (n 8) 182. The legality of reverse discrimination in the area of family reunification has also been challenged before constitutional courts with partial success in a number of Member States, such as Austria, Belgium, Germany and Spain. See, Groenendijk, 'Reverse Discrimination' (n 8) 178–79. On the ruling of the Belgian Constitutional Court, see EMN, 'Family Reunification with Third-Country National Sponsors in Belgium' (July 2017), 12 <https://emnbelgium.be/sites/default/files/publications/Final%20BE%20report%20on%20family%20reunification%20of%20TCN_%20July%202017.pdf> accessed 8 April 2024.

15 Case C-127/08 *Metock and Others* [2008] ECR I-06241, para 78.

16 Ibid para 76.

the CJEU by national courts. Reflecting the growing gap between the two sets of rights, the CJEU activity in this area reached its peak in the 2000s, when several Member States further tightened up their domestic family reunification rules. It is no coincidence that the majority of such cases originate in the Netherlands and the UK – two Member States with substantial differences between their national family reunification policies and provisions applicable to mobile EU citizens.

The following sub-sections will identify the main points of friction between the Court and Member States with regards to family reunion rights of EU citizens, as far as it is relevant to the topic of the present study. Along with exploring the Court's response to the Member State attempts to deny residence rights to EU citizens' family members, the chapter will also reveal if and how the concept of abuse of rights is reflected in the CJEU jurisprudence on the subject.

3 The Substance of Marriage

As observed in Chapter 1, the EU has been continuously privileging married couples over unregistered partners, enabling mobile EU citizens to live with their TCN spouses without having to satisfy any additional requirements.[17] One of the objections expressed by the Member States in this context concerned the retention of the right of residence of non-EU national spouses in cases of relationship breakdown. The issue was first addressed by the CJEU in its ruling in *Diatta*, handed down in the mid-1980s.[18] The case concerned a Senegalese spouse of a French national working in Germany. Having lived together for some time, the couple notified of their intention to divorce and moved into separate accommodations. When the Senegalese national applied for renewal of her residence permit, her request was declined on the basis that the couple no longer cohabited. The CJEU, however, preferred to adopt a formal approach to the issue, stating that a marital relationship is not regarded as dissolved as long as it has not been terminated by the competent authority and that the TCN spouse is not required to live together with the EU principal in order to qualify for residence rights.[19]

17 The structure of the CJEU case-law analysis in this and the subsequent sub-sections is partly borrowed from Elspeth Guild, 'Free Movement of EU Citizens and Their Family Members' (2016) 7 *New Journal of European Criminal Law* 231.

18 Case 267/83 *Diatta* [1985] ECR 00567.

19 Ibid paras 20, 22.

Having confirmed its position in subsequent case law,[20] the Court delivered its judgment in *Ogieriakhi* where it specified that the non-EU spouse continues to benefit from the Treaty rights even if both spouses cohabit with other partners, as long as their marriage is not officially terminated.[21] In other words, the CJEU jurisprudence shows that the TCN spouse of a Union citizen is entitled to a residence permit irrespective of the fact of cohabitation[22] and the quality of the relationship between the spouses.[23] The Court's approach is commendable, provided that many couples may choose to live separately for a variety of reasons, such as different job locations. Further, as the claimant sensibly argued in *Diatta*, even if the relationship between the spouses has deteriorated, it is not for the state authorities to decide whether reconciliation is still possible.[24] In addition, the requirement for the spouses to live together would leave the TCN party unprotected and entirely dependent on their EU citizen partner who could cause her expulsion simply by depriving her a roof.[25]

4 Returning Member State Nationals

Another major point of friction between the EU and Member States remains the position of EU citizens who return to their country of origin from another Member State, bringing with them their TCN family members. The first and principal ruling in this regard is *Surinder Singh*, delivered in 1992.[26] The case involved an Indian national who got married to a British national and then travelled with her to Germany where both worked before returning to the UK a couple of years later. Soon after their return, the couple separated and started divorce proceedings. Although the marriage had still not been dissolved, the UK authorities considered the situation in the domestic context, not the EU one, issuing a deportation order against the TCN spouse because the couple did not live together as foreseen by national immigration law. The UK court sought clarification from the CJEU, essentially asking if a Member State can

20 Case C-370/90 *Surinder Singh* [1992] ECR I-04265, para 12; Case C-40/11 *Iida* ECLI:EU:C:2012:691, para 58.

21 Case C-244/13 *Ogieriakhi* ECLI:EU:C:2014:2068, para 38.

22 There is nonetheless a requirement pursuant to the Citizenship Directive that the TCN spouse must be resident in the same Member State as the EU citizen, otherwise the spouse could not be regarded as accompanying or joining that citizen. *Iida* (n 20), para 64.

23 As long as their marriage is not found to be one of convenience.

24 *Diatta* (n 18), para 10.

25 Ibid.

26 *Surinder Singh* (n 20).

deny residence rights to the TCN spouse of its own national who moved, with that spouse, to another Member State, and then returned to his home country. The CJEU considered that such situations did indeed fall within the scope of Treaty rights. In the view of the Court, Member State nationals would be deterred from leaving their country of origin if, upon return, their family members were not also permitted to reside there under the same conditions as granted to them under the Treaty in another Member State.[27]

The judgment was subject to two interpretations.[28] According to the first one, supported by most commentators[29] and later apparently confirmed in subsequent case law,[30] the relevant intra-state movement the Court referred to was the UK national's initial movement from the UK to Germany. When viewed in this context, the significance of the element of deterrence was called into question. Alina Tryfonidou, for instance, argued that:

> Although there had been movement from one Member State to another that had an economic aim (Mrs Singh moved to Germany and was employed there for two years), nevertheless, if the Community right to be accompanied by her husband in the UK was not afforded to Mrs Singh, this would not have affected her decision to move to Germany in the first place. [31]

A number of scholars, nonetheless, opted for the second interpretation of the judgment, suggesting that the relevant movement the Court referred to was the one from Germany back to the UK. This logic was seen as more convincing. Since the couple was able to reside together in Germany by virtue of EU law, refusal of British authorities to grant Mr Singh a residence permit would indeed create an obstacle for his spouse to return to the UK.[32] Yet, without engaging into a discussion on the real rationale of the Court and its justifiability, it

27 Ibid paras 19–21.

28 For a detailed analysis, see, Alina Tryfonidou, *Reverse Discrimination in EC law* (Kluwer 2009) 99–101.

29 See among others, Miguel Poiares Maduro, 'The scope of European Remedies: The Case of Purely Internal Situations and Reverse Discrimination' in Claire Kilpatrick, Tonia Novitz and Paul Skidmore (eds), *The Future of Remedies in Europe* (Hart 2000); Nic Shuibhne (n 12) 744–48.

30 Case C-291/05 *Eind* [2007] ECR I-10719, paras 35, 36; *Iida* (n 20), para 70; Case C-456/12 *O and B* ECLI:EU:C:2014:135, para 54.

31 See for instance, Tryfonidou, *Reverse Discrimination in EC law* (n 28) 99.

32 For this view, see among others, Gavin Barrett, 'Family Matters: European Community Law and Third-Country Family Members' (2003) 40 *Common Market Law Review* 369, 379.

is important to underline that the CJEU has used a deterrence test to decide whether the TCN family members could benefit from Treaty rights.

During the proceedings, the UK authorities appeared extremely reluctant to give up control over the admission of non-Europeans into the country. British representatives argued against the application of EU law to 'returnees', claiming that granting residence rights to their spouses 'increases the risk of fraud associated with sham marriages',[33] irrespective of the fact that Mr Singh's marriage was not suggested to be such.[34] Whilst the Court rejected this argument, it nonetheless made a passing reference to the concept of abuse of rights, pointing out that, in principle:

> the facilities created by the Treaty cannot have the effect of allowing the persons who benefit from them to evade the application of national legislation and of prohibiting Member States from taking the measures necessary to prevent such abuse.[35]

The implications of the judgment for cross-border couples cannot be overstated. EU citizens unable to be together with their close ones due to restrictive national family reunification provisions now obtained an opportunity to avoid these by moving to another Member State and then returning to their home country. Such practices, rather unsurprisingly, caused growing discontent among Member States who were used to treat their own nationals worse than EU citizens. A decade after the delivery of the ruling in *Surinder Singh,* the CJEU handed down its judgment in *Akrich* where the UK authorities repeatedly sought to deny residence rights to a TCN spouse of a British national in a 'U-turn' situation.[36] The case involved a Moroccan national with a history of expulsion from the UK who clandestinely returned to the country and lived there undocumented before marrying a British national. Following that, he was detained for his irregular presence in the UK and deported, according to his wishes, to Ireland where his spouse had meanwhile moved. Having spent six months in Ireland, during which both spouses were employed, Mr Akrich applied for a UK entry visa as a spouse of a returning British national under the *Surinder Singh* rule. His application, however, was rejected because the couple

33 *Surinder Singh* (n 20), para 14.

34 Ibid para 12.

35 Ibid para 24. The Court referred to its previous case-law where it argued along the same lines: Case 115/78 *Knoors* [1979] ECR 00399, para 25 and Case C-61/89 *Bouchoucha* [1990] ECR I-03551, para 14.

36 Case C-109/01 *Akrich* [2003] ECR I-09607.

admitted that the purpose of their relocation to Ireland and back was to bring themselves within the scope of EU law to be able to benefit from its family reunion provisions. The UK authorities considered such an arrangement 'no more than a temporary absence deliberately designed to manufacture a right of residence for Mr Akrich'[37] which, in their view, constituted an abuse of EU law.

The CJEU disagreed. First, it reiterated its position in *Singh* that a Member State national may rely on EU law to claim family reunion rights upon return to their country of origin from another Member State.[38] As to the concept of abuse, the Court stated that the motives which may have prompted the person to take up employment in another Member State or return to their home country are irrelevant, as long as the employment activity is 'effective and genuine' – even where the non-EU spouse did not have residence rights in the EU citizen's home Member State, in the first place.[39] In the meantime, it was specified that:

> [T]here would be an abuse if the facilities afforded by Community law in favour of migrant workers and their spouses were invoked in the context of marriages of convenience entered into in order to circumvent the provisions relating to entry and residence of nationals of non-Member States.[40]

Yet, whilst confirming that reliance on the *Surinder Singh* route cannot be considered abusive, the Court made a surprising move by introducing the so-called 'prior residence rule' – a significant limitation of the EU citizens' right to family reunion. The CJEU held that, to fall within the scope of EU law, the TCN spouse must be already 'lawfully resident' in the first Member State before moving with the EU principal to another Member State.[41] In the view of the Court, EU law covered only freedom of movement within the Union, whereby first entry of non-EU nationals to their territory was to be regulated by Member State authorities. Absence of an EU right to family reunion was to be considered detrimental only in cases where the TCN spouse had a legal right to remain in one Member State in the first place, and the move to another Member State would result in the loss of the opportunity to live together.

37 Ibid para 37.
38 Ibid para 48.
39 Ibid paras 55–56.
40 Ibid para 57.
41 Ibid para 50.

Conversely, if the spouse of an EU citizen had no right to remain in the first place, their inability to benefit from EU rules in another Member State would not be regarded as less favourable treatment than they enjoyed before the movement. The same considerations were applied to returning EU citizens whose TCN spouses were not granted residence rights by the authorities of the host Member State.[42] In essence, that meant that the right of EU citizens to live with their family members was made entirely dependent on the national immigration law in their first country of residence. Importantly, the implications of the ruling not only concerned returning EU citizens but also nationals of other Member States who met their partners already in the host country and wished to continue living there.[43] Given that the relevant rules varied considerably across Member States, this created an odd situation where some couples did not face any particular obstacles in being together, while others were prevented from doing so.

The decision in *Akrich* was heavily criticised. Due to procedural flaws and inconsistency with prior case law,[44] Steve Peers called it 'the worst judgment in the long history of the Court of Justice'.[45] He also pointed out that, whilst suggesting a 'radical (or rather, reactionary)' re-interpretation of the scope of Treaty rights without adequate clarification, the decision was fundamentally unclear in its scope.[46] When interpreted broadly, the scope of the ruling would include not only EU citizens moving with their TCN partners to another Member State but also those who meet their partners already in the host country or cases where the family member joins the EU principal from a third country.

In two subsequent judgements, *Jia*[47] and *Eind*,[48] the Court, however, attempted to clarify and limit its decision in *Akrich*, before ultimately overturning it in *Metock*. In the latter case, which is discussed in detail in Section 5,

42 Ibid paras 52–54.

43 The position of the latter group is specifically addressed in Section 5 below.

44 Such as *Surinder Singh* (n 20); Case C-459/99 *MRAX* [2002] ECR I-06591; Case C-60/00 *Carpenter* [2002] ECR I-06279. For an analysis of *MRAX* and *Carpenter*, see, respectively, Sections 5 and 7.1.

45 Steve Peers, 'Free Movement, Immigration Control and Constitutional Conflict' (2009) 5 *European Constitutional Law Review* 173, 178.

46 Ibid. For criticism of *Akrich*, see also, Christophe Schlitz, 'Akrich: A Clear Delimitation without Limits' (2005) 12 *Maastricht Journal of European and Comparative Law* 241; Eleanor Spaventa, 'Case C-109/01, Secretary of State for the Home Department v. H Akrich.' (2005) 42 *Common Market Law Review* 225.

47 C-1/05 *Jia* [2007] ECR I-00001.

48 *Eind* (n 30).

the CJEU held that the right to family reunion under the Citizenship Directive could be enjoyed by mobile EU citizens irrespective of the prior residence status of the TCN spouse. As will be shown in Chapter 3, the ruling caused an outcry in several Member States; one of their main objections was the loss of control over their own nationals who bring their spouses back into the home country after having spent a very short time in another Member State.

The question about the duration of stay in another country, after which one could rely on the Citizenship Directive when moving home, was ultimately clarified six years later in *O and B*.[49] In that case, the CJEU linked the possibility to rely on EU law with the condition of 'sufficiently genuine' residence in the host Member State that would enable the citizen 'to create or strengthen family life'.[50] In the view of the CJEU, this requirement could only be fulfilled where the EU citizen settles in the home Member State under Article 7(1) of the Citizenship Directive. Tourists and other short-term visitors relying on Article 6(1), accordingly, were not deemed to be discouraged from moving to the host Member State if their TCN spouses were not granted the right of residence after returning home.[51] Whilst this reasoning has been subject to diverse views and interpretations,[52] it is another point that bears particular relevance to the present research. Having set out the principles for the operation of the *Surinder Singh* route, the Court recalled that 'the scope of Union law cannot be extended to cover abuses' and described the two-stage abuse test by explicit reference to *Emsland-Stärke*.[53] In spite of making this statement, the Court, however, appeared reluctant to apply the concept of abuse to the issue at stake, choosing to impose a general condition for family reunion under EU law instead. If the latter is not fulfilled, the situation concerned would simply fall outside the scope of the Directive, making the concept of abuse inapplicable in principle.

49 *O and B* (n 30).

50 Ibid para 51.

51 Ibid paras 52–56.

52 See among others, Nathan Cambien, 'Cases C-456/12 O. and B. and C-457/12 S. and G.: Clarifying the Inter-State Requirement for EU Citizens?' (*European Law Blog*, 11.04.2014) <https://europeanlawblog.eu/2014/04/11/cases-c-45612-o-and-b-and-c-45712-s-and-g-clarifying-the-inter-state-requirement-for-eu-citizens/> accessed 8 April 2024; Eleanor Spaventa, 'Family Rights for Circular Migrants and Frontier Workers: O and B, and S and G.' (2015) 52 *Common Market Law Review* 753.

53 *O and B* (n 30), para 58.

5 EU Citizens Forming Families in the Host Member State

An interrelated issue giving rise to Member States' migration-related anxieties is the position of nationals of other Member States who meet their future spouses when they are already in the host country. As will be demonstrated throughout this book, it is exactly this group that is typically associated with abuse of EU law via marriages of convenience, particularly where the TCN family members are overstayers or unauthorised migrants who can regularise their status by marrying an EU citizen.

Early CJEU case law on TCN family members of mobile EU citizens neither dealt with the question of in which (home or host) Member State family was formed, nor considered the immigration status of TCN family members prior to the acquisition of residency based on free movement provisions. In *MRAX* case,[54] delivered in 2002, a Belgian court asked the CJEU whether national authorities could deny residence rights to TCN spouses of mobile EU citizens if the former arrived at the border without a valid identity document or visa, or were already irregularly present in the country, and ask them to acquire national visas first. The Court answered the question in the negative. Relying on the literal interpretation of the relevant secondary law, it confirmed that the right of mobile EU citizens to live with their spouses is derived from a marital relationship alone.[55] Consequently, Member States are obliged to grant TCN spouses the right of entry and residence without any additional formalities, provided that they can prove their identity and marriage to an EU citizen.[56]

Rather surprisingly, the decision in *MRAX* was completely ignored in *Akrich,* where the CJEU imposed the controversial 'prior lawful residence' requirement on TCN family members. As noted above, the rule was denounced by the landmark judgment in *Metock,* handed down in 2008. The case was referred to the CJEU by the Irish High Court, which was hearing four appeals against the denial of residence rights to non-EU spouses of mobile EU citizens. Following the decision in *Akrich,* Ireland, along with ten other Member States, had linked the right of residence of non-EU family members to a prior lawful immigration status in a Member State.[57] The particular case concerned four couples,

54 *MRAX* (n 44).

55 Ibid para 59.

56 Ibid paras 62, 80, 91.

57 See Commission, 'Report from the Commission to the European Parliament and the Council on the application of Directive 2004/38/EC on the right of citizens of the Union and their family members to move and reside freely within the territory of the Member States' COM (2008) 840 final, 4.

all involving unsuccessful male asylum-seekers married to British, German, and Polish nationals working in Ireland. Their applications for residence cards were refused because they did not satisfy the condition of prior lawful residence in another Member State.

The case was decided under an accelerated procedure given the uncertainty over the validity of the Irish law preventing the couples from leading normal family lives. During the proceedings, the Irish authorities argued in favour of the principle imposed in *Akrich*. In their view, there was a division of competences between the Member States and the EU, under which the former have control over the admission of non-EU nationals upon their first entry into the EU, whereas the latter regulates the further movement of TCN family members within its territory.[58]

In the first question, the Court was asked to rule on the legality of the prior lawful residence requirement. In its reply, the CJEU stated that the ruling in *Akrich* needed to be reconsidered,[59] noting that 'if Union citizens were not allowed to lead a normal family life in the host Member State, the exercise of the freedoms they are guaranteed by the Treaty would be seriously obstructed'.[60] The Court then went on to argue that the refusal of the host Member State to grant family reunion rights to EU citizens would discourage them from exercising their free movement rights, even if their family members did not already have regular residence status in another Member State.[61] Conversely, if Member States retained exclusive competence upon granting residence rights to family members who did not satisfy the prior lawful residence condition, the freedom of movement of EU citizens would vary from one Member State to another, according to the national family reunification provisions. In the view of the Court, this would not be compatible with the objective of establishing the internal market, which implies the abolition of obstacles to the free movement of persons.[62] Moreover, it was stressed that such an interpretation would lead to a paradoxical outcome that a Member State would be obliged, under the Family Reunification Directive, 'to authorise the entry and residence of the spouse of a national of a non-member country lawfully resident in its territory where the spouse is not already lawfully resident in another Member State, but would be free to refuse the entry and residence of the spouse of a Union citizen in the same circumstances'.[63]

58 *Metock and Others* (n 15), para 44.
59 Ibid para 58.
60 Ibid para 62.
61 Ibid para 64.
62 Ibid paras 67, 68.
63 Ibid para 69.

Second, the CJEU was asked to clarify whether a TCN spouse can enjoy the right of residence if their marriage to an EU citizen has already taken place in the host Member State. The CJEU answered this question in the affirmative, confirming that this right was provided through EU law, 'irrespective of when and where their marriage took place and of how the national of a non-member country entered the host Member State'.[64] The Court reasonably argued that the refusal of the state to grant residence rights to the EU citizen's new spouse would discourage the EU citizen 'from continuing to reside there and encourage him to leave in order to be able to lead a family life in another Member State or in a non-member country'.[65] In other words, the CJEU held that the Directive applies even in cases when the couple have already met in the host Member State, and the non-EU party had previously lived in that country irregularly. Further, similarly to its previous case law in this area, the Court acknowledged that Member States may, in principle, derogate from provisions of the Directive in cases of abuse of rights,[66] yet did not even consider the applicability of Article 35 to the situation at stake.

Although the judgment in *Metock*, in fact, merely restored the previous *status quo* established in *MRAX*, it caused considerable controversy in several Member States. As will be shown in Chapter 3, it was exactly at this point that fears about perceived marriages of convenience involving mobile EU citizens escalated to an unprecedented level, ultimately resulting in the adoption of new EU-level measures aiming to calm the worries of national authorities. In this context, it is remarkable that, as expressly admitted by the Irish government, none of the marriages discussed in *Metock* were found to be ones of convenience.[67]

6 Visas for Non-EU Family Members Travelling to the UK

The issue of excessive visa requirements re-emerged before the CJEU a few years later, this time with respect to TCN family members who already hold residence cards issued by another Member State. In the *McCarthy* case,[68] a Colombian spouse of a dual British and Irish national living in Spain challenged British rules requiring all TCN family members of mobile EU citizens

64 Ibid para 99.
65 Ibid para 89.
66 Ibid para 75.
67 Ibid para 46.
68 Case C-202/13 *McCarthy* ECLI:EU:C:2014:2450.

to acquire entry visas before visiting the UK. In order to justify these measures, the British authorities claimed that there was a risk of systemic abuse of rights and fraud by 'those engaged in the "business of sham marriages"' who would use falsified residence cards to gain access to the UK.[69]

Having found that the wording of the Citizenship Directive exempts residence card holders from the visa requirement,[70] the CJEU proceeded to discuss the applicability of Article 35 to the present case. The Court, first, observed that examination of the potential abuse must be based on the two-stage test established in *Emsland-Stärke*[71] and carried out on a case-by-case basis, assessing the specific conduct of the individual concerned.[72] By contrast, the requirement to obtain UK visas could be regarded as an automatic measure of general prevention targeting all TCN family members of EU citizens, irrespective of whether their residence cards were authentic or not.[73] The court concluded that this norm, in effect, would obstruct the free movement rights of EU citizens and their family members, and therefore had to be abolished.[74]

7 Family Reunion Cases outside the Scope of the Citizenship Directive

Tensions between CJEU and Member States have also been observed in cases which, for some reason, are not covered by the Citizenship Directive. One category of persons falling outside its scope is third-country nationals who have no EU citizen family members. Apart from national immigration provisions, their position may be covered by EU immigration and asylum law, which is of limited interest to the present study. In the meantime, non-EU nationals who do have EU citizen family members may not benefit from the Directive in two cases: either because they find themselves in purely internal situations, or, less often, because, even if there is a cross-border element in their circumstances, it is not sufficient to trigger the application of the Directive.

---

69 Ibid paras 26–27.

70 Ibid paras 40–42.

71 Ibid para 54. The Court referred to its later case-law quoting the *Emsland-Stärke* test, such as Case C-364/10 *Hungary* v *Slovakia* ECLI:EU:C:2012:630, para 58, and *O and B* (n 30), para 58.

72 Ibid paras 52–53.

73 Ibid para 55.

74 Ibid paras 57–58.

7.1 *Different Forms of Free Movement*

The first group of persons who do not qualify as beneficiaries of the Directive are those whose situations are not precisely addressed by its provisions yet do include a cross-border element. Apart from the 'returnees', the CJEU has identified two more subcategories of such individuals: family members of EU citizens who work in more than one Member State (commonly referred to as '*Carpenter* cases') and family members of an EU citizen child who is exercising rights pursuant to the Directive in a host Member State (referred to as '*Chen* cases').

In *Carpenter*,[75] a British national residing in the UK was providing services to persons established in other Member States where he frequently travelled for the purpose of his business. When his Filipino wife applied for leave to remain in the UK as the spouse of a British national, the Home Office rejected her application because she had previously overstayed her visitor visa, and signalled an intention to deport her. In her appeal, Ms Carpenter argued that her situation fell within the scope of the Treaty rights, as her husband could more easily travel abroad while she was looking after his children from his first marriage. She accordingly claimed that her deportation would interfere with her husband's right to provide services.

First, the Court noted that the relevant secondary legislation (namely, Directive 73/148/EEC in force at the time) did not apply in this case, since the EU citizen's spouse physically remained in the Member State of his nationality.[76] It was nonetheless found that this situation could still trigger the application of Treaty provisions on the free movement of services. Having underlined the importance of protection of the family life of EU citizens to enable them to exercise their Treaty rights, the Court concluded, by reference to *Singh*, that 'the separation of Mr and Mrs Carpenter would be detrimental to their family life and, therefore, to the conditions under which Mr Carpenter exercises a fundamental freedom'.[77] Further, it noted that any national public interest measures that may hinder the exercise of Treaty rights had to comply with the fundamental rights observed by the EU, in this particular case the right to respect for family life protected under Article 8 of the ECHR.[78] The Court consequently considered that the decision to deport Ms Carpenter would be

75 *Carpenter* (n 44).

76 Ibid paras 28–36.

77 Ibid para 39.

78 European Convention for the Protection of Human Rights and Fundamental Freedoms, CETS No.005 (04.11.1950) (ECHR).

disproportionate, given that breach of national immigration rules was the only complaint related to her conduct.[79]

Along with the ruling in *MRAX* explored above, the Court's judgment in *Carpenter* contrasts strikingly with *Akrich* which was handed down only a year later. In *Carpenter*, the Court not only extended application of the deterrence test to situations involving a very limited element of physical movement, but also did not consider it necessary to substantiate its claim that expulsion of his TCN spouse could deter the EU citizen concerned from providing services in other Member States. Without going into much detail, the Court merely emphasised the link between the right to enjoy the freedom of movement and the right to family life, leaving the scope of the judgment rather uncertain.[80]

The issue was given more clarity in a similar case of *S and G*,[81] which dealt with family members of two Dutch nationals who resided in the Netherlands but who travelled regularly to other Member States for work. The first wished to secure residence for his Ukrainian mother-in-law who took care of his son in his absence, whilst the second claimed family rights for his Peruvian spouse with whom they had two children together. The Court found that the Court's interpretation of the Treaty provisions on the freedom to provide services in *Carpenter* could, by analogy, be equally applied to the freedom of movement of workers.[82] The CJEU, nonetheless, did not precisely follow its reasoning in *Carpenter*, concluding that it would be up to the national court to determine whether the refusal to grant TCN family members a derived right to reside would deter the EU citizen from exercising their fundamental rights.[83] Further, whilst in *Carpenter*, the role of family members as child-carers was not given any consideration, at all, in *S and G* the Court found that this was a 'relevant factor to be taken into account'.[84] Some scholars saw this as a substantial change of the approach established in *Carpenter*. For instance, Eleanor Spaventa argues that in *Carpenter*, the Court regarded the protection of the EU citizen's family as 'a value in itself (and the lack thereof could be construed as a barrier to movement) and no longer merely instrumental to the achievement of internal market objectives'.[85] By contrast, in *S and G*, it was considered that

79 Ibid paras 41–45.

80 For an analysis, see, Alina Tryfonidou, 'Mary Carpenter v Secretary of State for the Home Department: The Beginning of a New Era in the European Union?' (2003) 14 *King's Law Journal* 81.

81 Case C-457/12 *S and G* ECLI:EU:C:2014:136.

82 Ibid paras 39–40.

83 Ibid para 42.

84 Ibid para 43.

85 Spaventa, 'Family rights for circular migrants' (n 52) 767–68.

a mere fact of interference with the EU citizen's family life was insufficient to constitute an obstacle to free movement. In the application of the deterrence test, the Court now focused on the extent to which the relevant national measures could obstruct someone's exercise of their Treaty rights, with factors such as childcaring playing a crucial role in the assessment. In the opinion of Spaventa, such an approach 'restates the centrality of the market citizen whose non-market rights are protected only insofar as they facilitate her economic activity'.[86] Indeed, it is remarkable that in *S and G,* Article 8 of the ECHR was not mentioned at all.

Another contentious issue in this area relates to non-EU nationals deliberately giving birth in the particular Member State to enable the child to acquire its nationality. The key judgment illustrating this type of anxiety is *Chen,* which concerned a Chinese national who temporarily moved to Northern Ireland to give birth.[87] Similarly to applicants in *Akrich,* she expressly admitted that the purpose of such an arrangement was to ensure that her child would obtain Irish nationality on the basis of the *jus soli* principle which was in force in Ireland at the time. This, in turn, was expected to enable the mother to acquire the derived right of residence in the UK, where she intended to live. The Court first found that, as a Union citizen, the child was entitled to enjoy the right to free movement and residence protected by the Treaty, and the fact that she was born in the host Member State could not, 'for that reason alone, be assimilated to a purely internal situation'.[88] As she satisfied the self-sufficiency requirement (resources were provided by her TCN mother), she was also regarded as a beneficiary of Directive 90/364 (now, by analogy, Article 7(1)(b) of the Citizenship Directive).[89] The mother, on the other hand, was not dependent on her EU citizen child and, therefore, did not fall within the scope of direct family members listed in the Directive.[90] The Court nonetheless held that she was still entitled to the right to reside with her child in the host Member State since a refusal to allow a TCN parent to do so 'would deprive the child's right of residence of any useful effect'.[91]

Further, the UK government objected that provisions of EU law were not applicable in the situation at stake because the Chinese national mother's conduct constituted 'an attempt improperly to exploit' Treaty rights which,

86 Ibid 769.

87 C-200/02 *Zhu* and *Chen* [2004] ECR I-09925.

88 Ibid para 19.

89 Ibid paras 27–28.

90 Ibid paras 42–44.

91 Ibid para 45.

from the British perspective, fit the notion of abuse described in *Centros*.[92] The Court rejected this argument. Although in this particular case, the Irish nationality of the child was sought to be merely used as an instrument to secure residence rights under EU law, it was reiterated that acquisition of nationality fell within the competence of a particular Member State, and that other Member States were obliged to recognise it without any further conditions.[93]

7.2 *Static EU Citizens*

Although situations having no cross-border element at all will typically be entirely covered by national law, the CJEU has recognised some of them as falling within the scope of Treaty provisions on EU citizenship. This is viewed with unease by Member States who often perceive it as an intrusion into the sensitive area of their competence.

The key judgement giving rise to Member State anxieties in this context is *Ruiz Zambrano*.[94] The case concerned Mr Ruiz Zambrano, who, together with his spouse and child, arrived from Colombia and applied for asylum in Belgium. Their applications were refused, but they were allowed to temporarily remain in the country based on a *non-refoulement* clause. In the following years, Ms Ruiz Zambrano gave birth to two more children who acquired Belgian nationality since they were not registered at the Colombian consulate in Belgium. After unsuccessful attempts to rely on national law to take up residence in Belgium as their parents, Mr Ruiz Zambrano argued that he enjoyed the derived right of residence under the Citizenship Directive. The case was referred to the CJEU for clarification.

The CJEU first found that the situation at stake did not fall within the scope of the Citizenship Directive, since the EU citizen children resided in the Member State of their nationality and had never moved outside it.[95] Yet, the Court then proceeded to acknowledge the fundamental status of EU citizenship, stating that 'Article 20 TFEU precludes national measures which have the effect of depriving citizens of the Union of the genuine enjoyment of the substance of the rights conferred by virtue of their status as citizens of the Union'.[96] In

92 Ibid para 34. Article 35 of the Citizenship Directive was not discussed in the judgment, for it was delivered before the Directive came into force.

93 Ibid paras 36–39. The CJEU earlier held that Member States are obliged to recognise each others' nationalities, for the opposite would undermine their nationals' right to free movement. See, Case C-369/90 *Micheletti and Others* [1992] ECR I-04239, para 10; Case C-148/02 *Garcia Avello* [2003] ECR I-11613, para 28.

94 Case C-34/09 *Ruiz Zambrano* [2011] ECR I-01177.

95 Ibid para 39.

96 Ibid paras 41–42.

the Court's view, this is precisely what would happen if Member State authorities denied residence to parents of dependent minor children who are static nationals of a particular Member State. Since such a refusal would force the TCN parents to leave the Union together with their children, it would preclude the latter from exercising their rights derived from EU citizenship.[97] In other words, that would mean that situations where a Member State national risks losing their core EU citizenship rights would fall within the scope of EU law, regardless of whether they are purely internal or not.

The Court's reasoning and possible implications of the judgment gave rise to much controversy, not least due to the lack of clarity in its scope and possible implications.[98] In its follow-up jurisprudence, the Court, however, confined the *ratione personae* of the *Zambrano* rule to exceptional cases. The key requirement in this context is the relationship of legal, financial or emotional dependency between the third-country national and the EU citizen concerned. Although it may not necessarily be limited to the one between a TCN parent and an EU citizen child, and may also include spouses,[99] the dependency threshold is high; a mere desire of a Union citizen alone, for economic or other reasons, to preserve the family unit in the EU territory would not be sufficient.[100] Further, this criterion would only apply to situations where the EU citizen concerned would be forced to leave not only the Member State of their own nationality but the territory of the Union as a whole.[101]

97 Ibid para 44.

98 For a discussion, see among others, Dimitry Kochenov, 'A Real European Citizenship: A New Jurisdiction Test: A Novel Chapter in the Development of the Union in Europe' (2011) 18 *Columbia Journal of European Law* 56; Iyiola Solanke, 'Using the Citizen to Bring the Refugee In: *Gerardo Ruiz Zambrano v Office national de l'emploi* (ONEM)' (2012) 75 *The Modern Law Review* 101.

99 Joined Cases C-356/11 and C-357/11 *O and S* ECLI:EU:C:2012:776, para 55; Case C-836/18 *Subdelegación del Gobierno en Ciudad Real* ECLI:EU:C:2020:119, para 54.

100 Case C-256/11 *Dereci and Others* [2011] ECR I-11315, paras 67–68; *O and S* (n 99) para 52; Case C-82/16 *K.A. and Others* ECLI:EU:C:2018:308, para 74; *Subdelegación del Gobierno en Ciudad Real* (n 99), para 57.

101 See among others, *Dereci and Others* (n 100), paras 65–67; Case C-86/12 *Alokpa* ECLI:EU:C:2013:645, para 36; Case C-87/12 *Ymeraga* ECLI:EU:C:2013:291, para 45; *K.A. and Others* (n 100), para 52; Joined Cases C-451/19 and C-532/19 *Subdelegación del Gobierno en Toledo* ECLI:EU:C:2022:354, paras 46, 54, 86. For a discussion on post-Ruiz Zambrano case law, see Stephen Coutts, 'Expulsion and Article 20 TFEU: Some Practical and Conceptual Issues' (2021) 23 *European Journal of Migration and Law* 29; Hester Kroeze and Peter Van Elsuwege, 'Revisiting Ruiz Zambrano: A Never Ending Story?' (2021) 23 *European Journal of Migration and Law* 1; Martijn van den Brink, 'Is It Time to Abolish the Substance of EU Citizenship Rights Test?' (2021) 23 *European Journal of Migration and Law* 13; Hanneke van Eijken, 'Connecting the Dots Backwards, What Did Ruiz Zambrano Mean for EU

8 Marriages of Convenience as the Only Form of Abuse of Rights?

As has been shown in the sections above, the CJEU has, in principle, confirmed the applicability of the concept of abuse to family reunion cases. Nonetheless, like in other relevant rulings in the area of free movement of persons, it consistently refused to give it effect. The Court's extreme reluctance to find abuse in this field has been explained by some commentators by its different approaches to economic transactions and human beings where the latter are considered to have 'a higher moral value'.[102] Further, as AG Geelhoed convincingly argued in *Akrich*, establishing the subjective purpose of enjoying the freedom of movement may prove nearly impossible, given that an EU citizen 'may have all kinds of reasons for installing himself in another Member State'.[103] AG also noted that the explicit admission of the motives by the individuals concerned in *Akrich* was rather exceptional; it could thus be assumed that in other cases the motives may be subject to manipulation.[104] Others, in the meantime, have been more critical of the Court's position, suggesting, for instance, that the situation described in *Chen* obviously contains an artificial element which would have deserved a more detailed assessment.[105]

Irrespective of the rationale of the CJEU approach, it follows that the scope of abuse in family reunion cases is *de facto* confined to marriages (or, by analogy, registered partnerships)[106] of convenience. As the CJEU has consistently

Citizenship and Fundamental Rights in EU Law?' (2021) 23 *European Journal of Migration and Law* 48.

102 Rita de la Feria, 'Introducing the Principle of Prohibition of Abuse of Law' in Rita De la Feria and Stefan Vogenauer (eds), *Prohibition of Abuse of Law: A New General Principle of EU Law?* (Hart 2011) xix. Rita de la Feria, 'Prohibition of Abuse of (Community) Law: The Creation of a New General Principle of EC Law through Tax' (2008) 45 *Common Market Law Review* 417–18; Katja S Ziegler, '"Abuse of Law" in the Context of the Free Movement of Workers' in Rita De la Feria and Stefan Vogenauer (eds), *Prohibition of Abuse of Law: A New General Principle of EU Law?* (Hart 2011) 310–13.

103 *Akrich* (n 36), Opinion of AG Geelhoed, para 179. For this view, see also, Ziegler (n 100) 308–309; Eleanor Spaventa, 'Comments on Abuse of Law and the Free Movement of Workers' in De la Feria and Vogenauer (eds), *Prohibition of Abuse of Law* (n 102) 317–18.

104 *Akrich* (n 36), Opinion of AG Geelhoed, paras 172, 174.

105 Jean-Yves Carlier, 'Case C-200/02, *Kunqian Catherine Zhu, Man Lavette Chen v. Secretary of State for the Home Department*' (2005) 42 *Common Market Law Review* 1121, 1127–28; Rita de la Feria, 'Prohibition of Abuse of (Community) Law' (n 102) 417.

106 The Commission in its Guidelines confirms that the 'definition of marriages of convenience can be extended by analogy to other forms of relationships contracted for the sole purpose of enjoying the right of free movement and residence, such as (registered) partnership of convenience'. Commission, 'Communication from the Commission to the European Parliament and the Council on guidance for better transposition and application of Directive 2004/38/EC on the right of citizens of the Union and their family

held, the finding of this type of abuse falls within the competence of Member States and must be based on an individual examination of the particular case. The CJEU, however, was never asked to elaborate on the substance of the concept of marriages of convenience,[107] or rule on the compatibility of specific aspects of the examination with EU law. This is unsurprising, provided that none of the cases discussed above involved an alleged marriage of convenience; moreover, in several judgments, it was explicitly noted that none of the marriages concerned was considered as such.[108]

In light of the consistent refusal of the Court to find abuse in the area of free movement of persons, the decision to single out marriages of convenience from the general rule inevitably invites a further question – namely, why this type of conduct is treated so remarkably different from other similar arrangements, most notably the one discussed in *Chen*.

To begin with, it is worth exploring whether the concept of marriages of convenience satisfies the general two-stage test of abuse, established in *Emsland-Stärke*.[109] The first element of the test requires proving that, despite formal compliance with the relevant conditions, the purpose of the rules concerned has not been achieved. As observed above, the underlying aim of the right to family reunion granted to mobile EU citizens is to enable them to enjoy family life. Where a marriage is a purely formal arrangement which has never had any substance but an immigration motive, the intended purpose is not achieved. The second element of the abuse test refers to the subjective intention to obtain advantage from EU law by artificially creating the necessary conditions. Although there are a great variety of motives for getting married,[110] one of them – obtaining an immigration advantage – is not accepted for the purposes of the Citizenship Directive, provided that this is the only reason for marriage and the couple does not intend to lead a family life. Whilst the

members to move and reside freely within the territory of the Member States', COM (2009) 313 final, 4.2.

107 The only exception is the ruling in *Chakroun* which concerned application of the Directive 2003/86/EC. The Court briefly noted that the marriage in question of nearly 34 years can 'hardly be compared to a marriage of convenience'. Case C-578/08 *Chakroun* [2010] ECR I-01839, para 54. It should, however, be noted that this was not alleged by the national authorities; the relevant passage was rather used by the Court to strengthen its argument in favour of abolishment of a general rule adopted by the Member State concerned.

108 *Surinder Singh* (n 20), para 12; *Metock and Others* (n 15), para 46. See also, *Carpenter* (n 44), Opinion of AG Stix-Hackl, para 75; *Ogieriakhi* (n 21), Opinion of AG Bot, para 32.

109 See Chapter 1, Section 4.2.1 for more details.

110 For a critical discussion on the concept of marriages of convenience, see Chapter 3, Section 2.

subjective intention is difficult to prove, it is considered an inherent part of the concept of marriages of convenience; therefore, the second element of the *Emsland-Stärke* test is, at least formally, equally met.

Irrespective of this finding, marriages of convenience as a form of abuse do not sit particularly well with the CJEU approach to the relevant nationality cases, such as *Chen*. First, it must be noted that both areas concerned – i.e., the conditions of entry into marriage and acquisition of nationality, respectively – are regulated exclusively by Member States. However, whilst marriages contracted for the 'wrong' purpose are considered abusive, Member States are obliged to automatically recognise each other's nationalities. The purpose of its acquisition is consequently deemed irrelevant; there is no concept of a 'nationality of convenience' even where, as in *Chen*, the bond with the state of nationality is a pure formality, and the nationality was acquired only to enable the individual concerned to benefit from the Treaty rights.[111] Of course, making acceptance of the nationality conditional upon the existence of a 'close' or 'genuine' link with the relevant state would undermine legal certainty of nationality regimes, which would adversely impact the position of the individuals involved. For instance, Cathryn Costello argues that in this case '[a]ll designations of nationality at birth had to predict a child's life course and where she will develop genuine links'.[112] Notwithstanding that, given the parallels between the concepts of nationality and marriage, the decision to single out marriages of convenience as the only form of abuse would arguably need further justification, both by the EU legislator and the Court.

9 Conclusion

This chapter has shown that the CJEU, with a few exceptions, continuously departed from the logic of elimination of all possible obstacles to family reunion, which was supposed to ensure that EU citizens could freely exercise their Treaty rights. In its efforts to achieve this aim, the Court extended the right to family reunion to EU citizens returning to their own Member State, as well as to several situations which did not involve an actual cross-border element.

---

111 See also, the CJEU judgment in *Collins* where a jobseeker in the UK sought to rely on his Irish nationality, although he had never lived or worked in Ireland and only visited the country on three occasions for a few days. The Court did not even discuss the issue of abuse in this case. Case C-38/02 *Collins* [2004] ECR I-02703.

112 Cathryn Costello, 'Citizenship of the Union: Above Abuse?' in De la Feria and Vogenauer (eds), *Prohibition of Abuse of Law* (n 102) 336.

The CJEU has also set a very high threshold for establishing abuse in the area of freedom of movement of persons, essentially rejecting the applicability of Article 35 in 'U-turn' situations and confining it to the exceptional cases of marriages (or, by analogy, registered partnerships) of convenience. In its landmark judgment in *Metock*, the Court explicitly stated that, as long as the marriage is not one of convenience, the TCN party benefits from the Citizenship Directive irrespective of their residence status in the Member State concerned, as well as of where and when the marriage took place.

With regards to marriages of convenience, the CJEU has established two key principles Member States must respect when targeting suspicious marriages. First, it confirmed that the relevant examination must only be carried out on a case-by-case basis, and systematic checks are prohibited. Second, the Court specified that a TCN spouse continues to benefit from the Directive even if the couple do not live under one roof or even if they cohabit with other partners as long as their marriage is not officially dissolved (provided that it was not contracted only to enable the non-EU national to obtain residence rights).

CHAPTER 3

After *Metock:* Marriages of Convenience as an Apple of Discord between the EU and Member States

1 Introduction

As briefly mentioned in Chapter 2, it was the CJEU judgment in *Metock* in 2008 that marked the turning point in bringing unprecedented attention to the perceived abuse of EU free movement law. Over the decade following *Metock*, the discontent of several governments with the liberal family reunion provisions under the Citizenship Directive[1] has led to repeated calls for EU institutions to limit these rights.

This chapter describes the political dialogue between the EU and a number of Member States, particularly Denmark, Ireland, and the UK, and looks at how far the Union has been prepared to go to accommodate their demands. First, it provides a brief insight into the controversy surrounding the normative distinction between 'genuine' marriages and those contracted for residence purposes. Second, it explores the Member States' positions on the alleged abuse of EU law and the EU institutions' responses to their concerns, which included the adoption of several legislative instruments addressing the issue of marriages of convenience. In this context, a separate section of the chapter is devoted to the pre-Brexit referendum settlement, agreed between the EU and the UK to persuade the latter to remain in the EU. The chapter also touches upon public and media narratives related to the issue of marriages of convenience, including the perceived link between the abuse of free movement rights and the trafficking of human beings.

1 Directive 2004/38/EC of the European Parliament and of the Council of 29 April 2004 on the right of citizens of the Union and their family members to move and reside freely within the territory of the Member States amending Regulation (EEC) No 1612/68 and repealing Directives 64/221/EEC, 68/360/EEC, 72/194/EEC, 73/148/EEC, 75/34/EEC, 75/35/EEC, 90/364/EEC, 90/365/EEC and 93/96/EEC [2004] OJ L158/77 (Citizenship Directive).

 | DOI:10.1163/9789004499263_005

2 All You Need Is Love? The Controversial Notion of Marriages of Convenience

Unlike the concept of abuse in EU law, the notion of marriages of convenience had first developed in Member States' national laws before finding its way in the EU instruments. In the contemporary Western European context, the fight against marriages for residence purposes began to intensify after the introduction of restrictions on labour migration in the 1970s and further expanded alongside the tightening of domestic family reunification provisions in the 1990s and 2000s. Controls of marriages between nationals (or residents) and foreigners consequently became an intrinsic part of migration policies in the majority of Western European states, most notably the UK,[2] Denmark,[3] Germany,[4] Austria,[5] the Netherlands,[6] Belgium,[7] and Norway.[8]

At the same time, it must be noted that marriages for residence purposes are not the only instance where marriages may be deemed to be contracted, either entirely or partly, for rational reasons. Such arrangements may equally find

2 See among others, Helena Wray, 'An Ideal Husband? Marriages of Convenience, Moral Gatekeeping and Immigration to the UK' (2006) 8 *European Journal of Migration and Law* 303. The case of the UK is discussed in more detail in Chapter 6.

3 Helena Wray, 'Regulating Spousal Migration in Denmark' (2013) 27 *Journal of Immigration, Asylum and Nationality Law* 143.

4 Laura Block, *Policy Frames on Spousal Migration in Germany* (Springer 2016) 256–57.

5 Daniela Digruber and Irene Messinger, 'Marriage of Residence in Austria' (2006) 8 *European Journal of Migration and Law* 281; Irene Messinger, *Schein oder nicht Schein: Konstruktion und Kriminalisierung von 'Scheinehen' in Geschichte und Gegenwart* (Mandelbaum 2012); Irene Messinger, 'There is Something about Marrying … The Case of Human Rights vs. Migration Regimes using the Example of Austria' (2013) 2 *Laws*, 376 <https://ideas.repec.org/a/gam/jlawss/v2y2013i4p376-391d29258.html> accessed 2 April 2024.

6 Saskia Bonjour and Betty de Hart, 'A Proper Wife, a Proper Marriage: Constructions of "Us" and "Them" in Dutch Family Migration Policy' (2013) 20 *European Journal of Women's Studies* 64–67.

7 Marie-Claire Foblets and Dirk Vanheule, 'Marriages of Convenience in Belgium: The Punitive Approach Gains Ground in Migration Law' (2006) 8 *European Journal of Migration and Law* 263; Federica Infantino, 'Bordering "Fake" Marriages? The Everyday Practices of Control at the Consulates of Belgium, France and Italy in Casablanca' (2014) 1 *Etnografia e ricerca qualitativa* 27; Maïté Maskens, 'Bordering Intimacy: The Fight against Marriages of Convenience in Brussels' (2015) 33(2) *The Cambridge Journal of Anthropology* 42; Mieke Vandenbroucke, 'Legal-Discursive Constructions of Genuine Cross-Border Love in Belgian Marriage Fraud Investigations' (2020) 17 *Critical Discourse Studies* 175.

8 Wencke Mühleisen, Åse Røthing and Stine H Bang Svendsen, 'Norwegian Sexualities: Assimilation and Exclusion in Norwegian Immigration Policy' (2012) 15 *Sexualities* 142–45; Helga Eggebø, 'A Real Marriage? Applying for Marriage Migration to Norway' (2013) 39 *Journal of Ethnic and Migration Studies* 773.

place in other areas of national law, such as tax, social security, welfare or pension law.[9] As Kerry Abrams explains, for lawmakers, marriage serves as a proxy for a committed, long-term, and possible economic dependency relationship that makes the parties worthy of receiving the benefit, such as tax advantages. However, the legally valid marriage alone is not always deemed sufficient for this. Whether authorities will subject marriages to further (functional) tests, largely depends on their perception of the risk that the party(ies) will use the marriage instrumentally in order to obtain the benefit, as well as the harm this would potentially cause the state.[10]

Indeed, it is possible that good friends living in a shared flat may decide to marry solely to obtain tax advantages, without any intention of founding a family. The government, however, may believe that the number of such couples is unsubstantial because of the low value of benefit compared with the legal obligations arising from marriage (e.g., liability to spouse's debts, obligation to support the spouse, equitable distribution of property in case of divorce). In addition, the parties continue to receive the benefit only as long as they stay married. It is therefore unlikely that the state will spend significant resources to investigate the purpose of the marriage, particularly given the general nature of the respective benefit in question.

By contrast, a marriage between a third-country national and a national or a permanent resident would provide the former with an opportunity to obtain an immigration advantage. This type of benefit is often considered substantial enough to subject the spouses to further (e.g., income) requirements and/or functional tests – especially in light of the political importance of immigration control where marriages of convenience are perceived as a brutal invasion of the polity by new members who would not otherwise be accepted there.[11] The fact that the TCN party would later be able to obtain an independent residence permit serves as a further justification for subjecting marriages to additional scrutiny. Furthermore, in comparison with the previous group, this category is much more limited, which makes it easier to target 'suspicious' cases.

Scholars from various disciplines have argued that the normative distinction between 'genuine' marriages and those of convenience is deeply problematic, particularly in light of the great variety of global relationship patterns. When exercising control practices, national authorities tend to impose onto couples their own value judgments of how a 'real' marriage should look like,

9 Kerry Abrams, 'Marriage Fraud' (2012) 100 *California Law Review* 3.

10 Ibid 37–39.

11 Ibid 53.

a process that Helena Wray designates as 'moral gate-keeping'.[12] By doing so, governments risk targeting not only artificial arrangements that have no other substance apart from an immigration motive, but also marriages which do not entirely fit their subjective perceptions, leading to significant intrusion into the couples' family life.[13] Further, the assessment of a marriage is commonly based on the simplistic juxtaposition between 'pure' marriages based on the Western ideal of romantic love and those contracted for 'ulterior' reasons, such as social or financial gain via immigration. In reality, however, the two sets of motives can hardly be separated. As Katharine Charsley and Michaela Benson underline, the reasons for marriage-related migration may include 'love, genuine affection, family unity, property, status, economic and financial considerations, stability (including for children), and future security, and are often difficult to disentangle from one another'.[14] Due to global inequality, the migration status of the potential spouse may make them appear more attractive, but this does not mean that such couples do not wish to create a family. In the words of Helena Wray, '[m]arriage to secure the ability to move is no more morally reprehensible and no more sham than aspiring to social advancement through marriage within a state'.[15]

12 Helena Wray, 'An Ideal Husband?' (n 2) 303.

13 On this point, see among others, Katharine Charsley and Michaela Benson, 'Marriages of Convenience and Inconvenient Marriages: Regulating Spousal Migration to Britain' (2012) 26 *Journal of Immigration, Asylum and Nationality Law* 10; Messinger, 'There is Something about Marrying' (n 5); Bonjour and de Hart (n 6); Helena Wray, 'The "Pure" Relationship, Sham Marriages and Immigration Control' in Joanna Miles, Perveez Mody and Rebecca Probert (eds) *Marriage Rites and Rights* (Hart 2015).

14 Charsley and Benson (n 13) 16.

15 Wray, 'The "Pure" Relationship, Sham Marriages and Immigration Control' (n 13) 145–46. On this point, see also, Anne-Marie D'Aoust, 'In the Name of Love: Marriage Migration, Governmentality, and Technologies of Love' (2013) 7 *International Political Sociology* 258; Georgie Wemyss, Nira Yuval-Davis and Kathryn Cassidy, 'Beauty and the Beast': Everyday Bordering and "Sham Marriage" Discourse' (2018) 66 *Political Geography* 151; Apostolos Andrikopoulos, 'Love, Money and Papers in the Affective Circuits of Cross-Border Marriages: Beyond the "Sham"/"Genuine" Dichotomy' (2019) *Journal of Ethnic and Migration Studies*; Saara Pellander, 'Buy Me Love: Entanglements of Citizenship, Income and Emotions in Regulating Marriage Migration' (2019) *Journal of Ethnic and Migration Studies*.

3 The Judgment in *Metock:* Opening a Pandora's Box

The issue of marriages of convenience found its way in EU law in the 1990s, although not in the context of free movement rights. The first attempt to consolidate policies specifically targeted at the phenomenon was made in 1993 with the adoption of a non-binding Resolution on the harmonisation of national policies on family reunification. The document contained a provision stating that Member States may refuse admission of TCN spouses if the marriage concerned was found to be 'contracted solely or principally for the purpose of enabling the spouse to enter and take up residence in a Member State'.[16] The Resolution, nonetheless, only applied to non-EU nationals already legally resident in a Member State who wished to be reunited with their TCN family members. It later transformed into the binding Family Reunification Directive,[17] which is of limited interest to the present study.

The next EU soft law document dealing with marriages of convenience was adopted several years later. In December 1997, the Council agreed on a Resolution on measures specifically targeting marriages of convenience[18] in light of the need to 'adopt equivalent measures to combat the phenomenon'.[19] The proposal for the document, brought up by the Luxembourg presidency, was seemingly initiated by the UK which abolished its 'primary purpose rule' in the same year.[20] The document narrows down the definition provided in the 1993 Resolution, stating that a marriage of convenience is:

> [A] marriage concluded between a national of a Member State or a third-country national legally resident in a Member State and a third-country national, with the sole aim of circumventing the rules on entry and

---

16 Ad Hoc Immigration Group, 'Resolution on the harmonisation of national policies on family reunification', SN 2828/1/93 WGI 1497 REV 1 (01.06.1993), principle 4 (as cited in Parliament, 'Free Movement of Persons in the European Union: Specific Issues' (Working document, 05–1999) (PE 167.028, 1999) 120).

17 Council Directive 2003/86/EC of 22 September 2003 on the right to family reunification [2003] OJ L251/12 (Family Reunification Directive).

18 Council Resolution of 4 December 1997 on measures to be adopted on the combating of marriages of convenience [1997] OJ C382/1 (Council Resolution on Marriages of Convenience).

19 Ibid, preamble.

20 Betty de Hart, 'Introduction: The Marriage of Convenience in European Immigration Law' (2006) 8 *European Journal of Migration and Law* 251, 252. For more details on the 'primary purpose rule', see Chapter 6, Section 3.

> residence of third-country nationals and obtaining for the third-country national a residence permit or authority to reside in a Member State.[21]

The 1997 Resolution also lists several hints indicating that this might be the case. The wording of the document suggests that it was not intended to apply to mobile EU citizens before 2004 when the concept of marriages of convenience was introduced in the Citizenship Directive. Such an interpretation would, in any event, be *ultra vires*.[22] Although the notion did finally appear in the area of free movement law, the debate on the Article 35 was not as intense as the parallel discussion on the provisions concerning marriages of convenience in the Family Reunification Directive, which was adopted one year before the Citizenship Directive.[23] It is therefore apparent that during the negotiations, concerns about marriages of convenience primarily focused on the spouses of legally resident third-country nationals, rather than to those of EU citizens.

From the perspective of some Member States, the CJEU judgment in *MRAX*, delivered in 2002, opened Pandora's box by apparently allowing irregular migrants to acquire residence rights in the country based on a marriage to a mobile EU citizen. *Akrich* provided a reassuring restriction of the earlier case law by introducing the 'prior lawful residence' requirement. The reversal of *Akrich* by the *Metock* judgment in 2008 thus came as an unwelcome surprise in some capitals. The decision caused unprecedented controversy in several Member States who appeared extremely reluctant to revoke the 'prior lawful residence rule'. By July 2008, when *Metock* was handed down, the rule had already been implemented in eleven Member States, either through a hard law instrument[24] or administrative guidelines.[25] The strongest opposition came

21 Council Resolution on Marriages of Convenience, art 1. For an analysis of the definition of marriages of convenience, see Chapters 4, 7, 8 and 10.

22 There is nevertheless evidence that some Member States, such as the UK, did investigate marriages involving mobile EU citizens and third-country nationals already in the 1990s. See Chapter 6 for more details. For a discussion on legal effects and principles of soft law instruments, see Chapter 4.

23 de Hart, 'Introduction: The Marriage of Convenience in European Immigration Law' (n 20) 257.

24 Denmark, Finland, Ireland and the UK. Commission, 'Report from the Commission to the European Parliament and the Council on the application of Directive 2004/38/EC on the right of citizens of the Union and their family members to move and reside freely within the territory of the Member States' COM (2008) 840 final, 4.

25 Austria, Czech Republic, Cyprus, Germany, Greece, Malta and the Netherlands. Ibid, supra note 14. From 2006 (the latest), however, the Netherlands stopped applying *Akrich* due to the opposition from national courts and postponed its introduction into the domestic hard law pending the decision in the *Jia* case. Kees Groenendijk and others, 'Draft Report on the Free Movement of Workers in The Netherlands in 2005' (Nijmegen: Centre for

from Denmark which claimed that the decision allowed foreigners to sidestep the country's immigration law. At the JHA Council meeting in September 2008, the Danish minister, supported by colleagues from Ireland, Germany, Austria and Cyprus, called the Commission to propose amendments to the Citizenship Directive. Some other Member States, such as the UK and the Netherlands, also strongly criticised the judgment but did not expressly ask for the Directive to be revised.[26]

The Member State concerns over the impact of *Metock* focused on two different scenarios. The first was the *Surinder Singh* route which, as some governments feared, could be used by their own nationals to circumvent restrictive domestic family reunification rules. The second reason for objections related to third-country nationals, who could now automatically regularise their position by marrying a mobile EU citizen residing in the host Member State. Such marriages were now increasingly perceived as abusive, contracted solely to enable the non-EU national party to stay in the EU.

The underlying reason why the anxieties of the Member States intensified so rapidly after *Metock* is largely found in the relevant developments in their own immigration laws. As noted above, in the early and mid-2000s, several Western European countries tightened up their national family reunification provisions and introduced new sanctions for those allegedly participating in marriages of convenience. In Denmark, the strongest opponent of the *Metock*, power was taken by the centre-right minority government, which depended on the support of the right-wing Danish People's Party which required them to accept some of their demands in exchange. This *inter alia* contributed to making Danish national family reunification policy one of the most restrictive in Europe.[27] The Danish government now feared that *Metock* would lead to a massive increase in couples who would try to sidestep domestic rules by moving temporarily to Sweden or Germany and later return to Denmark on the basis of *Surinder Singh*. Anders Fogh Rasmussen, the country's prime minister at the time, described the ruling as a 'hijacking' of national immigration law.[28] The then Danish integration minister, Birthe Rønn Hornbech, further argued

Migration Law, 2006) 744–45; Roel Fernhout, Kees Groenendijk and Paul Minderhoud, 'Report on the Free Movement of Workers in the Netherlands in 2006' (Nijmegen: Centre for Migration Law, 2007) 798–99.

26 Kees Groenendijk and Roel Fernhout, 'Vrij Verkeer, Europa-Route en Omgekeerde Discriminatie: Wie Houdt Wie voor de Gek?' [2010] (1) *Asiel & Migrantenrecht* 4, 5–7.

27 Ibid 5; Wray, 'Regulating Spousal Migration in Denmark' (n 3) 147–48.

28 'EU Court Ruling Threatens Denmark's Immigration Policy' (*EU Business*, 01.09.2008) (as cited in Anja Lansbergen, 'Testing the Limits of European Citizenship' (The Federal Trust for Education and Research, *European Policy Brief*, May 2009)).

that the ruling opened 'the way for wide-scale approval of illegal immigration' through marriages of convenience.[29] The Danish concerns about the potential growth of marriages of convenience, however, appeared to be unfounded; the country's authorities presented no evidence suggesting this might be the case.

The anxieties of the Danish authorities, however, mainly related to 'U-turn' situations. By contrast, Ireland was principally worried about the issue of marriages of convenience between mobile EU citizens and non-EU nationals – not least because the ruling in *Metock* came at the time of increasing arrivals from the countries that joined the EU in 2004 after Ireland immediately opened its labour market to this group. The Irish government, however, was not able to provide reliable statistics on detected marriages of convenience, presenting figures on 'suspicious-looking' applications instead. Just before the September JHA Council, the Commission set up a FREEMO expert group to encourage dialogue between Member State officials and the Commission on issues related to the application of the Citizenship Directive. During its first meeting, the Irish representatives informed that in the years before the judgment in *Metock*, 4,600 non-EU family members had claimed residence rights in the country under the Directive, of whom 2,000 had not met the 'prior lawful residence' requirement. It was further underlined that 18% of the applicants were asylum-seekers who had married 'when their residence was in jeopardy', with 'disproportionate numbers' of Nigerian nationals. Another group of spouses portrayed as suspicious were Pakistani students who had overstayed their visas. It was also stressed that around 10% of all EU citizen spouses were Latvian, half of whom had married Indian or Pakistani nationals.[30] The UK also raised concerns about this form of abuse, claiming at the Council that the judgment in *Metock* 'could have implications for efforts to tackle false marriages'.[31]

In the meantime, some other Member States indicated that the phenomenon of marriages of convenience was very rare there, whilst Swedish authorities argued that the requirement of prior lawful residence was not an appropriate

---

29 Ibid.

30 Commission, 'Draft minutes of the Meeting of the Group of Experts from Member States on Problems of Practical Application of Directive 2004/38/EC' (Meeting held on 22.09.2008) 2. Available at <https://ec.europa.eu/transparency/expert-groups-register/screen/expert-groups/consult?lang=en&do=groupDetail.groupDetail&groupID=2397> accessed 9 April 2024.

31 Letter from the Minister of State, Home Office (Liam Byrne MP) to the Chairman of the September 2008 JHA Council (03.10.2008). The text of the letter is found in Select Committee on European Scrutiny, Thirty-fourth Report of Session 2007–08 (2007–08, HC 16-XXX) 112–13). The UK was also concerned about 'U-turn' arrangements.

tool to fight irregular migration.[32] At the September JHA Council, the then presiding Member State, France, equally opposed the Denmark-led initiative to amend the Citizenship Directive. The Commission tried to calm the tensions down and win time by announcing its intention to present a report evaluating the transposition of the Directive and then, if necessary, draw up guidelines on combatting abuse.[33]

Against this background, it is important to note that Denmark, Ireland, and the UK had opted out of the Family Reunification Directive and could thus impose stricter requirements for family reunification of lawfully resident third-country nationals and their non-EU resident family members. Moreover, not being bound by the Directive also indirectly implied that the three states enjoyed absolute freedom in designing family reunification rules applicable to their static nationals, even if these provided less favourable treatment than that afforded to TCN residents under the Family Reunification Directive. This state of affairs, which further contributed to deepening reverse discrimination, can partly explain the fierce reaction of the respective governments to *Metock* and the different positions of Member States on the issue. In other Member States which do partake in the Directive, the latter sets a minimum standard not only for family reunification rules applicable to lawfully resident TCNs but also to their static nationals. A situation where their own nationals are treated worse with regard to family reunification than third-country nationals would be difficult to justify, both politically and legally, not least in the light of the prohibition of discrimination enshrined in Article 14 of the ECHR.[34]

In its report on the transposition of the Citizenship Directive, published in December 2008, the Commission was extremely critical of national transposition measures, describing them as 'rather disappointing' and underlining that '[n]ot one Article of the Directive has been transposed effectively and correctly

32 'Draft minutes of the Meeting of the Group of Experts from Member States on Problems of Practical Application of Directive 2004/38/EC.' (22.09.2008) (n 30) 3.

33 Groenendijk and Fernhout (n 26) 7; See also, Council, Document 12923/08 (Presse 250, 25.09.1986), 9.

34 European Convention for the Protection of Human Rights and Fundamental Freedoms, CETS No.005 (04.11.1950) (ECHR). For a more in-depth discussion on how different Member States reacted to *Metock*, as well as on the differences between Member States in perception of and dealing with reverse discrimination, see Kees Groenendijk, 'Reverse Discrimination, Family Reunification and Union Citizens of Immigrant Origin' in Elspeth Guild, Cristina Gortázar Rotaeche and Dora Kostakopoulou (eds) *The Reconceptualization of European Union Citizenship* (Brill 2014); Kees Groenendijk, 'Lessen van Metock in Nederland en elders in de EU' [2021] (6–7) *Asiel & Migrantenrecht* 344; Groenendijk and Fernhout (n 26).

by all Member States'.[35] This particularly concerned Chapter VI (on the restriction of rights on the grounds of public policy or public security) and Article 35. The Commission, however, did not consider it necessary to reopen the Directive and recalled that Article 35 already provided Member States with a possibility to prevent abuse. At the end, it was announced that Member States would be provided with guidelines on problematic issues,[36] an intention that was ultimately welcomed by the Council[37] and the European Parliament.[38] The guidelines, which contained a separate section on abuse of rights (and also briefly referred to marriages of convenience), were subsequently issued in June 2009.[39]

4 Exploitation of the Vulnerable? EU-8 Nationals in Focus

Irrespective of the objections described above, virtually all Member States who had imposed the condition of prior lawful residence brought their national legislation or administrative practices in line with *Metock* within weeks or months.[40] By contrast, the UK government did not implement the judgment until 2011, when the 'prior lawful residence rule' was removed from the respective regulations.[41] The adoption of the Commission guidelines, nonetheless, did not reduce Member State anxieties with regards to perceived marriages of convenience or 'U-turn' arrangements.[42] In several Member States, compliance with *Metock* was followed by the introduction of additional measures

35 COM (2008) 840 final 3.

36 Ibid 10–11.

37 Council, Document 16325/1/08 REV 1 (Presse 344, 27–28.11.2008), 27–28.

38 Parliament, 'Resolution of 2 April 2009 on the application of Directive 2004/38/EC on the right of citizens of the Union and their family members to move and reside freely within the territory of the Member States (2008/2184(INI))' [2010] OJ C 137 E/02, 16.

39 For more details on the Guidelines, see, Groenendijk and Fernhout (n 26) 8–9 and Chapter 4.

40 See Kees Groenendijk, 'Beschränkung der Freizügigkeit von Unionsbürgern?' in Klaus Barwig, Stephan Beichel-Benedetti and Gisbert Brinkmann (eds), *Freiheit* (Schriften zum Migrationsrecht 15, Nomos 2014) 56, 61.

41 Immigration (European Economic Area) (Amendment) Regulations 2011, SI 2011/1247, reg 2(4).

42 In 2011, the Netherlands came up with a position paper advocating for levelling down the family reunion rights of EU citizens under the Citizenship Directive to those granted to lawfully resident TCNs under the Family Reunification Directive. The proposal did not receive much support among other Member States. Groenendijk, 'Reverse Discrimination, Family Reunification and Union Citizens of Immigrant Origin' (n 34) 183.

addressing perceived marriages of convenience (primarily Ireland and the UK) or targeting family members of returning nationals (most notably, Denmark).[43]

In Ireland and the UK, couples involving nationals of EU-8 Member States and migrants from West Africa and the Indian subcontinent remained the principal group strongly associated with abuse. At the EU level, concerns about marriages of convenience remained on the agenda and have been expressed *inter alia* during the subsequent FREEMO group meetings,[44] within the framework of a European Migration Network (EMN) country study published in 2012,[45] as well as at JHA Council meetings.[46] The Irish and UK authorities regularly complained that since the judgment in *Metock*, there had been a 'highly unusual' trend of nationals from the Indian subcontinent marrying nationals of Eastern European Member States.

---

43 For a brief overview of the post-*Metock* developments in Denmark, Ireland, and the UK, see Aleksandra Ancite-Jepifánova (published under Aleksandra Jolkina), 'CJEU, Judgment of 25 July 2008, *Metock*: Subsequent Developments in Denmark, Ireland, and the UK' [2021] (6–7) *Asiel & Migrantenrecht* 338. The situation in the UK is explored extensively in Chapters 6 and 7.

44 See for instance, Commission, 'Final minutes of the fifteenth meeting of experts on the right to free movement of persons (Directive 2004/38/EC)' (Meeting held on 05.02.2013) 4–5. Available at <https://ec.europa.eu/transparency/expert-groups-register/screen/expert-groups/consult?lang=en&do=groupDetail.groupDetail&groupID=2397> accessed 9 April 2024. Commission, 'Meeting of the expert group FREEMO on the right to free movement of persons (Directive 2004/38 EC)' (Meeting held on 21.10.2016). Available at <https://ec.europa.eu/transparency/expert-groups-register/screen/expert-groups/consult?lang=en&do=groupDetail.groupDetail&groupID=2397> accessed 9 April 2024; Commission, 'Minutes. Virtual Meeting of the expert group on the right to free movement of persons (FREEMO) (Directive 2004/38/EC). Free movement and implementation of the Citizens' Rights Part of the Withdrawal Agreement' (Meeting held on 24.11.2021). Available at <https://ec.europa.eu/transparency/expert-groups-register/screen/meetings/consult?lang=en&meetingId=35216&fromExpertGroups=2397> accessed 9 April 2024; Commission, 'Minutes. Hybrid Meeting of the expert group on the right to free movement of persons (FREEMO) (Directive 2004/38/EC)' (Meeting held on 13.12.2023). Available at <https://ec.europa.eu/transparency/expert-groups-register/screen/meetings/consult?lang=en&meetingId=51575&fromExpertGroups=2397> accessed 9 April 2024.

45 Corona Joyce, *Misuse of the Right to Family Reunification: Ireland. EMN Focussed Study 1* (The Economic and Social Research Institute 2012); Elizabeth Pendry and Samantha Dowling (eds), *Misuse of the Right to Family Reunification: Marriages of Convenience and False Declarations of Parenthood* (Home Office 2012).

46 See for instance, 'Sham Marriages Leading to Abuses of EU Freedom of Movement Rights' (*Inis*, 09.06.2011) <https://merrionstreet.ie/en/category-index/sham-marriages-leading-to-abuses-of-eu-freedom-of-movement-rights.39421.shortcut.html> accessed 9 April 2024.

The bias against such pairings was further reinforced by the widespread narratives of vulnerable Eastern European women being exploited by individual 'fixers' or organised crime gangs who bring them to Ireland or the UK with a view of arranging marriages of convenience for financial gain. This discourse was backed up by the often sensationalist media reports exposing 'the world of fake marriages', operated by ruthless criminals taking advantage of poor and vulnerable Eastern European women.[47] In addition, governments of several EU-8 Member States regularly voiced serious concerns about their nationals tricked into such arrangements and called on receiving countries to intensify their efforts to tackle marriages of convenience. The perceived link between marriages of convenience and human trafficking became the focus of a transnational study, co-funded by the EU programme 'Prevention of and Fight against Crime' (ISEC) and published by the Helsinki-based European Institute for Crime Prevention and Control, affiliated with the United Nations (HEUNI).[48] Its findings were presented in 2016 and covered the relevant developments in five Member States: Estonia, Latvia, Lithuania, Slovakia, and Ireland, with the first four identified as countries of origin and Ireland as a destination country. Although the UK was equally described as a destination country, it did not partake in the project. The main information sources featured in the study are NGOs providing assistance to victims of human trafficking and exploitation, the Latvian embassy to Ireland, and the police.

According to the report, the women involved in perceived marriages of convenience were targeted by 'fixers' either online or via personal connections. Many of them were young, had little education, very low incomes, and little or no English skills. Some had learning disabilities. In the beginning, the study introduces the term 'exploitative sham marriage', intended to be approached from a sociological, rather than a legal perspective. The notion is referred to a broad range of situations, including both cases with clear elements of human trafficking (e.g., when women are initially unaware of any marriage arrangements and approached with a promise of a job abroad, or where women are

47 See among others, 'My Big Fat Fake Wedding' (BBC One, Panorama, 24.03.2011); 'Paul Connolly Investigates: Ireland's Sham Marriages' (TV3 Ireland, 2011); 'The Sham Wedding Crashers' (Channel Five, 30.10.2014); 'The Sham Marriage Racket: How to Buy Your Way into Britain' (ITV, Exposure, 02.07.2015). For a more in-depth discussion on how UK media approach the issue, see, Wemyss, Yuval-Davis and Cassidy (n 15).

48 Minna Viuhko and others (eds), *Exploitative Sham Marriages: Exploring the Links Between Human Trafficking and Sham Marriages in Estonia, Ireland, Latvia, Lithuania and Slovakia* (Publication Series No. 82, HEUNI 2016).

forced into marriage),[49] and cases which cannot be identified as trafficking but involve 'exploitative elements'.[50] For instance, the study describes anecdotal cases where women initially consented to the marriage, but later the promised financial reward was not paid, or they were physically, emotionally or sexually abused by their non-EU national husbands.[51] Further, a significant emphasis is placed on so-called 'unilateral sham marriages' where 'the victim is misled by the illusion of a genuine relationship'.[52] The report quotes Latvian social service providers who believe this to be a widespread strategy of recruitment and claim that the deception is often exposed once the residence permit is obtained, which is often the point when the behaviour of the deceptive spouse becomes more violent. Whilst pointing out that such cases are difficult to prove, the study lists several features suggesting that the marriage had been 'genuine' only for one party, such as 'the prospective husband has hastened the woman into marriage and to giving birth to a child' or that 'the relationship is subordinated to visiting migration services to receive the residence permit'.[53]

The Latvian government has also been the most active in bringing the perceived problem to the attention of the Irish authorities, calling them to tighten up domestic marriage laws. Most notably, calling for them to criminalise marriages of convenience and permit marriage registrars or the police to intervene in cases where the intended marriage looks 'suspicious'.[54] In 2014,

---

49 The definition of THB is provided in art 2 of the Directive 2011/36/EU of the European Parliament and of the Council of 5 April 2011 on preventing and combating trafficking in human beings and protecting its victims, and replacing Council Framework Decision 2002/629/JHA [2011] OJ L101/1.

50 Minna Viuhko, Anni Lietonen and Anniina Jokinen, 'Happily Ever After? From Sham Marriages to Human Trafficking' in Viuhko and others (eds) (n 48), 19.

51 Inese Šūpule, 'Human Trafficking and Sham Marriages in Latvia' in Viuhko and others (eds) (n 48), 216–26.

52 Ibid 248.

53 Ibid 217.

54 For instance, Latvia made the respective recommendations to Ireland within the framework of the UN Universal Periodic Review Process on 6 October 2011 in Geneva. See Latvian Embassy to Ireland, 'Fiktīvās Laulības – Cilvēktirdzniecības Forma' ('Fictitious Marriages as a Form of Human Trafficking') (Presentation to the Latvian Parliament, 12–13.06.2012), on file with the author; 'Ireland Addresses Sham Marriages – Significant Amendments to the Civil Registration Act of Ireland' (*Cilvektirdzniecība.lv*, 15.04.2016) <http://www.cilvektirdzniecība.lv/en/ireland-addresses-sham-marriages-%E2%80%93-significant-amendments-to-the-civil-registration-act-of-ireland> accessed 9 April 2024. The Latvian Ministry of Foreign Affairs also issued a statement in 2010 urging Ireland to intensify its efforts to tackle 'sham marriages'. See 'New Guidelines on "Sham Marriages" Introduced' (*TheJournal.ie*, 09.10.2010) <https://www.thejournal.ie/new-guidelines-on-sham-marriages-introduced-32919-Oct2010/> accessed 9 April 2024.

Ireland indeed amended its Civil Registration Act by introducing a definition of marriages of convenience and empowering civil registrars to form an opinion of the nature of an intended marriage.[55] As will be shown in Chapter 7, similar legislation has been introduced in the UK. Additionally, in 2013, Latvia amended its legislation to criminalise those involved in marriages of convenience for immigration purposes, including where these are intended to be contracted abroad. The relevant provisions cover both organisers of such marriages and their parties.[56]

Linking forced marriages and human trafficking with the concept of marriages of convenience, however, is deeply problematic. Chapters 6–10 will show that couples consisting of nationals of EU-8 Member States and migrants from the Indian subcontinent are disproportionately targeted by measures designed to curb marriages of convenience, which, in many cases, is nothing short of discrimination of the groups concerned. Furthermore, whilst cases of trafficking EU citizens to another Member State with a view to force them to enter into marriage with a non-EU national are reported; their numbers appear to be low. For instance, the HEUNI study reveals that from 2007 to 2014, there were as few as 59 Latvian nationals allegedly tricked into marriages abroad who were subsequently identified as victims of human trafficking – i.e., on average, less than ten per year.[57] Moreover, such situations can be effectively addressed by instruments other than marriage controls. Forced marriages have recently been criminalised in both Ireland[58] and the UK,[59] and are considered 'voidable' in UK family law.[60] Likewise, the cases falling within the definition of trafficking in human beings should arguably be dealt with in the particular legal setting[61] or, if necessary, through mutual cooperation within Europol and

55 Civil Registration Act 2004, s 58 as amended by Civil Registration (Amendment) Act 2014, s 18. For more details, see Ancite-Jepifánova (published under Jolkina) (n 43), 343.

56 Krimināllikums (Criminal Law), s 285^2.

57 Šūpule (n 51) 204.

58 Domestic Violence Act 2018, s 38.

59 Anti-Social Behaviour, Crime and Policing Act 2014, s 121. An in-depth analysis of the rationale and implications of the criminalisation of forced marriages in the UK is outside the remit of the present study.

60 Under s 12(1)(c) of the Matrimonial Causes Act 1973, a marriage may be rendered 'voidable' where either of the parties has not validly consented to it *inter alia* 'in consequence of duress'. The UK High Court has explicitly confirmed that the notion of 'duress' is applicable to situations where a person is forced into marriage. *NS v MI* [2006] EWHC 1646 (Fam), [2006] Fam Law 839. For more details on the link between the concept of marriages of convenience and UK family law, see Chapter 7, Section 3.7.

61 Such as Modern Slavery Act 2015 in the UK and Criminal Law (Human Trafficking) Act 2008 in Ireland.

Eurojust.[62] Notably, the link between marriages of convenience and organised crime has been already highlighted in various Europol and Eurojust notifications and reports.[63]

Second, as implicitly acknowledged by the authors of the HEUNI study, the term 'exploitative sham marriages' is legally problematic.[64] As will be demonstrated in Chapter 4, the concept of marriages of convenience for the purposes of the Citizenship Directive is narrowly defined and principally limited to arrangements having no other content apart from the immigration motive. There is, however, lack of statistics on how many marriages have been found to be such, and no reliable estimates as to the numbers of EU-8 Member State nationals who have been brought to the UK or Ireland by marriage 'fixers'. Furthermore, it is admitted that many women whose marriages have been organised by facilitators develop an intimate relationship with their TCN husbands and have children with them. Anecdotal evidence suggests that this may be the case even if initially the sole purpose of the intended marriage is to help the non-EU national party obtain residence rights.[65]

In addition, even if an EU citizen initially consents to marry a non-EU national for a financial reward, their intentions may not necessarily exclude founding a family should the couple like each other and get on well.[66] Furthermore, the notion of 'unilateral sham marriages' frequently referred to in the study is highly confusing. As will be argued in Chapter 4, this concept does not easily fit within the legal definition of marriages of convenience found in the Citizenship Directive. In addition, claims that many intimate relationships

62 A similar opininion has been expressed by Marcello Di Filippo, 'Can EU Free Movement Rights be Abused? Critical Remarks on the "Marriages of Convenience Clause"' in Antonio Marcello Calamia (ed) *L'Abuso del Diritto* (G.Giappichelli Editore, 2017) 74.

63 See for instance, Eurojust, 'Report on National Legislation and Eurojust Casework Analysis on Sham Marriages' (January 2024); Europol, 'Marriages of Convenience: A link between facilitation of illegal migration and THB' (Early Warning Notification 2014/8, March 2014); Europol, 'Trafficking in Human Beings in the EU' (Document No: 765175, February 2016) 29–30.

64 This term has nevertheless been endorsed by the Commission, which adopted the same terminology whilst linking marriages of convenience with trafficking in human beings. See Commission, 'Second report on the progress made in the fight against trafficking in human beings (2018) as required under Article 20 of Directive 2011/36/EU on preventing and combating trafficking in human beings and protecting its victims', COM (2018) 777 final, 14–15.

65 The author came across this type of situations during her work as a journalist in 2009–2010. For a discussion of the compatibility of such cases with the definition of marriages of convenience, see Chapters 4 and 10.

66 This is also suggested by Andrikopoulos (n 15).

with or without children are 'unilateral sham marriages' are only based on subjective and normative judgments by the social service providers and should be approached with caution. Having a gender dimension, such assumptions tend to largely deny the agency of the women involved, who are instead portrayed as passive victims and castigated as naïve for failing to recognise that a residence status is the only reason for the marriage.[67] Quite strikingly, there are cases where Latvian social service providers claim that women have been deceived even if they themselves do not believe so.[68]

The language used by NGO representatives quoted in the report also suggests that there is a strong bias against marriages with non-Europeans who are typically perceived as abusers and perpetrators exploiting vulnerable women. This is perhaps unsurprising in light of the strong anti-immigrant sentiments in some Eastern and Central European Member States.[69] The need to protect the family reunion rights of their nationals, which constitutes an indispensable element of their freedom of movement, meanwhile appears to be completely ignored, both by the drafters of the study and their informants.

Evidence about women encountering various forms of exploitation, however, is also anecdotal and can by no means be generalised. In the author's view, such situations can equally be addressed by instruments other than marriage controls, such as laws on domestic violence. Alternatively, Member States of origin may preventatively target their nationals via awareness-raising campaigns, aimed at revealing the potential risks of such arrangements and helping the individuals concerned make an informed choice. Over 2009–2013, such campaigns were already conducted in Latvia and considered efficient, since the number of perceived 'exploitative sham marriages' is reported to have decreased since then.[70]

67 Several scholars have shown that such perceptions of female principals are rather common amongst migration policy makers who then use the need to protect women as an argument in support of restrictive family reunification policies. See among others, Bonjour and de Hart (n 6) 65–66; Natasha Carver, '"For her Protection and Benefit": The Regulation of Marriage-Related Migration to the UK' (2016) 39 *Ethnic and Racial Studies* 2758.

68 See Šūpule (n 51) 226.

69 For instance, in the Migrant Integration Policy Index 2020, Latvia was ranked 47th out of 52 participating countries which included all EU Member States, other European countries (including Serbia, Russia, Turkey, and Ukraine), several Asian and South American countries, as well as Canada, Mexico, the US, Australia, and New Zealand. Giacomo Solano and Thomas Huddleston, 'Migrant Integration Policy Index 2020' (CIDOB and MPG) 13–14, 155–58.

70 Šūpule (n 51) 228.

Overall, the subsequent chapters will demonstrate that discourses on marriages of convenience between women from Eastern Europe and men from the Indian subcontinent may lead to general stigmatisation of these groups and target many genuine couples, as well as create what Helena Wray has described as a 'self reinforcing cycle'.[71] The latter implies that depiction of such nationality pairings as suspicious may further intensify the state focus on this group; this, in turn, will most likely result in an increase in reports of marriages of convenience allegedly contracted between partners of the relevant nationalities.

In this light, it is important to mention that the normative perception of large cultural differences between such partners tends to dwell on the erroneous premise that partner choice is solely dictated by cultural or ethnic considerations. Meanwhile, scholarship has long identified similar social status and education as other major factors influencing partner choice.[72] The increase in mixed-status marriages involving EU citizens and foreigners could, therefore, be explained *inter alia* by the overall increase in short-term mobility and transnational connections.[73] As noted in the introduction to this book, unlike France or Germany, the UK and Ireland did not hesitate to allow nationals of EU-8 Member States full access to their labour markets immediately after the respective countries joined the EU in 2004. Provided that after arrival, many mobile EU citizens share social, work and study spaces with non-EU nationals, it is indeed unsurprising that some of them end up forming a relationship with TCN partners who happen to possess a short-term or irregular status.

5 UK and Three Other Member States Demanding Change

In response to the continued concerns of Member States over perceived marriages of convenience, the Commission signalled its intention to provide further, more detailed guidance specifically addressing the matter. In May 2012, the JHA Council agreed on a document, 'EU Action on Migratory Pressures – A Strategic Response',[74] which identified several strategic priority areas of the Union, such as border management, cooperation on return practices, and

71 Wray, 'The "Pure" Relationship, Sham Marriages and Immigration Control' (n 13) 154.

72 See for instance, Matthijs Kalmijn, 'Intermarriage and Homogamy: Causes, Patterns, Trends' (1998) 24 *Annual Review of Sociology* 395.

73 For a general discussion, see among others, Eleonore Kofman, 'Family-Related Migration: A Critical Review of European Studies' (2004) 30 *Journal of Ethnic and Migration Studies* 243, 249–52.

74 Council, Document 9650/12 (10.05.2012).

prevention of abuse of free movement by third-country nationals. One of the intended activities mentioned in the document was the preparation of 'a handbook on marriages of convenience, including indicative criteria to assist in the identification of sham marriages'.[75] In March 2013, a preliminary draft of the handbook was sent to the Irish Presidency and the Chair of the LIBE Committee of the European Parliament,[76] as well as presented to the Member States for informal feedback.[77]

Yet, in April of the same year, the UK, together with Austria, Germany, and the Netherlands, made another attempt to achieve a more restrictive interpretation of the free movement rights. In their letter to the Irish Presidency of the Council and three European Commissioners, the interior ministers of the four Member States called for a more restrictive interpretation of the free movement provisions. This was based on the claims that economically inactive EU citizens were placing a strain on local services and social welfare systems, as well as that the host societies lacked the necessary legal tools to fight abuse and fraud.[78] It is no coincidence that the letter was written a few months before the forthcoming removal of transitional restrictions for citizens of Romania and Bulgaria,[79] the two poorest EU Member States.[80] Although the main focus in the document was placed on the perceived need to prevent 'unwanted' EU citizens from claiming benefits, it also called for the introduction of more restrictive means to tackle systematic abuse or fraud, such as expulsion and re-entry bans.[81] The tone of the letter was further reinforced by the striking change in terminology: whilst in the first lines, the four ministers

---

75 Ibid 19.

76 See Council, Document 10316/13 (31.05.2013) 6.

77 See Commission, 'Draft Minutes of the Sixteenth Meeting of Experts on the Right to Free Movement of Persons (Directive 2004/38/EC)' (Meeting held on 25.03.2013) 4. Available at <https://ec.europa.eu/transparency/expert-groups-register/screen/expert-groups/consult?lang=en&do=groupDetail.groupDetail&groupID=2397> accessed 9 April 2024.

78 Letter from the Ministers of the Interior of Austria, Germany, the Netherlands and the UK to the Irish Presidency (April 2013) <http://docs.dpaq.de/3604-130415_letter_to_presidency_final_1_2.pdf> accessed 9 April 2024.

79 While the UK did not apply transitional restrictions on EU-8 workers, it did so with respect to nationals of Bulgaria and Romania, two Member States which joined the EU in 2007. The transitional period for them ended on 1 January, 2014.

80 See Eurostat, 'GDP Per Capita in the EU in 2013: Seven Capital Regions Among the Ten Most Prosperous' (News release 90/2015, 21.05.2015) <https://ec.europa.eu/eurostat/documents/2995521/6839731/1-21052015-AP-EN.pdf/c3f5f43b-397c-40fd-a0a4-7e68e3bea8cd> accessed 9 April 2024.

81 The UK began advocating for such measures already in the aftermath of the judgment in *Metock* in 2008, yet at the time its proposal did not receive much support in the Council. For an analysis see among others Groenendijk and Fernhout (n 26) 7–8.

acknowledged the rights of 'Union citizens' who move across the EU to work or study,[82] the undesirable groups of mobile Member State nationals were further referred to as 'immigrants',[83] essentially implying that EU citizenship was no longer considered their primary status.[84] Finally, the Member States requested the Presidency to put their letter on the agenda of the forthcoming JHA meeting in June 2013 and called upon the Commission 'to draw up proposals swiftly which can be submitted to the Member States for further consultations'.[85]

The Commission responded to the letter in May 2013 highlighting the key legal principles of free movement and stating that the four ministers did not present evidence of systematic abuse through marriages of convenience, fraud or benefits tourism.[86] The letter was discussed over lunch at the JHA Council in June, but most of the remaining Member States apparently showed little support for the initiative.[87] The Council invited the Commission to prepare a report on the implementation of free movement rules and present it by the end of the year.[88]

Upon the subsequent Commission request, the UK, along with several other Member States, provided the data intended to support its claims. In their letter to the Commission of 16 September 2013,[89] the British authorities argued that '[c]laims that abuse of free movement is not widespread ignore the reality that such abuse exists, and if not dealt with effectively is likely to increase' and '[t]he existence of serious fraud and abuse of free movement also has a serious and deleterious impact on the public perception of free movement'.[90] Having provided statistics of forged EU documentation and described one police operation uncovering social benefits fraud, the UK authorities went at great length to discuss the issue of alleged marriages of convenience. The document noted that there was 'significant evidence to suggest that the phenomenon of

82 Letter from the Ministers of the Interior of Austria, Germany, the Netherlands and the UK to the Irish Presidency (n 78) 1.

83 Ibid 2.

84 This point has also been stressed by Kees Groenendijk. Groenendijk, 'Beschränkung der Freizügigkeit von Unionsbürgern?' (n 40) 58.

85 Letter from the Ministers of the Interior of Austria, Germany, the Netherlands, and the UK to the Irish Presidency (n 78) 3.

86 Council, Document 10316/13 (n 76).

87 Kees Groenendijk, 'Recent Developments in EU Law on Migration: The Legislative Patchwork and the Court's Approach' (2014) 16 *European Journal of Migration and Law* 313, 320.

88 Council, Document 10461/13 (Presse 234, 06.-07.06.2013) 22.

89 The document is found in Select Committee on European Scrutiny, Thirty-first Report of Session 2013–14 (2013–14, HC 83-XXVIII).

90 Ibid 20.

sham marriage is linked with serious organised criminal activity' and followed the 'exploitation' narrative discussed above by stating that such arrangements mostly involve vulnerable women from Eastern European Member States who are 'tricked, coerced or forced' into marriages with non-EU nationals.[91] The letter then proceeded to describe several anecdotal cases illustrating the phenomenon, for instance, the story of a Church of England vicar who was found guilty of knowingly solemnising up to 360 alleged 'sham marriages',[92] or the case involving a Slovakian woman of Roma descent who was kidnapped in Hungary and trafficked to the UK for the purpose of being forced into a marriage with a Pakistani man.[93] At the end of the letter, the British government provided statistics of 'suspicious' cases reported by marriage registrars, their numbers reaching 1,891 in 2012.[94] Meanwhile, statistics of detected cases of marriages of convenience were not given, at all. The relevant figures of identified cases provided to the Commission by a few other Member States appeared to be low. For instance, over the period 2010 to 2012, Cyprus recorded 174 marriages of convenience, and Portugal, 144.[95]

In a Communication in November 2013, the Commission concluded that the data received showed no factual evidence of widespread abuse of free movement rights or large numbers of EU citizens relying on social assistance. Having underlined that mobile EU citizens pay more in tax contributions than they receive in benefits, it reiterated its earlier position and invited Member States to address cases of potential fraud or abuse on a case-by-case basis under the existing legal rules.[96] The Commission also reminded of its intention to publish the Handbook on tackling marriages of convenience.[97] During the JHA Council in December 2013, the majority of Member States agreed that 'the free movement of persons is a core principle of the European Union' and that 'individual cases of abuse have to be combated within the existing legal framework.'[98]

In addition, the Visegrad Countries (Czech Republic, Hungary, Poland, and Slovakia) issued a joint statement in which they voiced strong opposition to the British claims and underlined that the UK economy has hugely benefitted

91 Ibid 21.

92 Ibid 27.

93 Ibid 22.

94 Ibid 43. For more details on the Home Office statistics, see Chapter 6.

95 Commission, 'Free movement of EU citizens and their families: Five actions to make a difference' (Communication) COM (2013) 837 final, supra note 43 at 7.

96 Ibid 3–9.

97 Ibid 10.

98 Council, Document 17342/13 (Presse 534, 05.-06.12.2013) 8.

from the arrival of EU citizens from Central and Eastern Europe and that 'the selective application of core freedoms by Member States leads to an erosion of the single market'.[99] The letter of the UK and the other three Member States to the Presidency was no longer discussed during the subsequent Council meetings. In September 2014, the Commission published a Handbook on marriages of convenience that will be discussed in detail in Chapter 4.

6 Pre-referendum Settlement: an Unprecedented Concession to the UK

Whilst Chapter 4 will show that the content of the Handbook is not always without problems, in 2013 the Commission remained true to its role as guardian of the Treaties, showing resistance to the pressure of Member States by upholding the fundamental rules and principles of EU law protected by existing legislation. Yet, only two years later, in an unprecedented move, it reversed its position in response to the same requests of the UK who was now threatening to leave the EU altogether.

Already in early 2013, the then British prime minister and leader of the Conservative party, David Cameron, promised that if he was re-elected in the general election in 2015, the UK would hold a referendum on its membership of the EU. In his speech, he argued that the Union needed to reform to address the challenges it was facing and that the 'power must be able to flow back to Member States'.[100] With this purpose, he pledged to enter into negotiations with the EU for a new settlement and, should the British demands be met, campaign for the UK to stay in the EU.[101]

At the May 2015 election, the Conservative party obtained an absolute majority. In November 2015, Cameron outlined his demands in a formal letter to the president of the European Council, Donald Tusk. In the document, the UK prime minister set out four areas where he was seeking reforms: economic governance, competitiveness, sovereignty (which implied ending the UK's obligation to work towards an 'ever closer union' and enhancing the role

99 Council, Document 17395/13 (04.12.2013).

100 'David Cameron's EU Speech – Full Text' (*Guardian*, 23.01.2013) <https://www.theguardian.com/politics/2013/jan/23/david-cameron-eu-speech-referendum> accessed 9 April 2024.

101 Ibid.

of national parliaments), and 'immigration'.[102] Like in the 2013 letter explored above, the term 'immigration' was used here to refer to free movement rights of Union citizens, expressly transforming them into foreigners who need to fulfil certain conditions to obtain the privilege to reside in the country.[103] Cameron then argued that arrangements needed to be found 'to reduce the current very high level of population flows from within the EU into the UK' which have been 'unplanned and (…) much higher than forecast'.[104] Another priority named by the prime minister was 'to crack down on the abuse of free movement', including the introduction of more restrictive and lengthy entry bans for those involved in fraud or 'sham marriages', as well 'addressing the fact that it is easier for an EU citizen to bring a non-EU spouse to Britain than it is for a British citizen to do the same'.[105]

On 2 February 2016, following the negotiations that started only after the December 2015 European Council, Donal Tusk presented a draft Decision concerning a new settlement for the UK within the EU.[106] The document was then adopted in an astonishingly speedy procedure that attracted a lot of criticism due to its obvious democratic deficit and disregard of the ordinary legislative process in the EU.[107] Already on 19 February 2016, the Heads of State or Governments of the 28 Member States came up with the final Decision that was aimed to support the 'remain' option without changing the Treaties.[108]

Whilst the purpose of the deal was to persuade the UK to remain in the EU, the proposed changes would have equally applied to the remaining 27 Member States. Published in the form of an international agreement, rather than a decision of the European Council, the document was annexed to the Council Conclusions and organised in four main sections: Economic Governance, Competitiveness, Sovereignty, and Social Benefits & Free Movement. The latter section, for the first time in the Union's history, introduced several measures

---

102 Letter from David Cameron to Donald Tusk (10.11.2015) <https://assets.publishing.service.gov.uk/government/uploads/system/uploads/attachment_data/file/475679/Donald_Tusk_letter.pdf> accessed 9 April 2024.

103 On this point, see also, Elspeth Guild, *Brexit and its Consequences for UK and EU Citizenship or Monstrous Citizenship* (Brill 2016) 14–15.

104 Letter from David Cameron to Donald Tusk (n 102) 4.

105 Ibid 5.

106 Council, Document EUCO 4/16 (02.02.2016).

107 For criticism, see Guild, *Brexit and its Consequences for UK and EU Citizenship* (n 103) 16–32; Kees Groenendijk, 'Brexit: Free Movement of Union Citizens and the Rights of Third-Country Nationals under Threat?' in Carolus Grütters, Sandra Mantu and Paul Minderhoud (eds), *Migration on the Move* (Brill 2017) 287–88.

108 Council, Document EUCO 1/16 (19.02.2016).

designed to significantly limit the free movement rights of EU citizens, such as an 'emergency break' on the access of newly arriving EU workers to non-contributory in-work benefits or enhanced powers to expel EU citizens under the public policy provisions.

The most significant changes, however, were intended to be introduced in the area of family reunion. The Decision stated that '[t]hose enjoying the right to free movement shall abide by the laws of the host Member State' and that national governments can address not only fraud or abuse of rights such as marriages of convenience, but also 'U-turn' arrangements to bypass national family reunification rules.[109] These points were further elaborated in the attached Declaration by the Commission in which the latter undertook to adopt a proposal to amend the Citizenship Directive:

> [I]n order to exclude, from the scope of free movement rights, third country nationals who had no prior lawful residence in a Member State before marrying a Union citizen or who marry a Union citizen only after the Union citizen has established residence in the host Member State.[110]

It was further specified that in such cases, the position of couples would be governed by national immigration law.[111] This is a serious offence against the CJEU case law which would effectively mean the re-introduction of the infamous 'prior lawful residence rule' which was abolished in *Metock*.

Further, the Commission sought to extend the definition of a marriage of convenience to marriages which are not only contracted but also maintained for the purpose of enjoying a right of residence by a TCN spouse.[112] This clearly violates the CJEU jurisprudence in *Diatta* and *Ogieriakhi* and essentially suggests that marriages, entered into to found a family, may later become ones of convenience. Such an approach is highly dangerous, particularly because of the lack of legal certainty of what constitutes a marriage of convenience and the unprecedented breadth of the powers given to the governments who would then be free to deeply intrude into the private and family life of the EU citizens, attacking any marriage which does not conform to their perceptions of how a 'genuine' couple should behave. Finally, the Commission would allow the governments to address 'specific cases of abuse' involving their own nationals relying on the *Surinder Singh* route in case 'residence in the host

109 Ibid 21.

110 Ibid, Annex VII at 35.

111 Ibid.

112 Ibid.

Member State has not been sufficiently genuine to create or strengthen family life and had the purpose of evading the application of national immigration rules'.[113] This passage equally disregards the CJEU judgment in *O and B*, which does not make this right conditional upon such requirements.

The proposed rules, however, never entered into force. Following the referendum on 23 June 2016 in which the British people voted in favour of the UK leaving the EU, the agreement was annulled.[114] However, the significance of the Decision should not be underestimated. Having agreed to attack the key elements of free movement together with the long-standing jurisprudence of the CJEU, EU institutions created a dangerous precedent showing how much they would be prepared to sacrifice to accommodate the (very poorly justified) demands of the UK. It is thus possible that this signal is relied upon in the future by other Member States who may equally attempt to enforce their wishes and exclude the unwanted categories of EU citizens from the scope of free movement rights.[115]

7 Conclusion

The 2008 ruling in *Metock* exacerbated tensions between the EU and several Member States who claimed that the CJEU was encroaching upon their competences in immigration matters. Two principal issues are perceived as problematic in this regard: 'U-turn' arrangements enabling individuals to avoid domestic family reunification provisions which were tightened up during the 2000s, and the possibility for non-EU nationals to automatically regularise their status in the country by marrying a mobile EU citizen. The latter group of marriages were now increasingly portrayed as suspicious and associated with the exploitation of female nationals of EU-8 Member States and organised crime.

The UK has always been among the countries voicing the strongest concerns about perceived abuse of EU free movement law, a narrative that further intensified in the climate of growing Euroscepticism. Following *Metock*, there have been several attempts to persuade EU institutions to reduce the family reunion rights of EU citizens under the Citizenship Directive. The first two such proposals received little support within the Commission and the

113 Ibid.

114 Council, Document 381/16 (24.06.2016).

115 This point has been particularly emphasised in, Groenendijk, 'Brexit: Free Movement of Union Citizens and the Rights of Third-Country Nationals under Threat?' (n 107) 297.

rest of the Council – particularly due to the absence of evidence of the widespread abuse that would justify the restriction of fundamental rights. Instead, the Commission adopted two soft law documents aimed at assisting Member States in identifying marriages of convenience.

However, already in 2016, as part of the pre-Brexit referendum deal concluded to persuade the UK to remain in the EU, the Commission appeared willing to sacrifice its role as guardian of the Treaties. The proposed agreement foresaw a severe reduction of the family reunion rights of mobile EU citizens, including broadening up the definition of marriages of convenience and the re-introduction of the infamous 'prior lawful residence rule', abolished in *Metock*. Although the deal ultimately never entered into force, it set a striking precedent of attacking fundamental rights and long-standing CJEU case law, a signal that may potentially be used by other Member States willing to narrow down the scope of Treaty rights.

CHAPTER 4

Europeanisation of Relationship Standards? Marriages of Convenience in EU Soft Law

1 Introduction

Chapter 3 described the political conflict between the CJEU and a small group of Member States, including the UK, who felt that EU law was encroaching upon their sovereignty in immigration matters. In the years following the CJEU judgment in *Metock*, the pressure of Member States resulted in the European Commission adopting two soft law instruments addressing their concerns: the Guidance on better application of the Citizenship Directive,[1] issued in 2009[2] and the Handbook on addressing the issue of alleged marriages of convenience, published in 2014.[3] By focusing on these documents, this chapter explores how the Commission has responded to the tensions between the CJEU and national governments and to what extent it has been ready to accommodate the concerns of Member States. The principal attention of the chapter is concentrated on the Handbook, which is the key non-binding legal instrument in this field.

The chapter will begin with a general overview of EU soft law, including its definition, functions, and legal effects. It will then move on to specifically examine the content of the Commission Handbook and, to a lesser extent, Guidelines, as well as discuss the potential implications arising from it.

1 Directive 2004/38/EC of the European Parliament and of the Council of 29 April 2004 on the right of citizens of the Union and their family members to move and reside freely within the territory of the Member States amending Regulation (EEC) No 1612/68 and repealing Directives 64/221/EEC, 68/360/EEC, 72/194/EEC, 73/148/EEC, 75/34/EEC, 75/35/EEC, 90/364/EEC, 90/365/EEC and 93/96/EEC [2004] OJ L158/77 (Citizenship Directive).

2 Commission, 'Communication from the Commission to the European Parliament and the Council on guidance for better transposition and application of Directive 2004/38/EC on the right of citizens of the Union and their family members to move and reside freely within the territory of the Member States', COM (2009) 313 final.

3 Commission, 'Staff Working Document – Handbook on addressing the issue of alleged marriages of convenience between EU citizens and non-EU nationals in the context of EU law on free movement of EU citizens' SWD(2014) 284 final.

 | DOI:10.1163/9789004499263_006

2 EU Soft Law in a Nutshell

2.1 *The Concept of European Soft Law*

The concept of 'soft law' first emerged in the domain of public international law in the early 1970s as a response to the need to accommodate the diverse interests of various state and inter-state actors in a globalising postcolonial world.[4] The term equally found its way into the then EC law soon after the establishment of the Community. At present, soft law has become an integral part of the EU legal order, with some estimates suggesting that it accounts for over 10% of all EU legislative acts.[5] Traditionally such tools are actively adopted in areas of strong competence of the EU where the Commission retains exclusive competences, such as competition law or state aid. During the past years, however, the use of regulatory soft law instruments expanded to other sectors, such as labour, tax, welfare, education, healthcare, migration and environment, where the power of the EU remains limited.[6]

The very term 'soft law' is ambiguous, for the general aim of law is not, by its very nature, to express 'soft' rules of conduct, but to impose mandatory measures. Soft law differs from this. Linda Senden has explained the core contradiction as follows: 'soft law without legal effects is not law and soft law with legal effects is hard law'.[7] A range of scholars has attempted to address this issue by providing several definitions of the concept.[8] The most frequently quoted one is given by Francis Snyder who argues that soft law consists of 'rules of conduct which, in principle, have no legally binding force but which nevertheless may have practical effects'.[9] However, the most precise interpretation of the

4 For an overview of the relevant literature, see, Oana Stefan and others, 'EU Soft Law in the EU Legal Order: A Literature Review' (2010) SoLaR Working Paper, 5–8 <https://papers.ssrn.com/sol3/papers.cfm?abstract_id=3346629> accessed 9 April 2024.

5 Armin von Bogdandy, Felix Arndt and Jürgen Bast, 'Legal Instruments in European Union Law and their Reform: A Systematic Approach on an Empirical Basis' (2004) 23 *Yearbook of European Law* 91, 112.

6 Oana Stefan, 'Helping Loose Ends Meet? The Judicial Acknowledgment of Soft Law as a Tool of Multi-Level Governance' (2014) 21 *Maastricht Journal of European and Comparative Law* 359, 364; Corina Andone and Sara Greco, 'Evading the Burden of Proof in European Union Soft Law Instruments: The Case of Commission Recommendations' (2018) 31 *International Journal for the Semiotics of Law* 79, 83.

7 Linda Senden, *Soft Law in European Community Law* (Hart 2004) 109.

8 For a discussion on the definition of 'soft law', see among others, Fabien Terpan, 'Soft Law in the European Union – The Changing Nature of EU Law' (2015) 21 *European Law Journal* 68, 70–77; Oana Stefan and others, 'EU Soft Law in the EU Legal Order' (n 4) 5–17.

9 Francis Snyder, 'The Effectiveness of European Community Law: Institutions, Processes, Tools and Techniques' (1993) 56 *The Modern Law Review* 19, 32.

concept, in the author's view, is the one proposed by Senden: in her fundamental book on the subject she designates soft law as '[r]ules of conduct that are laid down in instruments which have not been attributed legally binding force as such, but nevertheless may create certain (indirect) legal effects, and that are aimed and may produce practical effects'.[10]

2.2 *General Rule: No Derogation from Hard Law*

The distinction between EU hard law and soft law can be observed *inter alia* in Article 288 of the TFEU, which lists key legal acts of the Union. In doing so, it refers to regulations, directives and decisions as binding instruments, and refers to recommendations and opinions as those deprived of legally binding force. Nevertheless, EU institutions also rely on other non-binding tools that equally fall within the soft law concept. For instance, a European Parliament working document explains that:

> At EU level, soft law ranges from Green and White Papers, Council Conclusions, Joint Declarations, Council Resolutions, Codes of Conduct, guidelines, communications and recommendations to the phenomenon known as 'co-regulation'.[11]

The main aim of non-binding interpretative instruments supplementing primary or secondary EU law is to provide (normative) guidance for its proper interpretation, ensure its uniform application, and describe the relevant legal acts with greater specificity.[12] Yet, notwithstanding its positive effects, soft law has been frequently criticised. For instance, it has been argued that the legal effects of non-binding measures cannot be determined, which impacts negatively on legal certainty.[13] A further point of criticism relates to the legitimacy deficit of soft law instruments. Notably, the Commission can generally adopt its guidelines without undergoing the scrutiny of the European Parliament and the Council, or the comitology control. In its 2007 Resolution, the European Parliament even went as far as to claim that:

> [T]he use of soft law is liable to circumvent the properly competent legislative bodies, may flout the principles of democracy and the rule of law

10 Senden, *Soft Law in European Community Law* (n 7) 3.

11 Parliament, 'Working Document on institutional and legal implications of the use of "soft law" instruments' (PE 384.581v02-00, 14.02.2007) 2.

12 Senden, *Soft Law in European Community Law* (n 7) 147, 312–16.

13 Ibid 461.

> under (…) EU Treaty, and also those of subsidiarity and proportionality under (…) EC Treaty, and may result in the Commission's acting *ultra vires*.[14]

The last point is particularly important since, in principle, soft law instruments of this type should not aim to create new legal effects apart from those already stemming from the hard law provisions they are interpreting. Nevertheless, as Senden notes, there are 'various gradations of interpretation'[15] and 'varying degrees of "newness"'.[16] In the first scenario, soft law may indeed merely restate and explain the relevant hard law provisions governing the area in question and summarise the relevant CJEU jurisprudence. Meanwhile, the second scenario envisages that the Commission provides a more subjective interpretation of EU legislation and comes up with new rules, which are not necessarily contained in the existing body of law.[17]

In this context, an important question arises: is there any limit to the degree of subjectivity and 'novelty', when it comes to the guidance offered by soft law? In other words, to what extent is the Commission allowed to provide its own interpretation of the underlying body of hard law, and is it bound by any restrictions? The answer to this question is apparently found in the general rule which says: a soft law act is valid as long as it does not derogate from primary or secondary law provisions of EU law or CJEU jurisprudence.[18]

This brings us to the next question, namely, if and how the legality of a soft law measure can be challenged before the CJEU. To begin with, it should be noted that enforcement of legal acts deprived of binding force is generally considered problematic. Due to the high 'legal effects' threshold, provided for in Article 263 of the TFEU, the applicability of traditional judicial review mechanisms, such as an action for annulment, remains largely confined to hard

14 Parliament, 'Resolution of 4 September 2007 on institutional and legal implications of the use of 'soft law' instruments (2007/2028(INI))' [2008] OJ C187 E/75, X. For a similar view, see, Linda Senden, 'Soft Post-Legislative Rulemaking: A Time for More Stringent Control' (2013) 19 *European Law Journal* 57.

15 Senden, *Soft Law in European Community Law* (n 7) 144.

16 Ibid 145.

17 Ibid.

18 This principle has been confirmed by CJEU. See for instance, Case 149/73 *Witt* [1973] ECR 01587, para 3; Case C-226/94 *Grand Garage Albigeois* [1996] ECR I-00651, para 21. For an analysis see Oana Stefan, 'European Competition Soft Law in European Courts: A Matter of Hard Principles?' (2008) 14 *European Law Journal* 753, 764–65; Oana Stefan, 'Hybridity before the Court: A Hard Look at Soft Law in the EU Competition and State Aid Case Law' (2012) 37 *European Law Review* 49, 60.

law instruments.[19] With limited options for direct review, the only available alternative for challenging the validity of EU soft law is a preliminary ruling procedure prescribed in Article 267 of the TFEU. The existence of such a possibility has been confirmed by the CJEU on a number of occasions.[20] Some commentators nonetheless argue that the literal reading of both articles 263 and 267 of the TFEU restricts their applicability only to acts adopted by EU institutions. It is therefore unclear if this condition would also be met by documents co-authored by EU institutions and Member States, such as Commission guidance.[21]

2.3 *Legal Effects of EU Soft Law at the National Level*

Although soft law instruments generally lack legally binding force, they can nonetheless become binding if translated into national law. The questions related to the interpretation of EU soft law instruments by courts and regulatory authorities of the Member States have been addressed by the CJEU on several occasions.

With respect to the Member States' judiciary, the CJEU held in *Grimaldi* that 'national courts are bound to take recommendations into consideration (…), in particular where they cast light on the interpretation of national measures adopted in order to implement them or where they are designed to supplement binding Community provisions'.[22] This essentially meant that whilst national courts were not obliged to comply with the Commission recommendations, they were under the duty to take the measures into account. In its later jurisprudence, the CJEU extended the *Grimaldi* approach to other EU soft law instruments, including Commission guidelines, reiterating the original wording 'bound to take' into account.[23] Two other rulings, however, further added to the confusion over the issue. In *CFK*, the Court concluded that the national court

19 For criticism of this situation see Mariolina Eliantonio and Oana Stefan, 'Soft Law Before the European Courts: Discovering a "Common Pattern"?' (2018) 37 *Yearbook of European Law* 457, 464–67, 469. Emilia Korkea-aho, 'National Courts and European Soft Law: Is *Grimaldi* Still Good Law?' (2018) 37 *Yearbook of European Law* 470, 473.

20 Case C-322/88 *Grimaldi* [1989] ECR 04407 para 8; Case C-258/14 *Florescu and Others* ECLI:EU:C:2017:448, para 30; Case C-16/16 *Belgium v Commission* ECLI:EU:C:2018:79, para 44.

21 Joanne Scott, 'In Legal Limbo: Post-Legislative Guidance as a Challenge for European Administrative Law' (2011) 48 *Common Market Law Review* 329, 349–50; Stefan, 'Helping Loose Ends Meet? (n 6) 367; Eliantonio and Stefan (n 19) 465.

22 *Grimaldi* (n 20), para 18.

23 Case C-410/13, *'Baltlanta' UAB* ECLI:EU:C:2014:2134, para 64. For an analysis see Korkea-aho (n 19) 485.

'may' take account of the Commission guidelines.[24] In contrast, in *Koninklijke,* the CJEU adopted a more restrictive position, stating that a national court may depart from Commission recommendations 'only where (…) it considers that this is required on grounds related to the facts of the individual case'.[25] Emilia Korkea-aho explains the differences in the CJEU approach by the nature of the soft law act in question. She argues that the Court imposes a duty to take soft law into account only where 'either primary or secondary law confers on the institutions (…) the task of providing further guidance, or where soft law guidance is in other ways foreseen in the underlying legislation'.[26] Meanwhile, in cases where the adoption of the relevant soft law instrument is not prescribed in primary or secondary law, national courts enjoy more discretion in deciding whether the measure at stake should be given any weight, at all.[27] Notably, whilst in *CFK,* the Commission guidelines were not derived from a primary or secondary legal instrument, in *Koninklijke,* the recommendations were adopted pursuant to the relevant framework directive. The latter explicitly suggested that the Commission was expected to issue recommendations,[28] and Member States needed to ensure that the national authorities take these into account.[29]

Apart from that, European soft law can become binding as a result of its implementation into national legislation. Yet, even in the absence of direct transposition into national law, EU soft law instruments may serve as a tool to reinforce certain values, norms, and practices and therefore transform the behaviour of national authorities. Practical effects of soft law in the national domain may range from policy changes to more subtle implications, such as the development of new discourses and policy principles.[30]

24 Case C-308/11 *Chemische Fabrik Kreussler* (*CFK*) ECLI:EU:C:2012:548, para 26.

25 Case C-28/15 *Koninklijke* ECLI:EU:C:2016:692, para 42.

26 Korkea-aho (n 19) 490.

27 Ibid 494.

28 Directive 2002/21/EC of the European Parliament and of the Council of 7 March 2002 on a common regulatory framework for electronic communications networks and services (Framework Directive) [2002] OJ L 108/33, art 15.

29 Ibid art 19. For an analysis, see, Korkea-aho (n 19) 490–91.

30 Oana Stefan, 'European Union Soft Law: New Developments Concerning the Divide Between Legally Binding Force and Legal Effects' (2012) 75 *The Modern Law Review* 881. The CJEU has also acknowledged that EU soft law instruments can have some effect on the practice of the national authorities. See for instance Case C-360/09 *Pfleiderer* [2011] ECR I-05161, para 23.

3 EU Soft Law on Marriages of Convenience

3.1 *Commission Guidelines and Handbook as Interpretative Tools*

As noted in the introduction to this chapter, two soft law instruments issued by the Commission – the 2009 Guidelines and the 2014 Handbook – are of particular relevance to the present study. According to the classification proposed by Senden,[31] both documents fulfil a post-law function and fall within the group of interpretative and decisional instruments. Both the Guidelines and the Handbook were published in the aftermath of the adoption of a secondary legal act – the Citizenship Directive – and aim to serve as guidance for its interpretation and application, particularly when it comes to implementation of Article 35. Since their publication was not originally foreseen in the Directive, national courts are not obliged to, and instead, *may* take these documents into account should they wish to do so.[32]

Issued following an unsatisfactory Commission report on the transposition of the Citizenship Directive, the 2009 Guidelines pursue a broad aim 'to provide guidance to Member States on how to apply Directive 2004/38/EC (…) correctly'.[33] The document contains a separate section on abuse and fraud,[34] the main part of which deals with the concept of marriages of convenience. It is, however, rather brief, and merely seeks to provide a general overview as to the application of the relevant concepts in the context of the Citizenship Directive.

The principal soft law instrument in this context is the 2014 Handbook which is devoted entirely to the issue of alleged marriages of convenience between mobile EU citizens and non-EU nationals. As noted in its introduction, the aim of the Handbook is:

> [T]o help national authorities effectively tackle individual cases of abuse in the form of marriages of convenience while not compromising the fundamental goal of safeguarding and facilitating free movement of EU citizens and their family members using EU law in a *bona fide* way.[35]

The document is 47 pages in length and structured into four sections. While the first three provide a comprehensive summary of the applicable legal

31 Senden, *Soft Law in European Community Law* (n 7) 118–20.

32 Emphasis added.

33 COM(2009) 313 final, 2.

34 Ibid s 4, 14–19.

35 SWD(2014) 284 final, 4.

framework and procedural safeguards Member States must respect when fighting abuse; the last 'operational' section contains a list of subjective hints that may indicate the marriage is not acceptable for the purposes of EU law. In addition, both the Guidelines and the Handbook seek to clarify the scope of the definition of marriages of convenience provided in the Citizenship Directive.

3.2 *Definition of Marriages of Convenience: the 'Sole Purpose' Test*

Although the Citizenship Directive does not contain a self-standing definition of 'marriages of convenience', this term shall be understood for its purposes as marriages entered into with the only aim being to regularise the stay of a third-country national in the EU. Whilst Article 35 of the Directive entitles Member States to adopt measures to tackle marriages of convenience, the wording of its Preamble makes clear that these are marriages 'contracted for the sole purpose of enjoying the right of free movement and residence'.[36] This definition has also been reproduced in the Commission Guidelines and Handbook. According to the latter, marriages of convenience are formally valid marriages 'contracted for the sole purpose of conferring a right of free movement and residence under EU law on free movement of EU citizens to a spouse who would otherwise not have such a right'.[37]

It is also reiterated that marriages of convenience are regarded as a specific form of abuse where 'abusive conduct is linked to the absence of intention to create a family as a married couple and to lead a genuine marital life'.[38] The Handbook further clarifies that the abusive character in this case is represented by '*mala fide* of the spouses prior to and at the moment they enter into the marriage.'[39] The cases where, in addition to the right of residence, the purpose of a marriage is to acquire other 'unfair advantages', e.g., a tax advantage, may also be considered 'abusive'.[40]

The Handbook then goes on to state that the '"sole purpose" is an autonomous concept of EU law', whereby 'a marriage cannot be considered a marriage of convenience simply because it brings an immigration advantage'.[41] It is

36 Citizenship Directive, recital 28.

37 SWD(2014) 284 final, 8. Similar wording is found in the 2009 Guidelines which reiterate that '[r]ecital 28 defines marriages of convenience for the purposes of the Directive as marriages contracted for the sole purpose of enjoying the right of free movement and residence under the Directive that someone would not have otherwise'. COM(2009) 313 final, 16.

38 SWD(2014) 284 final, 8.

39 Ibid.

40 Ibid.

41 Ibid 9.

further noted that '[w]hen an EU citizen genuinely marries a non-EU national, it should not be surprising that they want to live together somewhere, often in a country in which the other spouse had no legal right of residence before the marriage'.[42] In another passage, however, the Commission argues that:

> [T]he notion of 'sole purpose' should not be interpreted literally (as being the unique or exclusive purpose) but rather as meaning that the objective to obtain the right of entry and residence must be the predominant purpose of the abusive conduct.[43]

Several points of criticism can be made in this regard. First, the assertion that the 'sole purpose' is an autonomous concept of EU law has no basis in EU hard law. Given that the CJEU has never designated the concept of the 'sole purpose' as autonomous, the relevant passage of the Handbook is rather puzzling, particularly because the development of autonomous concepts in EU law is arguably not a matter of soft law. It is nonetheless true that, when examining the concept of abuse, the Court has consistently employed the narrow 'sole purpose' or, in other words, 'wholly artificial arrangements' test, referring to abuse as 'wholly artificial arrangements which (...) are set up with the sole aim of obtaining (...) advantage'.[44] This interpretation has been further confirmed by AG Poiares Maduro who referred to the 'sole purpose' paradigm as excluding situations where the activity in question 'may have some explanation other than the mere attainment' of the relevant advantage.[45] In addition, it is only where the conduct concerned does not have any other motive apart from obtaining such an advantage, that the objective of the relevant EU rules is not achieved.[46]

Against this background, the notion of the 'sole purpose' in the context of the Citizenship Directive shall be understood as referring to purely artificial arrangements having no content other than an immigration motive. Hence, obtaining an immigration benefit must be the only aim of the marriage, rather

42 Ibid.

43 Ibid.

44 Case C-653/11 *HMRC v Paul Newey* ECLI:EU:C:2013:409, para.46. See also, Case C-196/04 *Cadbury Schweppes* [2006] ECR I-07995, paras 55, 75; Case C-504/10 *Tanoarch* [2011] ECR I-10853, para 51; Case C-326/11 *J.J. Komen en Zonen Beheer Heerhugowaard* ECLI:EU:C:2012:461, para 35.

45 Case C-255/02 *Halifax* [2006] ECR I-01609, Opinion of AG Poiares Maduro, para 89.

46 On this point see Chapter 2, Section 8. See also, Richard Lyal, '*Cadbury Schweppes* and Abuse: Comments' in Rita De la Feria and Stefan Vogenauer (eds), *Prohibition of Abuse of Law: A New General Principle of EU Law?* (Hart 2011) 431.

than one among many. This is logical, given the fact that the state typically privileges marriage when it comes to family reunion and many couples get married just to be able to live together in one country, its choice often affected by various factors, including economic ones.[47] The Commission is therefore right in stating that a marriage cannot be considered to be one of convenience simply because it allows the TCN party to obtain a residence status. Indeed, the fact that an immigration advantage may be a consequence of marriage or even one motive for it does not mean that that the couple does not intend to lead a family life.[48] Against this background, the Commission's reference to the predominant purpose is highly confusing and seems to suggest that the Handbook seeks to expand the definition of a marriage of convenience found in the Citizenship Directive.[49] Going further than the Directive, however, constitutes a clear breach of EU law.[50]

Following the controversial passages discussed above, the Handbook proceeds to warn that some genuine marriages can sometimes be incorrectly considered marriages of convenience and distinguishes several situations where this may be the case. One particular example is arranged marriages.[51] It is noted that, although some characteristics of such marriages may resemble those of convenience (e.g., for example, where spouses have not met before the marriage or met only briefly), these should not be considered such, as long as they are the 'result of free will and wish of the spouses to create together a durable family unit as a married couple and to lead an authentic marital life'.[52]

Next, the Handbook refers to proxy marriages where one or both spouses are not physically present at the wedding ceremony and are usually represented by another person, a 'proxy'. After pointing out that such practice is uncommon in the EU and even unlawful in some Member States but rather common in several non-EU countries, the Handbook states that:

47 For more details, see Chapter 7, Section 2.5. See also, Helena Wray, 'The "Pure" Relationship, Sham Marriages and Immigration Control' in Joanna Miles, Perveez Mody and Rebecca Probert (eds) *Marriage Rites and Rights* (Hart 2015) 152.

48 See Chapter 3, Section 2.

49 A Commission representative involved in drafting the Handbook has confirmed that, in their view, a marriage of convenience may indeed be understood as the one contracted for the predominant purpose of obtaining residence rights (a follow-up email to an informal discussion with the author held in Brussels on 3 March 2017).

50 This point has also been highlighted in Marcello Di Filippo, 'Can EU Free Movement Rights be Abused? Critical Remarks on the "Marriages of Convenience Clause"' in Antonio Marcello Calamia (ed) *L'Abuso del Diritto* (G. Giappichelli Editore, 2017) 67.

51 SWD(2014) 284 final, 11.

52 Ibid 11.

> The reasons for marriage by proxy can be genuine (for example when one spouse cannot attend the ceremony for reasons of military service or imprisonment or is unable to travel due to serious health issues) but they can also be nefarious (such as to quickly contract a marriage of convenience without the EU spouse having to travel to another country for the wedding ceremony).[53]

The Handbook then goes on to list several possible scenarios of marriages of convenience, depending on the mode in which they have been set up. It is stressed that the list is not exhaustive.

The first scenario is labelled as a 'standard' marriage of convenience. In this case, both spouses are 'willing accomplices, freely consenting to enter into a relationship designed to abuse EU law'.[54] The Handbook suggests that this is probably the most common *modus operandi* related to marriages of convenience. It is nevertheless noted that '[t]he degree to which the EU citizens freely consent to enter into a marriage of convenience can significantly differ'.[55]

The second category encompasses the so-called 'marriages by deception'. As the Handbook explains, in such cases 'the EU spouse is deceived by the non-EU spouse to genuinely believe that the couple will lead a genuine and lasting marital life'.[56] According to the document, '[s]uch marriage is a marriage of convenience and should be tackled accordingly, with due regard to the innocence of the EU spouse'.[57] It is further stated that '[s]uch marriages typically, but not necessarily, follow a short relationship on the internet, or after the EU citizen has met the non-EU spouse in a foreign country on holidays' and 'may involve violence and threatening behaviour, particularly if the EU spouse has started to have concerns and is unwilling to participate in the immigration process'.[58]

The third and fourth categories concern forced marriages and marriages which include elements of human trafficking and/or are linked to organised crime. These groups typically overlap. The Handbook points out that EU citizens can sometimes be coerced into marriage without their consent or against their will, which is often considered trafficking in human beings. Meanwhile, it is noted that organised crime groups may also exploit the vulnerability of

53 Ibid.

54 Ibid 12.

55 Ibid.

56 Ibid.

57 Ibid.

58 Ibid 12.

EU citizens (such as poverty, outstanding debt, homelessness, drug addiction, unemployment or psychological vulnerability) to make them enter into a marriage of convenience.[59]

The Commission approach to the situations described above, however, is not unproblematic. First, the depiction of proxy marriages as a potential route of abuse may have adverse implications for couples who wish to lead a family life. As will be argued in Chapter 7, these are hostile and disproportionate Member State policies targeting perceived marriages of convenience that may prompt many couples to enter into marriage by proxy to avoid separation.

The author's major objection, however, relates to the Commission's decision to place so-called 'marriages by deception' within the scope of marriages of convenience. In the author's view, it is unclear how the situation at stake fits within the narrow definition of marriages of convenience found in the Citizenship Directive. First, in the absence of any additional remarks, the wording of both Article 35 and Recital 28 suggests that marriage is understood here as a holistic concept, i.e., a union entered into by two individuals. Accordingly, abuse in this situation presumably refers to the conduct of both spouses – both of them should be aware that a marriage is entered into with the only purpose to legalise the stay of the TCN party in the EU.

Second, even if this interpretation is incorrect and the motives of the spouses are to be examined separately, the concept of a 'marriage by deception' typically implies that the parties have already developed a relationship before the marriage, irrespective of the motives of the non-EU national. This essentially means that the authorities would need to prove that, at the point of the wedding, the only intention of one of the parties to an already existing relationship is to obtain an immigration advantage. These elements, however, seem to be mutually exclusive, which makes the task difficult and highly controversial. Moreover, it is highly likely that the TCN party would also intend to maintain a relationship with the EU spouse after the wedding. This is because, under the Citizenship Directive, a non-EU national spouse is normally able to obtain an independent right of residence only after three years of marriage. Such a situation, hence, cannot be regarded as one having no content other than an immigration motive. In the particular case, legalisation of the stay of a third-country national in the EU should not be considered a sole motive of marriage but rather a primary one (since a non-EU national also aims to maintain a relationship with the EU spouse). Accordingly, by including 'marriages of deception' into the scope of marriages of convenience, the Commission has

59 Ibid 12–13.

again unilaterally broadened the definition contained in the Directive and therefore derogated from hard law provisions.

Last, the very fact of deception, i.e., the intention to leave after obtaining the residence permit, by definition, can only be established in retrospect, after the residency has been granted to the TCN spouse.[60] Yet, investigations of obviously ongoing relationships at the application, let alone the pre-wedding stage based solely on the fear that unscrupulous TCN applicants are taking advantage of naïve EU citizens, may appear highly unjustified, discriminatory and disproportionate, and may lead to intense scrutiny of cases involving certain elements, e.g., where the parties have met online or only shortly before the wedding.

3.3 *Relationship between the 'Sole Purpose' Test and the CJEU Case Law*

As noted in Chapter 1, once it has been established that the marriage was not contracted only for the purpose of enabling the non-EU national to benefit from the Treaty rights, its substance is considered immaterial. According to CJEU case law, the spouses are recognised as family members for the purposes of the Citizenship Directive based only on their legal status, e.g., as long as the marriage has not been officially terminated, even if they already live with other partners.

The CJEU position has also been summarised in the Commission Handbook. In particular, it clarifies that:

> Marriages which started off as genuine marriages but later descended into something that is merely of form should not be considered as marriages of convenience even where a marriage that would otherwise have been terminated by divorce is maintained for the sole purpose of continuing to confer on the non-EU spouse a right of residence under EU law on free movement of EU citizens.[61]

Such an approach is logical, given that a marriage of convenience is defined as one entered into with the sole purpose of obtaining an immigration advantage. Once it has been established that the marriage in question cannot be classified as such, it is hard to imagine another legal reason why the spouses concerned would not be able to benefit from the Treaty rights, as long as the EU citizen

60 On this point see Wray, 'The "Pure" Relationship, Sham Marriages and Immigration Control' (n 47) 150.

61 SWD(2014) 284 final, 8–9.

satisfies the conditions laid down in Article 7 of the Citizenship Directive and the marriage has not been terminated.

Yet, although both the 'sole purpose' rule and the CJEU position with regard to the substance of marriage seek to protect couples from state interference into their marital life, the combination of the two approaches creates several challenges when it comes to detecting marriages of convenience.

As discussed above, the 'sole purpose' rule is concerned with the motive at the time of entry into the marriage. It requires proving a state of mind at a particular moment, something which, by definition, is based on subjective judgments by immigration authorities and open to misconceptions. Apart from that, such an approach creates several legal challenges, their character depending on the point the marriage is (potentially) subject to checks. In general, three basic points of control can be identified: (1) before the marriage; (2) at the point of application for a residence card; and (3) after the residence card has been issued.

With regards to pre-marriage controls, the Handbook specifies that the ECtHR case law allows national authorities to scrutinise intended foreigner-involved marriages in order to establish whether or not these are of convenience and prevent them from being registered where they are found to be such.[62] This approach may appear convenient from the immigration control perspective in that is prevents marriages from taking place. Furthermore, given the difficulties of determining the intentions of the couple *post factum*, the authorities may feel that carrying out pre-wedding checks is an easier solution. It should, however, be stressed that yet unmarried partners of EU citizens do not fall within the scope of direct family members under the Citizenship Directive, and as a consequence, do not enjoy the protection of EU law with regards to potential scrutiny of their relationship. In this context, a reference to pre-marriage controls in the Handbook is somewhat confusing, particularly because Member States are not obliged to respect the EU law safeguards listed in the document (the Handbook, however, does not specify this). As will be demonstrated in Chapters 5–9, national authorities enjoy a wide margin of discretion when carrying out checks on intended marriages. In several cases, this has resulted in significant interference in the right to marry and in the private life of the individuals involved.

In the second and third scenario, controls are exercised post-marriage, and the authorities face a difficult challenge of determining the motives of

62 Ibid 21. For an analysis of the concept of marriages of convenience in human rights law, see Chapter 5.

the couple in retrospect. As far as the 'sole purpose' is concerned, evidence obtained during the investigation shall only be relevant to the extent that it casts light on the motivation for the wedding. However, this is not always the case: Chapters 9 and 10 will show that the UK authorities frequently draw conclusions about the motives at the time of the wedding based on the nature of an already existing marriage, a practice which can lead to significant intrusion into the couples' private matters. Yet while such information may indeed, to a certain extent, shed light on the initial motivation of the parties, it is only of secondary importance: there is no direct correlation between the intentions before the marriage and the current state of the relationship.

Secondly, and most importantly: both the definition of marriages of convenience and the CJEU case law suggest that the nature of marriage becomes irrelevant immediately after the wedding. Following this logic, the spouses are not obliged to maintain the relationship and are even allowed to cohabit with other partners already at the application stage, which would still enable the TCN spouse to qualify as a family member of a Union citizen (provided that the purpose of marriage was to lead a family life and the marriage is not officially terminated). Conversely, denying the right of residence solely based on the fact that the relationship is non-existent at the present stage, would constitute a breach of EU law.

In this context it must be stressed that the Directive was apparently drafted with a very simple situation in mind: a marriage that was entered into with the only aim to obtain an immigration advantage and that was presumed to have no other content after the wedding. A standard example of a marriage of convenience is described in the 2009 Guidelines:

> S., a third country national, was ordered to leave in one month as she had overstayed her tourist visa. After two weeks, she married O., an EU national who had just arrived to the host Member State. The authorities suspect that the marriage might have been concluded only to avoid expulsion. They contact the authorities in O.'s Member State and find out that after the wedding his family shop was finally able to pay a debt of 5000 EUR, which it had been unable to repay for two years.
>
> They invite the newly-weds for an interview, during which they find out that O. has meanwhile already left the host Member State to return home to his job, that the couple is not able to communicate in a common language and that they met for the first time one week before the marriage.

> There are strong indications that the couple may have married with the sole purpose of contravening national immigration laws.[63]

Meanwhile, as noted in Chapter 3, the perceived phenomenon of marriages of convenience in the EU context is far more complex than the traditional understanding of the concept. In particular, there may also be cases where a marriage, initially entered into with the sole purpose of securing a right of residence for a TCN spouse, later transforms into a close relationship and appears to have characteristics considered to belong to family life, such as cohabitation, intimate relationship, joint finances, common plans for the future, etc. In such cases, application of the 'sole purpose' rule may appear challenging, particularly if there are indicators suggesting a marriage may be one of convenience, e.g., the involvement of organised crime.

In this regard, it is possible to identify several situations where the combination of the 'sole purpose' rule and the CJEU case law may make identifying marriages of convenience particularly difficult:

a) The marriage is entered into only for the purpose of securing an immigration advantage for the third-country national. However, at the application stage, it contains elements of a close relationship that may hold emotional significance for the parties involved. This may happen if, e.g., some time passes between the wedding and the application for a residence permit.
b) The marriage is entered into for the purpose of creating a family. However, at the application stage, the spouses have already separated and, possibly, even cohabit with other partners. This may happen, e.g., if the time has elapsed between the wedding and application for a residence permit, for instance, when the TCN spouse joins the EU citizen from another country.
c) Elements of a close relationship are present both at the wedding and application stage. In the meantime, there are indicators suggesting a marriage may be one of convenience, such as the involvement of organised crime. This may occur, e.g., where the couple initially intend to enter into marriage only for the purpose of obtaining residency but develop a relationship during the period between their meeting and the wedding (for example, in Ireland the parties to the proposed marriages must give a minimum of three months notification to a registrar,[64] which is sufficient time for developing a

63 COM(2009) 313 final, 17.
64 Civil Registration Act 2004, s 46(1)(a)(i).

relationship even if both initially had an intention to enter into a marriage of convenience).

It is therefore possible to assume that from a legal perspective, the combination of the two approaches may lead to a paradoxical outcome where non-EU nationals leading a real family life may be denied residency (cases (a) and (c)), whereas those separated with no intention of reconciliation may have it granted (case (b)). Chapter 10 will show that, in some cases, the literal interpretation of the definition of marriages of convenience by UK judiciary has indeed had such an effect. In the author's view, to achieve the aim of the Citizenship Directive, the definition should not be interpreted literally. To designate a marriage as one of convenience, two conditions must be satisfied: a) the sole purpose of the couple before and at the moment of the wedding should be to enable the non-EU national to obtain an immigration advantage; and b) the marriage should have no other content after the wedding. Such an interpretation is consistent with the overarching purpose of the right to family reunion granted to mobile EU citizens – namely, to provide them with an opportunity to live with their family members in a country of their choice, which would, in turn, facilitate free movement and their integration into the host Member State. Even a hypothetical situation where point (b) is absent, i.e., where a marriage, initially entered into with a sole purpose of securing a right of residence for a TCN spouse, later transforms into a real relationship, would still be consistent with this aim.[65] In contrast, refusal to grant a TCN spouse a residence permit would create unnecessary hardship for an EU citizen and, quite possibly, prompt the couple to move elsewhere, which would interfere with the principal's free movement rights.

3.4 *Investigation of Marriages: Limitations and Procedural Safeguards*

Having dealt with the definition of marriages of convenience, the Commission proceeds to provide a detailed overview of the procedural safeguards and limitations enshrined in EU law that the national authorities must respect when tackling potential abuse. The applicable legal framework is described at length in Section 3 of the Handbook. It begins by clarifying that derogations from free movement rights must be interpreted narrowly, whereby any measure adopted

65 Such an interpretation has also been endorsed by a Commission representative involved in drafting the Handbook. They expressed an opinion that situations where a marriage was entered into with the sole aim of securing an immigration advantage but later transformed into a real relationship should not be designated as marriages of convenience (Brussels, 3 March 2017).

under Article 35 of the Citizenship Directive must be proportionate and subject to procedural safeguards. It is further stressed that the principle of proportionality prohibits measures of general prevention and requires a case-by-case assessment where the decisions must be based 'exclusively on the personal conduct of the individuals concerned'.[66]

One of the key issues highlighted by the Commission in this context is the question of who bears the burden of proof. Both the Guidelines and the Handbook explicitly state that when investigating a potential marriage of convenience, the onus of proof rests on the authorities of the Member State seeking to restrict rights under the Citizenship Directive. Whilst the Guidelines address the issue only briefly,[67] the Handbook contains a separate subsection on evidential burden and burden of proof. It starts with a general observation that, in the absence of a unified EU approach to the issue, the evidential requirements to demonstrate that a marriage is one of convenience vary across Member States. It is nevertheless noted that national authorities must consider the collected evidence in its entirety and 'review all various elements that might constitute evidence to support or oppose the conclusion that a marriage of convenience has been contracted'.[68]

The Handbook then proceeds to note that the burden of proof is twofold. First, it is up to the non-EU national to prove that they are a beneficiary of EU free movement law. To do so, they are required to present supporting documentation proving their identity, the fact of their marriage to an EU citizen, and that they accompany an EU citizen who will be exercising free movement rights or join an EU citizen already doing so. Next, it is emphasised that the above list of documents is exhaustive and EU citizens and their family members enjoy the benefit of the assumption and the presumption of innocence, meaning that couples cannot be required, as a rule, to present evidence that their marriage is not abusive. Regardless of whether any suspicions exist, non-EU spouses are formally only asked to present proof of a valid marriage.[69] The Handbook accordingly states that 'the burden of proof clearly rests on the national authorities who suspect that a non-EU national has entered into a marriage of convenience with an EU citizen'.[70]

It is only where national authorities have 'well-founded suspicions as to the genuineness of a particular marriage, which are supported by evidence

66 SWD(2014) 284 final, 17.
67 COM(2009) 313 final, 17.
68 SWD(2014) 284 final, 26.
69 Ibid 26–27.
70 Ibid 27.

(such as conflicting information provided by the spouses)', that they can invite the couple to produce further documentation.[71] The term 'well-founded suspicions', however, is rather vague and lacks legal certainty. According to the Handbook, spouses are obliged to cooperate with authorities.[72] Nonetheless, failure to provide evidence that would dispel suspicions or even refusal to provide it at all 'cannot form the sole or decisive reason to conclude that the marriage is of convenience'.[73]

The Handbook proceeds to clarify that an investigation into a marriage can only be launched if there are 'reasonable doubts about its genuineness'.[74] Meanwhile, once an investigation has been carried out and led to the conclusion that the marriage is one of convenience, rights under free movement rules can be refused 'only where this is duly established by the national authorities concerned, in compliance with the relevant evidential standard', which may vary in accordance to the legal nature of the objective pursued (e.g., when the abusive conduct is addressed in the context of criminal proceedings or under immigration, administrative or civil status law).[75]

Other subsections provide an overview of the relevant principles and instruments of European and international human rights law. Having briefly explored the extent to which control practices are permitted under Articles 12 and 8 of the ECHR,[76] the Handbook warns that Article 3 of the ECHR[77] requires national authorities to respect the integrity of the individuals concerned and refrain from degrading or humiliating investigation techniques.[78] Further, Member States are reminded that discrimination on nationality, race, colour, ethnic or social origin is prohibited, as it would violate Article 14 of the ECHR.[79]

A separate subsection is devoted to the protection of the rights of the child. It begins with a statement that '[h]aving a child from the marriage is a strong "*counter-indication*" of abuse'.[80] It is nonetheless admitted that there may still

71 Ibid.
72 Ibid.
73 Ibid 28.
74 Ibid.
75 Ibid.
76 European Convention for the Protection of Human Rights and Fundamental Freedoms, CETS No.005 (04.11.1950) (ECHR). Or arts 9 and 7 of the Charter of Fundamental Rights of the European Union [2000] OJ C364/01 (EUCFR), respectively. For an analysis, see Chapter 5.
77 Or art 4 EUCFR.
78 SWD(2014) 284 final, 25.
79 Or article 21 EUCFR. Ibid.
80 Ibid 23.

be 'some marriages of convenience involving children, *mostly* from previous relationships of the spouses'.[81] While this wording apparently still leaves room for the possibility that marriages of convenience may involve children from the same relationship, it is difficult to imagine what this would mean in practice. In the author's view, the very fact of pregnancy and/or childbirth *per se* signifies that the parties, at least temporarily, had been in an intimate relationship, which is inconsistent with the narrow definition of a marriage of convenience. It is therefore regrettable that the Commission fails to explicitly exclude marriages involving pregnancy and childbirth from the scope of the concept.

Notwithstanding the above, the Handbook notes that, when deciding upon removal of one or both parties to an alleged marriage of convenience, the best interests of their children must be given primary consideration. It is specified that the relevant principle derives both from Article 24 of the EUCFR and, most notably, the UN Convention on the Rights of the Child[82] – the principal instrument of international law in this context. Article 3(1) of the Convention provides that '[i]n all actions concerning children, whether undertaken by public or private social welfare institutions, courts of law, administrative authorities or legislative bodies, the best interests of the child shall be a primary consideration'. The Handbook then notes that in cases of alleged marriages of convenience it would typically be in the best interests of the child to be able to continue to reside in the host Member State with both parents, particularly where the child is well integrated there. This, nonetheless, does not mean that the final decision of national authorities must inevitably comply with the child's best interests.

Yet, although Member States are allowed to assess if the strength of other considerations would outweigh those of best interests of the child, the former must be very substantial to decide in favour of the parent's removal. Moreover, under Article 9 of the Convention, the state needs to ensure that children are not separated from their parents against their will. Last, the Handbook warns that children who are nationals of the host Member State benefit from additional protection prohibiting the states from expelling their own nationals[83] or, in exceptional cases, from the principle established in *Ruiz Zambrano*.[84]

81 Ibid. Emphasis added.

82 Convention on the Rights of the Child, 1577 UNTS 3 (20.11.1989).

83 Art 3 of Protocol No.4 ECHR.

84 SWD(2014) 284 final, 23–25.

3.5 *'Operational' Measures*

The final section of the Handbook lists an extensive catalogue of possible indicators of marriages of convenience which may trigger the launch of an investigation by national authorities.[85] In the beginning, it is underlined that the hints are 'distilled from national practices across the Member States' and 'should serve as a toolbox of solutions allowing Member States to set up tailored operational schemes fitting their specific needs and available resources'.[86]

The Handbook then explains that in the case of doubts about the nature of a particular marriage and with a view to deciding whether to trigger an investigation, 'a number of hints could constitute one of the elements guiding the authorities'.[87] It is, however, stressed that the hints never automatically and inevitably confirm the abusive nature of the marriage but may merely 'trigger an open-ended investigation, with no pre-determined outcome'.[88]

In selecting the hints of abuse provided in the Handbook, its drafters followed the approach where '[a]n effective hint of abuse relates to conduct which abusive couples are reasonably expected to exhibit significantly more often than genuine couples'.[89] For example, it is clarified that the spouses not having a joint bank account or having a large age difference could not be considered as effective hints of abuse, as this can also be the case in many genuine marriages. On the other hand, the spouses not knowing crucial personal information about each other may be considered as an effective hint of abuse. Accordingly, that means that there are no 'safe' hints of abuse that can be triggered only by abusive couples, as any single hint will also be triggered by some genuine couples. However, 'while a typical genuine couple may trigger several hints of abuse, typical abusers will trigger substantially more hints of abuse'.[90] It is underlined that the hints of abuse 'must therefore only be seen and understood in their entirety in order to be relevant for triggering an investigation'.[91]

The Handbook further explains that it cannot be excluded that the national authorities 'will be confronted with atypical but genuine couples that will score a comparable number of hints of abuse as some abusive couples'.[92] This, in itself, is not considered a 'proof of their "guilt", just a signal that an

85 Similar indicators are provided in the 2009 Guidelines, although the list is much shorter. COM(2009) 313 final, 16–17.

86 SWD(2014) 284 final, 32.

87 Ibid 33.

88 Ibid.

89 Ibid.

90 Ibid.

91 Ibid.

92 Ibid 34.

investigation could be launched to look into the case in more detail'.[93] When making a decision, all pieces of evidence must be assessed together as a whole in a neutral and unbiased manner. The evidence which supports the conclusion that the suspected marriage is abusive should clearly outweigh the one supporting the view that it is not. The corroborating evidence can be used for prosecution if it is strong enough to meet the respective burden of proof.[94] The investigation techniques mentioned in the Handbook involve simultaneous interviews of questionnaires, document and background checks, inspections by law enforcement, and community-based checks.[95]

The Handbook then goes on to provide a number of hints of abuse that could trigger an investigation into a marriage. The hints are divided into several groups according to the 'inherent stages of "the life cycle" of marriages of convenience',[96] starting from stage 1 before the future spouses meet for the first time, and ending with stage 6 when the parties divorce because the right of residence of the non-EU spouse is well established.[97] It, therefore, follows that the couples, in principle, can be subjected to scrutiny at any stage of their residence in the host Member State.

Further, it will be demonstrated that the hints provided by the Handbook refer not only to the character of marriage, but also to the personal characteristics of its parties. Based on the criteria, it is possible to distinguish several broad categories of persons whose marriage has significantly higher chances to be considered 'suspicious' and, consequently, become subject of closer scrutiny. These include:

a) Third-country nationals who have not lawfully resided in another EU Member State before seeking residency in the host Member State;
b) EU citizens finding themselves in a 'vulnerable position'; and
c) Persons whose marriages have been organised by individual facilitators or organised crime groups.

3.5.1 Third-Country Nationals Who Have Not Lawfully Resided in Another EU Member State

Although the condition of prior lawful residence in another Member State was found to be in breach of the Citizenship Directive,[98] this factor subsequently

93 Ibid.
94 Ibid 35.
95 Ibid 42–44.
96 Ibid 36.
97 Ibid 36–40.
98 Case C-127/08 *Metock and Others* [2008] ECR I-06241.

appeared in the Handbook as one of the crucial elements while drawing a distinction between 'safe' and 'suspicious' TCN spouses of Union citizens. When pointing to the elements suggesting a marriage may be one of convenience, the Handbook consistently focuses on non-EU nationals who, before the application for a residence permit as a family member of an EU citizen, have not lawfully resided in another EU Member State. A particular emphasis is placed on those having a short-term or irregular status.

Aiming to minimise the risk of an erroneous decision, the Handbook suggests employing the so-called 'double-lock' approach. Accordingly, in the case of suspicions that the marriage is one of convenience, the national authorities should not focus primarily on hints of abuse 'to support their initial gut feeling' or predetermined assumption.[99] Rather, they are first recommended to verify the hints that there is no abuse, which, by analogy, reflect conduct which is 'much more likely to be exhibited by genuine couples than abusive couples'.[100] Only where this has not *prima facie* confirmed the 'genuine' nature of the marriage, should the authorities proceed to examine the hints of abuse.

The Handbook then lists a number of hints that there is no abuse. It is stated that, in comparison with abusive couples, 'genuine' couples are more likely:

1) To consist of a non-EU spouse who has previously lawfully resided with the EU citizen in another Member State;
2) To be in a close relationship for a long time;
3) To share parental responsibilities for one or more children and to be equally involved in their exercise;
4) To have a common domicile or household or to maintain regular and frequent contact if they do not live together;
5) To have entered a serious long-term legal or financial commitment together (e.g. a mortgage to buy a home); and/or
6) To have their marriage lasting for a long time.[101]

The non-EU nationals satisfying the condition of prior lawful residence in another Member State are therefore portrayed as 'safe' and have significantly lower chances of becoming an object of additional scrutiny. This point reflects the post-*Metock* concerns of some Member States who expressed fears that the abolishment of the prior lawful residence rule would encroach upon their sovereignty in immigration matters.[102]

99 SWD(2014) 284 final, 34.
100 Ibid 34.
101 Ibid 35–36.
102 See Chapter 3.

Formally, only the hint N1 explicitly refers to this group of persons. However, upon closer inspection, it becomes obvious that other characteristics, to a large extent, equally exclude couples who have not previously resided together elsewhere in the EU. If the couple meets in the host Member State and the third-country national has a short-term or irregular immigration status, it is likely that the insecurity associated with this will prompt the couple to enter into a marriage and apply for a residence permit as soon as possible, just to be able to reside together in one country – without having the chance to be in a close relationship or marriage for a long time. Similar considerations apply to the hint N3: if the couple is hastened into marriage, as well as given the uncertainty surrounding their status, the probability of having children at this stage is less likely in comparison with those who have already enjoyed a stable life in another Member State. Likewise, an uncertain situation is likely to prevent the former from entering into a serious financial commitment.

Out of the hints listed above, only one – the hint N4 – seems equally applicable both to TNC spouses with or without prior lawful residence in another Member State. It should be, however, remembered that according to CJEU case law, the spouses are not obliged to have a common domicile or household to qualify under the Citizenship Directive.

It is thus possible to conclude that newly-weds who have not lawfully resided together in another Member State may find themselves in a more disadvantaged position when it comes to the authorities deciding whether to proceed with further examination of the marriage in question. One can assume that in cases where the authorities have a 'gut' feeling that the marriage may be one of convenience, most couples who have already met in the host Member State may be unable to satisfy most of the 'no-abuse' criteria and would therefore be referred for further inspection – this time, their conduct and personal characteristics would be measured against the hints of abuse.

In selecting the hints of abuse, the drafters of the Handbook apparently followed the same approach. In particular, it is explained that TCN parties to an intended marriage of convenience are more likely:

1) To have been unsuccessful in previous entry or residence applications through other migration channels;
2) To have previously migrated or be currently residing irregularly in an EU Member State; and/or
3) To be currently faced with imminent expiry of their legal residence.[103]

103 Ibid 36.

These criteria repeatedly focus on the residence status of the non-EU spouse, with a particular emphasis on those with a short-term or irregular status. In general, however, all non-EU nationals who have not previously resided in another Member State are potentially regarded as a risk group. When explaining the reasons and motivations behind marriages of convenience, the Handbook argues that '[f]or some non-EU nationals, a marriage of convenience with an EU citizen offers a route towards a right of residence which may be more stable and protected than other channels of migration, regular or irregular'.[104] It is therefore expected that all non-EU nationals who do not have permanent residence status in the first place – e.g., those with a work visa – would fall into this category. The breadth of its scope is deeply problematic, particularly given that those who already have an independent right of residence in the host Member State, would by definition have no incentive to apply for a residence permit as family members of EU citizens. Further, in a number of Member States, the limited legal avenues for obtaining long-term residence rights, low asylum approval rates, bureaucratic delays in considering residence applications, and the legal & practical complexity of removal procedures results in substantial numbers of non-EU nationals living in legal limbo for many years.[105] In this context, it is indeed unsurprising that many of them start families in the country they live – *inter alia* with EU citizens. The stigmatisation of people with 'adverse immigration history' as potential parties to marriages of convenience may therefore result in significant difficulties for EU citizens who wish to lawfully live with their family members in the host Member State.[106]

3.5.2 History of Abuse or Fraud

The qualities of non-EU nationals are also assessed against such elements as a previous sponsorship, history of abuse, or forgery. According to the Handbook, where national law foresees banns of marriage or secular pre-marriage registration requirements, 'abusers' are more likely:

1) To have discrepancies in the documents provided which raise concerns of forgery;

---

104 Ibid 32.

105 For an analysis of the situation in the UK, see for instance, Franck Duvell, Myriam Cherti and Irina Lapshyna, 'Does Immigration Enforcement Matter? Irregular Migration and Control Policies in the UK' (Final Report, Centre on Migration, Policy and Society, University of Oxford, October 2018). For UK and EU asylum statistics see 'Asylum Statistics' (House of Commons Library Briefing Paper SN01403, 01.03.2024) <https://commonslibrary.parliament.uk/research-briefings/sn01403/> accessed 9 April 2024.

106 A similar view is expressed by Di Filippo (n 50), 68.

2) To provide a false local address; and/or
3) To have one of the prospective spouses registered in several municipalities as about to enter into marriage with a different person.[107]

Furthermore, the Handbook explains that 'abusers' are more likely (1) to have a history of previous marriages of convenience or other forms of abuse or fraud, or (2) to have family members with such a history.[108]

It must be stressed that the phrase 'other forms of abuse or fraud' lacks legal certainty and may potentially be interpreted broadly – for instance, as applicable even to those charged with minor offences unrelated to their marriage or immigration status. Similarly, a reference to their relatives is potentially over-inclusive. It increases the risk of considering an individual suspicious just based on the involvement of their family members in unlawful activities. Meanwhile, the scope of such family members is not specified.

As to the EU citizen parties to perceived marriages of convenience, the Handbook notes that they are not only more likely to have been previously involved in marriages of convenience[109] but also to have concluded short marriages with non-EU nationals as such.[110] Yet, even if 'serial cheaters' do exist, their number is likely to be low, given that the non-EU national can only obtain an independent right of residence after three years of marriage. Whilst it is not specified what period may be regarded 'short', it should be assessed with caution, provided that many marriages entered into for the purpose of creating a family, end up in divorce after a few years or even months.

3.5.3 EU Citizens in a Vulnerable Position

In the meantime, 'suspicious' EU citizens are portrayed in the Handbook as individuals in a bad financial situation whose vulnerability is often exploited by non-EU nationals or facilitators. Accordingly, the main reason why EU citizens may assist foreigners in contracting a marriage of convenience is deemed to be financial gain. It is stressed that:

> EU citizens finding themselves in a vulnerable position (poverty, outstanding debt, homelessness or drug addiction) are more likely to be

107 SWD(2014) 284 final, 37.
108 Ibid 36.
109 Ibid 39.
110 Ibid 36.

> convinced to contract a marriage of convenience in order to improve their situation. In many such cases, there are elements of human trafficking.[111]

This construct apparently reflects the discourses that have gained prominence in several Member States. As explored in Chapter 3, several governments have described the phenomenon as closely linked to human trafficking, where vulnerable Eastern European women are maliciously exploited by both intermediaries and third-country nationals. However, this factor may well appear overinclusive. There is a danger that the terms 'poverty' and 'vulnerable position' can be easily attributed to a vast number of EU citizens exercising their Treaty rights. This, in turn, would potentially subject their marriages to closer scrutiny, amounting to discrimination based on their social class.

3.5.4 Involvement of Facilitators or Organised Crime

The (c) and (d) categories are largely interrelated, as perceived exploitation of vulnerable EU citizens has been closely linked to organised crime. The Handbook addresses the latter issue in a separate sub-section.[112] The Commission underlines that marriages of convenience frequently involve elements of human trafficking, as well as provides the definition of human trafficking enshrined in the Directive 2011/36/EU.[113] It is also noted that besides what is 'typically considered as trafficking in human beings (for example, women brought to the host EU country and forced to marry someone)', organised crime groups may exploit the vulnerability of EU spouses to make them contract a marriage of convenience.[114]

Another sub-section has been specifically devoted to facilitators who may be involved in a marriage of convenience and whose main motivation is financial gain.[115] The Handbook consistently refers to organised crime throughout the stages of marriages of convenience. During the pre-marriage phase, for instance, 'abusers' are more likely, *inter alia*:

1) To never have met in person before the marriage; and/or
2) To have got together through the services of a disreputable marriage agency with suspected connections to organised crime or through an informal network within non-EU national communities which is known to be acting as facilitator.[116]

111 Ibid 32.

112 Ibid 12–13.

113 Directive 2011/36/EU of the European Parliament and of the Council of 5 April 2011 on preventing and combating trafficking in human beings and protecting its victims, and replacing Council Framework Decision 2002/629/JHA [2011] OJ L101/1, art 2.

114 SWD(2014) 284 final, 13.

115 Ibid 33.

116 Ibid 36–37.

Likewise, during the wedding stage, 'abusers' are more likely:

1) To use a marriage venue which is known to be prone to abuse or has possible connections to organised crime;
2) Where relevant – to have their wedding organised by a third party who does not seem to fit this purpose (e.g. not a friend/relative or a specialised agency) or who has suspected connections to organised crime;
3) To celebrate their wedding ceremony together with other couples with whom they do not seem to have anything in common, possibly with the same witness(es);
4) To have previously initiated procedures to wed another EU spouse;
5) To have the EU citizen flown to the country only a short time before the marriage without any plausible reason or leave the country shortly after the marriage has been conducted without any plausible reason;
6) To have their travel arrangements organised by a third party with possible connections to organised crime; and/or
7) To hand over an 'unexplained' sum of money or gifts in order for the marriage to be contracted (with the exception of money or gifts given in the form of a dowry in cultures where this is common practice) that could be considered as 'payment for abuse' to the EU spouse and facilitators.

While the hints provided may indeed be applicable to marriages involving elements of human trafficking, several risk factors can be identified. First, the hint of having never met in person before the marriage may disproportionately target arranged marriages where the couple may see each other only on the wedding day. Furthermore, at present, the abundance of alternative means of communication (e.g., messenger apps and social media) makes it possible to form and maintain long-distance relationships without meeting each other in person.[117]

Next, with respect to the hint N5, one should be careful not to infer that the marriage is one of convenience only because the EU citizen maintains some ties to another Member State. It must be stressed that the right of EU citizens to live in the host Member State is not subordinated to a period of uninterrupted physical presence in that country. As long as they are considered 'qualified persons' for the purposes of the Citizenship Directive, checks of their

117 For a similar view, see, Di Filippo (n 50) 68.

presence in the host Member State are unnecessary and may even prompt EU citizens to refrain from frequent travelling out of the fear that their marriage can be considered as one of convenience. This may also put obstacles to their right to free movement.

In addition, as pointed out above, there is a danger of not recognising the complexity of the phenomenon and oversimplifying it. As mentioned in Chapter 3, the involvement of facilitators or organised crime does not necessarily mean that the marriage has no content other than an immigration motive.

Finally, the Handbook lists several 'universal' hints that appear to be attributable to any category of the individuals concerned. These include:

1) Absence of a common language understood by both or evidence that they are making some efforts to establish a common basis for communication;
2) Parties give conflicting, inconsistent or false information about each other on:
    a. crucial personal matters (name, date of birth and age, nationality, address, closest family members, possible previous marriages and cohabitation, education, profession or job/unemployment);
    b. the circumstances of their first meeting which can be verified;
    c. the wedding ceremony and celebration (list of wedding guests, names of witnesses);
    d. common plans for their future, for the establishment of genuine marital life and how they (plan to) assume some of the responsibilities resulting from the marriage (such as those of financial nature);
3) Parties do not maintain their matrimonial cohabitation or continue living separately after their marriage without any plausible reason (for example work, children from previous relationships living abroad);
4) One of the spouses lives with someone else;
5) Parties show lack of contribution to the responsibilities and practical obligations arising from the marriage;
6) Parties make no plans for their financial stability;
7) Parties do not wish to effectively share parental responsibility for one or more children.[118]

118 SWD(2014) 284 final, 37–40.

As to the first hint, it is unclear who will be capable of carrying out a professional assessment of the couple's language and communication skills; it is doubtful that immigration officers are trained to do so. Furthermore, there are plenty of online translation tools that enable meaningful communication between parties who do not share a common language. The hints are also highly normative, of very general nature, and refer to elements that are difficult to assess. The CJEU has explicitly confirmed that couples must be free to arrange their marital life as they wish, including living separately or even cohabiting with other partners, as long as their marriage is not officially terminated.

Overall, the approach suggested by the Commission raises several points of concern. First, it is unclear how any of the hints mentioned in the Handbook can trigger the authorities' suspicions, given that the states are prohibited from systematically requesting married couples to provide evidence of their relationship at the application stage. As noted above, spouses of EU citizens only need to present their passport, marriage certificate and proof that the EU citizen is exercising their Treaty rights or intends to do so. The information that can be obtained from these documents is essentially limited to nationality, the residence status of the non-EU national and the length of their marriage. Yet, the former two elements cannot serve as the only grounds for suspicions as this would amount to blatant discrimination of certain groups of applicants. The principle of the presumption of innocence and the Commission's approach in presenting the list of 'suspicions-triggering' indicators are therefore mutually exclusive.

The author's second objection relates to the nature of the hints. Notwithstanding the safeguards and precautions stressed in Section 3 of the Handbook, the hints listed in its 'operational' part focus on detecting potential 'abusers' rather than on the need to minimise the risk of an erroneous decision and state interference into the family life of EU citizens. Such an approach is problematic, as it creates an artificial division between 'pure' and 'abusive' marriages and contributes to the reproduction of stereotypes and the normative, traditional perception of how 'real' couples should behave.[119] Accordingly, the main risk associated with the respective policies is that they usually target a much broader category of couples – primarily those whose profiles do not correspond to the 'standard' models of behaviour.

---

119 For criticism, see also, Di Filippo (n 50) 68; Betty de Hart, 'The Europeanization of Love. The Marriage of Convenience in European Migration Law' (2017) 19 *European Journal of Migration and Law* 296.

Moreover, although the drafters of the Handbook claim it was prepared in close cooperation with Member States,[120] a number of governments have been reluctant to share the relevant information in writing with the Commission, for instance, the detailed questions they ask during the interviews. The main concern was the need for confidentiality, as national authorities feared that disclosure of such information could play into the hands of potential 'abusers'.[121] As a result, when selecting criteria, the Commission largely relied on the information provided by the UK authorities who appeared ready to collaborate. In general, the drafting process was characterised by a lack of clear methodology, with Commission officers relying on anecdotal evidence[122] and, to an extent, validating control practices of the British government. As will be demonstrated in Chapter 9, UK domestic law indeed follows the spirit of the Handbook. Furthermore, the Commission's normative perception of the conduct which abusive couples exhibit 'significantly more often than genuine couples'[123] is not substantiated by any statistical evidence.

In the meantime, it must also be recalled that Member States are first advised to look for the hints that the marriage is genuine, which can be evaluated positively. Notwithstanding that, although the burden of proof lies on the national authorities, the latter do not need to prove that a marriage is one of convenience beyond all reasonable doubt, as is commonly required in criminal cases. To exclude the non-EU national spouse from the scope of the Citizenship Directive, it is sufficient to employ the balance of probabilities test. Yet, in light of the narrow definition of marriages of convenience provided in the Citizenship Directive and the fundamental nature of the rights at stake, the author advocates for a narrower approach. In the author's view, the main focus should not be placed on detecting abuse but on reducing the risk of targeting couples who do (or did) intend to lead a family life but whose behaviour does

120 SWD(2014) 284 final, 3. A Commission representative involved in drafting the Handbook further clarified in an informal conversation that, whilst the Commission consulted Member States, the draft was not subject to their formal agreement (Brussels, 3 March 2017).

121 Commission, 'Draft Minutes of the Sixteenth Meeting of Experts on the Right to Free Movement of Persons (Directive 2004/38/EC)' (Meeting held on 25.03.2013) 4. Available at <https://ec.europa.eu/transparency/expert-groups-register/screen/expert-groups/consult?lang=en&do=groupDetail.groupDetail&groupID=2397> accessed 9 April 2024. This was also confirmed by the Commission representative involved in drafting the Handbook. (Brussels, 3 March 2017).

122 Informal conversation with a Commission representative involved in drafting the Handbook (Brussels, 3 March 2017).

123 SWD(2014) 284 final, 33.

not conform to the prevailing stereotypes of how a 'genuine' marriage should look like, or where its quality is deemed 'insufficient'. Hence, in contrast to what is permitted in the Handbook, it would be more reasonable to require the authorities to show that the marriage does not have, and has never had, any other content apart from an immigration motive. Therefore, a marriage should be considered genuine in the absence of any reliable evidence that it has been a purely artificial arrangement and/or in the presence of *any* elements suggesting there is (or used to be) a close relationship between the parties, such as cohabitation, joint finances, common plans for future, financial and/or emotional support, intimate relationships, etc.[124]

In general terms, by including into the Handbook an extensive list of indicators suggesting that the marriage may be one of convenience, the Commission has made a significant concession to Member State authorities. In doing so, it has, to some extent, shifted its emphasis from the necessity to protect the fundamental rights of EU citizens and their family members to *de facto* validation of a normative division between marriages contracted for 'right' or 'wrong' reasons, endorsed by several governments. A Commission representative involved in drafting the Handbook stressed that the Commission was under intense pressure from Member States who demanded more clarity as to the measures they are allowed to take to tackle the perceived abuse. The representative accordingly admitted that limiting the list of measures to the EU law safeguards and the fundamental rights the Member States must respect would be useful legally but not necessarily useful politically.[125]

4 Conclusion

The drafters of the Commission Handbook – the principal EU soft law instrument addressing the issue of marriages of convenience – faced a difficult challenge in striking a balance between accommodating Member State concerns about the perceived abuse and protecting the free movement rights of EU citizens and their family members. To a certain extent, the Commission showed resistance to Member States by providing a detailed overview of the procedural safeguards and general principles of EU law that the national authorities must respect when tackling potential abuse. So far, the content of the Handbook can be evaluated positively.

124 Emphasis added.

125 Informal conversation with a Commission representative involved in drafting the Handbook (Brussels, 3 March 2017).

However, the Commission does not limit itself to merely restating the relevant provisions but supplements them with its own understanding of the concept of marriages of convenience. The analysis of the relevant measures has shown that some of them are highly contradictory and may produce adverse legal effects. For instance, extending the scope of the definition of marriages of convenience to those contracted with the primary purpose of obtaining an immigration advantage is arguably *ultra vires*, yet the options to challenge the relevant provision before the CJEU are limited. The second concern relates to the 'operational' part of the Handbook, where the Commission goes to great lengths to describe hints that may trigger suspicions, as well as provides recommendations on the choice of investigation tools. By doing so, the Handbook effectively reinforces the traditional discourses on how married couples should behave, as well as creating a distinction between 'safe' and 'suspicious' categories of persons: whilst the former are unlikely to be scrutinised by national authorities, the latter, such as those with an unstable residence status, have a good chance of becoming the focus of attention of the relevant state. The decision to include the catalogue of indicators in the Handbook represents an important concession to Member States' authorities.

As a soft law instrument that correspondingly escaped the scrutiny of the European Parliament and the Council, the Handbook should be understood as a voluntary interpretation aid. Notwithstanding that, it may have wide-ranging consequences for the individuals concerned if implemented into domestic legislation or used as a reference source by domestic policymakers or the judiciary. As will be shown in Chapter 10, the Handbook has already produced adverse legal effects at the national level. The analysis of UK case law suggests that the document has been influential in British courts where judges have relied on its most problematic passages to undermine the definition of marriages of convenience under the Citizenship Directive. By doing so, they have effectively incorporated the erroneous approach into domestic hard law.

CHAPTER 5

The Concept of Marriages of Convenience and European Human Rights Law

1 Introduction

When addressing perceived marriages of convenience, Member States are not only bound by the relevant constraints enshrined in EU law but also by the principles of international human rights law. The right to live with their family members has been guaranteed to individuals by nearly all core international human rights instruments, most notably the UDHR,[1] the ICCPR,[2] and the ECHR.[3] In the EU, the principal sources of this set of rights are the ECHR and the EUCFR,[4] the latter of which has acquired a legally binding force with the Lisbon Treaty.

As shown in Chapter 4, the Commission Handbook[5] has already pointed to some elements of human rights the state authorities must pay regard to when exercising marriage controls. This chapter aims to explore the relevant legal framework in more detail and show if and how human rights can protect couples from hostile state practices. The analysis will focus on two basic rights that are most likely to come into tension with government measures targeting perceived marriages of convenience. These are the right to respect for private and family life, guaranteed by Article 8 of the ECHR and Article 7 of the EUCFR, and the right to marry and to found a family, found in Article 12 of the ECHR and Article 9 of the EUCFR. Where relevant, the chapter will also explore the compatibility of the respective state policies with other fundamental rights, such as the prohibition of discrimination (Article 14 of the ECHR and Article 21 of the EUCFR) and the right to respect for human dignity (Article 1 of the EUCFR).

1 Universal Declaration of Human Rights, GA Res. 217 A (III) (10.12.1948) (UDHR).

2 International Covenant on Civil and Political Rights, 999 UNTS 171 (16.12.1966) (ICCPR).

3 European Convention for the Protection of Human Rights and Fundamental Freedoms, CETS No.005 (04.11.1950) (ECHR).

4 Charter of Fundamental Rights of the European Union [2000] OJ C364/01 (EUCFR).

5 Commission, 'Staff Working Document – Handbook on addressing the issue of alleged marriages of convenience between EU citizens and non-EU nationals in the context of EU law on free movement of EU citizens' SWD(2014) 284 final.

 | DOI:10.1163/9789004499263_007

The chapter begins by briefly defining the scope of Articles 8 and 12 of the ECHR, as well as providing a short overview of the relevant ECtHR case law in the context of immigration control. Then, the chapter explores the ECtHR position on the government measures targeting marriages of convenience and identifies problematic issues arising from it. Finally, the chapter looks at the relationship between the ECtHR jurisprudence on marriages of convenience and EU free movement law, focusing on the implications the Strasbourg court's approach may have for couples involving (mobile) EU citizens and non-EU nationals.

2 Articles 12 and 8 of the ECHR in a Nutshell

2.1 *The Right to Marry and to Found a Family*

Article 12 of the ECHR reads: 'Men and women of marriageable age have the right to marry and to found a family, according to the national laws governing the exercise of this right'. Like many other rights protected under the Convention, the right to marry and to found a family originates from the UDHR.[6] Both instruments were adopted in the immediate aftermath of the Second World War,[7] a period when the then-recent violations committed by the Nazis and other fascist regimes created a pressing need to de-legitimise their ideology. This objective also implied outlawing one of its key elements, namely, Nazi family policy which manifested itself in a ban of mixed marriages, as well as the curtailment of the reproductive rights of certain groups.[8] It is against this background that the drafters of both the UDHR and the ECHR not only wished to protect the right to privacy in general but also addressed the right to marry and found a family in a separate article.[9] The respective clauses can thus be viewed as guaranteeing classic human rights that protect individuals against government interference in their marital and family life.[10]

The right to marry and to found a family has equally found its way into the EUCFR. The wording of Article 9 of the Charter is similar to that of the ECHR and reads as follows: 'Right to Marry and Right to Found a Family shall

6 Art 16 UDHR. A similar provision is found in Art 23(1) ICCPR.

7 The UDHR was adopted in 1948, whilst the ECHR was drafted in 1950 and entered into force in 1953.

8 On this topic, see among others, Lisa Pine, *Nazi Family Policy 1933–1945* (Berg Publishers 1997).

9 Bart van der Sloot, 'Between Fact and Fiction: An Analysis of the Case-Law on Article 12 of the European Convention on Human Rights' (2014) 26 *Child and Family Law* 397, 399.

10 Ibid 401.

be guaranteed in accordance with the national laws governing the exercise of these rights'. Although the core elements of family law remain within the competence of Member States, Article 9 has a general application in all fields where these rights may be indirectly affected. One can distinguish several areas of often overlapping competences where indirect development of these concepts takes place, such as: (1) equal treatment and protection from discrimination, (2) the cross-border recognition of marriages, partnerships and parenthood, and the impact it has on the free movement of EU citizens and their TCN family members, and (3) admission of non-EU family members within the framework of the Citizenship Directive[11] or the Family Reunification Directive.[12]

The Explanations to the Charter state that Article 9 is based upon Article 12 of the ECHR, yet the right to marry and to found a family are clearly separated. The wording is said to be modernised to cover cases where national legislation recognised arrangements other than marriage for founding a family. It is also specified that Article 9 'neither prohibits nor imposes the granting of the status of marriage to unions between people of the same sex'.[13] Hence, whilst the scope of those rights under the Charter may be wider than under the ECHR, if the national law so provides, it is also made clear that they should always fall within the ambit of the minimum protection level guaranteed under Article 12 of the ECHR.[14]

Up to the present date, the CJEU has delivered several rulings indirectly addressing the issues linked to Article 12 of the ECHR – most notably, LGBT rights in the area of non-discrimination and the right to reproductive care within the field of free movement of goods and services. At present, the scope of Article 9 is principally determined by the ECtHR jurisprudence on Article 12 and, to a certain extent, Article 8 of the Convention, where the issue in question falls within the scope of both articles, such as LGBT rights and the right to adoption.[15] In a judgment delivered in late 2021, the CJEU confirmed

11 Directive 2004/38/EC of the European Parliament and of the Council of 29 April 2004 on the right of citizens of the Union and their family members to move and reside freely within the territory of the Member States amending Regulation (EEC) No 1612/68 and repealing Directives 64/221/EEC, 68/360/EEC, 72/194/EEC, 73/148/EEC, 75/34/EEC, 75/35/EEC, 90/364/EEC, 90/365/EEC and 93/96/EEC [2004] OJ L158/77 (Citizenship Directive).

12 Council Directive 2003/86/EC of 22 September 2003 on the right to family reunification [2003] OJ L251/12 (Family Reunification Directive). For an analysis, see Shazia Choudhry, 'Article 9 – Right to Marry and Right to Found a Family' in Steve Peers and others (eds), *The EU Charter of Fundamental Rights: A Commentary* (Hart/Beck 2014), 268–71.

13 Explanations relating to the Charter of Fundamental Rights [2007] OJ C303/17 (Explanations to EUCFR).

14 EUCFR, art 53.

15 For an analysis, see, Choudhry (n 12).

that, under Article 9, the rules governing the exercise of the right to marry fall within the competence of Member States. It was nevertheless reminded that, when exercising that competence, each Member State must recognise a marriage concluded in another Member State in accordance with its law.[16]

2.2 *The Right to Respect for Private and Family Life*

Although the areas of their application frequently overlap, the scope of Article 12 ECHR is quite distinct from Article 8 of the Convention. Whilst the former deals exclusively with those who wish to enter into marriage and found a family, the latter guards over individuals seeking authorisation based on the already existing family relationship.

Article 8 ECHR accordingly stipulates:

> 1. Everyone has the right to respect for his private and family life, his home and his correspondence.
> 2. There shall be no interference by a public authority with the exercise of this right except such as is in accordance with the law and is necessary in a democratic society in the interests of national security, public safety or the economic well-being of the country, for the prevention of disorder or crime, for the protection of health or morals, or for the protection of the rights and freedoms of others.[17]

The wording of its first paragraph is nearly identical to that of Article 7 of the EUCFR which provides that '[e]veryone has the right to respect for his or her private life, home and communications'.[18] Although a limitation clause set out in Article 8(2) of the ECHR is absent from the corresponding article of the EUCFR, an equivalent provision is found in Article 52(1) of the latter which lays down the scope and general principles for the Charter interpretation. Article 52(3) of the Charter and its Explanations further specify that the meaning and scope of Article 7 are the same as those guaranteed by Article 8 of the ECHR, including the limitations set out in its second paragraph. It, therefore, follows that Article 7 of the Charter must be interpreted in line with the ECtHR Article 8

---

16 Case C-490/20 *V.M.A. v Stolichna obshtina, rayon 'Pancharevo'* ECLI:EU:C:2021:1008, paras 51–52.

17 Similar provisions are also found in Art 17 ICCPR. In addition, Art 23(1) ICCPR stipulates that '[t]he family is the natural and fundamental group unit of society and is entitled to protection by society and the State'.

18 Except for the word 'correspondence' in Art 8 ECHR, which is substituted by 'communications' in Art 7 EUCFR to reflect technological developments. See Explanations to EUCFR.

case law,[19] although the EU is not precluded from granting an individual wider protection.[20] Of the four components of both Articles, two – namely, private and family life – are of particular importance to this study.

3 Articles 8 and 12 of the ECHR and Immigration Control

It is a general principle that the state has a power to control the entry and residence of foreigners into its territory, subject to its obligations under international law.[21] Further, governments are not obliged to guarantee a non-national the right to settle in the country.[22] Notwithstanding that, the state power to exercise immigration control may be limited in some situations, including where an individual has developed a family and/or private life in the host state.

To be able to invoke the family life limb of Article 8 of the ECHR in the migration context, the individual, first, must show that their respective ties constitute a family life within the meaning of the Convention. When determining the scope of Article 8, the ECtHR has privileged two forms of relationships by recognising them as families without requiring any further functional tests: (a) married couples and (b) minor children born of a marital or non-marital relationship, whereby the latter are regarded as *ipso jure* part of that family from the moment of their birth, even if their parents have separated.[23]

In addition, the Court extends its protection to *de facto* families, such as unmarried couples, on the condition that they can demonstrate the existence of close personal ties. The factors employed by the ECtHR in its assessment include cohabitation (although this is not a requirement),[24] the length of the relationship, the fact of having children together or the ability to demonstrate their commitment by other means.[25] A mere desire to found a family would not be sufficient to trigger the application of Article 8.[26] The only exceptions

---

19 Such an interpretation of Art 7 has also been confirmed by the CJEU. Case C-400/10 *PPU* [2010] ECR I-08965, para 53; Joined Cases C-92/09 and C-93/09 *Volker und Markus Schecke GbR and Hartmut Eifert* [2010] ECR I-11063, paras 51–52.

20 Art 52(3) EUCFR.

21 See, for instance, *Boujlifa v France* (2000) 30 EHRR 419, para 42.

22 *Jeunesse v Netherlands* (2014) 60 EHRR 17, para 103.

23 *Berrehab v Netherlands* (1988) 11 EHRR 322, para 21; *Keegan v Ireland* (1994) 18 EHRR 342, para 44; *Al-Nashif v Bulgaria* (2003) 36 EHRR 37, para 112.

24 See, among others, *Vallianatos and Others v Greece* (2014) 59 EHRR 12, paras 49, 73; *Schembri v Malta* App no 66297/13 (ECtHR, 19.09.2017), para 47.

25 See among others, *Kroon and Others v Netherlands* (1995) 19 EHRR 263, para 30; *Al Nashif v Bulgaria* (n 23), para 112.

26 *Marckx v Belgium* (1979) 2 EHRR 330, para 31; *Schembri v Malta* (n 24), para 46.

to this rule are a potential relationship which could be developed between a child born out of wedlock and their biological father,[27] or parties to a 'lawful and genuine'[28] marriage if the family life 'has not yet to be fully established'.[29]

Nevertheless, the recognition of the existence of family life by the ECtHR, taken alone, does not protect an individual from removal. The Court has recognised immigration control as a legitimate ground for derogation under Article 8(2) and confirmed that the Convention does not guarantee a foreign national the right to choose the country of their matrimonial residence and/or enjoy family reunion in its territory.[30] Article 8 claims from individuals who have developed family life in the host country but do not have a valid residence status there are thus typically rejected by the Court, save for exceptional situations[31] – most notably, where the applicant has shown that there are 'insurmountable obstacles' to enjoying family life in their country of origin.[32] Further, if at the point of creation of the family life, the couple was aware that it could be obstructed due to the foreign national party's insecure residence status, the removal of the latter would be regarded as a violation of Article 8 only in 'the most exceptional circumstances'.[33] The only factor overriding the restrictive approach is the best interests of any minor children involved. As stipulated by the Court, these must be given sufficient weight when deciding upon the proportionality of the non-national parent's removal by virtue of Article 3 of the UN Convention on the Rights of the Child.[34] As noted in Chapter 4, the Commission Handbook also specifies that, before deciding to remove a party to an alleged marriage of convenience, the state authorities must consider the best interests of any children involved.[35]

Notwithstanding the above, family life is not the only Article 8 component that a non-national may invoke to challenge the state's authority in exercising immigration control. In early ECtHR case law, certain elements of private life

27 *Nylund v. Finland* App no 27110/95 (ECtHR, 29.06.1999).

28 This point is further elaborated in Section 4.1 below.

29 *Abdulaziz, Cabales and Balkandali v United Kingdom* (1985) 7 EHRR 471, para 62.

30 See among others, *Gül v Switzerland* (1996) 22 EHRR 93, para 38; *Nunez v Norway* (2011) 58 EHRR 17, para 66; *Jeunesse v Netherlands* (n 22), para 107.

31 For a concise overview of the relevant ECtHR jurisprudence, see Mark Klaassen, 'Between Facts and Norms: Testing Compliance with Article 8 ECHR in Immigration Cases' (2019) 37 *Netherlands Quarterly of Human Rights* 157.

32 The relevant approach has been summarised, among others, in *Nunez v Norway* (n 30), paras 68–70.

33 *Rodrigues da Silva v Netherlands* (2007) 44 EHRR 34, para 39.

34 Convention on the Rights of the Child, 1577 UNTS 3 (20.11.1989). See among others, *Nunez v Norway* (n 30), paras 78, 84; *Jeunesse v Netherlands* (n 22), paras 109, 118.

35 SWD(2014) 284 final, 24–25.

were only addressed as part of family life considerations.[36] The Court, however, has since altered its original approach and made a clear distinction between these concepts. The notion of 'private life' within the meaning of Article 8 accordingly covers personal relationships (such as those between the individual and their extended family or adult children who normally do not fall within the concept of 'family life'),[37] as well as economic and social ties. To establish the latter, the Court may take into account such factors as the length of residence, education, employment, and the fact of marriage or giving birth in the host state.[38] The threshold set up by the ECtHR, nonetheless, is high; before one can successfully invoke the 'private life' grounds, the individual concerned must normally have lived in the host state for many years and even decades.[39]

Irrespective of the distinction between the scope of Articles 8 and 12 ECHR, when addressing the issue of immigration control, the Court has approached both provisions in a similar manner. Under the ECtHR case law, the states are equally permitted to impose far-reaching restrictions of the right of foreigners to marry and to found a family. The first key principle established by the Convention institutions is that the ECHR does not guarantee the right to marry in a particular country. In *A v United Kingdom*,[40] a disabled UK national living on benefits sought to challenge the refusal of the British authorities to grant entry clearance to his Filipino fiancée whom he had only corresponded with but never met.

The ground of refusal was that she had limited means to support herself, whereas the relevant domestic rules permitted entry in order to marry only in cases where the third-country national would not create an extra burden on public funds. The EComHR pointed out that Article 12 'does not, in principle, include the right to choose the geographical location of the marriage', and that there was no evidence of any legal obstacles preventing the applicant from marrying his fiancée in the Philippines. Furthermore, the limitation of the right of entry only to those who would definitely be able to survive without assistance from public funds was not considered unreasonably discriminatory under Article 14. In the view of the EComHR, whilst this requirement did not

36 See for instance, *Moustaquim v Belgium* (1991) 13 EHRR 802, paras 45–47.

37 See for instance, *Slivenko v Latvia* (2004) 39 EHRR 24, para 97.

38 Ibid, paras 96, 123.

39 For instance, in *Slivenko v Latvia* (n 37) and *Sisojeva v Latvia* (2006) 43 EHRR 33 the applicants had resided in the respective state for nearly 30 years. For a discussion on the applicability of the concept of 'private life', see Alan Desmond, 'The Private Life of Family Matters: Curtailing Human Rights Protection for Migrants under Article 8 of the ECHR?' (2018) 29 *European Journal of International Law* 261.

40 *A v United Kingdom* (1982) 5 EHRR 296 (Commission Decision).

apply to existing dependent spouses, their situation was different from the one where the applicant was 'seeking to establish a new relationship with a foreign person whom he has never actually met'. The complaint was consequently rejected.

The same principle was upheld in *App No 10914/84 v Netherlands*.[41] In contrast to the previous case, both applicants were present in the Netherlands and complained that they would be prevented from marrying there because of the decision to expel the prospective husband to Morocco. The EComHR held this did not constitute a breach of Article 12, for it did not guarantee the right to marry in a particular country or under a particular legal system.

4 The Legality of Targeting Marriages of Convenience for Immigration Purposes

4.1 *Marriages of Convenience in ECtHR Case Law*

A separate line of Strasbourg case law deals with the issue of marriages of convenience for immigration purposes. First, the Convention institutions have confirmed that states may subject proposed marriages involving foreign nationals to scrutiny to establish whether they would be ones of convenience and, if necessary, prevent them. Three judgments, delivered in the context of pre-marriage controls, are of relevance in this respect.

In *Sanders v France*,[42] a Turkish-French couple who lived together in Turkey, complained of delays encountered in a French consulate general in Istanbul in obtaining a certificate of capacity to marry as required under French law. The aim of such a certificate, to be issued by the French authorities, was to make sure the intended marriage was not one of convenience. The EComHR found the complaint manifestly ill-founded. In particular, it was held that the issue concerned substantive rules, the purpose of which was *inter alia* to preclude marriages of convenience between French nationals and foreigners, a limitation which did not violate Article 12. In the view of the Commission, the delay, although regrettable, did not impair the very essence of the right to marry. It, therefore, follows from the judgment that national authorities are authorised to delay an intended marriage between a national and a foreigner for a reasonable period to examine its nature.

41 *App No 10914/84 v Netherlands* (1986) 8 EHRR 308 (Commission Decision).

42 *Sanders v France* (1996) 87 B-DR 160.

Likewise, in *Klip & Krüger v Netherlands,*[43] a Dutch-German couple living in the Netherlands sought to challenge a Dutch law on addressing marriages of convenience. The respective Act sought to establish a systematic examination of all intended marriages where one of the parties did not hold Dutch nationality, and to that end required completion of a standard questionnaire. Apart from their personal details, the foreign national would be asked to provide information as regards to the period they had already resided in the Netherlands and their residence status. Dutch authorities would then verify their immigration history. Only where the authorities had reasonable suspicions that the intended marriage was one of convenience, would the parties be checked against more detailed criteria. The public prosecutor was, therefore, able to oppose a marriage where the primary purpose of one or both parties was to obtain entry into the Netherlands.

The applicants complained that the exercise of their right to marry was unjustly delayed on discriminatory and humiliating grounds, i.e., an investigation into the motives of their marriage. The EComHR rejected their claim. In its view, prevention of marriages of convenience for immigration purposes served a legitimate aim, because the Netherlands immigration policy was 'clearly related to the economic well-being of the country, in particular to the authorities' concern, given the population density in the Netherlands, to regulate the labour market'. Hence, it was argued that the applicant's obligation to submit a statement did not amount to a breach of Article 12. Furthermore, it was considered that the resulting difference in treatment between Dutch nationals who wished to marry another Dutch national and those who wished to marry a foreign national had 'an objective and reasonable justification' and therefore did not violate Article 14. In other words, the Commission upheld its previous decision in *Sanders v France,* essentially authorising systematic scrutiny of intended marriages with a view of establishing their motives.

Yet the most recent and relevant case in this respect has been the ECtHR judgment in *O'Donoghue v United Kingdom,*[44] delivered in late 2010 and specifically addressing the Certificate of Approval (CoA) scheme, which was in force in the UK from 2005 to 2011.[45] At the time of the application, the scheme had already been revised several times, but the final appeal at the domestic level was still pending. The case brought before the ECtHR concerned a Nigerian national who wished to marry his partner, a dual Irish-British national. At the time they became engaged in May 2006, the TCN party had no valid leave to

43 *Klip & Krüger v Netherlands* (1997) 91 A-DR 66.

44 *O'Donoghue and Others v United Kingdom* (2011) 53 EHRR 1.

45 For more details, see Chapter 6, Section 5.

remain and, for this reason, could not qualify for a CoA (permission from the Home Office to marry). After the scheme was revised to include this group, he did apply for a certificate but meanwhile asked for a waiver of the £295 fee, an amount that he could not afford. After the Home Office dismissed the latter request, the applicants lodged a complaint with the ECtHR. Although the couple eventually managed to borrow the money from friends and successfully obtained the Certificate of Approval, the Strasbourg court decided to rule on the compatibility of the scheme with the ECHR anyway.

The Court began its assessment by confirming that, according to the previous case law, the states may be entitled to prevent marriages of convenience, entered solely to secure an immigration advantage. Consequently, the national authorities will not necessarily breach Article 12 if they subject marriages involving foreign nationals to scrutiny – e.g., by requiring them to notify the authorities of an intended marriage, and if necessary, asking them to submit information relevant to their immigration status and the nature of the marriage. Hence, it was held that the requirement for non-EU nationals to obtain a CoA before being permitted to marry in the UK was not inherently objectionable.[46]

Notwithstanding that, the Court reiterated that such interference must meet the criteria of proportionality and must not otherwise deprive a person or a category of persons of full legal capacity of the right to marry with partners of their choice.[47] It then went on to remark that the first two versions of the CoA scheme imposed a blanket prohibition on the exercise of the right to marry by all persons having a short-term or irregular residence status, irrespective of the nature of the proposed marriage and without any attempt to investigate it. The Court considered such limitations unjustified and falling outside the margin of appreciation granted to the states under ECHR – 'even if there was evidence to suggest that persons falling within these categories were more likely to enter into marriages of convenience for immigration purposes'.[48] Furthermore, it was held that a sizeable fee which a needy applicant could not afford could impair the essence of the right to marry.

Provided that by the time the judgment in *O'Donoghue* came out, the CoA scheme was already declared unlawful by the House of Lords, the ECtHR ruling did not have a significant impact on the rights of foreigners to marry in the UK. Nevertheless, the importance of this case cannot be underestimated.

---

46 *O'Donoghue and Others v United Kingdom* (n 44), para 87.

47 Ibid, paras 83, 84.

48 Ibid, para 89. The Court remarked that no such evidence was provided by the UK government during the proceedings.

Whilst the Strasbourg court ruled that national authorities are entitled to carry out pre-marital checks on bi-national couples (including those of systematic nature), it also made clear that migrants with an irregular or short-term status, already present in the state, cannot be automatically banned from marrying there.

Meanwhile, the permission granted to the state to carry out checks to attest the 'genuineness' of the marriage is not confined solely to pre-marital situations. The ECtHR jurisprudence on Article 8 suggests that already married couples involving foreigners may equally be subjected to scrutiny. Although the Court has recognised parties to a marriage as *de jure* families, it has repeatedly emphasised that the concept of family life protects only those marriages that are 'lawful and genuine',[49] and excluded marriages of convenience from the scope of Article 8. For instance, in *Schembri v Malta,* it upheld the decision of the national authorities that the marriage concerned was one of convenience and 'there was not a committed relationship which was sufficient to attract the application of Article 8'.[50] In examining the facts of the case, the ECtHR concluded that it did not appear that the couple 'genuinely wished to cohabit and to lead a normal family life'.[51]

4.2 *Methods of Investigation and Human Dignity*

Another issue bearing a direct relevance to the subject of this study is the human rights constraints on investigation methods employed by the authorities to determine the nature of a marriage. Whilst governments are allowed to carry out such checks, this power is not unlimited. As mentioned in Chapter 4, the Commission Handbook grants Member States substantial discretion over the choice of investigation techniques, yet refers to Article 4 of the EUCFR (Article 3 of the ECHR) to emphasise that these must not subject the individuals to degrading treatment.[52]

This point is elaborated in more detail in the CJEU judgment in *A, B & C* which deals with methods for determining the sexual orientation of asylum-seekers whose claims are based on the fear of prosecution on the grounds of homosexuality.[53] First, the Court held that the applicant's declaration on their

49 *Abdulaziz, Cabales and Balkandali v United Kingdom* (n 29), para 62; *Berrehab v Netherlands* (n 23), para 21.

50 *Schembri v Malta* (n 24), para 53.

51 Ibid. A similar position regarding marriages of convenience was expressed by the EComHR as early as 1992. *Benes v Austria* App no 18643/91 (Commission Decision, 06.01.1992).

52 SWD(2014) 284 final, 26.

53 Joined Cases C-148/13 to C-150/13 *A, B and C* ECLI:EU:C:2014:2406.

sexual orientation alone might not appear sufficient and thus can merely serve as a starting point in the assessment process.[54] Yet, it then proceeded to stress that the assessment techniques employed by the authorities must respect the fundamental rights protected by the EUCFR – namely, the right to respect for human dignity (Article 1) and the right to respect for private and family life (Article 7).[55] According to the CJEU, detailed questioning as to the applicants' sexual practices would violate these principles and should be prohibited;[56] likewise, the Court declared the illegality of personality tests aimed to determine their homosexuality, as well as the use of visual evidence of applicants performing sexual acts, even if these are provided of their own free will.[57]

Although the case was delivered in a different context, its findings may well be applicable to marriage investigations. This view was first expressed by Betty de Hart, who draws parallels between the homosexuality checks and methods of assessing the 'genuineness' of the marriage. She observes that both are exercised in the context of immigration control and 'involve the investigation of private matters, subjective feelings, as well as sexual and relational behaviour'.[58] Indeed, highly intrusive and degrading questions, such as those of a sexual nature, would arguably amount to a violation of fundamental rights and should not be used in marriage investigations.

5 ECtHR Case Law on Marriages of Convenience vs EU Free Movement Law

The ECtHR case law on marriages of convenience may have serious implications for (prospective) marriages between (mobile) EU citizens and non-EU nationals. The principal issue is a very wide margin of discretion left by the ECtHR to national authorities, who are now free to impose on couples their own understanding of how a marriage of convenience may look like.

First, it should be remembered that, for the purposes of family reunion under the Citizenship Directive, marriage has been accepted as a central organising principle. Accordingly, the Directive guarantees protection only to

54 Ibid para 49.

55 Ibid para 53.

56 Ibid para 64.

57 Ibid para 65. On the prohibition of homosexuality tests, see also, Case C-473/16, *F* ECLI:EU:C:2018:36.

58 Betty de Hart, 'The Europeanization of Love. The Marriage of Convenience in European Migration Law' (2017) 19 *European Journal of Migration and Law* 283.

spouses of mobile EU citizens, whereby treatment of their unmarried partners entirely depends on the laws of the host Member State.[59] 'Durable partners' seeking to benefit from residence rights under the Directive are normally subject to close scrutiny[60] and need to comply with certain requirements. Yet even if the couple intended to enter into marriage, the authorities of the host Member State would enjoy absolute discretion in this matter. Among other things, this would also mean the absence of the EU safeguards the Member States should respect when addressing the issue of marriages of convenience. It is thus somewhat confusing that the Commission Handbook refers to the judgment in *O'Donoghue*[61] but fails to mention that the safeguards provided by the Handbook do not apply to (yet) unmarried couples.

One of the problematic issues involves defining marriages of convenience that are yet to be contracted. Whilst in *O'Donoghue,* the ECtHR referred to a marriage of convenience as one 'entered *solely* for the purpose of securing an immigration advantage',[62] this passage appears rather vague. Consequently, when investigating prospective marriages, Member States may employ a broader definition, potentially targeting unions where, e.g., residence is not the sole but primary purpose. Secondly, states may systematically examine all intended marriages involving foreigners, a measure that cannot be applied to already existing marriages under EU law. As will be shown in Chapters 7 and 8, the UK authorities indeed conduct systematic checks on almost all couples involving non-EU nationals who give a marriage notice at a register office.

The right of EU citizens to marry may be further obstructed by detention and removal of their TCN partners prior to the wedding due to their irregular immigration status. Chapter 7 will demonstrate that such practices are not uncommon in the UK and are principally aimed to stop the non-EU national from regularising their situation via marriage. Yet the compatibility of such measures with the ECtHR is questionable, provided that irregular migrants cannot be automatically precluded from marrying in the respective state. It is true that Member States, subject to certain conditions, may be entitled to expel a non-EU national without valid leave to remain.[63] Notwithstanding that, as long as the non-EU national does not leave the territory of Member State, they should still be allowed to solemnise their marriage according to

59 Case 59/85 *Reed* [1986] ECR 01283. For a discussion, see Chapter 1, Section 3.3.

60 For more details, see Chapter 7, Section 2.5.

61 SWD(2014) 284 final, 21.

62 *O'Donoghue and Others v United Kingdom* (n 44), para 83. Emphasis added.

63 Even in cases where this would disrupt their intended marriage. See *App No 10914/84 v Netherlands* (n 41).

the domestic rules. To the present date, the ECtHR has not directly addressed this matter; yet such a conclusion can be inferred from its case law which *inter alia* states that the fact of being in detention *per se* cannot prevent an individual from marrying.[64] Soon-to-be-expelled detainees, however, may not always be provided with such an opportunity, for a marriage to their EU partner would automatically enable them to stay in the country – a rather unwelcome scenario for the national authorities who strive for the opposite outcome.

Finally, excessive formal requirements may also create additional barriers to the solemnisation of marriages involving migrants. For instance, irregular migrants and asylum-seekers may arrive in Europe without the relevant identity documents, such as a birth certificate and/or passport. They may also be asked to present proof of their address, a requirement particularly difficult to satisfy for those irregularly present in the state.

Overall, the possible implications of the ECtHR approach for unmarried couples involving EU citizens and non-EU nationals cannot be underestimated. Due to the lack of protection guaranteed to their married counterparts under the Citizenship Directive, restrictive national measures aimed at preventing marriages of convenience may eventually result in the separation of yet unmarried couples or prompt them to move to another country. This, in turn, would seriously obstruct the exercise of free movement rights by EU citizen parties and hence run contrary to the logic of the CJEU expressed *inter alia* in *Metock*. Likewise, the human rights law provides little protection to already married couples whose marriage is found to be one of convenience. Although they may still seek protection on the basis of Article 8 of the ECHR, their claim does not have much of a chance to succeed, particularly where the authorities had previously disqualified the relationship as not 'genuine'.

6 Conclusion

This chapter has demonstrated that human rights instruments provide married couples with much weaker protection than EU free movement law. In contrast to the latter, the ECtHR jurisprudence neither precludes governments from subjecting foreigner-involved marriages to systematic checks nor obliges them to observe any other safeguards concerning targeting perceived marriages of convenience (with highly intrusive questions as the only exception).

64 *Frasik v Poland* App No 22933/02 (ECtHR, 5 January 2010); *Jaremowicz v Poland* App no 24023/03 (ECtHR, 5 January 2010).

Married EU citizens exercising their Treaty rights, therefore, may find themselves in a privileged position compared with static nationals of a particular Member State.

By contrast, the (yet) unregistered partners of EU citizens do not qualify for the protection reserved to 'direct family members' under the Citizenship Directive. Admission of this group is subject to the discretion of national authorities, who may require unmarried couples to comply with certain conditions and undergo an extensive examination of their personal circumstances. The insecurity associated with their status may prompt them to enter into marriage, a legal construct that is privileged in EU law over non-marital relationships. Yet, although the right to marry is protected by both the ECHR and the EUCFR as a fundamental right, its exercise may appear difficult, particularly where national authorities suspect the couple seeks to enter into a marriage of convenience for residence purposes.

When deciding upon the legality of state-imposed restrictions for non-nationals to marry in the country, the Strasbourg court has attempted to strike a balance between protecting fundamental rights and acknowledging the state prerogatives in respect of immigration control. In its landmark judgment in *O'Donoghue*, the ECtHR stressed the fundamental nature of the right to marry, prohibiting Member States from imposing blanket prohibitions on marriages by persons with an irregular residence status. In the meantime, however, the Court upheld the right of national authorities to prevent alleged marriages of convenience from being celebrated, granting the state nearly absolute discretion in this matter. As will be shown in Chapters 7 and 8, this approach, along with the lack of protection offered to prospective spouses at the EU level, has created hardship for a substantial number of EU citizens and their TCN partners in the UK – particularly if the latter has entered the country irregularly, outstayed their visas, or are (failed) asylum-seekers. Given the hostile policies pursued by the British state coupled with an extremely low level of protection guaranteed to foreigners under Article 8 of the ECHR, many unmarried couples involving mobile EU citizens risk separation, which, in turn, may prompt them to move to another country where they could enjoy family life. This situation arguably does not sit well with the aim of eliminating all existing and potential obstacles to free movement, as set out in CJEU case law on the right of EU citizens to family reunion.

PART 2

UK Law

CHAPTER 6

Historical Development of Family Reunification Provisions in UK Law

1 Introduction

The UK had a long history of reverse discrimination, subjecting its own nationals to more restrictive family reunification provisions than EU citizens. Over the pre-Brexit years, the British government had grown increasingly suspicious towards in-country marriages between mobile EU citizens and third-country nationals with an unstable or irregular residence status. In a widespread climate of Euroscepticism, the rights of family reunion protected by the Citizenship Directive[1] were openly denounced in the UK as a 'loophole' that enables dishonest individuals to enter into marriages of convenience and circumvent restrictive national immigration provisions.

To help better understand the rationale behind the UK approach to perceived marriages of convenience, this chapter offers a brief historical insight into the development of UK domestic family reunification rules with a particular focus on their alleged abuse. Starting with the post-WWII period and ending with pre-Brexit years, the chapter traces the evolution of the construct of marriages of convenience (or sham marriages) in British law, particularly where it concerns intended and existing marriages between EU citizens and non-EU nationals. The key phases covered in the chapter include the post-WWII years, which marked the end of free movement for Commonwealth nationals, the two decades of the so-called 'primary purpose rule' (1977–1997), the period following its abolishment, and the introduction of the Certificate of Approval scheme, a tool of pre-wedding controls which existed from 2005 to 2011. Lastly, the chapter describes the developments in 2012–13, which saw the growing gap between the right to family reunion in EU law and the restrictive UK family reunification provisions. This period was consequently marked by the UK

1 Directive 2004/38/EC of the European Parliament and of the Council of 29 April 2004 on the right of citizens of the Union and their family members to move and reside freely within the territory of the Member States amending Regulation (EEC) No 1612/68 and repealing Directives 64/221/EEC, 68/360/EEC, 72/194/EEC, 73/148/EEC, 75/34/EEC, 75/35/EEC, 90/364/EEC, 90/365/EEC and 93/96/EEC [2004] OJ L158/77 (Citizenship Directive).

 | DOI:10.1163/9789004499263_008

government's increasing focus on the Citizenship Directive and its portrayal as a means to circumvent domestic rules.

2 1948–1977: the End of Free Movement for Commonwealth Nationals

The historical development of UK domestic family reunification provisions has largely been shaped by Britain's heritage as a postcolonial state.[2] The roots of the present legislation date back to the 1940s, a period that was marked by growing calls for independence in British colonies. The principal legal instrument in this context is the British Nationality Act 1948, which classified all previous subjects of the Crown – nationals of the United Kingdom and Colonies and nationals of independent Commonwealth countries – as British subjects, and consequently, *de facto* reaffirmed their right to enter and settle in the UK (along with their family members). The purpose of the Act, however, was not to facilitate migration to the UK. Rather, it pursued two interrelated aims: (a) to provide a uniform basis for nationality and to consolidate the piecemeal citizenship law that had developed after acquisition of different territories by the colonial power, and (b) to reassert Britain's leading role within the Commonwealth.[3]

Yet, over the following years, a greater number of Commonwealth citizens exercised their right of entry into Britain than had ever done before, most of them looking for labour opportunities.[4] The first wave of immigration from the Caribbean was followed by a large number of entrants from the Indian subcontinent, whose annual rate of entry by the 1960s began to exceed that of the former group. The increased migration was met with hostility both by the public and the government: migrants categorised as non-white were widely perceived as a cause of social and economic problems. It was soon concluded at the cabinet-level that there was a need to end the 'open-door policy', which

2 For a comprehensive overview of the historical development of the British migration control system, see Evan Smith, 'From the Aliens Act to the "Hostile Environment": The Making of the British Border Control System' in Kahina Le Louvier and Karen Latricia Hough (eds), *UK Borderscapes: Sites of Enforcement and Resistance* (Routledge 2024).

3 For an analysis of the Act, see Randall Hansen, *Citizenship and Immigration in Postwar Britain: The Institutional Origins of a Multicultural Nation* (Oxford University Press 2000), 35–56.

4 Sanjiv Sachdeva, *The Primary Purpose Rule in British Immigration Law* (Trentham Books Ltd 1993), 18.

eventually led to the adoption of the Commonwealth Immigrants Act in 1962 which introduced a work voucher scheme for Commonwealth migrants.

The imposition of controls on this group can be regarded as a point after which family migration became an issue. The adoption of the work voucher scheme effectively eliminated the so-called rotating migration where male Commonwealth migrants came to the UK to work for a while before returning home again.[5] The removal of the ability to leave with a possibility of a later return effectively meant that many men chose to stay and call on their wives and children to join them in the UK. Given that the Act did not provide any restrictions on the right to be joined by one's family members, this subsequently led to a vast increase in family migration. Furthermore, children of migrants over time became of age to marry and started to look for a spouse in the country of their ancestors.[6]

As a consequence, the focus of British immigration control soon turned from primary to secondary immigration, i.e., the entry of family members. As early as 1965, family migration was perceived as a problem. The entry of husbands and fiancés caused particular suspicion due to the fears that men were entering the UK for work, using marriage as a pretext.[7] In 1969, instructions were issued to immigration officers to limit the admission of husbands and fiancés from the Commonwealth to those 'presenting special features'.[8] The new measures predominantly affected black and Asian families, as white British women were better able to plead such features, arguing that they could not move to live in a foreign environment.[9]

The process of transforming the status of Commonwealth citizens into that of migrant workers was completed with the adoption of the Immigration Act 1971, which officially brought an end to primary immigration from the Commonwealth.[10] The Act effectively created five new categories of British subjects, of which only one, the 'patrial' citizen, had a 'right of abode' in Britain. This category comprised of all those having a British grandparent – thus preserving

5 Ibid 21; Smith (n 2) 24–25.

6 Sachdeva (n 4) 21; Helena Wray, '"A Thing Apart": Controlling Male Family Migration to the UK' (2015) 18 *Men and Masculinities* 424, 430.

7 Helena Wray, *Regulating Marriage Migration into the UK: A Stranger in the Home* (Ashgate 2011) 48.

8 Ibid; Sachdeva (n 4) 47.

9 Ann Dummett and Andrew Nicol, *Subjects, Citizens, Aliens and Others* (Wiedenfeld and Nicholson 1990) 206–207 (as cited in Helena Wray, 'An Ideal Husband? Marriages of Convenience, Moral Gate-keeping and Immigration to the UK' (2006) 8 *European Journal of Migration and Law* 305).

10 Sachdeva (n 4) 27.

ties to the Old Commonwealth,[11] where larger numbers of British persons had emigrated in the first place.[12] Their descendants retained an opportunity to return to Britain, unlike New Commonwealth citizens whose status was now increasingly equated with that of foreigners. Meanwhile, husbands and fiancés of female Commonwealth citizens could still not be admitted, unless 'special features' were present. By 1974, due to the pressure for reform, the Labour government lifted the ban, so that the position of foreign husbands was equated to that of foreign wives.[13] Husbands were now to be admitted except for reasons of criminal records or the public good.[14]

3 The 'Primary Purpose Rule' (1977–1997)

Yet, this liberal turn proved to be short-lived – efforts to prevent the migration of husbands took a new turn already in 1977 with the introduction of the so-called 'primary purpose rule', later described as one of the most controversial components of historic immigration control. The new system, which developed out of the notion of marriages of convenience, eventually had the double effect of reducing the numbers of entry clearances granted to applicants and of introducing new but not necessarily subtler forms of discrimination.[15]

The concept of marriages of convenience seems to have been known in the UK since the Second World War. For instance, Ian MacDonald refers to some earlier cases of marriages for immigration purposes, mostly involving alien women seeking to settle in Britain.[16] A reference to such marriages, apparently, was first introduced into British immigration law in 1970. The relevant instructions provided that a husband of a British woman could be admitted in the UK if *inter alia* the immigration officer was satisfied 'that the marriage is not one of convenience, entered into to obtain a lodgement here'.[17]

11 The term 'Old Commonwealth' refers to Australia, New Zealand, South Africa and Canada.

12 Ian MacDonald, *Immigration Law and Practice in the United Kingdom* (1st edn, Butterworth 1983), 15.

13 For an analysis see Wray, *Regulating Marriage Migration into the UK* (n 7) 51–53.

14 MacDonald, *Immigration Law and Practice in the United Kingdom* (1st edn) (n 12) 219.

15 Sachdeva (n 4) 54–55.

16 Ian MacDonald, *Immigration Law and Practice in the United Kingdom* (2nd edn, Butterworth 1987), 228.

17 Aliens: Instructions to Immigration Officers, Cmnd 4296, para 43 (as cited in Dave Marrington, 'Legal Decisions Affecting Ethnic Minorities and Discrimination – No.24' (1985) 12 *New Community* 536, 537).

Whilst the early case law on marriages of convenience concerned women, in the 1970s the emphasis gradually shifted to men. The idea that many men from the subcontinent would readily arrange a marriage with a British-settled woman only to be able to live in Britain clearly came into prominence during the immigration debates in 1976.[18] In 1977, stricter rules were re-imposed on husbands. The new measures required the applicant to show that the primary purpose of the marriage was not for the husband to obtain admission in the UK, as well as introduced a probationary period of 12 months.[19]

In 1980, after the election of a Conservative government, a new set of immigration rules came into force. First, a slight change was made to the 'primary purpose rule' which allowed British national women born in the UK and with one parent born in the UK to sponsor husbands. As Sanjiv Sachdeva argues, this introduced a 'two-tier citizenship' and was clearly designed to allow white British women to sponsor husbands while still preventing most non-white women from doing so. The new rules also laid down a requirement that the parties should have met. The main idea behind these provisions was to reduce the number of women entering into arranged, as well as proxy marriages, although there was no founded reason to doubt that parties to such marriages genuinely wished to establish a family life.[20]

Given its restrictive nature, it is rather unsurprising that the 'primary purpose rule' was eventually challenged before the ECtHR. In its decision in *Abdulaziz* in 1985, the Court nonetheless found that the UK authorities had not violated Article 8 of the ECHR,[21] since there was no obligation on contracting states to respect the choice by married couples of the country of their residence.[22] With regards to Article 14, the Court, in principle, accepted the UK argument that the 'primary purpose rule' had the legitimate aim of protecting the domestic labour market.[23] It nonetheless held that the UK had not provided weighty enough reasons to differentiate between men and women and therefore was in breach of the principle of non-discrimination on the grounds of sex.[24] The response of the British government was not to amend the rules so that the more stringent requirements would no longer be applied to husbands

18 MacDonald, *Immigration Law and Practice in the UK* (1st edn) (n 12), 219.

19 Wray, *Regulating Marriage Migration into the UK* (n 7) 57.

20 Sachdeva (n 4) 76. For an analysis, see also, Wray, *Regulating Marriage Migration into the UK* (n 7), 59–62.

21 European Convention for the Protection of Human Rights and Fundamental Freedoms, CETS No.005 (04.11.1950) (ECHR).

22 *Abdulaziz, Cabales and Balkandali v United Kingdom* (1985) 7 EHRR 471, para 68.

23 Ibid, para 78.

24 Ibid, paras 79–83.

and fiancés, but to extend them so that they applied equally to wives and fiancées as well.[25]

4 After the 'Primary Purpose Rule': Focus on Pre-wedding Controls

The 'primary purpose rule' was ultimately abolished after the election of a Labour government in 1997. For the party, this step represented a win-win situation: it enabled it to gain credit by resolving a matter of high symbolic value without significantly affecting the total immigration numbers.[26] The positive effects of the denouncement of the discriminatory provision, however, were soon offset by new restrictive measures countering perceived marriages of convenience, an issue that began to play an increasingly prominent role in public debates.

At the heart of the government's concerns was the same old perception of the widespread abuse of British immigration rules by men predominantly from the Indian subcontinent. With the alleged aim to prevent abuse, the government adopted a number of measures effectively making family reunification in the UK more difficult and putting obstacles to secondary migration. The Immigration and Asylum Act 1999 introduced a broad definition of a 'sham marriage'[27] and placed a significant focus on pre-wedding controls, aimed to prevent such marriages from taking place. In contrast to the prior measures that foresaw a possibility for civil registrars to submit reports in case of suspicions, section 24(1)(da) of the Act imposed a duty on them to report to the Home Office if they have 'reasonable grounds for suspecting that the marriage will be a sham marriage'.[28] It was also provided that parties to a prospective marriage had to give notice of at least 15 days before their planned wedding by personally attending the registry office.[29] This rule did not apply to those marrying in the Church of England.

The decision to impose a requirement on registrars to carry out immigration control functions is problematic. The main task of a civil servant is to assist in the registration of a marriage and not to make judgments on the quality

25 For an analysis, see, Wray, *Regulating Marriage Migration into the UK* (n 7), 66.

26 Ibid 156.

27 Immigration and Asylum Act 1999 (IA 1999), s 24(5). For an analysis of the definition, see Chapter 7, Section 2.2.

28 The report form is found in Reporting of Suspicious Marriages and Registration of Marriages (Miscellaneous Amendments) Regulations 2000, SI 2000/3164, sch 1.

29 IA 1999, ss 160–63.

of the proposed union and determine the motivation of the TCN party. The latter point appears particularly controversial since the determination of what should constitute 'reasonable grounds' for suspicion was entirely left to the discretion of the registrar. As will be demonstrated below, such an approach not only results in the lack of legal certainty for the individuals involved, but also leads to the discrimination of certain groups perceived as particularly suspicious.

5 Certificate of Approval Scheme: Tarring Everyone with the Same Brush

The mid-2000s marked a new phase of targeting alleged marriages of convenience via pre-wedding controls. A new piece of legislation, known as the Certificate of Approval scheme, introduced blanket measures severely restricting the rights of non-EU nationals to marry within the UK. The new Asylum and Immigration (Treatment of Claimants, etc.) Act 2004, which came into force in February 2005, explicitly targeted persons with an unstable immigration status. The couples covered by the new regime were now required to give notice to a registrar in one of the specified registration districts. The registrar, however, would not accept the notice if at least one of the prospective spouses was subject to immigration control. All non-EU nationals, except those with a fiancé(e) or marriage visit visa[30] or indefinite leave to remain, were, at considerable cost,[31] required to obtain written permission from the Home Office to marry.[32] The chances for the application to be approved now only depended on the residence status of the third-country national. The relevant permission could only be granted to those whose initial leave to enter was more than six months long and who had at least three months leave remaining. All overstayers or irregular migrants, visitors with short-term leave, or those whose leave was about to expire had to leave the UK and either marry abroad or apply for a fiancé(e) or a marriage visitor visa.[33]

30 A fiancé(e) visa provides the non-EU national with a possibility to remain in the UK after the wedding, whereas a marriage visitor visa is granted for a temporary entry in order to marry.

31 The CoA initially cost £135, a fee which was later increased to £295. This was on top of the fees for the actual marriage which was £103.50. See *O'Donoghue and Others v United Kingdom* (2011) 53 EHRR 1, para 24.

32 Asylum and Immigration (Treatment of Claimants, etc.) Act 2004, s 19.

33 Immigration Directorate Instructions (February 2005) ch 1, s 15 and Annex NN.

The CoA scheme effectively excluded from its scope asylum-seekers still waiting for the outcome of their application, as the majority of them did not have leave to enter. If their claim was rejected (and subsidiary status not granted), the permission to marry would still be denied.[34] The only exception from the scheme was granted to those getting married in the Church of England: the government argued that there was no evidence of marriages of convenience taking place there, since people who wished to marry were normally known to the priest of the church.[35]

During this period, the public discourse increasingly identified marriages of convenience as a serious problem that had reached epidemic proportions, often associated with organised crime. This perception seems to be largely fuelled by media reports that quoted various estimates that lacked a solid foundation. One claim widely reported in the press and later mentioned during parliamentary debates was that one in five marriages in London (or around 8,000 marriages per year) was one of convenience. The figure was presented by the Superintendent Registrar at Brent Register Office, Mark Rimmer, based on the results of the survey carried out amongst marriage registrars.[36] Yet, this research was never published and was later described as 'impressionistic',[37] which made it impossible to properly evaluate the claims.

The intensified focus on marriages of convenience nonetheless resulted in the government presenting its scheme to make it 'more difficult for such marriages to take place'.[38] It ultimately appeared that the major aim of the new scheme was the reduction of the growing number of in-country marriages between third-country nationals and EU citizens, a group that was barely mentioned in the early debate but eventually turned out to be the principal target of the new policy. In this context it is important to note that marriages involving EU citizens were not exempt from suspicions already during the 1990s. As

34 Ibid. The only exception was reserved for asylum-seekers who were awaiting a decision on their application or appeal for at least 18 months, or those who could not be expected to travel abroad due to 'exceptionally compassionate' circumstances, such as pregnancy, illness, or life expectancy of less than twelve months.

35 HC Deb 12 July 2004, vol 423, col 1225.

36 HC Deb 13 May 2004, vol 421, cols 563–64; Home Affairs Committee, 'Immigration Control' (HC 2005–06, 775–I) para 316. See also, '"One in Five Marriages is Bogus"' (*BBC*, 10.06.2004) <http://news.bbc.co.uk/2/hi/uk_news/england/london/3794379.stm> accessed 11 April 2024; Isabel Oakeshott, 'One in Five Weddings May be Migrant Fraud' (*Evening Standard*, 10.06.2004). <https://www.standard.co.uk/news/one-in-five-weddings-may-be-migrant-fraud-6983676.html> accessed 11 April 2024.

37 Wray, 'An Ideal Husband?' (n 9) 315.

38 Explanatory Memorandum to the Immigration (Procedure for Marriage) Regulations 2005, para 2.1.

early as 1993, there were reports of anecdotal cases where the Home Office investigated already contracted marriages between then EC citizens and TCNs. One such case involved a Spanish-Zimbabwean couple who worked at the same place. According to an ILPA report, the immigration service, on no apparent suspicion, arrived at their workplace and interviewed the employer, who then subsequently dismissed the Zimbabwean national to avoid any problems with the authorities. At the time, however, such practices did not appear to be widespread, with a Home Office representative claiming that couples involving then EC citizens would be investigated only in exceptional circumstances.[39] For example, in the period between 1993 and May 1994, a total of 39 EEA citizens and their spouses were called for an interview regarding the genuineness of their marriages.[40]

In the same period, however, the UK authorised post-marriage controls in domestic legislation implementing the then EC directives in the area of free movement of persons. The Immigration (European Economic Area) Order 1994, the first instrument of this kind, defined the term '[EEA] national's spouse' as excluding 'a party to a marriage of convenience'.[41] This clause was reproduced in the successor Immigration (European Economic Area) Regulations, enacted in 2000,[42] 2006,[43] and 2016.[44] Given that, prior to the introduction of the Citizenship Directive in 2004, there was no concept of marriages of convenience in EU free movement law, the relevant UK domestic instruments lacked any legal basis for such exclusion and consequently violated EU law as it stood at the time. Furthermore, neither the 1994 Order nor the 2000 or 2006 Regulations contained the definition of marriages of convenience, which further undermined legal certainty. The definition of the concept first appeared only in the 2016 Regulations and will be discussed in the context of the pre-Brexit period legislation in Chapter 7.

Notwithstanding the above, throughout the 1990s, marriages between mobile EU citizens and third-country nationals did not seem to be the focus of public debate. This changed in the early 2000s when the UK experienced

39 Minutes of the ILPA European Group Meeting (15.09.1993) 4–6.

40 See ILPA letter to Lord McIntosh (15.07.1994) 1.

41 Immigration (European Economic Area) Order 1994, SI 1994/1895, art 2(2).

42 Immigration (European Economic Area) Regulations 2000, SI 2000/2326 (EEA Regulations 2000), reg 2(1).

43 Immigration (European Economic Area) Regulations 2006, SI 2006/1003 (EEA Regulations 2006), reg 2(1).

44 Immigration (European Economic Area) Regulations 2016, SI 2016/1052 (EEA Regulations 2016), reg 2(1).

significant growth in applications for asylum, as well as undocumented migration.[45] A number of persons who stayed in the UK without leave married UK-based EU citizens. The government increasingly viewed this practice as problematic, not least due to the overall climate of hostility towards non-European asylum-seekers who were widely portrayed as disguised 'economic migrants' seeking to abuse the system by submitting protection claims. The negative perception of this group in the UK further intensified after the 9/11 attacks and the subsequently declared 'War on Terror', which fuelled Islamophobic sentiments and fears that the asylum route may be exploited by potential terrorists.[46]

In the Lords, Lord Rooker argued that '[r]eports from registrars and other intelligence sources suggest that fixers of sham marriages are increasingly favouring this EEA route'.[47] In support of his claim, he quoted the latest Home Office figures suggesting that in May 2004, over 60% of all reports submitted by marriage registrars involved mobile EU citizens. In his view, this trend emerged because, contrary to TCN spouses of British nationals, those married to EU citizens enjoyed an automatic right of residence irrespective of their immigration status at the time of marriage. Lord Rooker proceeded to note that the investigation of suspicious marriages was 'a very difficult and resource-intensive activity', particularly given that in EU cases, the burden of proof lay with the Home Office.[48] Accordingly, he claimed: '[I]f we are to stop spouses of EEA nationals abusing immigration law through sham marriages, the most effective option is to stop them from getting married in the UK in [the] first place'.[49]

The government response to the perceived abuse appeared to be highly disproportionate to the proven extent of the problem. Whilst cynically admitting that investigating suspicious marriages on a case-by-case basis was too resource intensive, the Home Office chose to impose blanket preventative measures, affecting all EU citizens who wanted to live in the UK with short-term or irregular migrants. Meanwhile, the right of mobile EU citizens to enjoy family life with their intended TCN spouses in the country of their residence was not given any attention at all. By ignoring the position of EU citizens as

45 For an analysis see, for instance, Franck Duvell, Myriam Cherti and Irina Lapshyna, 'Does Immigration Enforcement Matter? Irregular Migration and Control Policies in the UK' (Final Report, Centre on Migration, Policy and Society, University of Oxford, October 2018). For UK and EU asylum statistics see 'Asylum Statistics' (House of Commons Library Briefing Paper SN01403, 01.03.2024). <https://commonslibrary.parliament.uk/research-briefings/sn01403/> accessed 9 April 2024.

46 See Smith, 'From the Aliens Act to the "Hostile Environment"' (n 2) 29–30.

47 HL Deb 6 July 2004, vol 663, col 725.

48 Ibid.

49 Ibid.

principals and excessively focusing on that of their (prospective) family members, the new policies not only prevented couples from being together but also arguably ran contrary to the spirit of free movement rights.

The introduction of the CoA scheme led to a significant drop in the number of marriages. By June 2005, there were about 60% fewer notifications of marriage in some London Boroughs and around 25% fewer in areas such as Birmingham or Leicester.[50] The number of registrar reports also fell from 3,578 in 2004 to 452 in 2005 and did not exceed this figure over the following years.[51] Although many presented this as evidence that marriages of convenience were widespread,[52] this claim was impossible to prove. The requirement to obtain a CoA led to considerable delays, particularly for those who did not fall into the scope of the scheme and had to leave the UK and marry elsewhere or apply for entry clearance for the purpose of marriage. Statistics suggest that many preferred the first option.[53]

The new regime was strongly criticised by immigrant organisations[54] and was successfully challenged in courts shortly after its introduction. Already in 2006, the High Court found it incompatible with Articles 12 and 14 of the ECHR, a decision that was subsequently upheld by the Court of Appeal, and ultimately, the House of Lords. In its judgment in *Baiai*, the High Court admitted that preventing marriages of convenience was a sufficiently important objective to justify limiting the fundamental right to marry;[55] yet, it found an infringement of Article 12 of the ECHR due to the absence of a rational connection between the scheme and the legislative objective. The Court considered the new measures over-inclusive in that 'all marriages of a party, who requires a CoA, are to be regarded automatically as actual or potential marriages of convenience'.[56] It was further noted that the new scheme did not foresee any

---

50 'Initial Evidence Indicates a Sharp Drop in the Number of Marriages After New Rules Came into Force last February' (*Migration News Sheet*, June 2005) 5 (as cited in Wray, 'An Ideal Husband?' (n 9) 318).

51 Letter from UK Minister for Immigration, Damian Green, to the Chair of the Human Rights Joint Committee (21.12.2010) <https://publications.parliament.uk/pa/jt201011/jtselect/jtrights/111/11110.htm> accessed 11 April 2024. The only exception was 2009 when there were 561 reports.

52 See, e.g., Duncan Gardham, 'Tough Rules Expose Scale of Bogus Marriages' (*The Telegraph*, 16.05.2005) <https://www.telegraph.co.uk/news/uknews/1490071/Tough-rules-expose-scale-of-bogus-marriages.html> accessed 11 April 2024.

53 See, e.g., Wray, *Regulating Marriage Migration into the UK* (n 7) 161–67.

54 For instance, the Joint Council for Welfare of Immigrants which later intervened in the judicial proceedings.

55 *Baiai and Others, R (On the Application Of) v SSHD* [2006] EWHC 823 (Admin), para 73.

56 Ibid para 76.

investigation of the circumstances of the couple, other than the determination of their immigration status and any compassionate grounds preventing one or both of the parties from returning to their home country and applying for admission into the UK.[57] Evidence that, e.g., the parties were in a long-term relationship during which they might have had children or bought a house together was thus ignored by the scheme.[58] The Court also noted that it was unclear why applicants were required to leave the UK if their application could just as easily be checked after the marriage within the country, 'without the disruption and expense caused by the need for the parties to have to go abroad'.[59] Furthermore, the Court found that the exemption for Church of England marriages breached Article 14 of the ECHR on the grounds of religion and nationality since persons of non-British nationality were less likely to marry in an Anglican religious ceremony.[60]

The position of persons who had no valid leave to remain was considered in a separate judgment of the Court of Appeal that concluded that the right to marry had to be guaranteed to anyone present in the country, irrespective of their immigration status.[61] Whilst, in theory, the requirement to leave the country and then apply for entry clearance from abroad (either with the purpose of marriage or after getting married elsewhere) did not prevent the marriage from taking place, this was considered a lengthy and complicated process which would become 'a very strong deterrent to exercising marriage rights', going well beyond the limits permitted by the ECHR.[62] After this view was confirmed by the House of Lords,[63] the Home Office considered there was no value in continuing to operate the scheme which no longer served its original purpose. The Asylum and Immigration (Treatment of Claimants, etc.) Act 2004 and the respective Regulations[64] were repealed by a Remedial Order under Section 10 of the Human Rights Act 1998,[65] thus abolishing the respective measures altogether. The CoA scheme officially ceased to exist in May 2011.

57 Ibid para 99.
58 Ibid para 85.
59 Ibid para 103.
60 Ibid para 137.
61 *SSHD v Baiai & Others* [2007] EWCA Civ 478, para 46.
62 Ibid.
63 *Baiai and Others, R (On the Application Of) v SSHD* [2008] UKHL 53.
64 Immigration (Procedure for Marriage) Regulations 2005, SI 2005/15.
65 Asylum and Immigration (Treatment of Claimants, etc) Act 2004 (Remedial) Order 201, SI 2011/1158.

6 The Blame Misplaced: Citizenship Directive as a 'Loophole'

The period after the abolishment of the CoA scheme was marked by the populist and nationalistic rhetoric of UK policy-makers who placed emphasis on such topics as the impact of migration on public finances, potential threats to national security, and concerns about the perceived abuse of UK immigration laws.[66] The Conservative/Liberal coalition in power from 2010 to 2015 came up with a pledge to reduce net migration from above 200,000 to 'tens of thousands' a year by attracting only 'the brightest and the best', an aim set up in the Conservative party's 2010 manifesto.[67] Given that free movement of EU citizens to the UK did not fall within its competence, the government focused its attention on non-EU nationals. Over the preceding few years, spouses of both UK nationals and settled persons and EU citizens constituted the largest category amongst this group.[68]

In July 2011, the government launched a public consultation on family migration, which was followed by significant legislative changes for spouses and unmarried partners of static British nationals or settled persons. In 2012, the Home Office increased the probation period before indefinite leave to remain could be granted from 2 to 5 years, as well as introduced the requirement for the relationship to be 'genuine and subsisting'.[69]

The most far-reaching measure, however, was the introduction of the onerous financial requirements for British nationals who wished to live in the UK with their TCN spouses. To sponsor a foreign national, one now had to earn at

66 For an analysis, see among others, Rebecca Partos and Tim Bale, 'Immigration and Asylum Policy under Cameron's Conservatives' (2015) 10 *British Politics* 169.

67 'Invitation to Join the Government of Britain: The Conservative Manifesto 2010' <https://conservativehome.blogs.com/files/conservative-manifesto-2010.pdf> accessed 11 April 2024. Although by 2015 the promise was not fulfilled, it was repeated in the party's 2015 manifesto. 'Strong Leadership. A Clear Economic Plan. A Brighter, More Secure Future. The Conservative Party Manifesto 2015' <http://ucrel.lancs.ac.uk/wmatrix/ukmanifestos2015/localpdf/Conservatives.pdf> accessed 11 April 2024.

68 In 2009, for instance, there were 61,485 grants for settlement issued to foreigners in their own right or on a discretionary basis and 77,380 grants issued to spouses of UK nationals or settled persons. Home Office, 'Control of Immigration: Statistics. United Kingdom 2009' (Home Office Statistical Bulletin 15/10, August 2010) <https://assets.publishing.service.gov.uk/government/uploads/system/uploads/attachment_data/file/116016/hosb1510.pdf> accessed 11 April 2024, 87.

In addition, 25,015 non-EU national family members of EU citizens were recognised as having a right to reside in the UK, with spouses most likely constituting a significant fraction of this group. Ibid, supplementary Table 4b <https://www.gov.uk/government/statistics/control-of-immigration-statistics-united-kingdom-2009> accessed 11 April 2024.

69 See Statement of Changes to the Immigration Rules HC 194 (June 2012).

least £18,600 per year (plus extra for sponsoring children),[70] a threshold that would be difficult to meet by a large part of the working-age population.[71]

Apart from that, the couples continued to be subject to the already existing domestic family reunification rules which required them to show (1) their intention to live together permanently as husband and wife, (2) that they have met, and (3) their ability to maintain and accommodate themselves without recourse to public funds. The burden of proof in these cases remained on the applicant. Furthermore, the 'no-switching rule', introduced in 2002 with a view to tackling marriages of convenience involving UK nationals,[72] prohibited non-EU nationals with leave to remain of up to six months from switching to the marriage category within the UK and required them to leave the country and apply from abroad.[73]

The new measures created a significant dichotomy between the treatment of UK nationals and EU citizens, further deepening the reverse discrimination of the former group. In the official discourse, EU citizenship was increasingly portrayed as a threat to British sovereignty and a 'loophole' enabling the circumvention of domestic immigration laws via marriage migration.[74] This perception was fuelled, not least, by the CJEU judgment in *Metock* in 2008, after which the UK had to renounce its discriminatory provision which put obstacles to EU citizens who wished to live in the UK with their TCN spouses with a short-term or irregular status.[75] The two issues identified as the most problematic in

70 Ibid.

71 Mariña Fernández-Reino & Madeleine Sumption, 'The Minimum Income Requirement for British Citizens Sponsoring Partners to Live With Them in the UK' (*Migration Observatory: COMPAS, University of Oxford* 13.04.2023) <https://migrationobservatory.ox.ac.uk/resources/commentaries/the-minimum-income-requirement-for-british-citizens-sponsoring-partners-to-live-with-them-in-the-uk/> accessed 11 April 2024. For a discussion on the *Surinder Singh* route, see also, Helena Wray, Eleonore Kofman and Agnes Simic, 'Subversive Citizens: Using EU Free Movement Law to Bypass the UK's Rules on Marriage Migration' (2019) *Journal of Ethnic and Migration Studies*.

72 Home Office, 'Secure Borders, Safe Haven: Integration with Diversity in Modern Britain' (Cm 5387, 2002), 7.11.

73 Statement of Changes to the Immigration Rules HC 538 (March 2003).

74 For instance, the 2013 ICIBI report quotes an immigration officer who described marriages of convenience as a 'massive loophole in the Immigration Rules.' ICIBI, '*A Short Notice Inspection of a Sham Marriage Enforcement Operation:* 14–24 October 2013' (January 2014), 13. On this point, see also, Anne-Marie D'Aoust, 'A Moral Economy of Suspicion: Love and Marriage Migration Management Practices in the United Kingdom' (2018) 36 *Environment and Planning D: Society and Space* 40.

75 For an analysis, see Chapters 2 and 3. The UK implemented the judgment in 2011 when the 'prior lawful residence rule' was removed from the EEA Regulations 2006. Immigration (European Economic Area) (Amendment) Regulations 2011, SI 2011/1247, reg 2(4). It should be nonetheless noted that the prior lawful residence requirement was abolished

this respect were the reliance of British nationals on the *Surinder Singh* route to bring themselves within the scope of EU law, and perceived marriages of convenience between mobile EU citizens and third-country nationals.

The latter, *inter alia*, found its reflection in the perception of the problem by civil registrars. In 2012, nearly 60% of section 24 reports involved nationals of another EU Member State, the rest being British nationals.[76] Among the TCN spouses of EU citizens, the main focus was placed on men coming from former British colonies. In 2012, the top nationals most frequently identified by registrars as suspicious were Pakistani, Nigerian and Indian, who collectively accounted for two-thirds of the total number of section 24 reports that year.[77] Along with foreigners with short-term or irregular status, students became another group viewed with particular suspicion. In 2012, nearly half of all section 24 reports involved non-EU nationals studying in the UK. The Home Office linked this development with the tightening of rules on extending student leave which non-EU nationals attempt to bypass by entering suspected 'sham marriages'.[78]

In addition to elements of racial, class and gender profiling of non-EU nationals, the discourse of suspicion also expanded to certain categories of their EU partners, effectively turning them into 'second class' EU citizens. The first such group involved naturalised EU citizens marrying migrants from their countries of origin, such as Nigeria, Ghana, and Pakistan, all former British colonies.[79] Particular suspicion was cast on those married by proxy.[80] Such marriages are not allowed in the UK but are legal in some countries, such as Ghana and Nigeria, provided that the ceremony with the participation of the appointed proxy takes place in that country with regards to the necessary

by the Court of Appeal already before the Regulations were amended. *ZH (Afghanistan) v SSHD* [2009] EWCA Civ 1060.

76 Home Office, 'Sham Marriages and Civil Partnerships: Background Information and Proposed Referral and Investigation Scheme' (November 2013), 45.

77 Ibid.

78 Home Office, 'Tackling Sham Marriage: Impact Assessment' (HO0090, 11.09.2013), 5.

79 See, for instance, ICIBI, 'The Rights of European Citizens and their Spouses to Come to the UK: Inspecting the Application Process and the Tackling of Abuse. October 2013 – January 2014' (June 2014), 37.

80 Ibid 22, 39. In this connection is should be noted that marriages in foreign consulates and other diplomatic premises in the UK are not regarded as being outside the UK. See, *Radwan v Radwan (No 2)* [1973] Fam 35, [1972] 3 All ER 1026. Such venue, however, needs to be listed in an 'approved premises' list for the purposes of s 26(1)(bb) of the Marriage Act 1949. See Immigration Directorate Instructions (July 2012), ch 8, s 1, Annex B, para 1.1.

formalities. Although in this case the marriage is recognised in the UK as valid,[81] the UK authorities began to consistently associate proxy marriages with abuse. For instance, as part of the evidence of the perceived abuse of free movement, provided to the European Commission in 2013, UK authorities noted that, in a selected sample of residence card applications, 16% involved marriages by proxy, a number that was considered disproportionate. The government expected that the 'normal' circumstances for choosing such a form of marriage would be 'relatively rare', limited to situations such as military service, incarceration, or inability to travel due to medical issues. It was, therefore, suggested that proxy marriages were used to avoid the scrutiny of civil registrars who may raise concerns about the nature of the intended marriage.[82]

The second group of EU citizens treated with particular suspicion were female nationals of EU-8 Member States marrying men from African countries and the Indian subcontinent who the women met when the men were already in the UK. Among mobile EU citizens, the top nationalities referred by the registrars to the Home Office in 2012 were Hungarians, Lithuanians, and Polish.[83] In this context, the UK authorities started to frequently express concerns about 'a pattern of East European brides matched with men from very different cultures', most notably Pakistani, Indian, Bangladeshi, Ghanaian and Nigerian nationals,[84] and often link this trend with human trafficking.[85]

During this period, the Home Office strategy at the pre-marriage stage continued to involve liaising with civil registrars and preventing perceived 'sham marriages'. Immigration officers appeared in the registry office before the ceremony and interviewed suspicious couples. In case it was concluded that their intended marriage was not 'genuine', it was not allowed to proceed; parties with no valid leave in the UK were issued removal notices. Such operations were normally conducted on an ad hoc basis following a section 24 report by a registrar.[86] As an example, under the 'Operation Mellor' initiative, which ran in the first nine months of 2013, the Home Office carried out 500 enforcement

81 Immigration Directorate Instructions (July 2012), ch 8, s 1, Annex B, para 3. This has also been confirmed in *Awuku v SSHD* [2017] EWCA Civ 178.

82 See Select Committee on European Scrutiny, Thirty-first Report of Session 2013–14 (2013–14, HC 83-xxviii) 23.

83 Home Office, 'Sham Marriages and Civil Partnerships' (n 76), 45.

84 See for instance ICIBI, 'The Rights of European Citizens and their Spouses to Come to the UK' (n 79), 36. See also, Georgie Wemyss, Nira Yuval-Davis and Kathryn Cassidy, 'Beauty and the Beast': Everyday Bordering and "Sham Marriage" Discourse' (2018) 66 *Political Geography* 151.

85 For criticism of this approach, see Chapter 3.

86 ICIBI, 'The Rights of European Citizens and their Spouses to Come to the UK' (n 79), 13.

operations which lead to 334 arrests and 78 removals.[87] In total, there were over 650 arrests made in 2013 as a result of marriage abuse enforcement visits.[88]

The practice of aggressively disrupting intended weddings may have targeted many couples in a close relationship. Not least due to the time restraints, the decisions on the nature of a marriage were made hastily and without due care, which provided a reason to seriously doubt their credibility. This can be best illustrated by paradoxical situations where non-EU nationals were first prevented from getting married but were then granted a residence card on the basis of a durable relationship with an EU citizen. One such case concerns a national of Bangladesh who arrived in the UK in 2011 with student leave and met a woman from Latvia whilst working at a car wash. After the couple moved in together in 2012, his leave was curtailed because the college had its sponsor licence revoked. In July 2012, the couple attempted to marry at a registry office but were intercepted by six immigration officers who interviewed them separately and ultimately did not allow the marriage to proceed. The same happened four months later when the parties made a second attempt to marry. Having been unable to obtain a legal status that would enable him to live in the UK with his EU partner, the non-EU national made an application as a durable partner of an EEA national. His claim was ultimately approved by the Upper Tribunal in 2016. By then, the couple were already cohabiting for over three years and had a child together.[89]

7 Conclusion

The British authorities have a long history of regulating family migration by imposing restrictive conditions on mixed-status couples who wished to live together in the UK, as well as by adopting measures addressing perceived abuse of family reunification provisions. Family migration has been viewed as a matter of concern already since the 1960s, with the entry of husbands and fiancés being perceived as particularly problematic. There was a widespread belief that men from former British colonies would readily marry a British-settled woman only to be able to obtain residence rights in the UK. Such anxieties

87 ICIBI, 'A Short Notice Inspection of a Sham Marriage Enforcement Operation' (n 74), 10.

88 Jessica Elgot, 'Warning Home Office Could Be Raiding Genuine Weddings in Sham Marriage Panic' (*Huffington Post*, 24.07.2014) <https://www.huffingtonpost.co.uk/2014/07/23/sham-marriage-home-office_n_5614057.html> accessed 11 April 2024.

89 *Miah v SSHD* [2016] UKUT 21503 (IAC); IA/21503/2014. See also, *Molina, R (On the Application Of) v SSHD* [2017] EWHC 1730 (Admin).

manifested themselves in the adoption of several legislative measures, most notably the 'primary purpose rule', which required the applicant to demonstrate that the primary purpose of their marriage was not to settle in the UK.

The 'primary purpose rule' was abolished in 1997 and later substituted by the Certificate of Approval scheme, which came into force in 2005 and focused on pre-marriage controls. Under the scheme, all irregular migrants, short-term visitors and those whose leave was about to expire were prevented from marrying in the UK and had to leave the country to marry abroad or apply for a fiancé(e) or marriage visitor visa. The principal target of the new rules appeared to be couples involving third-country nationals and mobile EU citizens, a group that was now increasingly associated with abuse. The indiscriminate provisions had serious implications for mobile EU citizens by not only preventing couples from enjoying family life in the UK but also prompting them to relocate and, thus, running contrary to the spirit of free movement rights.

Due to its blanket nature, the CoA scheme continuously received massive criticism from human rights organisations. It was ultimately successfully challenged in the courts and abolished in 2011. This was followed by the tightening up of UK domestic family reunification provisions, which included the introduction of an onerous minimum income requirement for British national sponsors.

The new requirements further deepened the gap between the treatment of UK nationals and mobile EU citizens, whereby the Citizenship Directive became increasingly portrayed as a 'loophole' enabling people to circumvent the restrictive national rules via marriages of convenience. Particular suspicion in that regard was cast on couples involving female nationals of EU-8 Member States and men from African countries and the Indian subcontinent, as well as naturalised EU citizens marrying migrants from their countries of origin. The Home Office's strategy during this period was preventing perceived 'sham marriages' from taking place by liaising with civil registrars and appearing in the registry office before the ceremony. Such practices continued until the introduction of the 'referral and investigation scheme' in 2014, which will be discussed in Chapter 7.

CHAPTER 7

Marriage Controls during the Pre-Brexit Period

1 Introduction

Chapter 6 has shown that starting from the mid-2000s, marriages between mobile EU citizens and non-EU nationals were perceived in the UK as a problem and frequently associated with abuse. This chapter examines the UK's approach to marriage controls during the years immediately preceding Brexit. Its first part discusses the implications of the so-called 'referral and investigation scheme', the most recent set of rules which target prospective marriages and were introduced in 2014 as part of the then 'hostile environment' policy. The chapter accordingly explores the definition of 'sham marriages' under the scheme, the possible implications of giving a marriage notice in the UK and the interplay between the scheme and EU law. The second part of the chapter explores post-marriage controls and assesses whether the relevant UK legislation conforms with the Citizenship Directive.[1] With this aim, the chapter provides an analysis of the procedures for family reunion with EU citizens in the UK and the concept of marriages of convenience in the EEA Regulations, a legislative instrument implementing the Directive in UK law. The final sections of the chapter discuss the right to appeal against a marriage of convenience determination, the repercussions faced by EU citizens accused of being involved in such a marriage, as well as how the concept of marriages of convenience intersects with UK family law.

2 Pre-marriage Controls: 'Referral and Investigation Scheme'

2.1 *Immigration Act 2014: 'Sham Marriages' and 'Compliant Environment'*

The Immigration Act, adopted in 2014, marks a more recent phase of targeting persons with a precarious residence status. The government's preoccupation

1 Directive 2004/38/EC of the European Parliament and of the Council of 29 April 2004 on the right of citizens of the Union and their family members to move and reside freely within the territory of the Member States amending Regulation (EEC) No 1612/68 and repealing Directives 64/221/EEC, 68/360/EEC, 72/194/EEC, 73/148/EEC, 75/34/EEC, 75/35/EEC, 90/364/EEC, 90/365/EEC and 93/96/EEC [2004] OJ L158/77 (Citizenship Directive).

 | DOI:10.1163/9789004499263_009

with irregular migrants allegedly abusing the system resulted in creation of the so-called 'hostile environment' – a set of wide-ranging exclusionary measures with the overall aim to 'reduce illegal immigration and to take a tougher approach to dealing with those who have either entered the country illegally or overstayed their visa'.[2] Whilst welcoming 'the brightest and the best', the government intended to make the life of those who were deemed unwanted more difficult, 'encouraging them to depart'.[3] The provisions of the new Immigration Act *inter alia* denied irregular migrants the right to access to basic services, such as rented accommodation,[4] bank accounts[5] or issuance of driving licenses.[6] Landlords were required to check the residence status of their prospective tenants, facing considerable civil penalties for non-compliance.[7] In addition, the Act introduced a new scheme aiming to prevent 'sham marriages',[8] increased the powers of authorities to identify persons without leave and remove them,[9] and limited appeal rights only to those who had made an asylum or human rights claim.[10] Many of these measures were further reinforced by the Immigration Act 2016.

Rather unsurprisingly, the 'hostile environment' policy has long been subject to considerable criticism.[11] The growing discontent over the adverse impact of such measures reached its peak in late 2017 to early 2018, amidst the scandal concerning the treatment of the so-called 'Windrush generation' – the term commonly referred to Commonwealth citizens who had arrived in the UK prior to 1973.[12] In response to public and opposition

2 Home Office, 'Overarching Impact Assessment – Immigration Bill' (HO0097, 14.10.2013), 1.
3 Ibid, 3.
4 Immigration Act 2014 (IA 2014) s 21.
5 Ibid s 40.
6 Ibid s 46.
7 Ibid ss 23–28.
8 Ibid ch 1. This is the term used by the Home Office for the purposes of the scheme. For more details, see Section 2.2 below.
9 Ibid ss 1, 4, sch 1.
10 Ibid s 15.
11 See for instance, United Nations, 'End of Mission Statement of the Special Rapporteur on Contemporary Forms of Racism, Racial Discrimination, Xenophobia and Related Intolerance at the Conclusion of Her Mission to the United Kingdom of Great Britain and Northern Ireland' (11.05.2018) <https://www.ohchr.org/EN/NewsEvents/Pages/DisplayNews.aspx?NewsID=23073&LangID=E> accessed 12 April 2024.
12 The scandal unfolded following the reports of wrongful detention, denial of rights and deportation of such individuals. For more details, see 'Windrush Generation' (House of Commons Library Debate Pack CDP-2018-0111, 01.05.2018) <https://researchbriefings.files.parliament.uk/documents/CDP-2018-0111/CDP-2018-0111.pdf> accessed 12 April 2024.

pressure,[13] the government launched a scheme aiming to confirm the right of such individuals to live in the UK,[14] as well as suspended or reduced the scope of some of its 'hostile environment' measures. The government also softened its language and substituted the term 'hostile environment' with 'compliant environment'.[15]

Nevertheless, softening or abolishing its most controversial measures does not mean that the policy has come to a halt.[16] For instance, the Home Office has announced no plans to review the so-called 'referral and investigation scheme' – provisions targeting suspected sham marriages. The latter form three separate chapters of the 2014 Immigration Act and, with some amendments pertaining to their personal scope, continue to remain in force after Brexit.[17] The scheme significantly altered the prior system and introduced systematic checks of all intended marriages involving foreigners who, in the view of the government, could gain from the union 'an immigration advantage'.[18]

The pressing need for change was repeatedly explained by the growing number of section 24 reports since the abolishment of the CoA scheme and the lack of Home Office capacities to act thereupon. According to the Home Office, there were 1,891 reports received in 2012, an increase of 8.6% from 2011, and 110% from 2010,[19] whereby over half of them involved EU citizens. Meanwhile, it was argued that the 15-day notice was too short for the Home Office to assess the information and act before the marriage took place – e.g., arrange a home visit or register office attendance.[20] The registrars also believed that there was

13 See for instance, 'Windrush: Corbyn Says PM Ignored Immigration Policy Warnings' (*BBC*, 22.04.2018) <http://www.bbc.co.uk/news/uk-politics-43857089> accessed 12 April 2024.

14 Immigration and Nationality (Requirements for Naturalisation and Fees) (Amendment) Regulations 2018, SI 2018/618.

15 See, Steven Poole, '"Compliant Environment": Is This Really What the Windrush Generation Needs?' (*The Guardian*, 03.05.2018). <https://www.theguardian.com/books/2018/may/03/compliant-environment-is-this-really-what-the-windrush-generation-needs> accessed 12 April 2024.

16 An equality impact assessment of the 'compliant environment' policies, published by the Home Office in 2023, shows that such policies disproportionately affected Indian, Pakistani, and Nigerian nationals. Home Office, 'Overarching Equality Impact Assessment of the Compliant Environment' (09.02.2023), 26 <https://assets.publishing.service.gov.uk/media/63e5311ed3bf7f05bdd3091a/FINAL_Overarching_CE_EIA_.pdf> accessed 12 April 2024.

17 For a detailed analysis of the post-Brexit developments, see Chapter 8.

18 Home Office, 'Sham Marriages and Civil Partnerships: Background Information and Proposed Referral and Investigation Scheme' (November 2013), 3.

19 Ibid 11.

20 Ibid 51.

significant underreporting of suspected marriages of convenience since they did not interview the couples in-depth.[21]

Against this background, the numbers provided by the Home Office in support of their initiative deserve closer attention. To begin with, there was a lack of comprehensive and reliable statistics of marriages identified as 'sham' by immigration authorities. The respective determinations on individual cases were not aggregated in national reporting systems and were only held with paper case files or within the notes sections of the Home Office databases. However, manual case searches to collate the data would, in the view of Home Office, be 'disproportionately expensive'.[22] In the meantime, the obviously more easily obtained estimates of the occurrence of sham marriages appear inaccurate, misleading, and largely unfounded.[23] First, it should be noted that the rise in section 24 reports is not necessarily linked to the real-life increase in the number of sham marriages, as suggested by the Home Office. Rather, it reflects the growing perception of such an increase by civil registrars and the development of 'risk profiles' where certain combinations of nationality or immigration status of a non-EU national were seen as particularly suspicious. Furthermore, it is quite likely that the very fact of a TCN partner having an irregular status frequently resulted in section 24 reports,[24] whilst the CoA scheme, in force from 2005 to 2011, effectively banned irregular migrants from marrying in the UK. It should be noted that in 2004, immediately prior to the introduction of the scheme, the Home Office received 3,578 such reports, nearly twice as many as in 2012.[25]

Another figure frequently quoted by the Home Office was that 4,000 to 10,000 applications a year to stay in the UK were made on the basis of sham marriages.[26] However, the calculation methodology used by the Home Office is highly questionable at best.[27] Yet, despite the lack of reliable statistical evidence that sham marriages indeed pose a significant threat to immigration control, the Home Office estimates have been used as a foundation for new rules which came into force in March 2015.

---

21 Ibid 3.

22 HC Deb 13 February 2014, col 764W.

23 For a similar view, see, Colin Yeo, 'Minister Misleads on Sham Marriage Numbers' (*Free Movement*, 16.12.2014) <https://www.freemovement.org.uk/minister-misleads-sham-marriages-numbers-statistics-1300/> accessed 12 April 2024.

24 For the 'risk profiles' used by the Home Office to assess marriages, see Chapter 9.

25 Home Office, 'Sham Marriages and Civil Partnerships' (n 18), 11.

26 Ibid, 43; Home Office, 'Tackling Sham Marriage: Impact Assessment' (HO0090, 11.09.2013), 3.

27 For an analysis, see Annex 1.

Part 4 of the 2014 Immigration Act imposed a duty on civil registrars to refer to the Home Office, all proposed marriages involving non-EU nationals without a permanent immigration status or a valid marriage visitor or fiancé(e) visa.[28] All couples involving non-EU nationals irrespective of their residence status,[29] were now required to give notice of a marriage at one of the 'designated' register offices (DROs).[30] Ecclesiastic marriages were also included in the scope of the Act: the right to marry following banns or by common license was only reserved to nationals of the UK and EU Member States. All other couples were now allowed to marry in the Church of England only after completing civil preliminaries, similarly to those using other religious services.[31] The rationale for this was that civil registrars would be better equipped to determine the immigration status of a non-EU national.[32]

In addition to the duty to refer to the Home Office, all intended marriages covered by the scheme, the registrars continue to be required to submit section 24 reports. The 2014 Immigration Act extended this requirement to cases where a sham marriage is suspected before notice has been given. For example, when the couple visits the register office to make an appointment.[33] In addition, schedule 6 of the Act provides that a civil registrar may disclose any information or supply any document to the Home Office for immigration purposes (e.g., about a foreigner without leave) while registering a birth or death.[34]

To provide the Home Office with more time to carry out checks, the scheme also extended the marriage minimum notice period from 15 days to 28 for all couples undergoing a civil ceremony within the country, irrespective of their immigration status.[35] The Home Office will then consider whether there are

28 IA 2014, s 49. After the end of the transition period, this requirement was also extended to certain groups of EU citizens. For more details, see Chapter 8.

29 Except those 'exempt from immigration control' as defined in s 3 of the Proposed Marriages and Civil Partnerships (Meaning of Exempt Persons and Notice) Regulations 2015, SI 2015/122. These include persons who have the right of abode in the UK under s 2(1)(b) of the Immigration Act 1971, members of a diplomatic mission or their family members, or members of HM forces or of Commonwealth forces undergoing training, or members of visiting forces.

30 There were 76 DROs in England and Wales. All register offices in Scotland and Northern Ireland were DROs. After the end of the transitional period, all offices have been made designated.

31 Since the end of the post-Brexit transition period, this requirement also applies to certain groups of EU citizens. See Chapter 8 for more details.

32 See Home Office, 'Sham Marriages and Civil Partnerships' (n 18), 28.

33 IA 2014 s 56(2).

34 Ibid sch 6, pt 2.

35 Ibid sch 4, para 9. As explained by the Home Office, this was done to ensure that 'there is no unlawful discrimination between couples on the grounds of nationality and to

'reasonable grounds' for suspecting that the intended marriage is a sham and whether to investigate the case. If the Home Office decides not to investigate, it will notify the register office, and the couple will be able to marry once the 28-day notice period has expired.

In contrast, if the marriage is to be investigated, the notice period will be extended to 70 days, during which the couple may be required to undergo an investigation. If the parties, without 'reasonable excuse', fail to comply with the investigation, e.g., by not attending the interview or not providing the documents/information requested, they will be unable to marry and will need to give notice again should they still wish to do so.[36]

Where the Home Office is satisfied that the parties have complied with the investigation, they will be allowed to marry, even where the Home Office believes that their marriage is a sham. However, in this case, the Home Office may take enforcement action against either relevant party, or both of them, before or after the end of the 70-day period.[37] Yet even if the enforcement decision is not taken and the alleged marriage of convenience is allowed to proceed, the Home Office would normally refuse any subsequent residence application made by the relevant non-EU national on the basis of marriage.[38] This approach signalled a shift of emphasis from disrupting intended sham marriages at register offices[39] to preventing a non-EU national from obtaining leave to remain on this basis. The Home Office claimed that the new scheme would act as a significant deterrent against such unions, as well as help disrupt organised crime groups who arrange sham marriages for profit.[40]

---

simplify procedures for registration officials when taking notices (…), especially where they deal both with those who are subject to immigration control and those who are not'. Home Office, 'Sham Marriages and Civil Partnerships' (n 18), 7. This, in fact, meant that all couples wishing to marry in the UK (285,400 in 2011) had to wait longer to allow the Home Office to investigate a very low number of suspected sham marriages.

36 Proposed Marriages and Civil Partnerships (Conduct of Investigations, etc.) Regulations 2015 (Proposed Marriages Regulations), SI 2015/397, reg 17(1).

37 Ibid reg 18(1)(c).

38 Ibid reg 18(1)(e).

39 For instance, 2020 Home Office guidelines reiterate that '[i]t is unlikely that visits to register offices to investigate marriages will be necessary since the introduction of the Immigration Act 2014 requiring registry officials to refer suspicious proposed marriages and civil partnerships for investigation where a spouse is a foreign national'. Home Office, 'Enforcement Visits' (Version 3.0, 22 December 2020).

40 Home Office, 'Tackling Sham Marriage: Impact Assessment' (n 26), 1.

2.2 *Definition of a 'Sham Marriage'*

In contrast to the Citizenship Directive, UK domestic immigration law continues to employ the term 'sham marriage' to designate marriages contracted for immigration purposes. The 2014 Immigration Act amended the definition of a 'sham marriage' under the existing legislation to cover those seeking to obtain the right of residence based on the Citizenship Directive, as transposed in UK law. The amended definition reads as follows:

> A marriage (whether or not it is void)[41] is a 'sham marriage' if –
> a) either, or both, of the parties to the marriage is not a relevant national,[42]
> b) there is no genuine relationship between the parties to the marriage, and
> c) either, or both, of the parties to the marriage enter into the marriage for one or more of these purposes –
>   i. avoiding the effect of one or more provisions of United Kingdom immigration law or the immigration rules;[43]
>   ii. enabling a party to the marriage to obtain a right conferred by that law or those rules to reside in the United Kingdom.[44]

Apart from supplementing the earlier definition with the additional provision (ii) with an apparent reference to EU Treaty rights, the 2014 Act also specified that, for a marriage to qualify as a sham, there should be no 'genuine relationship' between the parties. The wording of this definition is similar to the one provided by the Citizenship Directive and the Commission Handbook, yet the two do not exactly match. Two key differences can be distinguished: (1) in the reference to the purpose of the marriage under the Immigration Act, the word 'sole' is omitted, and (2) the EU law definition does not include a specific provision as to the genuineness of the relationship. It should be remembered, however, that, marriages that are yet to be contracted escape the ambit of EU law; hence, Member States are entitled to define marriages for immigration

41 For an analysis of the concept of 'sham marriages' in UK family law, see Section 3.7 below.

42 A 'relevant national' was originally defined here as a UK, EEA or Swiss national. Immigration and Asylum Act 1999 (IA 1999), s 24(6). This subsection was amended after Brexit to exclude certain categories of EU citizens from its scope. See Chapter 8 for more details.

43 'UK immigration law' was defined here to include EEA Regulations. See Immigration Act 2014, Explanatory Notes s 55(320).

44 IA 1999 s 24(5) as amended by IA 2014 s 55(2). A similar definition is provided for 'sham civil partnerships'. IA 1999, s 24A(5) as amended by IA 2014 s 55(3).

purposes without having regard to the definition provided in the Citizenship Directive. As explored in Chapter 5, the ECtHR has equally left the contracting states wide discretion in this matter; therefore, choosing their own definition of 'sham marriages' does not result in the breach of Article 12 of the ECHR.[45] Notwithstanding that, the definition of 'sham marriages' found in national immigration law may lead to important implications for prospective marriages involving EU citizens and their TCN partners.

First, it is regrettable that the Immigration Act definition omits the word 'sole' and only refers to the 'purpose' instead. Taken alone, such wording may cover situations where securing residence rights for the TCN spouse is not the sole but the primary purpose of the marriage. The conditions, however, are cumulative and this flaw is mitigated by the requirement of the absence of a 'genuine relationship' between the parties. Indeed, if the couple is in a relationship but wishes to get married to enable the TCN partner to stay in the UK with their spouse, their situation would not fall within the 'sham marriage' definition.

It should, however, be stressed that the absence of the relationship between the parties alone does not necessarily suggest that they do not intend to lead a family life. It must be recalled that the definition of 'marriages of convenience' provided in the Citizenship Directive is narrow and, in principle, does not require the couple to have a relationship at all – neither before, nor after the marriage.[46] What needs to be established is only that the sole purpose of the couple on the wedding day is to enable the TCN party to settle in the respective EU Member State. The situations where there is no relationship between the parties before the marriage may include arranged marriages or any other cases where parties refrain from having pre-marital relationships and/or cohabiting – e.g., due to religious or other beliefs. Hence, under the Immigration Act, couples in such situations enjoy less protection than guaranteed by the Citizenship Directive should it apply at the pre-marriage stage (and remain applicable post-Brexit). Moreover, given that arranged marriages are often entered into by EU citizens with foreign roots, an increasing suspicion towards this group may result in disguised discrimination on the basis of race and religion. The principal concern, however, relates to the interpretation of

45 European Convention for the Protection of Human Rights and Fundamental Freedoms, CETS No.005 (04.11.1950) (ECHR).

46 Although the Commission Handbook makes a puzzling reference to the 'predominant purpose' which is arguably a breach of the Citizenship Directive. See Chapter 4 for a discussion.

the concept of the 'genuine relationship', given a wide variety of relationship patterns and behaviours in the increasingly globalised world.

2.3 *Compliance with an Investigation*

If the Home Office decides to investigate a case, the couple may be required to contact its staff to arrange an interview.[47] The parties must be given at least three working days written notice of the date, place and time of the interview.[48] If the parties are unable or no longer able to attend the interview at the date proposed by the investigation officer, they may set an alternative time for it to take place.[49]

One of the most problematic issues in this context, however, is the pattern of excessive demands for additional documentary evidence at the interview stage. The solicitors interviewed complained about the standard Home Office letters containing a list of documents their clients were asked to bring with them on the interview day, a practice which was described as widespread.[50] Those unable to do so risked being considered non-compliant with an investigation.[51] In their letters, the Home Office required both parties to provide the following:

1) Passport(s) current and previous – covering the relationship duration;
2) Birth certificates for any dependant(s);
3) Marriage/divorce certificate and details of previous marriages;
4) Bank statements to cover the last six months from all accounts held, including any that are held overseas;
5) Details of any credit card(s) the person may have, and statements for them for the last six months;
6) Documentary evidence of tenancy/rental agreement to include named person(s) including evidence of payments plus details of

47 Proposed Marriages Regulations, reg 5. Immigration practitioners interviewed revealed that not all couples whose notices have been extended to 70 days were called for an interview, yet were nonetheless considered compliant with an investigation. Interview with David Tang, principal solicitor at David Tang & Co (London, 20 February 2019); interview with Nath Gbikpi, an associate solicitor at Leigh Day (London, 21 February 2019).

48 Proposed Marriages Regulations, reg 5.

49 Ibid, reg 11.

50 Interviews with David Tang (n 47) and Nath Gbikpi (n 47).

51 Such concerns were also raised by other legal practitioners quoted in UK media. See Robert Wright, 'Crackdown on Sham Marriages Leaves Migrants in Limbo' (*Financial Times*, 09.09.2018) <https://www.ft.com/content/3a724c10-ac47-11e8-94bd-cba20d673 90c> accessed 12 April 2024.

their Tenancy Deposit Scheme. Mortgage provider if appropriate (if renting, full details of landlord/letting agent are required – name, address telephone numbers and e-mail address);
7) Local authority/council tax payments to include the named person(s);
8) National Insurance card and number(s);
9) Full or provisional UK driving licence;
10) Evidence of employment in the form of wage-slips or employment contract;
11) Benefits/council entitlement payment(s);
12) Photos/family members where relevant; and
13) Any other evidence, either jointly or separately for consideration of cohabitation.

It was further noted that failure to provide the requested documents on the relevant day, without a reasonable excuse, might lead to non-compliance action and, consequently, the inability to get married.[52]

The list above is astonishing in its length, scope and degree of intrusion into the couple's private matters. The applicants are asked to reveal all their financial details to the authorities on the sole basis that their prospective marriage, for unknown reasons, was suspected to be a sham. Furthermore, most of the documents requested would be particularly difficult to provide for non-EU nationals with no legal right to live in the UK. In the view of the 'compliant environment' policy, landlords may appear extremely reluctant to sign an official rental agreement with someone irregularly in the UK, let alone reveal their own names and contact details to the Home Office. The parties may also live with their relatives or friends or have other types of informal arrangements. The requirement to provide bank statements from all accounts held is also highly problematic, e.g., where a person has not used an account for a long time.[53] Furthermore, irregular migrants who are not authorised to work and use their bank account for transactions may be reluctant to reveal it out of fear of having it blocked. Last but not least, couples were asked to provide documents within a short timescale, which could not always be possible for reasons outside of their control.[54]

The requirement to provide extensive documentation appears somewhat mitigated by the Home Office guidelines, which state that it may be possible to

52 An invitation letter to a marriage interview (December 2018), on file with the author.
53 Interview with David Tang (n 47).
54 Interview with Priya Solanki, a barrister at One Pump Court (online, 12 December 2023).

establish that the relationship is genuine even if the couple fails to present all the requested documents. In that case, officers should consider whether there is a 'reasonable excuse' for non-compliance and whether the missing documents would make a 'fundamental difference' to the assessment outcome. It is further reiterated that '[a]n inflexible approach to the provision of documents where they would not make a fundamental difference to the outcome of the genuineness decision, is likely to be unreasonable'.[55]

These principles, however, are not always applied in practice. There are cases where couples were rejected for purely bureaucratic reasons unrelated to the nature of their planned marriage. For instance, one couple that involved an unauthorised migrant from Albania was unable to submit his tenancy agreement as he was living rent-free with a disabled man he was helping. Their application was consequently rejected.[56] A solicitor interviewed recalls a case where an investigation officer saw the entry of money into a non-EU national's bank account, despite him not having a valid immigration status in the UK. When he confirmed he was working in the UK, the officer made a moral judgment about his activity, asking him if he regretted 'doing what he was not allowed to do'.[57] In another case, a person was ruled non-compliant with the investigation because he failed to provide bank statements covering the last six months for an account that was opened only four months earlier. Another example concerns a couple who were expecting a baby together but did not have a tenancy agreement as they lived with the non-EU national's sister. Her letter explaining their situation proved insufficient, whereby the Home Office did not even attempt to interview the parties.[58]

Immigration practitioners are nevertheless familiar with cases where the Home Office did accept an explanation of why the requested documents could not be delivered.[59] Irrespective of its approach, however, a fundamental problem with the list above is the absence of a direct link between the requested documents and the nature of a prospective marriage. According to the Home Office Regulations and Guidance, the purpose of an investigation is

55 Home Office, 'Marriage Investigations' (Version 8.0, 22 June 2023), 18.

56 Wright (n 51).

57 Interview with Nath Gbikpi (n 47).

58 Wright (n 51).

59 For example, a letter from a friend the applicants live with, giving evidence of that friend's identity and the right to occupy the property. Interview with Nath Gbikpi (n 47).

to determine whether a proposed marriage is a sham.[60] It is, however, unclear how this type of evidence would help the Home Office in reaching such a decision.

Moreover, excessive and unreasonable documentary requirements, as well as the lack of flexibility in arranging interviews amounts to a potential breach of Article 12 of the ECHR.[61] As explored in Chapter 5, the ECHR, in essence, allows a contracting state to require parties of the prospective marriage to undergo an investigation.[62] The ECtHR has not further elaborated on the scope of such a requirement; nonetheless, the fundamental nature of the right to marry suggests that the concept of lack of compliance must be interpreted narrowly – i.e., confined to a refusal to undergo an investigation whatsoever. Hence, preventing someone from getting married only because they are unable to attend an interview at offered dates or fail to provide bank statements or a tenancy agreement is clearly disproportionate. Furthermore, it represents a direct attack on their human rights which, most likely, would not stand a court challenge.[63]

The next key element that may determine the outcome of an investigation is the manner the interview is conducted in. Whilst this issue is extensively discussed in Chapter 9, at this point it is sufficient to note that failure to respond to any question asked during an interview (or a refusal to answer any further questions thereby bringing the interview to an end) may be regarded as non-compliance with the investigation, unless a 'reasonable excuse' is given.[64] This provision is highly problematic and may go beyond what is permitted under the ECHR. As ILPA rightly points out, there are many reasons for not answering the question, including confusion and embarrassment.[65] The person may also reasonably refuse to answer any highly personal or intimidating questions if they are asked by an immigration officer.

60 Proposed Marriages Regulations, reg 3(2); Home Office, 'Marriage and Civil Partnership Referral and Investigation Scheme: Statutory Guidance for Home Office Staff' (March 2015), 14; Home Office, 'Marriage Investigations' (Version 8.0), 17.

61 This view is also supported by David Tang (n 47) and Nath Gbikpi (n 47).

62 *Klip & Krüger v Netherlands* (1997) 91 A-DR 66.

63 Indeed, an immigration practitioner interviewed has seen cases where marriages have been accepted as not sham marriages but were not allowed to proceed because of incompliance with the formalities. Interview with Nath Gbikpi (n 47).

64 Proposed Marriages Regulations, reg 16(a); Home Office, 'Marriage Investigations' (Version 8.0), 18.

65 ILPA, 'Comments for the Chief Inspector of Borders and Immigration. Review of Sham Marriages' (31.08.2016).

2.4 *Implications of Giving a Marriage Notice in the UK*

The 'referral and investigation scheme' subjects couples involving foreign nationals to considerable uncertainty. EU citizens whose TCN partners have no valid leave to remain face a particularly high risk of being separated – both before and after Brexit. Paradoxically, the very fact of giving a marriage notice with the aim to live together lawfully in the country of their current residence will automatically mean coming to the attention of the Home Office, which may eventually lead to an opposite outcome.

As demonstrated above, it is compliance or lack of compliance with the investigation and not the nature of the prospective marriage that directly impacts on the couple's right to marry. Yet, irrespective of whether or not the couple has complied with an investigation and if it has even been started in the first place,[66] unauthorised migrants may be removed from the UK anytime before their marriage is registered. The relevant Home Office guidance, issued before the end of the transition period,[67] stated that the Home Office could take enforcement action where a person met all of the following criteria: (1) he/she was the 'genuine unmarried partner' of an EU citizen, (2) he/she did not yet hold an EEA residence card[68] issued on this basis, and (3) he/she was 'an immigration offender'. The latter designation included, 'overstayers, illegal entrants, [people who are in] breach of [immigration] conditions, and [people who have obtained] leave [to remain] by deception'.[69] In this case, the Home Office could start a standard administrative procedure under section 10(1) of the Immigration and Asylum Act 1999 which provides for the removal of a person who 'requires leave to enter or remain in the United Kingdom but does not have it'.

Before the end of the transition period, once a person was married to an EU citizen, they automatically qualified as a family member under the Citizenship Directive and could be removed only if their marriage was found to be one of convenience. The Home Office, however, frequently sought to remove 'undesirable' persons before this point, effectively preventing their

66 Immigration practitioners and media report about cases where the couple were informed that their relationship would not be investigated but their wedding was still interrupted by immigration officials with a view of detention and removal of a TCN partner. See, Diana Taylor and Frances Perraudin, 'Couples Face 'Insulting' Checks in Sham Marriage Crackdown' (*The Guardian*, 14.04.2019) <https://www.theguardian.com/uk-news/2019/apr/14/couples-sham-marriage-crackdown-hostile-environment> accessed 12 April 2024.

67 For an analysis of the legislation, applicable after the cut-off date, see Chapter 8.

68 For more details on EEA residence cards, see Section 3.4 below.

69 Home Office, 'Marriage Investigations' (Version 3.0, 13 February 2019), 6 and 24.

marriage from taking place even if it was accepted as genuine. Former paragraph 323(i) in conjunction with paragraph 322(5) of the Immigration Rules provided for curtailment of migrant's leave if their conduct, character or associations made it undesirable to permit them to remain in the UK but they did not reach the deportation threshold. Paragraph 322(5) did not only apply to criminal cases but also to non-EU nationals seeking to enter into a 'sham marriage'.[70] Once the investigation had confirmed that this was indeed the case, the file was passed on to the curtailment team who then decided whether the curtailment of leave was appropriate. This was done on the basis of the evidence provided by the immigration officers, such as the record of the marriage interview highlighting discrepancies in responses to their questions. The decision had to be made on the balance of probabilities, whereby the caseworker was required to 'fully evaluate the evidence provided by the ICE team, and any other relevant evidence or information about the migrant'.[71]

This requirement, however, was difficult to satisfy, given that the decision had to be already made on the same day as the referral, or the next day if impossible. As was explained in the guidance, '[t]he individuals concerned will usually have been arrested by ICE teams. If curtailment is appropriate in the circumstances of the individual case, a swift decision may allow them to be kept in detention and removed soon afterwards'.[72] It was further noted that curtailment should normally be with immediate effect.[73]

This approach was highly problematic. An erroneous assessment of the couple's circumstances, followed by a speedy curtailment and/or removal procedure would normally result in their separation, as well as deprive them of their fundamental right to marry. Yet the capability of curtailment caseworkers to evaluate the evidence is questionable, not only due to the time restraints, but also, more generally, because they are neither ready, nor expected to perform a thorough review of Home Office decisions concerning alleged sham marriages.

Apart from this category of persons, the prospect of being detained for removal at any point either before, during, or after the interview is faced by all non-EU nationals with no valid leave to remain, irrespective of whether their marriage is considered a sham – both before and after the end of the transition period.[74] Even if the TCN partner is not detained during the interview and

70 For changes after the end of the transition period, see Chapter 8.

71 Home Office, 'Curtailment' (Version 18.0, 19.12.2019), 19.

72 Ibid 18.

73 Ibid.

74 For instance, according to the facts of *Seferi & Anor, R (On the Application Of) v SSHD* [2018] EWHC 287 (Admin), the Home Office issued a notice stating that the couple had

has complied with an investigation, there is no guarantee that they will not be arrested on their wedding day which would effectively prevent them from marrying. Detention of a person pending their removal is allowed under paragraph 16(2) of Schedule 2 to the Immigration Act 1971.

Yet, where the couple have complied with an investigation, the very fact of detention of the TCN partner alone should not preclude them from getting married in the UK. There are two main routes of getting married prior to the TCN partner's removal from the state: arranging for a civil ceremony whilst in detention or doing so upon their release on bail. According to the relevant Home Office instructions, detainees should be allowed to marry, provided that the immigration removal centre (IRC) staff escorts the detainee both to give notice of the marriage at the local DRO and to the ceremony itself.[75] One of the immigration practitioners confirmed in an interview that their client was indeed escorted to the ceremony in handcuffs.[76] Alternatively, the couple can have a wedding ceremony if the detainee has been released on bail.[77]

Meanwhile, it should be stressed that the foreigner's options to challenge the decision to detain and remove them are limited. Before the end of the transition period, the rights of appeal were basically confined to (1) refusal of a human rights or asylum claim, (2) refusal of a visa and refusal to vary leave to remain in some situations, where the application was made before the Immigration Act 2014 was in force, (3) refusal to issue an EEA family permit,[78] and (4) deprivation of citizenship.[79] Unless any of these claims were made, an unauthorised migrant or someone whose leave was curtailed did not have a right of appeal. An alternative option would be to lodge judicial review proceedings that will normally suspend removal[80] and enable the couple to gain time, which, in some situations, could prove sufficient for them to undergo a marriage ceremony. A claim for judicial review, is, however, unlikely to be satisfied, particularly where the only reason for detention and removal is the

---

complied with an investigation only to detain the irregularly present TCN partner on the very same day.

75 Home Office, 'Marriage/Civil Partnership' (Detention Services Order 06/2015, Version 1.1, April 2016), paras 2, 5.

76 Interview with David Tang (n 47).

77 Under sch 10 of the Immigration Act 2016, the bail may be granted either by the Home Office or the First-tier Tribunal, provided *inter alia* that the person is not intended to be removed within 14 days of the bail hearing.

78 For more details on EEA family permits, see Section 3.3 below.

79 See Home Office, 'Rights of Appeal' (Version 8.0, 31.01.2020), 6. For developments after the end of the transition period, see Chapter 8.

80 See Home Office, 'Judicial Reviews and Injunctions' (Version 20.0, 10.10.2019), 30–31.

non-EU national's irregular status. The latter will also cover cases where a prospective marriage is found to be a sham. In *Seferi & Anor,* it was held that even where the conclusion about the adverse nature of their intended marriage 'infected' the Home Office's decision to remove the applicant, the legal basis for it was his adverse immigration status.[81]

To protect the position of unauthorised migrants before their marriage, solicitors recommend them to submit a human rights (e.g., under Article 8 of the ECHR) or protection claim immediately after giving a marriage notice.[82] Even if there is no realistic chance to succeed, this type of application will suspend removal. If it remains pending until after the end of the notice period, the non-EU national will be able to marry in the UK. The Home Office, however, tends to view this practice as a step taken by dishonest individuals to avoid removal, rather than a strategy pursued by couples who do not wish to be separated.[83]

2.5 *Interplay between the 'Referral and Investigation Scheme' and EU Law*

As explored above, due to the division of competences between the EU and Member States, pre-marriage controls escape the ambit of EU law, and Member States enjoy nearly absolute discretion in this matter. In the meantime, before the end of the transition period the UK 'referral and investigation scheme' had serious implications for (yet) unmarried EU citizens who enjoyed their free movement rights and wished to live together with their TCN partners. In the absence of protection reserved to married couples under the Citizenship Directive, British authorities used the legal lacuna to carry out systematic checks on almost all prospective marriages involving foreign nationals, subjecting such couples to considerable inconvenience and uncertainty.

For the purposes of the Citizenship Directive, UK immigration law used formal marital status as a proxy for serious long-term commitment. Accordingly, there were very limited opportunities for unmarried couples to stay together on different grounds: the non-EU nationals either needed to submit a human rights claim under Article 8 of the ECHR with rather low chances of succeeding,[84] or apply for a residence card as an extended family member of an EU

81 *Seferi & Anor* (n 74), paras 33, 34.

82 Interview with Nath Gbikpi (online, 12 December 2023).

83 See for instance, ICIBI, 'The Implementation of the 2014 "Hostile Environment" Provisions for Tackling Sham Marriage. August to September 2016' (December 2016).

84 For an in-depth analysis of Article 8 jurisprudence at UK Supreme Court level, see Helena Wray, *Article 8 ECHR, Family Reunification and the UK's Supreme Court* (Hart 2023).

citizen.[85] With respect to the latter, the EEA Regulations[86] implementing the Citizenship Directive in UK law provided no definition of 'durable partners', and the Home Office equated them to unmarried partners under the Immigration Rules.[87] To qualify for admission, the parties normally needed to have been living together 'in a relationship akin to marriage or civil partnership' for at least two years[88] and present extensive proof of cohabitation, joint finances or commitments, evidence of joint responsibility for children, etc.[89] For couples who had not lived together for two years, marriage frequently represented the only opportunity to stay together in the UK, particularly where the TCN partner had an irregular or a short-term status and was unable to acquire an independent right to work due to the UK restrictive labour migration policy.[90]

It is quite understandable that an EU citizen could wish to regularise the status of their partner and stop living in constant fear of separation, which may put a serious strain on their relationship. Furthermore, after the marriage, the non-EU national spouse acquired the right to work full-time, a key advantage which would enable them to support their family, and thereby, further contribute to their integration into the host Member State. Hence, by limiting alternative routes to family reunion, the state effectively forced such couples into marriage, although they might have preferred to postpone such a serious commitment to a later date or, for various reasons, avoid it.

Yet, rather paradoxically, the 'referral and investigation scheme' introduced by the Home Office acted (and continues to act post-Brexit)[91] as a significant deterrent to couples involving non-EU nationals. It should be remembered that, before the end of the transition period, TCN spouses of EU citizens did

85 It should be noted that, unlike spouses, unmarried partners did not have an automatic right to join or remain with the EU citizen partner in the UK. The respective rights were acquired only after the Home Office had granted the applicant an EEA residence card (or family permit) on this basis. An outstanding application for an EEA residence card as an extended family member of an EU citizen or an appeal against refusal to grant one would not suspend removal. This has been stressed *inter alia* in *Molina, R (On the Application Of) v SSHD* [2017] EWHC 1730 (Admin), para 103.

86 Immigration (European Economic Area) Regulations 2016, SI 2016/1052 (EEA Regulations 2016). For an analysis see Sections 3.1–3.6 below.

87 Immigration Rules (25.02.2016), pt 8, para 295A(i)(a)(i).

88 Ibid.

89 Home Office, 'Free Movement Rights: Extended Family Members of EEA Nationals' (Version 7.0, 27.03.2019), 14–15.

90 For a general overview of UK domestic immigration law, see Ian MacDonald and Ronan Toal, *Macdonald's Immigration Law and Practice* (9th edn, Butterworth 2014).

91 See Chapter 8 for more details.

not obtain an independent right of residence in the UK but derived it from the principal, whereby the right of mobile EU citizens to family reunion was regarded as a necessary pre-condition for the exercise of free movement rights. Yet instead of enabling EU citizens (and UK nationals) to live together with partners of their choice and, for example, providing the latter guarantees against pre-wedding removal, the Home Office placed the main emphasis on the fight against allegedly dishonest foreigners aiming to regularise their stay in the UK by all possible means. As a consequence, many unmarried couples involving irregular migrants could (and may still) prefer to live in limbo rather than risk imminent separation.

Some couples might have been able to overcome these barriers by marrying abroad. Provided that their marriage is recognised in the UK, a TCN spouse of a mobile EU citizen would then immediately qualify for admission into the country (unless public policy or public security grounds would apply or their marriage would be found to be one of convenience). For many, however, this option might not have been available for various reasons. Travelling to another EU Member State may be difficult for those UK-based short-term or irregular migrants or asylum seekers who require either a national or Schengen visa. In addition, this may prove an expensive and unsafe journey for both partners, as well as result in significant delays and inconvenience before their possible reunion in the UK. A further option would have been to contract a marriage by proxy if it were legal in the country where it would take place. Nonetheless, proxy marriages were treated as particularly suspicious when it came to the application for an EEA residence card.[92]

All in all, it is understandable that many EU citizens might have wished to marry in the UK, the country where they lived and where their friends, and possibly family members, were. Denying them such an opportunity was not only against the spirit of EU law[93] but also prompted them to live in legal limbo. Instead of respecting their partner choice and thus contributing to their integration and well-being in the host Member State, the British authorities disrupted unwanted families of EU citizens, forcing the latter to look for alternative solutions and in some cases, relocate.[94] Hence, although formally the UK pre-marriage controls did not breach the Citizenship Directive, the

92 See Chapter 9.

93 For an analysis of the situation after the end of the transition period, see Chapter 8.

94 For a discussion on the impact immigration enforcement may have on the lives of couples where one of the spouses is subject to removal, see, Melanie Griffiths '"My Passport is Just My Way Out of Here". Mixed-Immigration Status Families, Immigration Enforcement and the Citizenship Implications' (2019) *Identities*.

free movement rights of EU citizens might have nonetheless been seriously obstructed. The same refers to British nationals who could wish to relocate to another EU Member State with their TCN partners but needed to marry them to be able to do so.

3 Post-marriage Controls

3.1 *Procedures for Family Reunion with EU Citizens in the UK*

Before the end of the transition period, once partners had managed to enter into marriage, their situation moved from the domain of UK domestic immigration law to the ambit of the Citizenship Directive. In the years immediately preceding the cut-off date, the Directive was transposed into UK law by the Immigration (European Economic Area) Regulations 2016 (as amended), which came into force on 1 February 2017. In accordance with the Directive, the Regulations defined direct family members as including spouses or civil partners of EU citizens or returning British nationals,[95] as long as their union was recognised as valid in UK law.[96]

As was explained in the Regulations, a non-EU national obtained the right of entry and residence in the UK, provided that their EU citizen spouse was either (1) entitled to reside in the UK for an initial period of three months,[97] (2) considered a 'qualified person' – i.e., a jobseeker, worker, a self-employed person, a self-sufficient person, or a student,[98] (3) had a right of permanent residence[99] or (4) was a returning British national.[100] This also referred to family members who had retained the right of residence following the death of or divorce from the EU citizen.[101]

Those seeking to enter the UK from abroad were asked to either be in possession of a residence card issued by another Member State (if the couple had already lived there), or apply for an entry visa, the so-called EEA family permit. For the latter to be issued, the EU citizen principal either had to already be in the UK, or intend to travel there with their TCN spouse within six months

95 EEA Regulations 2016, regs 7(1)(a) and 7(4).

96 Unless an otherwise valid marriage was found to be one of convenience, see below. On recognition of marriages contracted abroad see Immigration Directorate Instructions (July 2012), ch 8, s 1, Annex B.

97 EEA Regulations 2016, reg 13.

98 Ibid, regs 6(1) and 14.

99 Ibid, reg 15(1).

100 Ibid, reg 9.

101 Ibid, reg 10.

of the application date.[102] In addition, the permit had to be granted to family members who had retained the right of residence or acquired the right of permanent residence.[103] In these situations, the non-EU nationals possessed residence rights in a personal capacity and did not need to show that they would be joining or accompanying an EU citizen.

The Regulations confirmed that non-EU nationals were not obliged to produce a family permit or residence card upon arrival, and the immigration officer had to allow the person to prove their family member status by other means.[104] In practice, however, the decision was subject to the discretion of an immigration officer, and spouses of EU citizens could be denied entry into the UK without the relevant permit.[105]

An EEA family permit was issued free of charge and was valid for six months, during which the TCN spouse could leave and enter the UK multiple times. Upon its expiry, the non-EU national could continue to reside in the UK, provided that they still met the conditions under the Regulations. In this case, they needed to apply for a residence card which had to be issued no later than six months after the application was received and was valid for five years,[106] following which, the foreign national could qualify for permanent residence.

3.2 *The Concept of Marriages of Convenience in the EEA Regulations*

When referring to marriages for immigration purposes, the EEA Regulations used different terminology from that of the Immigration Act, designating such unions as ones 'of convenience', the term used in the Citizenship Directive. The Regulations accordingly stipulated that the concepts of 'spouse', 'civil partner', and 'durable partner' of an EU citizen did not include a party to a marriage, civil partnership and durable partnership of convenience, respectively.[107] The reference to the 'durable partnership of convenience' was made in the Regulations for the first time: this designation is particularly puzzling, provided that the couple would have normally needed to live together for two years before the TCN partner could qualify for residence, as well as submit extensive evidence to prove that their relationship was subsisting. Furthermore, given that there was no equivalent concept in domestic statutes relating to unmarried partners

102 EEA Regulations 2016, reg 12(1).

103 Ibid, reg 12(3).

104 Ibid, reg 11(4)(b).

105 This has been confirmed by David Tang (n 47) and Nath Gbikpi (n 47).

106 EEA Regulations 2016, regs 18(1), 18(3) and 18(6)(a).

107 Ibid, reg 2(1). No corresponding provision exists in the Citizens Directive, although art 35 suggests the same.

of static UK nationals, the new provision arguably violated the principle of non-discrimination in EU law. The definition of the relevant terms read as follows:

> '[M]arriage of convenience'[108] includes a marriage entered into for the purpose of using these Regulations, or any other right conferred by the EU Treaties, as a means to circumvent –
> (a) immigration rules applying to non-EEA nationals (such as any applicable requirement under the 1971 Act to have leave to enter or remain in the United Kingdom); or
> (b) any other criteria that the party to the marriage of convenience would otherwise have to meet in order to enjoy a right to reside under these Regulations or the EU Treaties.[109]

It is likely that the definition was originally drafted to cover the same situations as the one provided in the Citizenship Directive. This is suggested, for example, by the relevant Home Office guidance which specified that there should have been 'no genuine relationship between the parties',[110] thus equating the definition found in the Regulations to the one of a 'sham marriage' provided in the Immigration and Asylum Act 1999. Yet the absence of the word 'sole' from the relevant hard law instrument was crucial and could have wide-ranging consequences for couples involving EU citizens. When interpreted literally, the scope of the definition appeared to be significantly broader than foreseen in EU law – i.e., limited only to marriages contracted for the sole purpose of securing the right of residence for the non-EU national. Moreover, it was also broader than the 'sham marriage' definition found in the Immigration Act: whilst in the latter, the word 'sole' is equally omitted, it expressly provides that there should not be a genuine relationship between the parties.

Conversely, the EEA Regulations referred to marriages of convenience as ones contracted for the purpose of enabling the non-EU national to circumvent immigration rules, irrespective of whether the couple intended, at least at the point of the wedding, to lead a family life. Formally, this definition reminded one of the infamous 'primary purpose rule', targeting literally every couple where the non-EU national would gain an immigration advantage from

108 The same wording was used to define a civil partnership or durable partnership of convenience, whereby the term 'marriage' was substituted with 'civil partnership' or 'durable partnership', respectively.

109 EEA Regulations 2016, reg 2(1).

110 Home Office, 'Marriage Investigations' (Version 3.0), 11.

the marriage, including those who are (or were) in a close relationship. The wording of the definition was, hence, arguably in breach of the Citizenship Directive.

Further, the EEA Regulations expressly permitted the Home Office to verify the right of residence of EU citizens and their family members. Regulation 22(3) provided that if a non-EU national spouse sought to avail themselves on Treaty rights on the basis of marriage to an EU citizen, the Home Office could invite them to attend an interview. A further provision allowed the Home Office to draw 'any factual interferences' about the non-EU national's right to reside if they, without good reason, on at least two occasions, failed to attend an interview[111] – an apparent reflection of a similar provision in domestic immigration law (see Section 2.3 above).

3.3 *Application for an EEA Family Permit*

Although formally family members of EU citizens were not required to apply for an EEA family permit prior to their first entry in the UK, most still chose to get an entry clearance beforehand, rather than risk being refused entry at the airport. The number of EEA family permits issued outside the UK reached its peak in 2018 and 2019, assumingly reflecting the rise in applications ahead of Brexit and the end of the transition period (see Table 1).

Home Office statistics did not specify how many of these included spouses of EU citizens nor provided the rate of refusals. Yet evidence suggests that the Home Office pursued an inconsistent approach when processing applications and refused people for reasons that were arguably incompatible with the Citizenship Directive.

For their application to be considered, the non-EU national spouse was asked to complete an online application form,[112] which, pursuant to regulation 21(2)(a), had to be accompanied or joined by the evidence of proof required by regulation 12. The relevant Regulation, however, only set out the categories of persons eligible for an EEA family permit without requiring any specific evidence. The list of documents required was meanwhile found in the application form. It included: a valid passport of the non-EU national, the passport or EEA national identity card of their principal, proof of their relationship (marriage certificate for spouses), and evidence that the principal was either living in the UK as a 'qualified person' or would be travelling to the UK within six months of the application date (for example, flight or hotel bookings). These

111 EEA Regulations 2016, reg 22(4).

112 Online application form was available at <https://visas-immigration.service.gov.uk/country-selection> accessed 26 August 2020.

TABLE 1 Total number of EEA family permits issued to non-EU nationals, 2014–2021

2015	30,302
2016	33,092
2017	27,106
2018	36,555
2019	45,692[a]
2020	16,122
2021	7,204

a On 30 March 2019, the UK launched the EU Settlement Scheme family permit scheme, an entry clearance route for certain family members of EU citizens resident in the UK by the end of the transition period. This was, expectedly, followed by a significant decrease in applications for EEA family permits and rise in applications for EUSS Family permits. See Chapter 8 for more details.

b Home Office, 'Why do People Come to the UK? (4) For Family Reasons' (Immigration Statistics, year ending December 2018, 28.02.2019) <https://www.gov.uk/government/publications/immigration-statistics-year-ending-december-2018/why-do-people-come-to-the-uk-4-for-family-reasons> accessed 12 April 2024; Home Office, 'Why do People Come to the UK? (4) For Family Reasons' (Immigration Statistics, year ending December 2021, 24.02.2022) <https://www.gov.uk/government/statistics/immigration-statistics-year-ending-december-2021/why-do-people-come-to-the-uk-for-family-reasons> accessed 12 April 2024.

SOURCE: HOME OFFICE[b]

requirements were largely consistent with the Citizenship Directive[113] and designed to ascertain the status of a direct family member of an EU citizen and that the latter was exercising their Treaty rights.

However, in addition, spouses of EU citizens were asked to provide further details about their relationship, such as: (1) where and when they had lived together within or outside the UK and if they cohabited at the particular moment; if not, they were required to provide reasons for why not, (2) how they kept in contact (e.g., by phone, email, social media, letters), (3) the date when they first met (month and year could be given if unsure of the exact date), (4) where they first met (e.g., work, school, social club), (5) when the relationship began (month and year could be given if unsure of the exact date), (6) how often they usually saw (met) their partner (for example, weekly,

113 Although there were some concerns as to the excessive requirements to demonstrate the 'qualified person' status. See Parliament, 'Obstacles to the right of free movement and residence for EU citizens and their families: Country report for the United Kingdom' (PE556.967, 2016).

monthly, three times a year), and (7) the date when they last saw their partner.[114] It followed that answering all these questions was mandatory since the EEA Regulations required all applications to be 'complete' to be accepted as valid.[115] Indeed, one could not proceed with the online application if the relevant fields were not completed.

At the end of the form, it was stated that non-EU nationals could also send in other documents 'to help support' their application, including evidence proving their relationship. For example, documents (such as bank statements, utility bills, rental or mortgage agreements, etc.) addressed to them jointly, in both names, or individual names, to the same address. Partners not living together at the particular time could provide evidence of having lived together in the past, as well as plans to marry or live together in the future. Although from the wording it followed that sending in these documents was not a requirement, the relevant Home Office guidance for entry clearance staff suggested otherwise. First, it is noted that an applicant could be requested to provide evidence about the relationship or attend an interview *if* it was suspected that their marriage was one of convenience.[116] However, this contradicted the next passage, which stated that when submitting their application, spouses and civil partners of EU citizens were required provide proof that their relationship was 'genuine and subsisting', e.g., evidence of cohabitation such as joint tenancy or mortgage agreements, utility bills, bank statements, or other documents.[117]

Taken together, this was highly confusing, adversely impacted legal certainty and arguably violated not only EU law but also the EEA Regulations. As explored above, systematic checks of marriages were prohibited both under domestic Regulations and the Citizenship Directive, whilst the burden of proof of establishing marriages of convenience had to rest with the national authorities.[118] Unlike those applying for a family visa under UK domestic immigration law, spouses of EU citizens should not have been asked to demonstrate that their marriage was 'genuine and subsisting'; hence, the relevant provision in the guidance clearly went beyond what was permitted under EU law. It was

114 EEA family permit application form, version as of 14 July 2019, on file with the author.

115 EEA Regulations 2016, regs 21(2)(b) and 21(4). This was further stressed in the Home Office Guidance which stated that, in order for an application to be valid, it had to be 'submitted on the specified application form, with all relevant sections completed'. Home Office, 'Processes and Procedures for EEA Documentation Applications' (Version 8.0, 14.02.2019), 6.

116 Home Office, 'EEA Family Permits: Guidance for Entry Clearance Officers' (Version 2.0, 13.03.2017), 10. Emphasis added.

117 Ibid, 11. Emphasis added.

118 This has also been confirmed by UK judiciary. See Chapter 10.

even more confusing given that the Home Office guidance on direct family members of EU citizens did rightly specify that if a marriage of convenience was suspected, it was for the Home Office to prove this.[119]

Moreover, by systematically requiring applicants to provide additional details of the relationship in the application form, the Home Office clearly went beyond the Citizenship Directive which only asks them to prove a family relationship through a valid marriage certificate. Not to mention that it was unreasonable to ask the couples to remember the exact date or month when they first met (particularly if it happened a long time ago, e.g., in childhood or adolescence) or began a relationship (there might be different perceptions as to how and when the relationship started). Remarkably, the Home Office also disregarded the domestic case law: it was already in 2012 when the Upper Tribunal explicitly outlawed such practices with regards to applications for an EEA family permit.[120]

Nonetheless, national authorities continued to frequently violate EU law by rejecting EEA family permit applications on the basis that the non-EU nationals had not proactively provided evidence that their marriage was 'genuine and subsisting'.[121] To reduce the risk of an adverse outcome, couples felt obliged to upload with their application, detailed evidence of their relationship; and immigration practitioners often advised this.[122] The relevant discussions on online forums[123] showed that the 'bundle' typically included screenshots of text messages; phone, WhatsApp and Facebook call logs; and chats showing that the couple had stayed in regular contact over a lengthy period (e.g., 4 to 6 screenshots per month). As one of the users explained, he chose 'the most normal bits of conversation – boring and silly emails to each other while at work, texts reminding to grab lunch that was on the table, sending ideas of cakes for [their] wedding and other wedding planning stuff'. Another user made screenshots of their Facebook chats at different times which included phrases like

119 Home Office, 'Free Movement Rights: Direct Family Members of European Economic Area (EEA) Nationals' (Version 9.0, 21.02.2020), 37.

120 *Papajorgji (EEA spouse – marriage of convenience) Greece* [2012] UKUT 38 (IAC).

121 This has been confirmed by David Tang (n 47) and Nath Gbikpi (n 47). See also, *Ussenbai v Entry Clearance Officer* [2019] UKUT 00472 (IAC); Conrad Duncan, 'Man Refused UK Visa to Visit Newborn Grandson Because He Did Not Send Photo of 1975 Wedding' (*The Independent*, 14.09.2018) <https://www.independent.co.uk/news/uk/home-news/uk-visa-wedding-photo-russian-grandson-refused-home-office-marriage-eea-family-permit-a8537946.html> accessed 12 April 2024.

122 Interview with Nath Gbikpi (n 47).

123 Most notably Immigrationboards.com and the Facebook group 'EU and Family Members EEA Permit Holders UK'.

'I love you' or 'I miss you', as well as attached screenshots of him searching the phrase 'I love you' which showed 10,000 results. This type of evidence was often accompanied by photos documenting every stage of the relationship (including pictures of travel, engagement, wedding, family events, etc.). In addition, applicants frequently submitted a cover letter explaining how their relationship developed, including, e.g., how they planned their wedding and why they preferred a small ceremony without families. Further evidence provided included proof of trips taken together or to see each other (hotel bookings, airplane tickets), or proof of cohabitation (tenancy agreement and utility bills).

The practice of submitting excessive levels of documentation gave reason for serious concern. In addition to violating EU law where the applicants enjoy the presumption of innocence, it put pressure on couples who felt obliged to reveal intimate details about their relationship. This alone could act as a significant deterrent for couples involving non-EU nationals, potentially keeping them apart and prompting them to choose another place of residence, which undeniably, negatively impacted the exercise of free movement rights by EU citizens.

3.4 *Application for an EEA Residence Card*

Where a non-EU national was already in the UK, they could wish to apply for a residence card as a confirmation of their right of residence (including the right to work) under EU law. To qualify for a residence card, the non-EU national was asked to complete an application form,[124] whereby regulation 21(2)(a) further noted that all applications had to be accompanied or joined by the 'evidence of proof required by this part'. The relevant part, however, did not contain any description as to what such evidence entailed, which seemed somewhat confusing. The evidential requirements were nonetheless specified in the application form and accompanying guidance notes. Apart from their own and their principal's personal details; date and place of their wedding; and details of their status, former and existing spouses of EU citizens were asked to answer *inter alia* the following questions:

1) When and where did you first meet your sponsor?
2) When did your relationship begin?

---

124 UKVI, 'Application for a registration certificate or residence card as the family member of a European Economic Area (EEA) or Swiss national' (EEA(FM), Version 03/2019) (EEA residence card application form), on file with the author.

3) Do you and your sponsor currently live together? If yes, when did you start living together? Were you in a relationship with each other when you started living together?
4) If you are not currently living together, why do you not currently live with your sponsor? Please include information on how often you meet, when you last saw each other, how you keep in touch and if you plan to live together in future.
5) Have you ever lived with your sponsor within or outside the UK? If yes, please provide details of when and where you previously lived with your sponsor.
6) When did you decide to marry or form a civil partnership with your sponsor?
7) Were you and your sponsor both present at the ceremony? If you were not, or your sponsor was not, present at the ceremony, please say why and explain where you were/your sponsor was at the relevant time.
8) Do you or your sponsor currently have another spouse or civil partner, or an unmarried or a same-sex partner with whom you or they are in a durable relationship? If yes, please give details of all other current or previous marriages/civil partnerships/relationships.[125]

Section 20 of the application form set out the list of documents that had to be submitted together with the application. With respect to spouses, these included identity documents for both the non-EU national and their EU citizen principal, marriage certificate as a proof of their relationship,[126] proof of the principal's status as a 'qualified person', as well as evidence of their marriage – e.g. marriage certificate, evidence of living together, evidence that any previous marriage or civil partnership had legally ended – e.g. divorce certificate. It was, however, noted that the full list of documents was available in the relevant guidance. The latter specified that, for those who were living together, it was advised to provide at least six items, from three different sources, that 'clearly show[ed]' that the spouses lived, or had lived, at the same address.[127] Those living with relatives or friends were asked to provide a letter from the relevant person confirming the spouses had been living with them. Those who

125 EEA residence card application form, s 5.

126 Persons who had retained their right of residence were asked to additionally submit the relevant evidence (e.g., the principal's death certificate, decree absolute or evidence of domestic violence).

127 UKVI, 'EEA(FM): Guidance Notes' (Version 4.0, February 2020), 4.

had not been living together were asked to tell the reasons for this and how they stayed in contact with each other, as well as provide any relevant supporting evidence. According to the guidance, suitable evidence included (but was not limited to):

1) Letters or other documents from government departments or agencies, for example, HM Revenue and Customs, Department for Work and Pensions, DVLA, TV Licensing;
2) Letters or other documents from a GP, a hospital or other local health service about medical treatments, appointments, home visits or other medical matters;
3) Bank statements/letters;
4) Building society savings books/letters;
5) Council tax, electricity and/or gas, water rates, telephone bills or statements;
6) Mortgage statements/agreement;
7) Tenancy agreement(s);
8) Photographs of the couple together – for example, on holiday or at a family celebration; and
9) Evidence of how they have kept in contact with each other during periods in which they have not lived together – for example, letters, printouts of emails or contact via social media, mobile phone bills showing they contacted each other, printouts of Skype (or similar) logs, etc.[128]

Whilst applicants were free to choose what type of documents to submit, it appeared that the option of not providing any such evidence at all was not permitted by the Home Office. In particular, it was stated that the applicant 'must' send the relevant evidence as specified in section 20 of the application form and the guidance notes.[129] The wording made it clear that a marriage certificate was not accepted as the only proof of the relationship, and it needed to be supported by other details. Furthermore, it followed that it was compulsory to answer all the relevant questions in the application form,[130] an apparent reference to the relevant provision in the EEA Regulations.[131]

128 Ibid.

129 EEA residence card application form, 2.

130 In particular, applicants were asked to '[c]omplete all relevant sections of the form as directed'. Ibid.

131 EEA Regulations 2016, regs 21(2)(b) and 21(4).

Similarly, as with the application form for an EEA family permit, the Home Office requirements were clearly disproportionate and went well beyond what is permitted under the Citizenship Directive. This not only amounted to systematic checks explicitly prohibited both under EU law and the EEA Regulations, but also breached EU law concerning the issues of burden of proof and the presumption of innocence. Furthermore, by subjecting all applicants to scrutiny, the government was deeply intruding into their private matters. In doing so, it placed a strong emphasis on cohabitation, although CJEU case law rightly permits couples to arrange their marital life as they wish and even live with other partners, as long as a decree absolute is not issued. This raised the question of whether those not cohabiting faced an increased risk of being treated as suspicious, which, in turn, reduced their chances of a positive outcome.

Another Home Office guidance set out various stages the caseworkers needed to follow when assessing applications from direct family members of EU citizens.[132] With respect to spouses, it was first required to assess evidence of their identity and nationality, and second, consider the proof of their relationship (a marriage certificate).[133] Importantly, the caseworker was allowed to proceed with assessing the status of the EU spouse only after making sure that the marriage was legally valid and not one of convenience.[134] If any suspicions arose, the Home Office was open to investigating individual cases.[135] Interestingly, the guidance further referred to the 'sole purpose' definition of marriages of convenience as provided in the Citizenship Directive, as well as specified that the burden of proof rested with the Home Office.[136] This was commendable, yet also confusing, given that applicants were required to supply extensive evidence of the relationship in advance and that the EEA Regulations used a broader definition instead.

A similar application form needed to be completed if a TCN family member was seeking to apply for a permanent residence card. The relevant form included the same questions about the quality of the relationship as the residence card application form.[137] It followed that TCN spouses of EU citizens

132 Home Office, 'Free Movement Rights: Direct Family Members of European Economic Area (EEA) Nationals' (Version 9.0).

133 Ibid, 9–10.

134 Ibid, 11.

135 Ibid, 37.

136 Ibid.

137 UKVI, 'Application for a document certifying permanent residence or permanent residence card under the EEA Regulations' (EEA(PR), Version 03/2019) (EEA permanent residence application form), s 11.

risked being accused of entering into a marriage of convenience at any stage of their residence, irrespective of whether their marriage had been previously investigated and found not to be one of convenience. In other words, one could never be confident that the state would not question the nature of their marriage, even if it was contracted years ago.

In this context, the position of those who got married in the UK deserved closer consideration, in particular with regards to unlawful detention and the removal of TCN spouses. As noted above, a marriage to an EU citizen provided someone with no valid leave in the UK an automatic right of residence. This was rightly confirmed in the Home Office guidance to its enforcement staff. The guidance stated that 'where there is evidence that a non-EEA immigration offender is now genuinely married to an EEA national, you must not serve enforcement papers' on them, regardless of whether they had applied for an EEA residence card.[138] This, however, was not always understood by Home Office officers who sought to detain and remove the TCN partner even after the marriage had been contracted, particularly where they were yet to submit an application for a residence card. As pointed out by immigration practitioners, Home Office officers wrongly believed that the status of the TCN spouse was not confirmed until they had been granted a residence card. In some cases, non-EU spouses were discovered in raids on properties and subsequently detained.[139] There were also cases where yet unmarried non-EU nationals, detained because of their irregular status, were escorted to the register office and brought back to the detention centre after marriage. These types of cases have been successfully challenged in courts, with plaintiffs able to win damages for unlawful detention.[140]

3.5 *Non-suspensive Appeal Rights*

A Home Office decision that the marriage to an EU citizen was one of convenience bore serious repercussions for their non-EU spouses. In this case, they were not considered family members for the purposes of the EEA Regulations, and their applications for a residence card or an EEA family permit were to be refused.[141] For those applying for a residence card, this would normally be

138 Home Office, 'Marriage Investigations' (Version 3.0), 24.

139 See for instance, ILPA, 'Comments for the Chief Inspector of Borders and Immigration. Review of Sham Marriages (n 65).

140 Interview with David Tang (n 47).

141 See Home Office,, 'Marriage Investigations' (Version 3.0), 23; Home Office, 'EEA Family Permits: Guidance for Entry Clearance Officers' (Version 2.0), 10.

followed by the curtailment of the existing leave to remain[142] (if any) and a standard non-EEA removal procedure.[143] In case an EEA family permit, residence card or a permanent residence card had already been issued, e.g., where the Home Office had previously recognised an EU right based on the marriage but later found it to be of convenience, the person could be removed under an administrative procedure foreseen by the EEA Regulations 2016. The latter provided for removal if the relevant person did not have or ceased to have a right to reside under EU law,[144] which automatically invalidated the existing residence card. In addition, they could become subject to a criminal investigation.[145]

One of the major issues with the Home Office decision on the nature of the marriage is that an appeal against the refusal of an EEA residence card, in most cases, would not have suspended removal. In 2015, the Upper Tribunal delivered a rather puzzling judgment in *Bilal Ahmed*[146] which concerned a Pakistan national in the UK on a student visa who was married to a Romanian national. After interviewing both parties separately, the Home Office concluded that the marriage was one of convenience and subsequently refused the TCN spouse's application for a residence card. By this point, his student leave had already expired, and he was detained and served with a removal notice. The applicant sought judicial review of the removal decision, as well as appealed against the refusal of an EEA residence card.

The main issue in the proceedings was whether the right of appeal against the EEA decision was suspensive of removal. With this respect, the UT argued that, since the executive found the marriage to be of convenience, the TCN party was not a 'spouse' for the purposes of the EEA Regulations and thus fell outside the protection of EU law. Consequently, according to the court, he was not entitled to an in-country appeal right even if it was provided by Article 31 of the Citizenship Directive.[147] In the view of the UT, the latter was not the case, for the respective article does not expressly preclude the Member State from removing the person concerned while their appeal is pending but only permits the latter to submit a 'defence in person', subject to public policy exceptions.[148]

142 Similarly as with those whose intended marriage is found to be a sham prior to its conclusion, the Home Office caseworker could curtail the non-EU national's leave under paragraph 323(i) of the Immigration Rules.

143 Under s 10 of the Immigration and Asylum Act 1999.

144 EEA Regulations 2016, reg 23(6)(a).

145 See Home Office, 'Marriage Investigations' (Version 3.0), 16.

146 *Ahmed, R (On the Application Of) v SSHD* IJR [2015] UKUT 436 (IAC).

147 Ibid paras 28–29.

148 Art 31 reads: '(1)The persons concerned shall have access to judicial and, where appropriate, administrative redress procedures in the host Member State to appeal against or seek review of any decision taken against them on the grounds of public policy, public security

Yet even if it did provide suspensive appeal rights, the applicant would not be considered a family member and therefore excluded from its scope. As the UT put it, Article 31 'has nothing whatsoever to say about a person who is not being expelled as a Union citizen or family member but who is appealing a decision that he or she is not such a family member'[149] and '[t]here is no principle of law, whether purely domestic or European, that confers a right on an individual to remain within a jurisdiction, regardless of his or her status, in order to pursue an immigration appeal'.[150]

This reasoning is obviously problematic. First, if the UT had any doubt as to the existence of general in-country appeal rights under Article 31, the correct way forward would be to refer the case to the CJEU for clarification. Secondly, and most importantly, the UT decision essentially meant that a person who was refused a residence card was not considered a spouse for the purposes of the Directive. As Elspeth Guild reasonably argued, by this logic, non-EU nationals should not have had appeal rights provided by the Directive, at all.[151] This was absurd, particularly given that non-EU nationals who have been successful in obtaining residence cards would rarely need an appeal. Further, by withdrawing EU procedural rights from a non-EU national solely because their marriage was believed to be one of convenience, the UT wrongly shifted the burden of proof to the individual concerned, although their marriage was perfectly valid under UK family law.[152] In this light, it was even more regrettable that the UT decision was later upheld by the Court of Appeal. In its ruling, the Court confirmed that, if a non-EU national did not have leave to remain, they could be removed pending their appeal against the refusal of a residence card.[153]

---

or public health', and '(4) Member States may exclude the individual concerned from their territory pending the redress procedure, but they may not prevent the individual from submitting his/her defence in person, except when his/her appearance may cause serious troubles to public policy or public security or when the appeal or judicial review concerns a denial of entry to the territory'.

149 *Ahmed* (n 146), para 28.

150 Ibid para 26.

151 This, however, was not the case, since they could still appeal against a negative EEA decision, which contradicts the logic adopted in *Bilal Ahmed* and thus made it even more puzzling. Elspeth Guild, 'Reflecting EU Law Faithfully? R (Bilal Ahmed) v SSHD IJR [2015] UKUT 00436 (IAC)' (*Free Movement*, 14.09.2015) <https://www.freemovement.org.uk/reflecting-eu-law-faithfully-r-bilal-ahmed-v-sshd-ijr-2015-ukut-00436-iac/> accessed 12 April 2024.

152 Ibid.

153 *Ahmed, R (On the Application Of) v SSHD* [2016] EWCA Civ 303, [2016] Imm AR 869.

3.6 *Deporting EU Citizen Spouses: Public Policy Test*

An accusation of being involved in a marriage of convenience could have serious implications not only for non-EU nationals but also for EU citizens who exercised their Treaty rights. Under regulation 23(6)(b) of the EEA Regulations 2016, an EU citizen or their family member could be removed from the UK *inter alia* on public policy grounds. The relevant Home Office guidance confirmed that it also covered persons 'involved' in a marriage of convenience: these were 'subject to a public policy decision' and could 'be removed from the UK by means of a time-limited deportation'.[154] Removal on these grounds was also foreseen for non-EU nationals who, in spite of being 'genuine family members' of EU citizens, facilitated marriages of convenience for someone else.[155] This also followed from paragraph 6(a) of schedule 1 of the Regulations which stated that it was consistent with public policy requirements to refuse, terminate or withdraw EU citizens' rights in cases of 'entering, attempting to enter or assisting another person to enter or to attempt to enter, a marriage, civil partnership or durable partnership of convenience'. According to regulation 23(8), a person deported from the UK on the grounds of public policy or public security would be prohibited from entering the UK until the revocation of the deportation order or the period specified in the order. The relevant Home Office guidance indicatively provided that 'facilitating immigration abuse where there is no criminal conviction, for example, marriages of convenience' could result in a re-entry ban of three years.[156]

The public policy approach towards this group[157] raised serious concerns. First, there was no definition of public policy neither in the Citizenship Directive, nor the EEA Regulations. The position of the UK was that, since there was no uniform scale of public policy values imposed on Member States,

154 Home Office, 'Marriage Investigations' (Version 3.0), 25. An 'involvement' was broadly understood here as entering, or attempting to enter a marriage of convenience, or facilitating it.

155 Ibid, 6.

156 Home Office, 'EEA Decisions on Grounds of Public Policy and Public Security' (Version 3.0, 14.12.2017), 37.

157 Under regulation 19(3)(c) of an earlier version of the EEA Regulations (Immigration (European Economic Area) Regulations 2006, SI 2006/1003), an EU citizen found to be involved in a marriage of convenience could be removed from the UK via an administrative removal procedure on the grounds of abuse of rights. This provision contradicted the Citizenship Directive. Unlike non-EU nationals, EU citizens enjoy an independent right of residence and do not obtain any advantage by marrying someone. It can thus be argued that in this situation, no abuse of free movement rights could occur on the part of an EU citizen.

the government enjoyed considerable discretion to define the relevant standards.[158] As noted in Chapter 1, the Directive nonetheless provides several safeguards that need to be observed when deporting EU citizens on public policy grounds. The relevant principles were found in regulation 27(5) and schedule 1 of the Regulations. The former *inter alia* provided that (1) the decision had to comply with the principle of proportionality and (2) the personal conduct of the person had to represent a genuine, present and sufficiently serious threat affecting one of the fundamental interests of society. Under paragraph 7(a) of schedule 1, 'preventing unlawful immigration and abuse of the immigration laws' was considered one of the fundamental interests of society in the UK. The relevant Home Office guidelines further specified that this interest included marriages of convenience, human trafficking, and facilitating the circumvention of the immigration system.[159]

This evaluation, however, was highly subjective and therefore speculative: it was not known how many UK residents would have agreed that preventing marriages of convenience was fundamental. When considering whether an individual posed a threat, the Home Office could take into account such factors as the nature of the offence, the length of sentence and rehabilitative efforts. Yet, according to the guidelines, a public policy or security decision could be made even if the person has not received any criminal convictions 'if there [was] sufficient, corroborated law enforcement evidence to underpin a decision'.[160]

Although a criminal investigation was normally required for the public policy test to apply, EU citizens could be deported under regulation 23(6)(b) even in the absence of any referral for prosecution.[161] Whilst any such decision

158 EEA Regulations 2016, sch 1, para 1.

159 Home Office, 'EEA Decisions on Grounds of Public Policy and Public Security' (Version 3.0), 19.

160 Ibid, 22.

161 In the UK, there is no specific criminal offence of entering into a sham marriage or marriage of convenience but there are other offences for which a person could be prosecuted for involvement in one. Parties to sham marriages/marriages of convenience can be charged with conspiracy under s 1(1) of the Criminal Law Act 1977, whilst those organising such marriages can be charged with assisting unlawful immigration (known as facilitation) under s 25 of the Immigration Act 1971. For more details, see Home Office, 'Criminal Investigations: Sham Marriage' (Version 2.0, 12.11.2019). Whilst a detailed analysis of these provisions falls outside the scope of this book, it should be noted that EEA caseworkers would refuse an application for a residence card if there had been a criminal investigation into a marriage that resulted in a conviction for any of the parties involved. See Home Office, 'Free Movement Rights: Direct Family Members of European Economic Area (EEA) Nationals' (Version 9.0), 38.

would have had to comply with the principle of proportionality, EU citizens could in principle be deprived of their Treaty rights on the sole basis that some Home Office officers believed that their marriage was one of convenience.

Another point of concern was that an appeal against the decision to deport an EU citizen on public policy grounds could only be exercised from outside the UK. As in the case of non-EU nationals, regulation 37 applied.[162] To cover the express provision under Article 31(4) of the Citizenship Directive, the EEA Regulations only permitted their temporary admission in the UK if they wished to make submissions before the tribunal in person.[163] As argued in Section 3.5 above, such an approach was highly problematic. By depriving a person of a suspensive right of appeal solely because the Home Office believed their marriage was one of convenience, the Regulations wrongly shifted the burden of proof to the EU citizen. Taken together, any EU citizen who wished to live with their TCN partner in the UK risked being deported from the country for up to three years with no right to challenge the decision whilst still in the country. This was not only a serious interference with the right to free movement, but could also deter EU citizens from marrying their TCN partners in the UK, and consequently, prompt them to move elsewhere.

3.7 *Marriages of Convenience and UK Family Law*

Another aspect worth closer inspection is the link between the concepts of a 'sham marriage' and 'marriage of convenience' and UK family law. As briefly noted above, marriages not involving non-EU nationals were (and continue to be after Brexit) subject to much less scrutiny by the British state. For a marriage to be valid, both parties must have reached a certain age, not be related within prohibited degrees, not be lawfully married to someone else, and comply with marriage formalities.[164]

In contrast to marriages involving third-country nationals, the nature of marriages between persons who are not subject to immigration control is never examined – neither before, nor after the ceremony. Indeed, there is no concept of a 'sham marriage' or 'marriage of convenience' in other areas of UK domestic law. In this respect, the British state obviously attributes to immigration control, much higher value than other domains where a marriage may

162 Provided that the Home Office had certified that removal pending the final determination of an appeal would not be unlawful under s 6 of the Human Rights Act 1998.

163 EEA Regulations 2016, reg 41.

164 The full marriage procedure is set out in the Marriage Act 1949 (for England and Wales), the Marriage (Scotland) Act 1977 and the Marriage (Northern Ireland) Order 2003.

equally confer on couples a number of advantages, such as inheritance[165] or tax law.[166] Although, in theory, some couples may also enter into marriage solely to obtain a certain benefit (for example, to claim a marriage allowance), they will only need to provide a marriage certificate to prove their status.

Moreover, the refusal of the Home Office or the courts to recognise a perceived marriage of convenience for immigration purposes does not result in its annulment in family law. Under the Matrimonial Causes Act 1973, governing marriages in England and Wales, a marriage may be declared null and void if either it was not validly contracted from the start (a so-called 'void' marriage)[167] or it possesses some 'flaws', although it was validly contracted ('voidable' marriage).[168] In the first case, the annulment of a marriage may be demanded by any interested party, including the state, whilst in the second scenario, this option is exclusively reserved for the parties to the marriage. Provided that marriages of convenience or sham marriages are normally understood as validly contracted, the state has no legal grounds to ask for their annulment. The validity of a marriage entered into for immigration purposes has also been explicitly confirmed in domestic case law.[169]

This creates an odd situation where marriages unaccepted for residence purposes continue to be recognised in other domains of British family law, with all the legal responsibilities emanating from them. For instance, a married partner with higher income may have a legal duty to support the other financially, and under certain conditions, continue to do so after divorce.[170] In

165 For instance, under the Inheritance (Provision for Family and Dependants) Act 1975, if one of the spouses dies without making a will, the surviving spouse inherits all or some of their estate. By contrast, the unmarried partner may not automatically inherit, unless the property was jointly owned. A broader discussion of the distinction between the rights of married and unmarried couples is outside the scope of this study.

166 Chs 3 and 3A of the Income Tax Act 2007 provide tax relief for married couples and civil partners.

167 Matrimonial Causes Act 1973, s 11.

168 Under the Act, a marriage may be rendered 'voidable' on the following grounds: it has not been consummated (does not apply to same-sex couples); either of the parties has not validly consented to it; either of the parties, at the time of the ceremony, suffered from a mental disorder that rendered them 'unfit' for marriage or a communicable venereal disease; the wife, at the time of the marriage, was pregnant by a person other than her husband; one party married without knowing that the other party had legally acquired a different gender from the one assigned at birth; or either party objects to the other party changing their gender during the marriage. Ibid, s 12. For the relevant procedures in Scotland and Northern Ireland, see the Marriage (Scotland) Act 1977 and the Matrimonial Causes (Northern Ireland) Order 1978, respectively.

169 *Vervaeke v Smith* [1983] 1 AC 145 (HL), paras 145, 152.

170 For England and Wales, see pt II of the Matrimonial Causes Act 1973.

this context, by perceiving foreigners primarily as dishonest individuals aiming to regularise their stay in the UK by all possible means, the British authorities tend to ignore the fact that marriage is a serious commitment which is normally entered into all but lightly – particularly given that even under EU law, one needs to stay married for at least three years before acquiring an independent right of residence in the UK.

4 Conclusion

Over the pre-Brexit period, the excessive preoccupation of the UK authorities over the perceived abuse of EU law via marriages of convenience has resulted in the adoption of several legislative measures, disproportionally and arbitrarily targeting couples involving mobile EU citizens.

First, this chapter has demonstrated that human rights were too weak to protect yet unmarried couples from the hostile policies of the UK government. Under the Citizenship Directive, spouses of EU citizens automatically acquire the right of residence, irrespective of their previous immigration status. To prevent allegedly dishonest non-EU nationals from benefitting from more generous Treaty rights, the UK introduced systematic checks of all intended marriages involving persons without indefinite leave. The relevant rules went well beyond targeting couples whose prospective marriage would fit the legal definition of a 'sham marriage'. Although formally, one was allowed to register marriage even if it is found to be a sham, in practice, many couples in a close relationship could face numerous hurdles depriving them of this fundamental right. Now, every couple not exempt from the scheme could be required to endure another 70 days of anxiety and undergo an intrusive investigation with an unknown outcome.

The respective rules were highly confusing and provided little legal certainty for EU citizens (or UK nationals) and their TCN partners, particularly where the latter had a short-term or irregular status in the UK. First, the couple could be denied the right to marry for non-compliance with the investigation for purely bureaucratic reasons unrelated to the nature of their marriage, which potentially amounts to a breach of the ECHR. Second, their prospective marriage could be erroneously considered a sham, a decision which is likely to lead to the couple's separation. Third, and most importantly, by giving a marriage notice, the foreigner automatically came to the attention of the Home Office: this was particularly risky for those irregularly present in the UK who could be removed at any point before their marriage was registered. Therefore, instead of respecting their partner's choice and protecting the family life of

UK-based EU citizens, the government sought to disrupt their families, prompting the couples to live in legal limbo or even relocate, which, in turn, seriously obstructed the free movement rights of EU citizens.

In contrast to UK domestic law, the Citizenship Directive prohibits systematic checks of marriages involving EU citizens. However, even at the post-marriage stage, the UK measures targeting perceived marriages of convenience went well beyond what was permitted under the Citizenship Directive and CJEU case law. First, to obtain an EEA family permit or residence card, the TCN spouses were required to submit excessive details about their relationship, although they did not need to do so under EU law. Yet, the refusal to grant the non-EU national a residence card bore serious implications for the couple, particularly since an appeal against the relevant decision would not have suspended removal. This was further aggravated by the fact that an EU citizen, allegedly involved in a marriage of convenience, could be deported from the UK on public policy grounds, an arbitrary and unprecedented measure that equally violated EU law.

One of the major issues with the UK approach is the co-existence of two different legal terms ('marriages of convenience' and 'sham marriage') and various definitions of the same concept. This is highly problematic in terms of clarity and legal certainty. As will be shown in Chapter 10, the problems created by this approach are best evident in interpretations of the concept by UK judges which have led to extremely perplexing outcomes. The second important paradox is that the terms 'sham marriage' and 'marriages of convenience' are only used in the domains of immigration and free movement[171] law; consequently, a marriage disqualified for residence purposes as a 'sham' or 'one of convenience', continues to be valid under UK family law with all the corresponding rights and responsibilities.

171 After the end of the transition period, the term 'marriages of convenience' continues to be used in the context of the Withdrawal Agreement, see Chapter 8.

CHAPTER 8

Marriage Controls after Brexit

1 Introduction

Chapter 7 has shown that, during the pre-Brexit period, British marriage control practices targeted a much broader group of couples than those whose circumstances could fit the narrow definition of a marriage of convenience under the Citizenship Directive.[1] It was demonstrated that such measures could lead to the disruption of families and discourage EU citizens from exercising their free movement rights.

This chapter focuses on the relevant changes in the UK after Brexit. Following the official end of its membership, the UK entered a transition period which ended on 31 December 2020. In March 2019, the UK opened the so-called EU Settlement Scheme, requiring all EU citizens and their family members who resided in the country by 31 December 2020 to register in order to continue living there. The chapter looks at these developments in more detail by focusing, specifically, on the position of family members of EU citizens in the UK after Brexit, the government's approach to the perceived marriages of convenience, as well as procedures following a marriage of convenience determination, applicable to different groups depending on the EU citizen's status after the cut-off date.

2 Position of EU Citizens in the UK after Brexit

In March 2017, nine months after the Brexit referendum held on 23 June 2016, the UK formally notified the European Council of its decision to leave the EU. This officially triggered the withdrawal procedure prescribed in Article 50 of the Lisbon Treaty. The latter provided that the leaving Member State and the EU should agree on the departure terms within two years after the notification date unless an extension was negotiated. In October 2019, following a slow and

1 Directive 2004/38/EC of the European Parliament and of the Council of 29 April 2004 on the right of citizens of the Union and their family members to move and reside freely within the territory of the Member States amending Regulation (EEC) No 1612/68 and repealing Directives 64/221/EEC, 68/360/EEC, 72/194/EEC, 73/148/EEC, 75/34/EEC, 75/35/EEC, 90/364/EEC, 90/365/EEC, and 93/96/EEC [2004] OJ L158/77 (Citizenship Directive).

 | DOI:10.1163/9789004499263_010

turbulent negotiation process and several extensions, the contracting parties approved a revised version of the EU-UK Withdrawal Agreement, a legally binding instrument of international law establishing the conditions for the UK's exit from the Union. The Agreement was accompanied by a non-binding Political Declaration setting out the framework for the future relationship between the UK and the EU.[2] On 23 January 2020, the UK Parliament passed the Withdrawal Agreement Act incorporating the Withdrawal Agreement into UK law.[3] This was done because the UK is a 'dualist state', which gives effect to an international treaty only after it is incorporated into its domestic law. Following this, the Agreement was signed by the UK and EU representatives, approved by the European Parliament, and ratified by the EU Council. Both the Agreement and the Act entered into force at 11 p.m. GMT on 31 January 2020, marking the official end of the British membership in the EU.

The Withdrawal Agreement covers a number of areas, including citizens' rights, the financial settlement, border arrangements and judicial and administrative procedures. To allow the parties time to negotiate a new trade deal, the Agreement provided for a transition period running from Brexit day to 31 December 2020. During that time, free movement continued to operate as normal, the UK remained in both the single market and the customs union, and the CJEU continued to have jurisdiction over the UK.

The end of the transition period on 31 December 2020 has effectively divided EU citizens (and UK nationals) into two groups who are now covered by separate sets of rights. The first group is comprised of nearly four million EU citizens who were resident in the UK[4] and approximately one million British

---

2 Political Declaration setting out the framework for the future relationship between the European Union and the United Kingdom (TF50 (2019) 65 – Commission to EU 27).

3 European Union (Withdrawal) Act 2018 (WA 2018) as amended by European Union (Withdrawal Agreement) Act 2020. The Act also implements the Agreement on arrangements between Iceland, the Principality of Liechtenstein, the Kingdom of Norway, and the United Kingdom of Great Britain and Northern Ireland following the withdrawal of the United Kingdom from the European Union, the EEA Agreement, and other agreements applicable between the United Kingdom and the EEA EFTA States by virtue of the United Kingdom's membership of the European Union [MS No.1/2020] (EEA EFTA Separation Agreement) and Agreement between the United Kingdom of Great Britain and Northern Ireland and the Swiss Confederation on citizens' rights following the withdrawal of the United Kingdom from the European Union and the free movement of persons agreement [CS Switzerland No.5/2019] (UK-Swiss Citizens' Rights Agreement) which protect the rights of citizens between the UK and Norway, Iceland, and Liechtenstein and the UK and Switzerland, respectively.

4 For statistics, see Mihnea Cuibus, 'EU Migration to and from UK' (*Migration Observatory: COMPAS, University of Oxford* 20.11.2023) <https://migrationobservatory.ox.ac.uk/wp-content/uploads/2020/10/MigObs-Briefing-EU-migration-to-and-from-the-UK.pdf> accessed 13 April 2024.

nationals who were living in the EU by this date.[5] The second group, on the other hand, is made up of those who arrived in the UK (or an EU Member State, respectively) after the deadline.

Those belonging to the first group have retained residence rights on the same terms as under the Citizenship Directive, provided that the individual already lived in or moved to the respective state before the end of the transition period[6] (this group is further referred to in this chapter as eligible EU citizens or UK nationals). EU citizens, UK nationals, and their family members[7] who have lived in the host state for a continuous period of five years obtain the right of permanent residence. The principle of non-discrimination continues to apply to all the aforementioned categories.[8]

In the UK, the residence guarantees to eligible EU citizens and their family members were not provided automatically. All beneficiaries of the Withdrawal Agreement (and correspondingly the Withdrawal Agreement Act) were (and in some cases still are)[9] required to apply for a new status online under the so-called EU Settlement Scheme, introduced as an Appendix EU to the UK Immigration Rules. Applications were accepted for a further six months after the end of the transition period, with 30 June 2021 set out as the final deadline. Under the scheme, those who could prove they had lived in the UK for five continuous years obtained the so-called 'settled status', or formally, indefinite leave to remain (ILR). Conversely, those who relocated to the UK prior to 31 December 2020 but had not yet reached the five-year residence threshold were granted 'pre-settled status' or limited leave to remain (LLR) for five years. Once the five-year continuous residence requirement is satisfied, the 'pre-settled status' can be upgraded to the 'settled status'.[10]

Although the holders of pre-settled or settled status continue to enjoy the core rights guaranteed under the Citizenship Directive, the new scheme has effectively transformed EU citizens into foreigners who need to comply with certain conditions to retain residence rights. One of the key differences between the EU citizenship and the settlement scheme is that the 'settled

5 'How Many British Citizens Live in the EU?' (*UK in a Changing Europe*, 21.09.2020) <https://ukandeu.ac.uk/the-facts/how-many-british-citizens-live-in-the-eu/> accessed 13 April 2024.

6 Although British nationals in the EU lose their ability to move freely between the Member States.

7 For more details on who qualifies as a family member for these purposes, see Section 3 below.

8 WA 2018, art 12.

9 See Section 3 below for more details.

10 From September 2023, people with a pre-settled status have their status automatically extended by two years before it expires if they have not obtained a settled status. Statement of Changes to the Immigration Rules HC 1496 (17 July 2023).

status' is lost after being outside the UK for over five years in a row, whereas an upgrade from the pre-settled status becomes impossible after spending two continuous years abroad. Those who do not meet residence requirements are expected to be excluded from the scheme and fall within the domain of UK immigration laws. The residence requirements hardly bear any resemblance to EU free movement law which provides for the possibility of freely leaving, moving to, or returning to any EU Member State at any time.

Further, as a general rule, the UK is no longer obliged to comply with any CJEU judgments handed down on or after 31 December 2020 unless the case is brought before the Court prior to this date.[11] When interpreting the Agreement provisions, the UK courts may nonetheless have regard to the subsequent CJEU jurisprudence (or any other EU legislation) if they wish to do so.[12] Further, British courts will be able to request from the CJEU preliminary rulings on the position of EU citizens resident in the UK for a further eight years from the end of the transition period. In such cases, CJEU decisions will be binding upon the UK.[13]

Notwithstanding their obvious limitations, however, the rights reserved for EU citizens who moved to the UK before 31 December 2020 are much more generous than those provided to nationals of EU Member States arriving in the UK after the deadline. The position of EU citizens and UK nationals who relocate to the host state after 31 December 2020 is not covered by the Agreement; the relevant rules are determined by the domestic immigration laws of the UK and EU Member States. The cut-off date on 31 December 2020 marked the revocation of the EEA Regulations 2016[14] and the end of free movement in the UK. In January 2021, the UK introduced a so-called 'points-based immigration system' under which EU citizens are now treated equally to third-country nationals and selected based on their skills, qualifications, and labour market needs.[15]

11 Withdrawal Agreement, art 86(1).

12 Ibid, art 4(5).

13 Ibid, art 158. Other EU Member States will also be able to refer to the CJEU cases concerning the position of UK nationals resident in their territory.

14 Immigration (European Economic Area) Regulations 2016, SI 2016/1052 (EEA Regulations 2016).

15 See CJ McKinney, Melanie Gower and Georgina Sturge, 'The UK's New Points-Based Immigration System' (House of Commons Library Research Briefing CBP-8911, 27.09.2022) <https://researchbriefings.files.parliament.uk/documents/CBP-8911/CBP-8911.pdf> accessed 13 April 2024.

In late 2023, the UK government announced a five-point plan aiming to significantly reduce net migration. Among other things, the changes include raising the minimum salary threshold for foreign skilled workers' visas. See 'Government Announces Major Changes to Legal Immigration, Raising Minimum Skilled Worker Salary and Income

3 Family Members of EU Citizens in the UK

The end of the transition period has divided EU citizens into several groups, not only with respect to their residence rights in the UK but also to their ability to live there with their family members. As noted in Section 2 above, according to the terms of the Withdrawal Agreement (and correspondingly the Withdrawal Agreement Act), EU citizens or UK nationals resident in the respective state before the cut-off date can continue living there on the same terms as under the Citizenship Directive. When it comes to their right to family reunion, however, the respective individuals *de facto* enjoy less protection than was previously afforded to them by virtue of EU free movement law. In this context, one can distinguish two sub-groups of EU citizens who have retained residence rights in the UK yet whose rights to family reunion differ, depending on when the relationship was formed.

The first and most privileged group of eligible EU citizens (or UK nationals) in this respect are those whose family members (as defined under Articles 2 and 3(2) of the Citizenship Directive) had already lived in the host state on the basis of the Treaty provisions by 31 December 2020 and continue to do so thereafter. Under the Withdrawal Agreement, this category of EU citizens retains the right to live with their close ones on the same conditions as under the Citizenship Directive, whereby their family members retain the same level of residence-related rights. In other words, if an Indian national spouse of a mobile EU citizen was already residing in the UK under the EEA Regulations 2016 before the cut-off date, the couple could continue living in the UK on the same terms. To continue enjoying these rights, the eligible family members equally needed to apply for the Settlement Scheme and acquire either a settled or pre-settled status. Residence cards previously granted to family members of EU citizens under the EEA Regulations 2016 have ceased to be valid.

Family members who did not reside in the relevant country before the cut-off date still have a right to join the eligible principal on the condition that their relationship began (e.g., marriage or civil partnership was registered) before 31 December 2020 and still continues to exist.[16] These criteria should also be met in order for the host state to facilitate the admission of durable partners after

Requirement for Spouse Visa to Over £38K' (*EIN*, 04.12.2023) <https://www.ein.org.uk/news/government-announces-major-changes-work-related-immigration-raising-minimum-skilled-worker> accessed 13 April 2024.

16 The only exception are Swiss citizens who are eligible for family reunion with their spouses or civil partners if the marriage or civil partnership was registered by 31 December 2025. UK-Swiss Citizens' Rights Agreement, art 10(1)(e)(iv).

the cut-off date. Family members joining the principal from abroad are asked to apply for a newly introduced EU Settlement Scheme family permit (EUSS family permit), which is valid for six months and, among other things, allows its holder to work in the UK. Should a family member wish to stay in the UK for a longer period, they need to apply to the Settlement Scheme after arrival.[17]

To sum up, the couple can enjoy the right to family reunion on the same terms as under EU free movement law only if a) the EU citizen principal relocated to the UK before the end of the transition period and b) the relevant relationship began before this date. Settled- or pre-settled status holders who establish a relationship with their spouse, civil, or unmarried partner after the deadline no longer benefit from the rights to family reunion guaranteed under the Withdrawal Agreement and the EU Settlement Scheme. To enjoy family life with their close ones in the UK, this group needs to comply with the restrictive British national family reunification provisions described in Section 6 of Chapter 6 above, such as the minimum income requirement and the requirement to prove that their relationship is 'genuine and subsisting'. Moreover, in late 2023, the UK Home Secretary announced the plan to raise the minimum income requirement for family reunification from £18,600 to £29,000 in spring 2024 and £38,700 in 2025.[18]

In this respect, individuals belonging to this category have been placed in the same position as EU citizens and UK nationals who move to the host state after 31 December 2020 and are treated as full-fledged foreigners. Since the latter are excluded from the scope of the Agreement, their rights to live with their family members are determined by the domestic immigration laws of the UK and EU Member States and, where applicable, EU law on third-country nationals, such as the Family Reunification[19] or Long Term Residents[20] Directives.

Returning to EU citizens who were residents in the UK before the deadline, one group that was particularly disadvantaged by the new system was unmarried couples involving EU citizens and non-EU nationals with a short-term or irregular residence status. To fall within the scope of the Agreement and EU Settlement Scheme, a spouse or a civil partner of an EU citizen needed to have

17 EEA nationals and holders of a valid UK-issued biometric residence card joining the principal can directly apply to the EU Settlement Scheme from outside the UK.

18 Home Office, 'Net Migration Measures – Further Detail' (Factsheet on net Migration Measures, 21.12.2023) <https://www.gov.uk/government/news/fact-sheet-on-net-migration-measures-further-detail> accessed 13 April 2024.

19 Council Directive 2003/86/EC of 22 September 2003 on the right to family reunification [2003] OJ L251/12 (Family Reunification Directive).

20 Council Directive 2003/109/EC of 25 November 2003 concerning the status of third-country nationals who are long-term residents [2004] OJ L16/44.

their marriage or civil partnership registered before the cut-off date; it is the day the marriage or civil partnership was entered into that is considered the start of the relationship under the scheme. Durable partners could be granted residence rights under the scheme only if the parties had already been living together for at least two years before the deadline or could show 'other significant evidence of the durable relationship' that existed before the cut-off date. According to the relevant Home Office guidance, the latter may include evidence of joint responsibility for a child, evidence of shared financial responsibilities, or evidence of regular communication and visits while living apart alongside definite plans concerning living together in the UK.[21]

For those whose marriage or civil partnership was registered only after 31 December 2020, the only possibility to qualify for the scheme was to provide extensive evidence of a durable relationship that existed before this date. If the non-EU national unmarried partner was living in the UK before the deadline and wished to apply for the scheme, they either needed to already have been granted an EEA residence card or a family permit as a durable partner of an EU citizen or apply for one before the cut-off date. In addition, they needed to present proof that they had a legal residence status in the country. These requirements were difficult or even impossible to satisfy – particularly where the foreign-national partner lived in the UK irregularly. An alternative option would be to leave the UK for six months and apply for an EUSS Family Permit as a joining family member of their EU citizen sponsor – on the precondition that their relationship could still be considered durable before the cut-off date. The latter option, however, would not be available for many, particularly those unable to move to any other country or whose relationship had only started recently. For such couples, marrying before the deadline was the only opportunity to bring themselves within the scope of the Withdrawal Agreement and secure their residence rights in the UK without having to worry about possible separation. Many, however, might not have been able to marry due to the hurdles created by the 'referral and investigation scheme' or the suspension of marriage registration because of the coronavirus outbreak.[22] Such difficulties are reflected in a line of recent Upper Tribunal decisions, which concerned

21 Home Office, 'EU Settlement Scheme: EU, Other EEA and Swiss Citizens and Their Family Members' (Version 23.0, 4 April 2024), 20. For an overview, see also, Nath Gbikpi, 'Who Qualifies as a "Durable Partner" under the EU Settlement Scheme?' (*Free Movement*, 18.08.2023) <https://freemovement.org.uk/who-qualifies-as-a-durable-partner-under-the-eu-settlement-scheme/> accessed 13 April 2024.

22 See Rebecca Probert and Stephanie Pywell, 'Love in the Time of Covid-19: A Case-Study of the Complex Laws Governing Weddings' (2021) 41 *Legal Studies* 676.

unsuccessful applications under the EUSS scheme as durable partners. In the relevant cases, the couples met or began a relationship before the cut-off date yet only managed to register their marriage after 31 December 2020 due to COVID-19-based restrictions.[23]

Another important change is that after the cut-off date, the new rules apply not only to non-EU nationals but also to EU citizen family members who could previously enjoy residence rights in their own capacity. If, after 31 December 2020, a Dutch national with a settled status in the UK marries another Dutch national who lives in the Netherlands, the couple will need to comply with UK domestic family reunification rules. In other words, to bring their spouse from the Netherlands to the UK, the British-resident party will need to satisfy the minimum income requirement and, among other things, show that their relationship is 'genuine and subsisting'. In addition, the refusal of the UK authorities to admit family members is no longer subject to appeal unless an Article 8 ECHR-based claim is lodged as part of the application.

On a broader level, the UK's continuous demands to narrow down the family reunion rights of EU citizens have ultimately been satisfied. It must be recalled that the 2016 UK-EU deal, created to persuade the UK not to leave the EU, foresaw the re-introduction of the infamous 'prior lawful residence rule', which was abolished in *Metock*.[24] According to the proposed rules, TCNs who a) did not have a lawful residence status in the UK before marrying an EU citizen or b) would marry an EU citizen only after the latter moved to the UK would be excluded from the scope of the Treaty rights. Under the Withdrawal Agreement, the scope of EU citizens who continue to benefit from generous family reunion rights guaranteed to them under EU law is essentially limited to those whose family members had already obtained a residence permit in the UK on this basis before the cut-off date. Another – much smaller – group includes settled- or pre-settled status holders who got married before the cut-off date and whose spouses wish to join them from abroad. EU citizens

23 See, among others, *Celik (EU exit; marriage; human rights)* [2022] UKUT 00220 (IAC); *SSHD v Hysenaj* [2022] UKUT 13962 (IAC); *SSHD v Meta* [2022] UKUT 12192 (IAC); *SSHD v Sam* [2022] UKUT 10691 (IAC); *Ul Abidin v Entry Clearance Officer, Islamabad* [2022] UKUT 12501 (IAC); *Dauti v SSHD* [2023] UKUT 11747 (IAC); *Qevani v SSHD* [2023] UKUT 15774 (IAC); *SSHD v Beshiri* [2023] UKUT 15942 (IAC); *SSHD v Consolacion* [2023] UKUT 13871 (IAC); *SSHD v Gjini* [2023] UKUT 11846 (IAC); *SSHD v Gjoni* [2023] UKUT 13239 (IAC); *SSHD v Hasmuca* [2023] UKUT 14985 (IAC). Immigration practitioners interviewed are also familiar with such cases. Interview with Nath Gbikpi, an associate solicitor at Leigh Day (online, 12 December 2023).

24 Case C-127/08 *Metock and Others* [2008] ECR I-06241. For an analysis of the case, see Chapter 2.

whose marriage is registered after 31 December 2020 now need to comply with highly restrictive British national family reunification provisions,[25] irrespective of whether they themselves were resident in the UK before the deadline or moved there at a later date. Since the cut-off date, all TCNs with a short-term or irregular residence status who meet EU citizens whilst they are already in the UK can no longer rely on generous EU family reunion provisions rights. This is precisely what was envisaged in the 2016 pre-Brexit referendum settlement between the UK and the EU. In addition, the *Surinder Singh* route for UK nationals has also been effectively abolished.[26]

Restricting the application of the Withdrawal Agreement only to couples whose relationship began before the cut-off date is a substantial departure from the approach established by the CJEU. In *Metock*, the Court explicitly stated that a TCN spouse would enjoy the right to family reunion under the Citizenship Directive irrespective of when their marriage to a mobile EU citizen took place.[27] The CJEU argued that the refusal of the state to grant residence rights to new spouses of EU citizens would encourage the latter to relocate to another country where they could lead a family life, a situation incompatible with the objective of removing all real or potential obstacles to free movement.[28] The relevant provisions of the Withdrawal Agreement go against this logic. It would not be surprising if a Dutch national with a settled status in the UK who marries an India-based Indian national after the cut-off date eventually decided to establish their marital home in one of the EU Member States, rather than trying to meet time-consuming and financially demanding UK family reunification requirements, risking prolonged separation.

It is understandable that from a political perspective, the UK authorities would find it difficult to justify the continuous preferential treatment of EU citizens, allowing the holders of pre-settled and settled status to rely on EU family reunion rules even if they get married after the cut-off date. From a purely legal perspective, however, denying this group such a possibility undermines legal certainty and contradicts the overarching principle of the Withdrawal Agreement, according to which EU citizens resident in the UK by 31 December

25 Unless they can provide evidence of a durable relationship that existed before the cut-off date.

26 Under the Immigration Rules, family members of returning UK nationals whose relationship started before the Brexit day had to return and apply to the EU settlement scheme by 29 March 2022; those whose relationship started after the Brexit day had to return by 31 December 2020, and apply by 30 June 2021.

27 *Metock and Others* (n 24) para 99.

28 Ibid paras 63, 64, 67, 68.

2020 retain their residence rights on the same terms as under the Treaties and the Citizenship Directive.

4 Marriages of Convenience Post-Brexit

The next issue bearing particular importance to this study is post-Brexit changes related to the concept of marriages of convenience and their implications for UK-based EU citizens and their (prospective) spouses. The following sub-sections will accordingly explore the relevant developments at both pre- and post-marriage level.

4.1 *Pre-marriage Controls*

As shown in Section 3 above, since the end of the transition period, foreign nationals can no longer automatically obtain residence rights in the UK by marrying a UK-based EU citizen. At the post-marriage stage, such couples will need to comply with restrictive national family reunification provisions, including the 'no-switching rule', the minimum income requirement, as well as the requirement to provide extensive evidence that the relationship is 'genuine and subsisting'. Given that couples involving mobile EU citizens and non-EU nationals were the principal target group of the 'referral and investigation scheme', introduced before the Brexit referendum, the system has largely stopped serving its purpose. The UK government, however, not only continues to operate the scheme but has even broadened its scope to include family members who are EU citizens without a settled or pre-settled status.

According to the 'sham marriage' definition found in the 1999 Immigration Act, the first criterion for a marriage to be classified as such is that either, or both, of its parties must not be a 'relevant national'. Under the pre-Brexit version of the Act, a 'relevant national' was defined as a UK, EEA, or Swiss citizen.[29] Since 1 July 2021 (the end of the six-month grace period), this definition has been updated to exclude EU citizens without a settled or pre-settled status or a pending application for that status to the EU Settlement Scheme.[30] EU citizens not covered by the Withdrawal Agreement, therefore, are now equally viewed as potentially ready to undergo a sham marriage. For instance, if a German national with a settled status wants to marry another German

29 Immigration and Asylum Act 1999 (IA 1999), s 24(6).

30 As amended by the Immigration and Social Security Co-ordination (EU Withdrawal) Act 2020 (Consequential, Saving, Transitional and Transitory Provisions) (EU Exit) Regulations 2020, SI 2020/1309.

national who had not lived in the UK before the cut-off date, their case will be referred to the Home Office for assessment. The same will happen if a marriage is to be contracted between a UK national and an EU citizen not covered by the Settlement Scheme or two EU citizens who relocate to the UK after the deadline.

The remaining criteria of a 'sham marriage' under the 1999 Act – namely, the absence of a genuine relationship between the parties and that the marriage is being entered into for the purpose of obtaining an immigration advantage – have not been altered and continue to apply as usual. Since 1 July 2021, all register offices in England and Wales have become 'designated', i.e., accepting marriage notices from couples where one of the parties is not a 'relevant national'.

4.2 *Post-marriage Controls*

Whilst the 'referral and investigation' scheme has been expanded to cover broader groups of EU citizens, pre-marriage controls continue to escape the ambit of the Citizenship Directive (and consequently, the Withdrawal Agreement). Meanwhile, post-marriage controls targeted at couples involving EU citizens are now regulated by either the Withdrawal Agreement or UK domestic law, depending on the residence status of the EU citizen involved.

The Withdrawal Agreement does not cover EU citizens who relocate to the UK after the cut-off date; consequently, the UK authorities no longer need to respect EU law safeguards when investigating marriages involving this group (unless another party is an EU citizen with a settled or pre-settled status). By contrast, EU citizens who do fall within the scope of the Withdrawal Agreement (i.e. those who were resident in the UK and whose marriage was registered before the deadline) enjoy the same level of protection from marriage checks as it is provided for under the Citizenship Directive.

The Withdrawal Agreement has not broadened the definition of marriages of convenience to include marriages that are not only contracted but maintained for immigration purposes, as was envisaged in the 2016 UK-EU deal.[31] Article 20(3) of the Withdrawal Agreement stipulates that the host state may adopt measures to combat fraud or abuse on the same conditions as set out in Article 35 of the Citizenship Directive and with respect to the same procedural safeguards listed in this document. As stated in the Agreement, its provisions must be interpreted and applied 'in accordance with the methods and general principles of Union law', including the relevant CJEU case law handed down

31 The pre-referendum settlement between the UK and the EU is described in detail in Chapter 3.

before the end of the transition period, which retains binding force in the UK.[32] Accordingly, when addressing perceived marriages of convenience within the framework of the EU Settlement Scheme, UK authorities may continue to consult the Commission Handbook addressing the issue. Further, when it comes to marriages involving the holders of settled or pre-settled status, the UK continues to be bound by the relevant constraints imposed by the CJEU, such as the prohibition of systematic checks, the burden of proof, and the absence of the cohabitation requirement.

Similarly to the revoked 2016 EEA Regulations, Appendix EU to the UK Immigration Rules provides that, for the purposes of family reunion under the EU Settlement Scheme, the terms 'spouse' and 'civil partner' exclude marriages or civil partnerships of convenience. These concepts are defined there as marriages or civil partnerships entered into to circumvent:

> a) Any criterion the party would have to meet in order to enjoy a right to enter or reside in the UK under the EEA Regulations; or
> b) Any other provision of UK immigration law or any requirement of the Immigration Rules; or
> c) Any criterion the party would otherwise have to meet in order to enjoy a right to enter or reside in the UK under EU law; or
> d) Any criterion the party would have to meet in order to enjoy a right to enter or reside in the Islands under Islands law.[33]

The wording of this definition is similar to the one previously found in the 2016 EEA Regulations and is equally problematic. It neither contains the word 'sole' as provided under the Citizenship Directive nor the passage that there should not be a 'genuine relationship' between the parties as stipulated in the Immigration Act 1999. Literally read, it covers not only marriages entered into only for the purpose of securing an immigration advantage for the foreign spouse and having no other content apart from an immigration motive but also situations where couples wish to lead a family life and residence status is only one of the motives for marriage. As noted in Chapter 4 and Section 3.2

32 Withdrawal Agreement, art 4(3). It is nonetheless stipulated in s 6 of the WA 2018 that the Supreme Court can depart from the retained CJEU case-law in the same exceptional circumstances in which the court would depart from its own case-law. Moreover, the UK government is granted significant powers to enact secondary legislation to determine how and to what extent the courts may depart from the retained EU case-law. For an analysis, see, Steve Peers, 'The Withdrawal Agreement Act: Implementing the Brexit Withdrawal Agreement in the UK' (*EU Law Analysis*, 17.02.2020) <http://eulawanalysis.blogspot.com/2020/02/the-withdrawal-agreement-act.html> accessed 13 April 2024.

33 Immigration Rules Appendix EU, Annex 1.

of Chapter 7, this interpretation is arguably in breach of Article 35 of the Citizenship Directive and, consequently, the Withdrawal Agreement and Agreement Act.

4.3 *Procedures Following a Marriage of Convenience Determination*

Similarly as prior to Brexit, a finding that a (prospective) marriage is not genuine has serious repercussions for the individuals involved. The key scenarios the latter may face include the curtailment or revocation of an existing leave to remain, deportation under the EEA Regulations, as saved, on public policy or conducive grounds, or administrative removal under section 10(1) of the Immigration and Asylum Act 1999. Since the end of the transition period on 31 December 2020, the relevant pathway in such cases is determined by the following criteria:

- The person's residence status
- Any protection they have under the Agreements
- Whether the 'relevant conduct' commenced before or after the end of the transition period.[34]

With respect to the third point, the Home Office guidelines note that the term 'relevant conduct' refers to taking part in a *mala fide* marriage or an attempt to do so. It is further explained that the start of the 'relevant conduct' 'does not have to be when a relationship began, or when a marriage or civil ceremony took place'. Instead, it can be considered to have started when the relevant persons 'confirmed to have first acted to gain an immigration advantage through the relationship' – for example, when they 'confirmed their intention to marry of form a civil partnership'.[35] In the case of a person who has allegedly facilitated a marriage of convenience, it is suggested that the start of the relevant conduct 'might be the earliest date for which there is evidence to show that they planned or took steps to assist the sham marriage, whether it was successful or not'.[36]

This formulation is vague, open to diverse interpretations, and grants the authorities a large margin of discretion in determining the conduct commencement date. To uphold the principle of legal certainty, however, the 'relevant conduct' should have been considered to have started at the marriage date – particularly given that a marriage contracted after 31 December 2020 no longer guarantees the TCN party an automatic right of residence under EU law.

34 Home Office, 'Marriage Investigations' (Version 8.0, 22 June 2023), 6.

35 Ibid, 42–43.

36 Ibid, 43.

4.3.1 'Referral and Investigation Scheme'

After the end of the transition period, couples involving TCNs with an irregular residence status continue to face a high risk of being separated by giving a marriage notice. Following a referral of their case to the Home Office, unauthorised migrants may be removed from the UK. The procedure used in this case is administrative removal under section 10(1) of the Immigration and Asylum Act 1999, applicable to a person who does not have leave to enter or remain in the UK. For this group, it is irrelevant when the conduct was committed and whether their prospective marriage was found to be a sham at all. Couples involving people with an irregular status, therefore, may be prompted to either avoid entering into marriage and live in legal limbo or relocate to another country. Among other categories of principals, this also refers to EU citizen holders of a pre-settled or settled status.

4.3.2 Non-EU Nationals with Protection under the Agreements

Even if the couple manage to enter into marriage, a finding that it is not genuine may still lead to their separation. With a few minor differences, the legislative provisions governing their situation post-Brexit are very similar to the ones that were in force before the end of the transition period.

If the marriage was found to be *mala fide* and the TCN party has applied to the EUSS scheme, the application will be reviewed for potential refusal alongside the removal action.[37] Under paragraph EU16(a) of the Appendix EU, an application to the EUSS scheme may be refused on so-called 'suitability' grounds if the applicant has submitted false or misleading information that is material to the decision to grant or refuse leave. The Home Office guidelines clarify that reliance on a marriage of convenience does fall within the scope of the relevant provision.[38]

Where a non-EU national has already obtained an EUSS leave on the basis of marriage that is subsequently found to be one of convenience, the leave will typically be lost. An EUSS family permit may be cancelled on the grounds that the applicant provided false or misleading information which was material to granting the relevant leave.[39] A pre-settled status may be curtailed on the same grounds.[40] Likewise, a settled status may be revoked if it was obtained by deception.[41]

37 Ibid, 34–35.

38 Ibid, 39.

39 Immigration Rules Appendix EU (Family Permit), para A3.5(a); Immigration Rules Appendix EU, para A3.4(a).

40 Ibid.

41 Immigration Rules Appendix EU, para A3.5(b); Nationality, Immigration and Asylum Act 2002, s 76(2).

In all these situations, the relevant decision can be appealed against under the Immigration (Citizens' Rights Appeals) (EU Exit) Regulations 2020.[42] After appeal rights have been exhausted, the person becomes liable for administrative removal under section 10(1) of the Immigration and Asylum Act.[43] Appeals under the Citizens' Rights Appeals Regulations are suspensive of the TCN party's removal,[44] which has been repeatedly reiterated in Home Office guidelines on approaching situations of alleged marriages of convenience.[45] This is an important change from the pre-Brexit period when an appeal in such cases, made under the EEA Regulations 2016, would typically be non-suspensive.

4.3.3 EU Citizens with Protection under the Agreements

Further, pre- and settled status holders[46] may lose their rights to live in the UK if their status was not obtained on the basis of a marriage of convenience but they have nonetheless been involved in one. This refers to EU citizens who have allegedly entered into a marriage of convenience with a TCN or who are deemed to have facilitated a marriage of convenience for someone else, whether or not it was successful.

In cases where the relevant conduct began before the end of the transition period, the same provisions as pre-Brexit apply. In particular, the person allegedly involved in a marriage of convenience is liable to deportation on public policy grounds under regulation 23(6)(b) of the EEA Regulations 2016, as saved and modified by The Citizens' Rights (Restrictions of Rights of Entry and Residence) (EU Exit) Regulations 2020.[47] A deportation order will invalidate the person's EUSS leave.[48]

---

42 Immigration (Citizens' Rights Appeals) (EU Exit) Regulations 2020, SI 2020/61. If there is a decision to remove taken under reg 23(6)(b) of the EEA Regulations 2016, the decision can be appealed under the respective Regulations.

43 Home Office, 'Marriage Investigations' (Version 8.0), 39.

44 Unless the decision has been either certified on national security grounds, or where a deportation decision has been made. See Home Office, 'EU Settlement Scheme Appeals: Certification in National Security and Deportation Cases' (Version 2.0, 17 August 2022), 5.

45 See, e.g., Home Office, 'Marriage Investigations' (Version 8.0), 39, 51, 52. See also, Home Office, 'EU Settlement Scheme Appeals: Certification in National Security and Deportation cases' (Version 2.0), 5.

46 As well as a person holding an entry clearance under Appendix EU (Family Permit); a person with permission as a service provider from Switzerland; and a person with permission as a S2 healthcare visitor, which can include an accompanying person who is providing care or support during the planned healthcare treatment.

47 Citizens' Rights (Restrictions of Rights of Entry and Residence) (EU Exit) Regulations 2020, SI 2020/1210.

48 Home Office, 'Marriage Investigations' (Version 8.0), 51.

Although the public policy approach to the issue is not without problems,[49] this cohort meanwhile continues to enjoy stronger protection against deportation in accordance with EU law. As described in Chapters 1 and 7, a person with settled status can only be deported on 'serious grounds of public policy' (e.g., if the person has participated in multiple marriages of convenience or has been convicted of facilitation).[50] After ten years of residence in the UK, involvement in such a marriage can no longer serve as grounds for deportation, for such conduct does not meet the 'imperative grounds of public security' threshold applicable in that case.[51]

If the relevant conduct began after the end of the transition period, this may lead to the cancellation of an EUSS leave to enter or the curtailment of a pre-settled status under paragraph A3.4(b) of Annex 3 to Appendix EU. The latter specifically provides that the pre-settled status may be curtailed if 'it is more likely than not that, after the specified date, the person has entered, attempted to enter or assisted another person to enter or to attempt to enter a marriage of convenience'. Following that, the person is liable to administrative removal under section 10(1) of the Immigration and Asylum Act, provided that no appeal is pending.[52]

4.3.4 Persons without Protection under the Agreements

For individuals who do not enjoy protection under the Agreements, an accusation of being involved in a sham marriage may also lead to the cancellation of other forms of permission to enter or stay previously granted to them under the Immigration Rules. The latter provide that the relevant (temporary) permission may be cancelled 'where the decision maker is satisfied that it is more likely than not the person is, or has been, involved in a sham marriage or sham civil partnership'.[53] Likewise, the Nationality, Immigration and Asylum Act 2002 provides for the revocation of indefinite leave to remain if it was obtained by deception, including as a result of a sham marriage.[54] Following that, the person can be administratively removed under section 10(1) of the Immigration and Asylum Act 1999.

---

49 For an analysis, see Chapter 7.

50 This has been stressed in Home Office, 'Marriage Investigations' (Version 8.0), 38.

51 Ibid.

52 Ibid, 51.

53 Immigration Rules (11.04.2024), pt 9, para 9.6.2.

54 Nationality, Immigration and Asylum Act 2002, s 76(2). See also, Home Office, 'Marriage Investigations' (Version 8.0), 49, 55.

Although the Agreements do not cover these types of situations, they may have serious implications for couples involving beneficiaries of the EUSS scheme – in particular, where an EU citizen with a settled or pre-settled status gets married to a foreign national[55] after the end of the transition period. Even where the TCN spouse has already been granted leave to stay in the UK on other grounds, an erroneous finding that a marriage is not genuine may effectively lead to its cancellation or revocation. The couple would then effectively find themselves in a more disadvantageous position than before the marriage – when the TCN party could stay lawfully in the UK on the basis of their permit. The situation is further aggravated by the fact that unlike the decisions made under the EUSS scheme, cancellation or revocation decisions under the Immigration Rules are not subject to appeal. As a consequence, the couple may get separated for a mere attempt to exercise their human right to marry, even where the marriage would not automatically provide residence rights to the TCN spouse, and the parties would first need to comply with restrictive UK domestic family reunification requirements. The inability to continue living together in the UK with their TCN partner may prompt the EUSS status holder to relocate. As noted in Section 3, this is against the spirit of EU free movement law and the Withdrawal Agreement that aims to secure the EU citizen's rights to stay in the UK on the same terms as under the Citizenship Directive.

4.3.5 Proportionality Considerations

With respect to all the situations described above, the Home Office guidelines stress that the powers to curtail or revoke someone's leave on sham marriage (or marriage of convenience) grounds and/or take enforcement action against them are discretionary and must comply with the proportionality requirements. For example, it is stressed that a person who is resident in the UK may have established a family or private life in the country regardless of their involvement in a *mala fide* marriage.[56] Hence, in cases where children may be potentially affected, the authorities must have regard to Article 3 of the UN Convention on the Rights of the Child[57] and give the child's best interests a primary consideration.[58] Furthermore, a deportation decision on public policy grounds must meet the EU public policy test, laid out in the saved EEA Regulations 2016.[59] The effectiveness of these safeguarding measures, however,

55 Including EU citizens who do not qualify under the EUSS scheme.

56 Home Office, 'Suitability: Sham Marriage or Civil Partnership' (Version 2.0, 10 November 2021), 7.

57 Convention on the Rights of the Child, 1577 UNTS 3 (20.11.1989).

58 Home Office, 'Marriage Investigations' (Version 8.0), 35.

59 Ibid, 44.

depends on how and to what extent they are applied in practice. For instance, Chapter 10 will show that, when examining cases of alleged marriages of convenience, UK judges do not seem to give any consideration to the rights of the children involved.

The Home Office guidelines also repeatedly emphasise that there are cases of so-called 'marriages by deception' where one party has been 'duped or deceived as to the true nature and purpose of the relationship'.[60] It is stressed that it would 'generally not be proportionate to take enforcement action against that person' (such as deport the EU citizen party on public policy grounds) and that 'enforcement action must only be considered against the culpable party'.[61] As discussed in Chapter 4, however, the concept of 'marriages by deception' is inherently problematic and arguably incompatible with the narrow definition of marriages of convenience under the Citizenship Directive.

5 Conclusion

The UK decision to leave the EU has profoundly transformed the position of UK-resident EU citizens and their family members. The principal instrument in this context is the EU-UK Withdrawal Agreement; the latter provided for a transition period until 31 December 2020, during which EU free movement law continued to apply in the UK as normal. The end of the transition period effectively created two groups of EU citizens covered by a separate set of rules: the Withdrawal Agreement, which includes similar rights to family reunion as provided under EU free movement law, and UK domestic immigration, including family reunification, rules.

Those belonging to the first group have retained their residence rights in the UK on the same terms as under the Citizenship Directive, on the condition that the relevant person was resident in the country by 31 December 2020. All beneficiaries of the Withdrawal Agreement were required to register under the so-called EU Settlement Scheme and obtain either settled or pre-settled status, depending on how long they had previously lived in the UK. EU citizens who relocate to the UK after the cut-off date are not covered by the Withdrawal Agreement and are treated equally to third-country nationals.

The Withdrawal Agreement (as incorporated into UK law by the Withdrawal Agreement Act) has also divided EU citizens into several groups with respect

60 Ibid, 34.
61 Ibid, 36.

to their ability to live in the UK with their family members. The first and most privileged group are settled or pre-settled status holders whose marriage to a TCN was registered by 31 December 2020. In that case, their foreign spouses are entitled to stay in the UK on the same terms as under the Citizenship Directive, which also includes the relevant EU law safeguards the UK authorities need to observe when addressing potential marriages of convenience (such as the prohibition of systematic checks and the burden or proof). Rather disappointingly, however, the UK Immigration Rules applicable to this group have introduced yet another definition of marriages of convenience; the latter is similar to the one previously provided in the EEA Regulations and broader than the one found in the Citizenship Directive.

Settled- or pre-settled status holders who get married after the cut-off date can no longer rely on the generous EU family reunion provisions and need to comply with restrictive UK domestic family reunification rules, such as the 'no-switching rule' and the minimum income requirement. In this respect, this group has been placed in the same position as EU citizens who relocate to the UK after 31 December 2020. Moreover, after the cut-off date, the new rules also apply to family members who are EU citizens and did not reside in the UK before the deadline. Further, the UK authorities no longer need to respect EU law principles when investigating marriages registered after the deadline.

In addition, the UK government continues to conduct systematic pre-marriage controls within the framework of the 'referral and investigation scheme'. Although after the cut-off date, new spouses of UK-resident EU citizens no longer obtain an automatic right of residence under EU law, the scheme not only continues to operate but has even been expanded to include family members who are EU citizens without settled or pre-settled status.

An alleged involvement in a *mala fide* marriage may have serious consequences for couples involving EU citizens and third-country nationals – irrespective of whether the marriage has been registered before or after the end of the transition period. Similarly as prior to Brexit, the main repercussions for foreign spouses of EU citizens include the curtailment or revocation of existing leave to remain and administrative removal. Further, in certain situations, EU citizen beneficiaries of the EUSS scheme, allegedly involved in a marriage of convenience, may lose their residence status in the UK and either be deported on public policy grounds or face administrative removal.

CHAPTER 9

Assessing the Nature of Marriage: Conduct of Investigation

1 Introduction

Previous chapters have offered a detailed analysis of the UK legislative framework regulating the position of couples involving UK-resident EU citizens and third-country nationals. It was demonstrated that couples may be referred for investigation both before and after their marriage is registered, an approach that has remained unchanged after Brexit. This chapter specifically focuses on the Home Office's practices in selecting and investigating marriages considered suspicious and evaluates the compatibility of the Home Office's approach with EU law. It starts by discussing the issues surrounding the 'suspicion-raising' criteria, relied on by the Home Office both at the pre- and post-marriage stage. It then proceeds to look at the investigation techniques employed by the UK authorities and identify their most problematic practices in that respect. In particular, the chapter offers insight into the questions a couple may be asked during a marriage interview, the role of home visits in assessing the nature of marriage, as well as the Home Office approach in cases involving pregnancy or childbirth.

2 'Risk Profiles' and Marriages Perceived as 'Suspicious'

Under the 'referral and investigation scheme', registrars must not only refer prospective marriages involving non-EU nationals to the Home Office but also conduct a short interview with the couple to decide if there are any grounds to additionally submit a section 24 report. The years after the introduction of the scheme saw a significant rise in such reports. In 2018, their number reached 2,868, a 40% increase from 2014.[1] The list of 'suspicion-raising' criteria communicated to the registrars by the Home Office is not publicly available. Such factors are nevertheless found in a Home Office document from 2017, which

1 Diana Taylor and Frances Perraudin, 'Couples Face "Insulting" Checks in Sham Marriage Crackdown' (*The Guardian*, 14.04.2019) <https://www.theguardian.com/uk-news/2019/apr/14/couples-sham-marriage-crackdown-hostile-environment> accessed 12 April 2024.

 | DOI:10.1163/9789004499263_011

contains a non-exhaustive list of possible grounds for suspicion and a section 24 report, mostly related to the couple's behaviour, interaction, ability to communicate in the same language, and the TCN party's residence status (the list is reproduced, with minor changes, in Table 2).

All cases referred by the marriage registrars to the Home Office as part of the scheme are initially assessed by the Marriage Referral and Assessment Unit (MRAU), which, under section 48(3) of the 2014 Act, must decide whether to carry out an investigation. The referrals contain information provided by the couple upon giving a marriage notice and a section 24 report if it is considered appropriate to submit one. To determine if there is a risk that the intended marriage is a sham, the MRAU assesses the cases against certain criteria. Home Office documents obtained by the independent legal charity Public Law Project (PLP) in response to a FOI request reveal that since at least 2019, this has been done using an automated triage system that processes the data and allocates the case either a green or red light. A red light outcome indicates that there are reasonable grounds for suspicions that the proposed marriage is not genuine, and there is a need for further investigation.[2]

The relevant Home Office guidance further explains that the criteria are drawn from section 24 reports, recent sham marriage-based enforcement and prosecution cases, and applications refused on the basis that the marriage is not genuine. The guidance notes that the criteria 'are kept under review and may change over time' but lists the possible factors they may reflect. In a nutshell, suspicions may be raised if either of the parties to the intended marriage has ever breached UK immigration law, has links to criminality, has been subject to a section 24 report, or has previously been sponsored by another spouse to enter or remain in the UK.[3] It is, however, stressed that the presence of one or more of these factors does not mean that the proposed marriage will automatically be investigated. Rather, this may mean that the case will be subject to additional scrutiny which involves manual assessment. It is further stressed that '[t]he assessment should be informed, but not solely determined,

2 Home Office, 'Borders Immigration Citizenship Systems: Equality Impact Assessment', available at <https://www.whatdotheyknow.com/request/sham_marriages_8/response/1693677/attach/3/61422%20Maxwell%20Annex%20C%20Redacted.pdf?cookie_passthrough=1> accessed 15 April 2024. See also, Home Office, 'MRAU Guidance' (Version 1.1) Available at <https://www.whatdotheyknow.com/request/sham_marriages_8/response/1693677/attach/4/61422%20Maxwell%20Annex%20D%20Redacted.pdf?cookie_passthrough=1> accessed 15 April 2024.

3 Home Office, 'Marriage and Civil Partnership Referral and Investigation Scheme: Statutory Guidance for Home Office Staff' (Version 3.0, 23 June 2023), 10.

TABLE 2 Possible grounds for suspicion and S24 report

Suspicion	Record as much information as possible, for example
One person knows very little about the other person. Or little interaction.	Were the couple referring to notes to answer questions about the other party? Was there little communication/ contact/ interaction between them?
Reluctance to provide evidence of name, age, marital status, or nationality.	Did reluctance relate to all information requested or only specific areas? What evidence was provided?
One of the parties struggles to give the full name or address of the other person.	What happened, and how was the information provided?
Parties unable to converse in the same language.	How did they communicate with one another? How did they understand what information was being requested? Was an interpreter used to aid communication between parties?
One of the couple may have exceeded their period of permitted stay in the UK.	What was seen or said to raise suspicions of their immigration position?
The couple arrive separately but doesn't want to be interviewed separately, or the couple leave separately after the ceremony.	What was seen or said?
One of the couple is seen to receive payment for the marriage.	What did the registration officer see? How was payment made and by whom and to which party?
Suspected use of a facilitator, for example a witness or a translator.	How often has the suspected facilitator attended? – Details of events attended, who was acting as a facilitator, and why does the registration officer think they were acting as a facilitator? Names and contact details, if known, should be included in the report.
An allegation by a credible third party such as an immigration officer, police officer, registration officers, etc.	Who is the credible third party, and what raised their suspicions? Is the registration officer content that a reasonable suspicion does indeed exist and is confident in the source of the data?

TABLE 2 Possible grounds for suspicion and S24 report (*cont.*)

Suspicion	Record as much information as possible, for example
Overall, the arrangements seem odd	The EU national turns up on their own, and the non-EU national has family friends in attendance and/or the timing of the marriage is suspicious.
Other possible indicators.	
Non-attendance at a planned ceremony.	This on its own would not normally be a reason for raising an S24/24A report.
Suspicions that forged documents have been provided.	This on its own would not normally be a reason for raising an S24/24A report but should be reported using guidance at MD3.51–67 and Annex E.
Visa about to expire.	This on its own would not normally be a reason for raising an S24/24A report.

a Home Office, 'Prevention and Detection of Offences', 7–8 (16.01.2017), on file with the author
SOURCE: HOME OFFICE[a]

by the presence of one or more of the factors mentioned above'.[4] When undertaking such an assessment, the decision maker shall consider all the available information about both parties to decide whether the case shall be referred for investigation.[5]

According to the Equality Impact Assessment, disclosed by the Home Office to PLP in 2020, at the time of its publication, the algorithm assessed the cases against eight criteria.[6] Whilst it is apparent that the possibility of an investigation is largely determined by the immigration history of the non-EU national, the Home Office has provided a redacted version of the document and refused to release the full list of criteria on the grounds that this would prejudice their ability to 'successfully detect and deter sham marriages' and would not be in

4 Ibid, 11.

5 Ibid. PLP representatives have confirmed that the manual assessment does take place, since not all of the cases flagged red are ultimately referred for further investigation. Interview with Carla Clarke, PLP's Legal Director, and Mia Leslie, PLP's Research Fellow (online, 23 November 2023).

6 Home Office, 'Borders Immigration Citizenship Systems: Equality Impact Assessment' (11 2), 6.

the public interest.[7] The only two criteria disclosed in the Assessment and apparently used by the Home Office were the age difference between the parties and any shared travel history.[8]

The opacity surrounding the list of criteria gives several reasons for concern. First, it arguably undermines procedural fairness of decisions to investigate,[9] particularly given that the criteria are amended over time. It is worth noting that PLP obtained the pro forma of the letter sent to couples who are being referred for further investigation, which does not inform them of an automated system or a triage tool that has been involved in the process.[10] Second, further disclosure would be necessary to assist in understanding whether and to what extent the automated model is discriminatory on nationality grounds. A graph included in the Home Office Equality Impact Assessment shows that, at the time, applicants of Albanian nationality had the highest rate amongst all non-EU nationals of failing triage – between 20% and 25%. The same percentage refers to EU citizens of Bulgarian, Greek, and Romanian nationality. Although the Home Office denies that nationality is included in the algorithm's criteria,[11] the system may nevertheless appear to be indirectly discriminatory if it is having a systemic negative impact on certain nationalities. As reasonably stressed by PLP, such practices would be contrary to sections 19 and 29 of the Equality Act 2010.[12] In this context, the disproportionate share of Albanian nationals is particularly concerning, given the increasingly hostile treatment of Albanian asylum seekers in the UK and negative narratives around this group in British media and political discourse.[13] Moreover, an interrelated issue is possible

---

7 Home Office response to a PLP FOI request (ref. 61422, 22.06.2021). Available at <https://www.whatdotheyknow.com/request/sham_marriages_8/response/1818059/attach/3/IR%2061422%20Jack%20Maxwell%20final%20response.pdf> accessed 15 April 2024.

8 Home Office, 'Borders Immigration Citizenship Systems: Equality Impact Assessment' (n 2), 7.

9 Tatiana Kazim, 'Home Office Refuses to Explain Secret Sham Marriage Algorithm' (*Free Movement*, 21.07.2021) <https://freemovement.org.uk/home-office-refuses-to-disclose-inner-workings-of-sham-marriage-algorithm/> accessed 15 April 2024.

10 The pro forma of the letter is available at: <https://www.whatdotheyknow.com/request/sham_marriage_triage_scheme/response/2143185/attach/4/71986%20Leslie%20Annex%20B.pdf> accessed 15 April 2024.

11 Home Office, 'Marriage and Civil Partnership Referral and Investigation Scheme: Statutory Guidance for Home Office Staff' (Version 3.0), 11.

12 Kazim (n 9).

13 See, e.g., Liri Kuci, 'Scapegoating: UK Immigration Policy Rests on Villifying Albanians' (*BIRN*, 15.02.2023) <https://balkaninsight.com/2023/02/15/scapegoating-uk-immigration-policy-rests-on-villifying-albanians/> accessed 15 April 2024; 'MiCLU: Hostile Environment Towards Albanian Asylum Seekers Poses Alarming Risk to Their Mental Health and Wellbeing' (*EIN*, 04.01.2024) <https://www.ein.org.uk/news/miclu-hostile-environment-towards-albanian-asylum-seekers-poses-alarming-risk-their-mental> accessed 15 April 2024.

'automation bias', where an official conducting an assessment may be more inclined to conclude that the marriage is not genuine if the algorithm has given the couple a red light.[14]

The Home Office's decision not to disclose the list of criteria was nevertheless upheld, first by the Information Commissioner[15] and later by the First-tier Tribunal (Information Rights). Although the Tribunal recognised that 'there will be some indirect discrimination' on nationality grounds, it did not agree that disclosure of the remaining criteria would help minimise or understand such bias[16] and argued that 'understanding the criteria could lead interested individuals or parties, to adapt their behaviour or answers to any questioning or subsequent investigation'.[17]

In view of the above, it must be emphasised that the number of detected sham marriages under the scheme is remarkably low. Between 2016 and 2022, there were nearly 107,500 intended marriages referred by the registrars to the Home Office, of which only 15,000 were extended for investigation. Of the latter group, as few as 1.2% (1,319) were found to be sham.[18] Prior to the end of the transition period, a similar pattern was observed among couples involving EU citizens, who could then rely on EU law to secure automatic residence rights for the foreign national spouse. In 2019, for instance, there were 16,889 marriage referrals received by the Home Office which included at least one non-EU national. Of these, over one-third (6,046) involved mobile EU citizens. Of the latter group, 15% (931) of intended marriages were extended for investigation. In over one-third (329) of these cases, the couples were considered non-compliant and were hence not allowed to marry. Yet it was only in 165 cases that the prospective marriage was found to be sham,[19] which constitutes as little as 2% of the total number of marriages intended to be registered between EU citizens and non-EU nationals.[20] In 2020, the last year before the end of the

14 See Kazim (n9).

15 The Information Commissioner's Office is an independent authority, charged with enforcing and promoting the data protection and freedom of information law in the UK.

16 *Public Law Project v The Information Commissioner* [2023] UKFTT 102 (GRC), para 56.

17 Ibid, para 54.

18 Jack Barton, 'Thousands of Couples Face "Humiliating" Home Office Sham Marriage Checks' (openDemocracy, 12.07.2023) <https://www.opendemocracy.net/en/home-office-immigration-sham-marriage-hostile-environment/> accessed 15 April 2024.

19 Although the criteria and methods of investigation employed by the Home Office may target many couples who do intend to lead a family life. See Sections 3–6 below.

20 Home Office responses to FOI requests, made by the author (on file with the author). In 2018, 4% of intended marriages involving EU citizens were found to be sham.

transition period, there were 14,607 cases flagged to the Home Office, of which nearly 6,000 involved EU citizens. Of the latter group, around 660 cases were extended for investigation. Sixty-five couples were determined non-compliant, whereby as few as six intended marriages were found to be sham.[21] The particularly low numbers in 2020 can also be partly explained by the suspension of the investigations between April 2020 and June 2021 due to the COVID-19 pandemic.[22]

These numbers raise questions as to the proportionality of the checks, not only from a legal but also from a public policy perspective. The government continues to invest substantial resources to tackle a problem that is not found to bear any statistical significance, particularly given that after 31 December 2020, marriage to an EU citizen no longer provides a foreigner with an automatic right of residence. Instead of its declared aim, the scheme appears to be used to identify and remove foreign nationals with an irregular residence status. Between 2016 and 2022, 2,400 of the people investigated under the scheme were detained for suspected immigration offences, and 2,211 individuals were removed from the UK, which significantly exceeds the number of detected sham marriage cases.[23]

The lack of transparency is also observed at the post-marriage stage. The Home Office guidance does not contain a publicly available list of indicators that the marriage may be one of convenience. Nonetheless, the author has been able to have a sight of such criteria in an anonymised extract from a Home Office file, obtained by an immigration lawyer as part of a subject access request on behalf of their client. It contains a list of reasons that might provoke referral to the interview. These include:

1) Proxy marriage;
2) London issued passport dated near marriage and no evidence of previous immigration history;
3) Child born shortly before/during marriage and the spouse is not the parent;
4) Bank statements show large unexplained payments near the date of marriage;
5) Applicant immigration history shows history of deception;
6) Marriage is bigamous;
7) Reasons to doubt the validity of documentary evidence;
8) Applicant married at a venue recorded on the Portal;

21 Ibid.
22 Ibid.
23 Barton (n 18).

9) Sponsor is self-employed or became self-employed following a previous refusal on Treaty rights;
10) The marriage took place in another EU Member State;
11) Applicant has a poor immigration history;
12) Plausibility in question (large age difference, cultural differences); and
13) The EU principal commenced employment shortly before marriage.[24]

Since the file is from 2015, it is unknown if the Home Office continues to employ the same criteria and which of them are relied on most frequently. Nonetheless, the document provides a valuable insight into the Home Office perception of 'suspicious' marriages. The indicators provided are very similar to the ones found in the 2014 Commission Handbook and gave various reasons for concern. First, similarly to the pre-marriage cases, the main emphasis was placed on the non-EU national's immigration history. The applications from those having no long-term leave were thus more likely to be investigated and accordingly refused. Quite strikingly, applicants could fall under suspicion even for marrying at a particular venue, or where their EU spouse was self-employed or started employment shortly before marriage. This indicator was highly discriminatory, for it targeted a broad category of EU citizens who exercised their Treaty rights as self-employed persons, or whose plans to marry had coincided with them getting a job in the host Member State. The same refers to a large age difference between spouses, which notably has not been included in the list of hints in the Handbook due to its over-inclusive nature.[25]

Second, whether a marriage would be considered suspicious would depend on its type. Rather unexpectedly, one could be referred to the interview because their marriage took place in another Member State. This approach is puzzling, not least because it covered all the cases where the EU citizen had already lived with their TCN spouse in another (including their home) Member State, a group that was traditionally construed as the least suspicious. Furthermore, an EU citizen could, quite understandably, wish to celebrate their marriage in their home Member State in the company of their family and friends. Alternatively, many couples could be forced to seek another Member State where they could undergo the marriage procedure more easily than in the UK, without facing the risk of separation before the ceremony. It seems, however, that the Home Office perceived this strategy as suspicious, albeit it is precisely the state that was responsible for its development.

24 Extract from an anonymised Home Office file, completed in 2015 (on file with the author).
25 Commission, 'Staff Working Document – Handbook on addressing the issue of alleged marriages of convenience between EU citizens and non-EU nationals in the context of EU law on free movement of EU citizens' SWD(2014) 284 final.

The same considerations apply to proxy marriages that continue to be construed as suspicious. The Home Office guidance specifically notes that '[m]arriages by proxy can be open to abuse and where encountered must be thoroughly investigated'.[26] Further, although the Home Office claims it does not officially practice nationality profiling, the factor of 'cultural differences', found in the Home Office file, was apparently used as a covert attempt to target nationals of countries considered 'high risk'. It is no coincidence that a significant number of the Upper Tribunal judgments analysed in Chapter 10 involve female nationals of Central and Eastern European Member States married to male nationals of countries such as Pakistan, India, Nigeria, or Albania. Overall, male migrants from the Indian subcontinent, African countries, or Albania are disproportionately represented amongst non-EU spouses of EU citizens appealing against adverse decisions of the Home Office and the lower courts. Immigration lawyers have also noted in the interviews that their clients whose marriages are considered to be ones of convenience predominantly involve nationals of Islamic countries who meet their EU citizen partners whilst already in the UK. In contrast, couples involving nationals of countries belonging to the Global North[27] are rarely examined.[28]

3 Interview Questions: Focus on Discrepancies and Cohabitation

If there are factors suggesting that the marriage may not be genuine, the couple may be referred to an interview. The interview assessment criteria are not publicly available either for the pre- or post-marriage stage. The Home Office guidance nevertheless specifies that, during the interview, the partners may be asked about:

1) The background to, history of and subsistence of their relationship;
2) Their general background and the immigration history;
3) Their living arrangements;
4) The arrangements for the proposed marriage; and

26 Home Office, 'Marriage Investigations' (Version 8.0, 22 June 2023), 10.

27 The designation 'Global North' is typically employed to refer to developed economies with high living standards, such as the EU, US, Canada, Australia, New Zealand, and Japan. For a critical discussion on the division between 'Global North' and 'Global South', see for instance, Matthew Sparke, 'Everywhere But Always Somewhere: Critical Geographies of the Global South' (2007) 1 *The Global South* 117.

28 Interview with David Tang, principal solicitor at David Tang & Co (London, 20 February 2019); interview with Nath Gbikpi, an associate solicitor at Leigh Day (London, 21 February 2019).

5) Their future plans.[29]

Evidence suggests that interviews with couples involving EU citizens, who got married before the end of the transition period, could frequently last for several hours, with applicants being asked well over 100 detailed questions.[30] These often related to such matters as to when and how the couple first met, how their relationship developed, the marriage proposal, the wedding day, what they knew about each other's backgrounds, and recent events.[31] A record of a post-marriage interview of a Bulgarian-Algerian couple obtained by the author includes questions such as how they spend their free time, when and what time they last went to a restaurant together, what TV programmes they watch together, what hobbies or interests they have, if the husband has a best friend, when and how they met and began living together, who paid for the wedding, and what hours they worked each day.[32] Yet the practice of questioning couples in much detail about their present relationship is problematic since according to EU law, at the post-marriage stage the parties are not obliged to spend their time together or be in a relationship at all.

Next, immigration practitioners complained that interviewers frequently placed their main focus on minor discrepancies, rather than questions where the answers matched. One lawyer commented that interviews appeared 'more designed to get wrong answers on trivial things than to test the genuineness of the relationship'.[33] Lawyers described cases where applications for EEA residence cards were refused following about a dozen minor differences in over 100 questions.[34] Couples could be asked to remember difficult things or the exact dates of certain events. For instance, recall the name of the coffee shop where they met many years previously, recall if the table at their wedding

29 Home Office, 'Marriage Investigations' (Version 8.0), 27.

30 See, e.g., *Virk v SSHD* [2018] UKUT 19843 (IAC); ILPA, 'Comments for the Chief Inspector of Borders and Immigration. Review of Sham Marriages' (31.08.2016); a marriage interview record from 2011 obtained by the author. There are also cases when the parties are asked even more questions. In one case, the TCN spouse was asked 641 question and her EU citizen husband 248 questions (*K v SSHD* [2017] UKUT 29770 (IAC), para 3). In another case, the EU citizen principal was asked over 300 questions over a period of nearly three hours (*Alex [A] v SSHD* [2018] UKUT 04343 (IAC), para 12). See also, *Hajdari v SSHD* [2022] UKUT 03750 (IAC), para 3; *Abdelmotaleb v SSHD* [2023] UKUT 01177 (IAC), para 5; *SSHD v Abdeaziz* [2023] UKUT 006527 (IAC), para 5. There is also a case where the couple was asked about 1000 questions (*[B S] v SSHD* [2017] UKUT 16879 (IAC), para 9).

31 E.g., *K v SSHD* (n 30), para 3; *A U v SSHD* [2017] UKUT 00052 (IAC).

32 Marriage interview record (n 30).

33 See ILPA, 'Comments for the Chief Inspector of Borders and Immigration. Review of Sham Marriages' (n 30).

34 Ibid.

ceremony was round or square, and recall what the colour of the walls and the shutter in the shop where the wife worked were. Spouses reported being asked complex questions about their partner's religion, education, country of origin that they had never visited, and the exact ages of their parents-in-law whom they had never met.[35]

In addition, couples were normally expected to know the exact date of their (proposed) marriage, whether their partners had been married before, as well as each other's financial affairs, as well as remember when they last went to the cinema or restaurant. It should be noted, however, that many couples in a close relationship may not recall or choose not to share such details with each other. EU citizens were also typically asked about their TCN partner's immigration history. A couple who later gave birth to a child was considered to be one of convenience *inter alia* because the EU spouse could not recall the exact date of their marriage, as well as did not know that her Egyptian husband had entered the UK using a false name and put forward an asylum claim as a national of Palestine.[36]

Moreover, in some of the interviews, couples were asked questions that were confusing, vaguely formulated or could be interpreted in many different ways. One lawyer reported his clients being asked when their relationship became serious, although the parties may perceive the word 'serious' differently: for some, it may mean kissing for the first time, for others – becoming intimate, moving in together, or deciding to get married.[37] Couples were also asked, for example, about each other's favourite colour,[38] although a person may not have one, and what plans they had for the future, although their answers would most likely differ. For instance, in one marriage interview, the husband said he wished to start his own business, whilst his wife wanted to have a baby.[39]

Further, when interviewing couples, the Home Office placed a significant focus on cohabitation, asking the parties to provide a detailed description of their claimed marital home. For instance, one marriage interview included 15 questions under the section 'home', including how many bedrooms the flat had, what floor was it on, what was in the bedroom, if they had a bath or shower in the bathroom, and what they could see when looking out of their bedroom window.[40] One couple was asked to give the number of pictures on

35 Ibid.

36 *Abouelhasaan v SSHD* [2019] UKUT 04931 (IAC), para 10.

37 Interview with David Tang (n 28).

38 Ibid.

39 Marriage interview record (n 30).

40 Ibid.

the wall of their sitting room;[41] another marriage was considered to be one of convenience *inter alia* because the husband described the electric toaster as white and the wife as silver.[42]

It must be recalled that, according to the Commission Handbook, Member States are first advised to look for the hints that the marriage is not one of convenience. Yet, it appears that this is has not been the approach pursued by the Home Office. Overall, the analysis above shows that the aim of the executive was not to avoid disproportionate intrusion into the lives of genuine couples who could be erroneously deprived of their fundamental rights, but to uncover perceived marriages of convenience – both at the pre- and post-marriage stage – even where there was no basis to believe one existed. Indeed, although the majority of couples interviewed within the framework of the 'referral and investigation scheme' were determined to be genuine,[43] Home Office officers still questioned the nature of their marriage and believed that offenders were simply too well-prepared to get caught.[44] The focus of the government, therefore, appears entirely misplaced.

4 Hostile Interviewing Style

Although Home Office officers are not permitted to ask inappropriate questions, such as about the couple's sex life,[45] there are numerous examples of personal and aggressive questioning. Such practices arguably amount to a violation of the rights to respect for human dignity and for private and family life (Article 1 and 7 of the EUCFR[46] respectively).[47] In a number of cases, immigration officers have asked the parties about their intimate relationships, including details about sexual positions and contraception.[48] In other situations, interviewees were threatened with arrest and removal from the UK. For

41 See ILPA, 'Comments for the Chief Inspector of Borders and Immigration. Review of Sham Marriages (n 30).

42 Ibid.

43 n 20. The Home Office has nonetheless declined to disclose statistics on detected marriages of convenience amongst applicants for EEA family permits and residence cards.

44 See for instance ICIBI, 'The Implementation of the 2014 "Hostile Environment" Provisions for Tackling Sham Marriage. August to September 2016' (December 2016).

45 Home Office, 'Marriage Investigations' (Version 8.0), 28.

46 Charter of Fundamental Rights of the European Union [2000] OJ C364/01 (EUCFR).

47 For an analysis see Chapter 5, Section 4.2.

48 See for instance, *Ait-Rabah, R (on the application of) v SSHD [2016] EWHC 1099 (Admin)*, para 53; Taylor and Perraudin (n 1).

instance, in one case, the Home Office officer set the tone of the interview by advising the principal that the penalties for an EU citizen entering into a marriage of convenience can include up to 14 years' imprisonment. The interviewer further warned her that her husband could be taken to a detention centre and then removed from the UK. The interrogation then proceeded to 125 questions and continued after the pregnant principal stated at question 112 that she wanted to stop the interview because she felt nauseous. The interviewer nevertheless continued to ask questions.[49]

Another case involved an EU citizen principal who could not answer the questions properly because she felt physically unwell during the interview due to her sugar levels dropping as she was diabetic. Overall, she was asked over 300 questions for nearly three hours. From question 180, she began to feel confused, and the officer had to repeat the questions. However, the officer did not stop the interview or change their intimidating style of questioning. At question 200, the interviewer aggressively asked how often the couple spoke on the phone in the period when their relationship developed saying: 'Which was what? Was it weekly? Was it daily? Was it fortnightly? How regular's regular to you?' It was only at question 206 when the officer apparently realised that the EU principal was unwell, asked if she needed to check her blood sugar, and issued a break, following which the interview continued. The principal was given food at question 219 and another break at question 229. The questioning then went on in spite of her indicating that she did not feel well enough to continue. The marriage was ultimately found to be one of convenience.[50]

5 Cases Involving Pregnancy or Childbirth

A particularly problematic category of cases involves situations where one of the spouses is pregnant, or the couple already has a child. As argued in Chapter 4, the very fact of pregnancy and/or childbirth alone signifies that the couple has been in a relationship, which is inconsistent with the restrictive definition of a marriage of convenience under the Citizenship Directive.[51]

49 *Virk v SSHD* (n 31), para 6.

50 *Alex [A] v SSHD* (n 31), paras 12, 20.

51 Directive 2004/38/EC of the European Parliament and of the Council of 29 April 2004 on the right of citizens of the Union and their family members to move and reside freely within the territory of the Member States amending Regulation (EEC) No 1612/68 and repealing Directives 64/221/EEC, 68/360/EEC, 72/194/EEC, 73/148/EEC, 75/34/EEC, 75/35/EEC, 90/364/EEC, 90/365/EEC and 93/96/EEC [2004] OJ L158/77 (Citizenship Directive).

Evidence, however, suggests that the Home Office frequently designated marriages involving pregnancy and children as ones of convenience.[52] In a number of cases, the Home Office concluded the marriage in question was of convenience despite the pregnancy of the EU citizen principal.[53] Lawyers interviewed claimed that Home Office officers tended to either not believe that the biological father of the child is the TCN husband, or claim that parties of marriages of convenience try to give birth to a child only to increase the opportunities of the TCN spouse to stay in the UK.[54]

Such assumptions are striking for a number of reasons. First, by questioning the paternity of the child, the Home Office is ignoring the presumption in English family law that states that the husband is considered to be the father of any child born in wedlock.[55] Secondly, as noted above, the very fact of pregnancy is inconsistent with the definition of marriages of convenience. Thirdly, having children is a serious commitment, and it is difficult to imagine that many would use it solely to obtain an immigration status. Last but not least, whilst attacking couples with children, the Home Office does not seem to give any consideration to the UN Convention on the Rights of the Child.[56]

6 Home Visits

The Home Office practices also suggest that immigration officers were often unaware of the CJEU judgments in *Diatta*[57] and *Ogieriakhi*,[58] which do not require the couple to live together under one roof. In several cases involving EU citizens (where the marriage was entered into before 31 December 2020), a TCN spouse's application for a residence permit was refused, or the existing residence permit revoked following a single visit to the couple's indicated home

52 This was also confirmed in interviews with David Tang (n 28) and Priya Solanki, a barrister at One Pump Court (online, 12 December 2023).

53 See for instance, ILPA, 'Comments for the Chief Inspector of Borders and Immigration. Review of Sham Marriages (n 30); *Virk v SSHD* (n 31); *Khan v SSHD* [2019] UKUT 03191 (IAC); *Resul [M] v SSHD* [2019] UKUT 07602 (IAC).

54 Interview with David Tang (n 28).

55 Child Support Act 1991, s 26(2). For Scotland and Northern Ireland see, respectively, Law Reform (Parent and Child) (Scotland) Act 1986, s 5 and The Children (Northern Ireland) Order 1995, N.I.2 1995/755, s 5.

56 Convention on the Rights of the Child, 1577 UNTS 3 (20.11.1989).

57 Case 267/83 *Diatta* [1985] ECR 00567.

58 Case C-244/13 *Ogieriakhi* ECLI:EU:C:2014:2068.

address where the spouses were not encountered. By doing so, the authorities failed to discharge the burden of proof and, hence, clearly breached EU law.

In one case, the officers noted that there was no furniture or signs of cohabitation at the property, and the bins were empty. It was thus believed the TCN applicant had provided the Home Office with a false address, thus preventing the authorities from verifying the nature of her marriage.[59] In another case, the refusal followed an immigration visit that took place two months after the couple had moved out, the Home Office having been informed of the new address. The officers claimed that 'a man said they had never lived there'.[60] In a line of other situations, neighbours have similarly struggled to recognise the couple or reported that one of the spouses lived there alone.[61] The heavy reliance by immigration officers on such accounts is all the more puzzling, since, especially in large cities, neighbours may not know each other, and in any event, should not be considered a credible information source.

An application may also be refused where only one of the spouses is absent from their claimed marital home. In one case, the Pakistani national husband was present at the time of the visit but said that his Slovenian wife was visiting her sister in her home Member State. The immigration officers observed there was scant evidence of a woman's presence at the house and there was lack of photographs and phone records. This made them conclude that their marriage was not 'genuine and subsisting', and, hence, was one of convenience.[62] In a similar case, the Home Office raided the TCN husband's sister's home where the couple claimed to live. The EU citizen wife was absent, but her Cameroon national husband was found hiding in a cupboard, which, in the view of the officers, indicated that his marriage was one of convenience.[63] Later at the court hearing, he said he was simply scared, an explanation that was accepted by the FtT judge who eventually allowed his appeal.[64]

In *Gill*, immigration officers noted that there was no evidence of the EU citizen spouse's presence in the property and that her TCN husband was sharing a room with another male. They also considered that messages on his mobile phone from his wife were not affectionate. Although the non-EU national

59 *SSHD v Okofor* [2016] UKUT 42725 (IAC), para 3. See also, *Agho v SSHD* [2015] EWCA Civ 1198, [2016] INLR 411, para 3.

60 ILPA, 'Comments for the Chief Inspector of Borders and Immigration. Review of Sham Marriages (n 31).

61 E.g., *De Vera v SSHD* [2017] UKUT 07000 (IAC), para 2; *Saeed v SSHD* [2017] UKUT 09715 (IAC), para 2; *Muhammad [M] v SSHD* [2019] UKUT 07160 (IAC), para 8.

62 *SSHD v Kashif* [2016] UKUT 19663 (IAC), paras 3–5.

63 *SSHD v Lekeate* [2019] UKUT 08363 (IAC), para 5.

64 Ibid, para 15.

claimed that his wife had gone to Hungary for a visit, the immigration officers concluded there was no satisfactory evidence of a subsisting relationship and arrested him. The TCN husband was subsequently served a removal notice under section 10 of the Immigration and Asylum Act 1999 as someone who did not have, or ceased to have, the right to reside under the EEA Regulations 2016.[65] This decision was ultimately overturned by the UT, which rightly argued that the adverse finding was only made on the basis of the appellant's current circumstances without any reference to the period when the marriage was entered into. The UT stressed that, under EU law, 'the appellant was entitled to continue to reside in the UK whatever the state of his relationship, provided that he was still married to his EEA national sponsor and that the marriage itself had not been one of convenience when entered into'.[66]

On the other hand, a number of judgments show that the mere fact of cohabitation was deemed insufficient for a marriage to be considered not one of convenience. For example, in one case, immigration officers encountered the spouses in a bedroom and observed the presence of both male and female clothes and photographs of the couple on a bedside table. Yet, there were some sheets laid out on the floor which, in view of the officers, suggested they were sleeping separately. This, together with the fact that the spouses could not remember the exact place where they married, made the officers believe their marriage was one of convenience.[67] In its decision, the Home Office not only failed to discharge the burden of proof and wrongly placed its main focus on cohabitation but also discussed their sleeping arrangements, a disproportionate interference with the applicant's right to respect for human dignity and private and family life.

7 Conclusion

This chapter has shown that the Home Office's practices of investigating marriages give numerous reasons for concern and, at least at the post-marriage stage, did not easily comply with the Citizenship Directive or the Commission's guidance on the issue.

One of the problems with the Home Office's approach is the opacity surrounding 'risk profiles', used at the pre-marriage stage to decide if there is a need for further investigation. All cases referred by the marriage registrars to

65 *Gill v SSHD* [2019] UKUT 07335 (IAC).

66 Ibid, para 19.

67 *Uddin v SSHD* [2017] UKUT 27273 (IAC), paras 22, 32.

the Home Office as part of the 'referral and investigation scheme' are assessed using an automated triage system against certain criteria, which the Home Office has refused to disclose. There is a risk, however, that the algorithm is directly or indirectly discriminatory on nationality grounds. Another potentially problematic issue is possible 'automation bias' where an official conducting a subsequent assessment may be more inclined to conclude that the marriage is a sham if the system had previously flagged the case as suspicious. In the meantime, the number of detected sham marriages under the scheme is very low, which raises a question about the government's rationale in continuing to operate the scheme not only from a legal perspective but also a public policy one.

Next, it was demonstrated that during the interviews, Home Office officers did not seek to reduce the risk of an erroneous assessment by looking for hints that the marriage was genuine; rather, they focused on discrepancies in responses to prove that the marriage was one of convenience. Furthermore, at the post-marriage stage, the executive wrongly approached the issue of the burden of proof, required the relationship to be 'genuine and subsisting', designated marriages involving children as ones of convenience, as well as disregarded CJEU case law by placing an excessive focus on the present state of the relationship and requiring the couple to live under one roof. In addition, some of the investigation techniques are particularly hostile and arguably violate the EUCFR. Further, the data obtained suggests that the Home Office measures disproportionately target(ed) men from the Indian subcontinent, West Africa, and Albania, as well as female nationals of EU-12 Member States and naturalised EU citizens.

CHAPTER 10

Legitimising the Illegitimate: Marriages of Convenience and the UK Judiciary

1 Introduction

Previous chapters have shown that the Home Office has frequently disregarded EU law when designating marriages as ones of convenience and subjected TCN spouses of UK-resident EU citizens to excessive scrutiny. The general climate of suspicion and hostility towards this group resulted in significant interference and, in many cases, disruption of the family life of Union citizens involved. This chapter considers how UK courts respond to the 'compliant environment' practices of the executive, how much weight is given to EU-level legislation on the issue, and whether or not the relevant domestic provisions implementing the Citizenship Directive[1] or, more recently, the Withdrawal Agreement,[2] are interpreted in conformity with EU law.

To answer these questions, the author conducted an analysis of 193 Upper Tribunal (UT) Immigration and Asylum Chamber (IAC) decisions in cases where TCN spouses of UK-based EU citizens were previously refused entry or residence in the UK on the grounds that their marriage was found to be one of convenience. The cases examined were delivered between July 2016 and December 2023 and selected using the keywords 'marriage of convenience' or 'sham marriage'.[3] In addition, the author has explored several high-profile cases on the issue, delivered by the former Asylum and Immigration Tribunal, the Court of Appeal, the High Court of England and Wales, and the Supreme Court.

The majority (162) of the cases analysed concern appeals brought by TCN spouses against post-marriage determinations made by the Home Office at

1 Directive 2004/38/EC of the European Parliament and of the Council of 29 April 2004 on the right of citizens of the Union and their family members to move and reside freely within the territory of the Member States amending Regulation (EEC) No 1612/68 and repealing Directives 64/221/EEC, 68/360/EEC, 72/194/EEC, 73/148/EEC, 75/34/EEC, 75/35/EEC, 90/364/EEC, 90/365/EEC and 93/96/EEC [2004] OJ L158/77 (*Citizenship Directive*).

2 Agreement on the withdrawal of the United Kingdom of Great Britain and Northern Ireland from the European Union and the European Atomic Energy Community [2019] OJ C384/1 (*Withdrawal Agreement*).

3 For the full list of UT decisions analysed, see Annex 3.

 | DOI:10.1163/9789004499263_012

different stages of their residence in the UK, which were then unsuccessfully challenged in the First-tier Tribunal. In around half of these, the UT either allowed the appeal or remitted the case to the FtT for rehearing. A minority of cases (31) deal with appeals brought by the Home Office against positive FtT decisions. Likewise, a FtT finding that the marriage was not one of convenience was upheld in around half of such decisions.

Whilst most judgments involve initial applications for residence cards as spouses of EU citizens, many deal with the retained right of residence following divorce, applications for permanent residence, or an EEA family permit. Following the end of the transition period, the Upper Tribunal has largely been dealing with appeals brought by TCN spouses of EU citizens covered by the Withdrawal Agreement Act.[4] These types of cases concern applications for pre-settled or settled status or an EUSS family permit (mostly where the couples got married relatively shortly before 31 December 2020) or appeals against already existing negative decisions previously made by the Home Office or FtT under the EEA Regulations.[5] Provided that marriages entered into after the cut-off date do not fall within the scope of the Withdrawal Agreement Act, it is expected that in the following years, the courts will gradually stop hearing cases on alleged marriages of convenience in the EU law context.

Pre-marriage cases specifically focusing on sham marriages are rarely dealt with in courts. This can be explained by the fact that the yet unmarried non-EU nationals are removed under section 10 of the Immigration and Asylum Act 1999 as persons without leave, irrespective of the adverse findings about the nature of their intended marriage.

It should be noted that, due to its limitations, the study only focuses on First-tier Tribunal decisions brought on appeal. Normally, Home Office decisions that are successfully challenged in the FtT are not passed on to a higher instance court (except for cases where the Home Office appealed against such judgments). In the absence of statistics on the relevant FtT decisions that have resulted in a favourable outcome for non-EU nationals or have not been further pursued for other reasons, it is difficult to provide a full picture of how the FtT courts deal with the concept of marriages of convenience. Notwithstanding that, the number of judgments analysed is sufficient not only to provide a comprehensive overview of the UT approach to the issue but also to identify the most problematic practices of lower courts.

4 European Union (Withdrawal Agreement) Act 2020.

5 Immigration (European Economic Area) Regulations 2016, SI 2016/1052 (EEA Regulations 2016).

As briefly noted in Chapter 9, a significant share of the UT judgments analysed involve female nationals of Central and Eastern European Member States (such as Bulgaria, Czech Republic, Hungary, Lithuania, Romania, or Slovakia), as well as Portugal, married to male nationals of countries such as Pakistan, India, Nigeria, or Albania. The cases also frequently involve naturalised EU citizens who marry nationals of their countries of origin. Of the decisions analysed,[6] only one involved a TCN applicant from a country belonging to the Global North – namely, a US citizen.[7] As pointed out in the previous chapters, such patterns raise concerns about potential discrimination on nationality grounds.

The first section of this chapter considers the application of the burden of proof, an issue that has been explicitly addressed in EU-level legislation on marriages of convenience. Second, the chapter explores how the courts deal with the executive's excessive focus on cohabitation and the present state of the relationship. Next, bearing in mind the co-existence of different definitions of marriages of convenience and terms describing the concept in UK and EU law, the chapter looks at how the concept is defined by UK judges and identifies problems associated with that. The last section is specifically devoted to cases involving pregnancy and childbirth, factors which make the finding that a marriage is one of convenience particularly problematic.

2 Burden of Proof

One of the key issues in cases involving alleged marriages of convenience concerns the establishment of the burden of proof. To begin with, it has long been confirmed by UK judiciary that the legal burden of proof in EU cases lies with the Home Office. A line of rulings can be distinguished in this regard, starting from the much-quoted UT decision in *Papajorgji*,[8] delivered in late 2011, and ending up with the more recent Supreme Court judgment in *Sadovska*.[9]

The judgment in *Papajorgji* concerned an Albanian-Greek couple who had been married for 12 years and had two children. Irrespective of this fact, the Albanian wife was refused entry clearance to accompany her husband on a visit to the UK on the grounds that their marriage was one of convenience. The decision was based on the fact that she failed to produce any documentary

6 Where the UT has disclosed the applicant's nationality.

7 *SSHD v Holmes* [2018] UKUT 07786 (IAC).

8 *Papajorgji* (*EEA spouse – marriage of convenience*) *Greece* [2012] UKUT 38 (IAC).

9 *Sadovska and another v SSHD* [2017] UKSC 54, [2017] WLR(D) 556.

evidence of the nature of her marriage, such as pictures of their wedding or life together, or documents in joint names.[10] The Upper Tribunal disagreed. It first confirmed that the applicant was not required to discharge the burden of proof in the absence of reasonable suspicions suggesting the marriage was of convenience. Second, the Tribunal stated that 'if there was such evidence, it was for the applicant to produce evidence to address the suspicions' and that 'such an approach can be described as one of an evidential burden in the first place on the respondent and then shifting to the claimant in the light of the relevant information rather than a formal legal burden'.[11] The judge rightly referred to the 2009 Commission guidelines[12] (the Handbook[13] was yet to be delivered at the time), which places the burden of proof on the state, and clarified that although adverse inferences may be drawn by a claimant's failure to address the suspicions, this cannot form the sole or decisive reason for the conclusion.[14]

This approach was further endorsed in the subsequent Court of Appeal (CoA) judgment in *Agho,* where the Court referred to *Papajorgji* to confirm that the legal burden of proof rested with the Home Office and that it was not discharged merely by showing a 'reasonable suspicion'.[15] The CoA nonetheless acknowledged that the evidential burden may shift to the applicant 'by proof of facts that justify the interference that the marriage is not genuine, and the facts giving rise to the inference may include a failure to answer a request for documentary proof of the genuineness of the marriage where grounds for suspicion have been raised'.[16]

This was further confirmed in the CoA decision in *Rosa*[17] and the Supreme Court ruling in *Sadovska*.[18] In the latter case, the FtT erroneously claimed that '[i]n immigration appeals, the burden of proof is on the appellant and the standard of proof required is a balance of probabilities'.[19] The Supreme Court

10 *Papajorgji* (n 8), para 3.

11 Ibid, para 20.

12 Commission, 'Communication from the Commission to the European Parliament and the Council on guidance for better transposition and application of Directive 2004/38/EC on the right of citizens of the Union and their family members to move and reside freely within the territory of the Member States', COM (2009) 313 final.

13 Commission, 'Staff Working Document – Handbook on addressing the issue of alleged marriages of convenience between EU citizens and non-EU nationals in the context of EU law on free movement of EU citizens' SWD(2014) 284 final.

14 *Papajorgji* (n 8), para 37.

15 *Agho v SSHD* [2015] EWCA Civ 1198, [2016] INLR 411.

16 Ibid, para 13.

17 *Rosa v SSHD* [2016] EWCA Civ 14, [2016] WLR(D) 6.

18 *Sadovska and another* (n 9).

19 Ibid, para 14.

corrected this error by reiterating that the FtT approach would generally be correct in cases involving domestic law yet did not apply where EU law came into play.[20]

Notwithstanding the line of judgments clarifying the issue, an analysis of the Upper Tribunal decisions suggests that FtT judges still frequently placed the burden of proof upon the applicant,[21] including cases where they correctly referred to the EEA Regulations or the Appendix EU to the Immigration Rules. In many cases, however, the FtT wrongly referred to the domestic immigration provisions (or even human rights grounds)[22] instead and/or required an applicant to demonstrate that their marriage was 'genuine and subsisting', claiming that the burden of proof lay on the non-EU national involved.[23] In such situations, the Upper Tribunal normally allowed the appeal by reiterating that the burden of proof rested with the Home Office and providing a reference to the relevant judgments in *Sadovska, Rosa, Agho* or *Papajorgji*.[24] The Commission Handbook has almost never been quoted in this context.[25] In one case, which concerned an application for an EUSS status, the UT has nevertheless explicitly clarified that the principles protected by EU law should equally apply in appeals brought under the Immigration (Citizens' Rights Appeals) (EU Exit) Regulations 2020.[26,27]

20 Ibid, para 31.

21 See among others, *Igwe v SSHD* [2016] UKUT 27335 (IAC), para 4; *Aziz v SSHD* [2017] UKUT 01427 (IAC), para 7; *SSHD v Michael [O]* [2018] UKUT 02107 (IAC), para 11; *Yeya v SSHD* [2018] UKUT 00515 (IAC), para 3; *Nasreen v SSHD* [2018] UKUT 25249 (IAC), para 11; *Ninsinghkhon v Entry Clearance Officer, Bangkok* [2018] UKUT 08937 (IAC), paras 8–9; *Muhammad [M] v SSHD* [2019] UKUT 07160 (IAC), para 19. *Isufaj (PTA decisions/reasons; EEA reg. 37 appeals)* [2019] UKUT 00283 (IAC), para 26; *Andrushkiv v SSHD* [2020] UKUT 07859 (IAC), para 9; *Shakeel v SSHD* [2022] UKUT 13405 (IAC), paras 5,7; *Khan v SSHD* [2023] UKUT 11835 (IAC), paras 5,6,13.

22 *Laizane v SSHD* [2019] UKUT 17910 (IAC), para 3.

23 See among others, *Rovillos v SSHD* [2017] UKUT 01821 (IAC), paras 9, 13; *Mahmood v SSHD* [2018] UKUT 02903 (IAC), para 2; *De Zoysa Siriwardana Nanediri v SSHD* [2019] UKUT 04892 (IAC), para 3; also *Ussenbai v Entry Clearance Officer* [2019] UKUT 00472 (IAC), para 8; *Sokoya v SSHD* [2019] UKUT 07559 (IAC), para 6; *Nakanwagi v Entry Clearance Officer, Pretoria* [2021] UKUT 01779 (IAC), para 20. In *Waseem v SSHD* [2020] UKUT 07454 (IAC), the FtT applied the 'genuine and subsisting' test whilst meanwhile referring to the EEA Regulations.

24 In one case, the UT nevertheless endorsed the 'genuine and subsisting' test whilst meanwhile correctly referring to the EEA Regulations. *Khan v SSHD* [2022] UKUT 06826 (IAC), para 24.

25 See *Letitia [G] v SSHD* [2020] UKUT 00458 (IAC) for an exception.

26 Immigration (Citizens' Rights Appeals) (EU Exit) Regulations 2020, SI 2020/61.

27 *Shakeel* (n 21), para 7.

2.1 *Evidential Burden*

Even where the judges did show awareness of the relevant case law, the application of the test in practice appeared problematic. In a number of judgments, FtT considered that in cases of 'well-founded' suspicions, the legal burden of proof rested with the non-EU national. In several cases, such decisions were set aside by the UT;[28] yet there are disappointing examples when the Upper Tribunal did concur with the FtT.[29]

Furthermore, the case law analysis shows that judges rarely followed the 'double-lock' approach described in the Commission Handbook. Instead of first looking for the hints suggesting that the marriage is not one of convenience, tribunals tended to endorse the position pursued by the executive – i.e., focus on alleged discrepancies and other perceived signs of abuse. In doing so, the judges typically relied on their stereotypes and highly normative perceptions of how a 'real' marriage should look like. In this light, their findings that the Home Office had discharged the burden of proof are rather questionable. Although the erroneous conclusions of the FtT were frequently overturned or set aside by the UT, this was not always the case.

Rajah is one of the rare cases where the UT explicitly referred to the positive and negative indicative criteria listed in the 2009 Commission guidelines (although the decision was delivered in 2018, the judge appeared to be unaware of the Handbook). The FtT previously found the marriage to be one of convenience mainly because the applicant was not found at home during the immigration visit, a decision that was ultimately rejected by the UT. Following the criteria provided in the Guidelines, the UT *inter alia* noted that the couple had a relationship before their marriage, the appellant already had a five-year UK visa, the couple were consistent about the circumstances of their first meeting, they had a common language, and it was not suggested that the principal was paid to marry her husband or that either of them had a previous history of fraud, abuse, or marriages of convenience.[30] Hence, on the balance of probabilities, the UT concluded that Home Office had not discharged the burden of proof.[31]

28 See for instance *Mubashar v SSHD* [2017] UKUT 00171 (IAC), para 2; *Mazhar v SSHD* [2017] UKUT 14102 (IAC), paras 12–13. *Mirush [K] v SSHD* [2020] UKUT 07293 (IAC), paras 10–13.

29 See for instance, *Sonde v SSHD* [2017] UKUT 32338 (IAC), para 10.

30 *Rajah [A] v SSHD* [2018] UKUT 08581 (IAC), paras 30–33.

31 Ibid, para 34.

In one case, the FtT judge endorsed the Home Office's finding that a marriage was one of convenience because *inter alia* the EU principal had limited knowledge of her TCN husband's academic career.[32] The UT, however, noted that the judge failed to consider the questions which the partners had answered correctly, as well as evidence from family and friends, photos, and evidence of their cohabitation. In this light, the UT doubted that the FtT considered whether the evidential burden had shifted to the appellant and if it had, whether the appellant had satisfied it, a procedure set out in *Papajorgji*. The decision was consequently set aside.[33]

In another case, the FtT judge found that a marriage was one of convenience *inter alia* because they considered the appellant's lack of knowledge about his wife's family was inconsistent with that 'normally expected of a husband'.[34] This is a highly normative and subjective position that was rightly criticised by the UT, particularly given that the wife explained that they did not talk about her father or brother due to 'abuse issues during her childhood'.[35] The appeal was consequently remitted to the FtT for re-hearing. Likewise, in *Ogbewi*, the FtT judge argued that the non-EU national's evidence that her sisters, who also lived in the UK, did not attend the wedding because they were working, was 'not indicative of a genuine wedding',[36] a highly subjective perception that the UT implicitly endorsed.

In some cases, both tribunals drew adverse inferences from the fact that the couple had a joint bank account and bills in joint names, opining that it was 'part of a package' to convince the Home Office that their marriage was not one of convenience.[37] In *Jamil*, the UT judge commented that a marriage that lasted for three years was 'on any way brief'.[38] This, together with other questionable evidence, made the judge believe it was one of convenience. In another case, both the FtT and UT found the marriage to be one of convenience solely because there was evidence of a direct link between the EU citizen principal and an organised gang that brought Lithuanian nationals to the UK to be married to non-EU nationals. From the decision, it does not follow

32 *[B S] v SSHD* [2017] UKUT 16879 (IAC), para 10.

33 Ibid, paras 8–11.

34 *Ahmed v SSHD* [2019] UKUT 01401 (IAC), para 5.

35 Ibid.

36 *Ogbewi v SSHD* [2017] UKUT 03381 (IAC), para 19.

37 *Habib v SSHD* [2018] UKUT 06534 (IAC), para 5; See also, *Marquez v SSHD* [2018] UKUT 00705 (IAC), para 9.

38 *Jamil v SSHD* [2017] UKUT 33121 (IAC), para 18.

that the judges had ever dealt with the purpose or substance of the particular marriage.[39]

In a number of cases, the FtT judges dismissed the claims *inter alia* on the grounds of their biased assessments of the photographic evidence. The judges tend to complain about the low number of photographs submitted or label them as 'staged'.[40] As a result, couples may feel pressured to take many pictures together even if they would not do so in normal circumstances, and then risk being considered not 'genuine' because of showing either too much or too little affection. In *Nasreen*, for instance, the FtT indicated that the couple did not seem comfortable with each other in their wedding photos. The UT judge later did not find this claim persuasive, explaining that the couple may have looked formal out of respect for the wife and her parent's strict religious background.[41] In another case, the UT rightly criticised the FtT judge who erred by saying she was surprised there were no photos from Christmas 2014, although the couple did not spend it together.[42] In a further case, which involved an unsuccessful application for an EUSS family permit, the FtT judge doubted the authenticity of the provided photographs and erroneously shifted the burden of proof onto the appellant to prove that the photo evidence was not forged. The UT pointed out that the allegation of forgery was unsupported by any expert evidence and clarified that '[i]t is not for the appellant to prove that his photographs are not doctored or that his marriage is genuine'.[43] The appeal was consequently allowed.

Furthermore, some judges placed significant weight on cultural differences between the spouses, a highly discriminatory position that is in no way linked to the purpose or content of the marriage. As UT reasonably argued in *Nasreen*, it was unclear why the FtT judge doubted that a Bangladeshi-Italian couple developed a relationship at a takeaway restaurant where he worked, and she was a customer, and they found they had a lot in common despite their different backgrounds.[44] Likewise, judges tend to follow the approach by the executive and act as language and communication experts, evaluating the parties' language skills and their ability to converse.

39 *Arif v SSHD* [2019] UKUT 06176 (IAC).

40 See among others, *De Vera v SSHD* [2017] UKUT 07000 (IAC), para 2; *Ogbewi* (n 36), paras 4–5; *Raja v SSHD* [2018] UKUT 35032 (IAC), para 14; *Marquez* (n 37), para 9; *Letitia* [*G*] (n 25), para 26.

41 *Nasreen* (n 21).

42 *Ogbewi* (n 36).

43 *Mohamud v SSHD* [2022] UKUT 03758 (IAC), para 19.

44 *Nasreen* (n 21), para 24. See also, *Jamil* (n 38), para 18.

In one case, the FtT judge dismissed the appeal on the grounds that the appellant's responses to the questions were 'incredibly vague' and the English of the principal – 'wholly inadequate'.[45] This led the judge to conclude that the spouses were unable to converse, a finding also accepted by the UT. In another case involving a Pakistani-Portuguese couple, the FtT found that the marriage was one of convenience because the couple gave inconsistent evidence and the wife spoke 'very little' English,[46] a finding that paradoxically outweighed the fact that the couple had a son. Although the wife said in evidence that her husband spoke very slowly to her, the judge held that 'the level of the EEA sponsor's knowledge of English is so low that a meaningful communication and conversation cannot be held between them', as well as erroneously relied on the 'genuine and subsisting' relationship test.[47] The UT reasonably argued that it was unclear how the judge proceeded to receive evidence from the wife without an interpreter and ultimately held that his analysis was 'tainted by legal error on the grounds of perversity'.[48]

3 Focus on Cohabitation and/or Present State of the Relationship

The issue of the evidential burden of proof is closely linked to another problematic approach adopted by the courts. As observed in Chapter 9, when investigating suspicious cases, the Home Office tended to dwell extensively on the current nature of the relationship, requiring the marriage to be 'genuine and subsisting' and placing the main focus on cohabitation as evidence of its genuineness. As will be shown below, both FtT and UT are inclined to support this erroneous position.[49] There are cases, however, where the UT has criticised such an approach by stressing that EU law does not require the couple to live together under one roof[50] or remain in a 'subsisting' and 'enduring'

45 *Aziz* (n 21), para 5.
46 *Adnan v SSHD* [2017] UKUT 25601 (IAC), para 3.
47 Ibid, para 4.
48 Ibid, para 8.
49 In some cases, however, such an approach appeared to be beneficial to couples who could demonstrate extensive evidence of cohabitation, which was accepted by judges as evidence that their marriage was not one of convenience. Interview with Priya Solanki, a barrister at One Pump Court (online, 12 December 2023).
50 See, for instance, *Faisal v SSHD* [2017] UKUT 00817 (IAC), para 13; *Azam v SSHD* [2019] UKUT 04634 (IAC), para 11, *Sokoya* (n 23), para 19; *Cunningham v SSHD* [2020] UKUT 06579 (IAC), para 5.

relationship.[51] Meanwhile, there are cases where both tribunals expressed an opinion that the mere fact of cohabitation is insufficient for a marriage to be considered 'genuine'.[52]

In a number of cases, the judges rightly held that the Home Office failed to discharge the burden of proof by considering the marriage to be one of convenience only because the spouses were absent from their claimed marital home during an immigration visit. In one case, the FtT judge endorsed the Home Office finding that the marriage was one of convenience which was made following a visit to the couple's address where a neighbour did not recognise either of the parties and claimed they had never lived there.[53] The UT judge was reasonably concerned that the FtT ignored the fact that the wife had meanwhile miscarried.[54] Furthermore, it was rightly argued that the neighbours' reports did nothing to illuminate the reasons for the marriage: after all, it was possible that the neighbours were misunderstood by immigration officials, did not trust them, or were untruthful.[55]

In another situation, the Home Office did not believe the TCN husband who said his wife had gone to her home Member State for a visit. The couple provided to the FtT, extensive evidence of cohabitation, including a return ticket for the principal, photographs, and a tenancy agreement in both names. As the FtT noted, the latter showed that they 'jointly occupy a small flat with a single bedroom' and '[i]t is not the case that they occupy different rooms in the same building'.[56] Furthermore, the couple were consistent about where the wife worked, as well as the bedroom furnishings, sleeping arrangements, and details such as what they had for breakfast. The appeal was subsequently allowed, with the finding later upheld by the UT.[57]

The above cases serve as clear examples of the erroneous approach of the Home Office in rejecting the applications of couples who were obviously in a relationship, without providing them with a fair opportunity to address the suspicions. Yet, whilst ultimately coming to the right conclusions, the tribunals still placed the main emphasis on the evidence of cohabitation without acknowledging that spouses are not obliged to live together in the first place.

---

51 *Aroyehun v SSHD* [2022] UKUT 05977 (IAC), para 29; *Khan v SSHD* [2023] UKUT 001516 (IAC), para 18.

52 See for instance, *Asghar v SSHD* [2019] UKUT 07181 (IAC), paras 13–14.

53 *Muhammad [M]* (n 21), paras 8–11.

54 Ibid, para 17.

55 Ibid, para 12.

56 *SSHD v Kashif* [2016] UKUT 19663 (IAC), para 13.

57 See also, *SSHD v Okofor* [2016] UKUT 42725 (IAC).

Likewise, the tribunals gave the main weight to the ongoing relationship, regarding it as a condition for the marriage to be treated as genuine, thus erroneously focusing on its substance rather than its purpose.[58]

For instance, in one case, the Home Office concluded that the couple was not 'genuine' because of a 'litany of discrepancies', including matters such as where they had spent New Year's Eve and when marriage had been proposed.[59] Following the cross-examination during the hearing, the FtT found that the vast majority of their answers were consistent. The parties were asked to state what their favourite food was, what hours they worked, and what they liked to do together. Taking all the evidence together, the FtT found that the burden of proof had not been discharged, and the UT upheld this judgment after the Home Office appealed against the FtT decision.[60]

Similarly, in another case, the UT accepted that the EU principal gave discrepant answers during the interview not because her marriage was one of convenience but due to her medical condition and the aggressive style of questioning she faced.[61] In its decision, the UT dismissed the discrepancies as insignificant – e.g., that the principal did not know the appellant was staying with a cousin on the very first occasion they met and assumed he was staying in a hotel, or that the TCN husband did not know why the sponsor moved to the Netherlands in 1980, as this was two decades before their relationship began. The UT consequently found, on the balance of probabilities, that the marriage was not one of convenience.[62] In doing so, the UT mentioned many indicators proving this, such as: a consistent account of the relationship and the marriage proposal; both parties knowing the names of each other's family members and the different addresses they lived at; both parties knowing the practical details of their current property; the description of the principal's work uniform and hours; as well as what they did last Sunday.[63]

In another case, the FtT accepted that the parties' answers to around 200 questions were largely consistent and that they were cohabiting.[64] Nonetheless, other factors were held against the appellant – i.e., the 'haste' with which

58 With some exceptions. For instance, in *Adi v SSHD* [2019] UKUT 09432 (IAC) the FtT concluded that the parties were not in a 'genuine and subsisting marriage'. The UT held that the FtT erred in law by failing to specifically consider the position at the date of marriage.

59 *SSHD v Chami* [2016] UKUT 12375 (IAC), para 2.

60 Ibid.

61 *Alex [A] v SSHD* [2018] UKUT 04343 (IAC), para 21.

62 Ibid paras 22–23.

63 Ibid para 25.

64 *Raza v SSHD* [2019] UKUT 03566 (IAC), para 5.

the parties married[65] and the lack of the wife's knowledge concerning her husband's finances, a factor which, in the view of the FtT, fundamentally undermined the validity of their relationship.[66] Furthermore, the FtT gave significant weight to the fact that the husband said he did not tell the principal he was living in the UK 'illegally', whilst the principal said that he told her on their first date.[67] This led the FtT to conclude that the marriage was one convenience, a finding that was dismissed by the UT. The latter underlined that these factors must be viewed in the context of all the evidence as a whole, and the UT did not regard them to have a determinative value. In particular, the UT noted that the TCN husband did not consider his status 'illegal' but simply told the principal that he did not have a visa, which matches with the principal's account.[68] Furthermore, the tribunal rightly emphasised that relationships may 'take many forms' and '[s]pouses have very different degrees of knowledge of each other's financial situation'.[69] The appeal was consequently allowed. In another case, the FtT went as far as to claim that a genuine marriage can later transform into a marriage of convenience. In particular, it found that, although the applicant might have entered into a genuine marriage, he 'was not living in anything more than a marriage of convenience' at a later stage, and there was no evidence that the relationship was 'genuine and subsisting'.[70] This reasoning was considered erroneous by the UT who stressed that '[a] marriage that was entered into for genuine reasons but subsequently ceases to subsist is not a marriage of convenience under EU law'.[71]

In other cases, however, the UT upheld the decision of the Home Office in concluding that the appellant's marriage was one of convenience. In *Gjana*, both tribunals reached this conclusion because the EU citizen spouse went for a holiday to her home Member State. The FtT judge, in particular, considered it 'noteworthy that she went for the month and not a shorter holiday so that she could spend time with her husband' and placed weight on the fact that it happened shortly after the couple moved into the same accommodation.[72] In the view of the judge, this suggested that 'her family visit was of more importance to her and undermine[d] that claim that this is a genuine relationship'.[73]

65 Ibid para 10.
66 Ibid para 28.
67 Ibid paras 26–27.
68 Ibid para 27.
69 Ibid para 28.
70 *Aroyehun* (n 51), para 13.
71 Ibid, para 29.
72 *Gjana v SSHD* [2019] UKUT 07850 (IAC), para 10.
73 Ibid.

This view was also upheld by the UT. Such an approach is striking in its subjectivity and clearly breaches EU law – both the evidential burden test and the CJEU case law in *Diatta*[74] and *Ogieriakhi*.[75] It should be recalled that the spouses are free to arrange their marital life as they wish and it is not for the judges to decide whether they can go on lengthy holidays on their own and how much time they need to spend together. In another case, the UT correctly noted that cohabitation is not a requirement under EU law but nonetheless stressed that the couple did not supply a tenancy agreement, evidence from family or friends, photographs, or other evidence of an 'ongoing relationship'.[76]

Another problematic category of cases is those where the relationship has deteriorated, or the spouses have chosen to maintain separate accommodation due to their work arrangements.[77] In *De Vera*, the Home Office refused to grant the TCN spouse a residence card after not having encountered the couple at their declared home address. During the hearing, the FtT judge placed weight on the fact that the appellant had said that she lived 'on and off with her husband', as well as expressed surprise by the fact that she was working in Essex, some distance from their marital home in the London borough of Hounslow. Although she did return to Hounslow for four days a week, the judge claimed that such an arrangement was 'wholly inconsistent with the appellant and her husband being a young couple who wish to spend their lives together in a genuine marriage', suggesting that she should have been able to find a job nearer to where she lived in London.[78] This finding was rightly dismissed by the Upper Tribunal as purely speculative, particularly in view of the explanation of the appellant about the difficulty of finding work and accommodation.[79] The marriage was ultimately found not to be one of convenience. Yet, although the UT rightly dismissed the erroneous conclusions of the FtT by reference to the extensive evidence produced by the couple, it did not refer to the CJEU case law which would have further strengthened its argument.

In a number of cases, a residence permit was revoked on the sole basis that the Home Office found that the spouses had separated, but their divorce was still pending. In *Iqbal*, the relevant Home Office decision was subsequently upheld by both the FtT and the UT, whereby the latter noted that the situation for the appellant had been made even more complicated in that there was

74 Case 267/83 *Diatta* [1985] ECR 00567.

75 Case C-244/13 *Ogieriakhi* ECLI:EU:C:2014:2068, para 38.

76 *Sokoya* (n 23), para 19.

77 This has also been confirmed by Priya Solanki (n 49).

78 *De Vera* (n 40), paras 3–4.

79 Ibid 10–11.

now 'a letter from his wife saying that they are no longer in a relationship'.[80] Irrespective of the nature of the marriage, this remark is confusing since separation must not affect the TCN spouse's entitlement to a residence permit as long as the marriage is not officially terminated. In some cases, however, the UT has rightly confirmed that even if the couple is estranged, under EU law, the status of a family member would only change with divorce.[81]

4 Definition of Marriages of Convenience

The analysis of case law suggests that very few judges attempted to establish a legal definition of marriages of convenience. This, in turn, undermined legal certainty and frequently lead to adverse outcomes. Those who did attempt to define a marriage of convenience, however, often struggled with providing a correct definition of the phenomenon in the context of EU free movement law. As observed above, in numerous situations, FtT appeared to be fully unaware of EU law or the domestic EEA Regulations on the issue and erroneously relied on the domestic immigration law instead, requiring the marriage to be 'genuine and subsisting'.[82] Whilst in several rulings, UT judges did quote the definition found in the EEA Regulations 2016,[83] in some cases, the UT stated that the Regulations did not define marriages of convenience and referred to the 1997 Council Resolution instead.[84] The latter approach is confusing not only because the Regulations did contain a definition of marriages of convenience but also because the judges appeared to be unaware of the 2014 Commission Handbook, even though the relevant UT decisions were delivered several years after its publication.

Yet even where the judges rightly focused on the position at the point of entry into marriage, the 'sole purpose' definition was frequently substituted by the 'primary purpose' approach, which is inconsistent with EU law. One of the cases illustrating this trend is *Papajorgji*, discussed in Section 2 above. The judgment was delivered in 2012 before the 2016 EEA Regulations came into force.

80 *Iqbal v SSHD* [2016] UKUT 09279 (IAC).

81 *Faisal* (n 50), para 13; *Tandel v SSHD* [2019] UKUT 05031 (IAC), para 8.

82 See, among others, *Nasreen* (n 21), para 9; *Ussenbai* (n 23), paras 5, 7; *Sokoya* (n 23), para 6. See also, *Rovillos* (n 23), para 9; *Mahmood* (n 23), para 2; *De Zoysa Siriwardana Nanediri* (n 23), para 3.

83 See, e.g., *Letitia* [*G*] (n 40), para 10; *Raza v SSHD* [2020] UKUT 00542 (IAC), para 12; *Nakanwagi* (n 23), para 31; *Usiobaifo v SSHD* [2021] UKUT 02875 (IAC), para 40.

84 *Entry Clearance Officer v Yuliia* [*Z*] [2019] UKUT 01734, para 10; *Josephine* [*O*] *v SSHD* [2019] UKUT 05252 (IAC), para 6; *Sidhu v SSHD* [2019] UKUT 07915 (IAC), para 6.

The UT argued that neither the Citizenship Directive nor the previous version of the EEA Regulations contained a definition of marriage of convenience, but that phrase 'has been construed in the context of the immigration rules as a marriage entered into without the intention of matrimonial cohabitation and for the primary reason of securing admission to the country'.[85] The concluding passage of the judgment provided a slightly reformulated definition, where a marriage of convenience was designated as a marriage 'contracted for the sole or decisive purpose of gaining admission to the host state'.[86]

Although the judge ultimately resolved the case in the appellant's favour and rightly held that 'a durable marriage with children and co-habitation' should not be considered a marriage of convenience,[87] the definition applied is nonetheless inconsistent with EU law. In the author's view, Article 35 of the Citizenship Directive, in conjunction with Recital 28 of its Preamble, clearly define it as a marriage concluded with the sole purpose to legalise the stay of a third-country national in the EU. Furthermore, the judge was obviously unaware of the 1997 Resolution or the 2009 Guidelines that had already been published at the time of the hearing and included the 'sole purpose' definition.

The 'primary purpose' definition provided in *Papajorgji* was further reproduced in the judgment of *Agho,* albeit it did not influence the favourable outcome for the applicant in a particular case.[88] In a subsequent ruling in *Rosa,* however, the judge adopted the correct approach by referring to the 'sole purpose' definition as provided in the 1997 Resolution (although the judge was obviously unaware of the 2009 Commission Guidelines or 2014 Handbook, already published at the time).[89]

However, in a subsequent line of high-level cases, the tribunals adopted a strikingly confusing approach, not least due to the apparent misinterpretation of the relevant EU guidance caused by its obvious ambiguity. The Supreme Court ruling in *Sadovska*[90] is an important case where Commission soft law became national hard law – in this particular situation, however, this has led to adverse implications for EU citizens and their TCN family members. The Court first described the phrase 'marriage of convenience' as 'a term of art' which is defined in the Citizenship Directive and 2009 Guidelines as one contracted for the sole purpose of enjoying Treaty rights.[91] Yet, the judge then went on to

85 *Papajorgji* (*EEA spouse – marriage of convenience*) *Greece* (n 8), para 14.
86 Ibid, para 30.
87 Ibid.
88 *Agho* (n 15).
89 *Rosa* (n 17).
90 *Sadovska and another* (n 9).
91 Ibid, paras 22, 24.

quote a passage from the 2014 Handbook which says that 'the notion of "sole purpose" should not be interpreted literally (as being the unique or exclusive purpose) but rather as meaning that the objective to obtain the right of entry and residence must be the predominant purpose of the abusive conduct'.[92] The Court then suggested that the Handbook expanded the definition provided in the Directive by stating that the entry and residence in the EU shall be not the sole, but the predominant purpose.[93] As mentioned in Chapter 7, such an interpretation is deeply problematic and arguably violates the Directive.

In the same month that the decision in *Sadovska* came up, the High Court delivered its judgment in *Molina*.[94] In its reasoning, the court further departed from EU law by rather paradoxically suggesting that a couple may enter into a marriage of convenience even if they are in a genuine relationship.

The case involved a Bolivian national who entered the UK in 2007 using a false passport and remained in the country since. Six years later, he began a relationship with an Italian national and moved in with her. The couple arranged to be married on 19 May 2015, but further to a section 24 report by a marriage registrar, they were approached on that date by immigration officers and subsequently interviewed. Following the interviews, a notice was served on the claimant, which stated that:

> [A]lthough there is a relationship going on it does not show that they have a relationship akin to marriage. [The claimant] will benefit from his union with [the EU citizen] and even though this may not be a sham marriage it is definitely a marriage of convenience to gain immigration advantage.[95]

The marriage was consequently prevented and the non-EU national detained. After a series of appeals, the FtT judge ultimately held that he was entitled to an EEA residence card as an extended family member of an EU citizen, as the judge was satisfied the couple were in a 'genuine and durable relationship'.[96] The Bolivian national nonetheless lodged judicial review proceedings, seeking to challenge the decision to prevent his wedding from taking place, as well as detaining and removing him.

92 Ibid, para 24.

93 Ibid, para 29.

94 *Molina, R (On the Application Of) v SSHD* [2017] EWHC 1730 (Admin).

95 Ibid, para 4.

96 Ibid, para 20.

The first issue directly dealt with the question of whether an intended marriage could be prevented on the grounds that it was a marriage of convenience even though the Home Office admitted the parties were in an ongoing relationship. The applicant argued that the decision to impede his marriage had been premised on a mistaken understanding that there is a difference between a 'sham marriage' and a 'marriage of convenience', which were, in truth, synonymous. In his view, neither could exist if there was a genuine relationship between the parties.

The Court disagreed. It recalled that under section 24(5) of the Immigration and Asylum Act 1999, 'the absence of a "genuine relationship between the parties to the marriage" is a pre-requisite to the marriage being a "sham marriage"'.[97] The judge then went on to observe that section 24 did not provide a statutory definition of a 'marriage of convenience'. However, the Court further noted that a non-exclusive definition was found in regulation 2(1) of the EEA Regulations 2016. In the view of the judge, although the EEA Regulations 2016 were not yet in force at the time Mr Molina's marriage was prevented, they did show that the underlying purpose of a marriage of convenience should be obtaining an immigration advantage.

In addition, the High Court relied on the case of *Baiai,* where the judge quoted the 'sole purpose' definition found in the 1997 Council Resolution.[98] Based on the above considerations, the judge concluded that 'there is a difference in principle between a "sham marriage" and a "marriage of convenience". It is clear from the statutory definition that a sham marriage can only be established if there is no genuine relationship between the parties'.[99] Yet, although 'a "marriage of convenience" may also entail a marriage which is not genuine', its hallmark is 'one that has been entered into (…) for the purpose of gaining an immigration advantage'.[100] The judge then stated:

> [A] 'marriage of convenience' may exist despite the fact that there is a genuine relationship and in the absence of any deception or fraud as to its existence. The focus is upon the intention of one or more of the parties and, in the present context, whether the sole aim is to gain an immigration advantage.[101]

97 Ibid, para 59.
98 Ibid, paras 60–62.
99 Ibid, para 64.
100 Ibid.
101 Ibid, para 73.

This made the Court conclude that the immigration officer was right in stating that the couple was in a genuine relationship but nevertheless intended to enter into a marriage for an immigration advantage, which, in the Court's view, was consistent with the legal definition of a 'marriage of convenience'. The decision to prevent the marriage from taking place was therefore considered lawful.[102]

Overall, the ruling is fundamentally flawed for a number of reasons. First, since the couple were not married yet, their situation did not fall within the scope of the EEA Regulations, and the only definition that applied to them was the one of a 'sham marriage', found in the Immigration and Asylum Act 1999. Therefore, by finding their marriage to be one 'of convenience', although there was no legal basis to consider the given definition as such, the judge clearly erred in law. Second, the intended wedding was supposed to take place a few weeks after the 'referral and investigation scheme' came into force. Since then, it is compliance with the investigation and not the nature of the intended marriage that can impact the individual's right to marry. Yet neither the Home Office nor the High Court showed awareness of the relevant rules.

Notwithstanding the above, the High Court entirely misinterpreted the 'sole purpose' principle established for the purposes of the Directive. The key issue here is the distinction between the sole and the primary purpose of a marriage in the context of both the EEA Regulations 2016 and the 1997 Council Resolution, the two legal instruments quoted by the judge. As argued in Chapter 7 above, it is indeed the case that the EEA Regulations did not contain the phrase 'sole purpose' and could potentially cover a broader range of situations contrary to what is envisaged under EU law. This has led to a puzzling conclusion that the definition of a 'marriage of convenience' in EU law is somehow broader than the one found in the UK Immigration Act, which in reality, is not the case. Nonetheless, the High Court also relied on the 'sole purpose' definition provided in the 1997 Resolution, which is formulated quite clearly. In this light, the outcome of the judgment is even more confusing.

The erroneous approach established in *Molina* was further applied in later case law. In its judgment in *Seferi & Anor*,[103] delivered in early 2018, the High Court adopted the same line of reasoning by holding that a couple may enter into a marriage of convenience if their wedding was planned predominantly for an immigration advantage. The facts of the case are similar to *Molina*. The appellant, Mr Seferi, was an Albanian national with no valid leave to remain.

102 Ibid.

103 *Seferi & Anor, R (On the Application Of) v SSHD* [2018] EWHC 287 (Admin).

In January 2015, he met Ms Zara, a Greek national and later started to cohabit with her. In 2017, they gave notice of their intention to marry, following which they were invited for an interview. After the interview, the Home Office issued a notice stating that they had now complied with the investigation. However, on the very same day, the Home Office detained Mr Seferi as an irregular migrant with a view to removing him. Mr Seferi issued a judicial review shortly before his intended removal date.

One of the main issues considered by the Court was whether there was a reviewable decision about the nature of the proposed marriage. To provide an answer to this question, the judge examined the Home Office decision letters relating to the removal and detention of the appellant. One of them, with relation to the marriage interview, concluded:

> Although elements of genuineness to the relationship were demonstrated, the overall application for marriage had been contrived, mainly by the sponsor [Ms Zara], as a vehicle to allow the applicant to remain in the UK legally. As such the relationship is deemed a sham to circumvent immigration officials.[104]

The High Court concurred with this evaluation. First, the judge endorsed the interpretation of the concepts of a 'sham marriage' and a 'marriage of convenience' found in *Molina*. Having referred both to the Immigration and Asylum Act 1999 and the EEA Regulations 2016, the judge concluded that 'a marriage of convenience under the 2016 Regulations may be entered into by a couple in a genuine relationship, and is different from a sham marriage as defined by the 1999 Act'.[105] Furthermore, the judge quoted the judgment in *Sadovska,* where it was stated that the immigration advantage must be the predominant purpose of the marriage.[106] In relation to the present case, the High Court noted that the terminology of the Home Office was somewhat confusing yet the letters suggested that 'the primary purpose of the marriage was to give Mr Seferi an immigration advantage'.[107] Therefore, in the view of the judge, 'even if it was not truly a sham marriage as defined by the 1999 Act, it was certainly a marriage of convenience as defined by the 2016 Regulations'.[108] Despite this, the Court concluded that the legal basis for the detention and intended removal

104 Ibid, para 23.
105 Ibid, para 16.
106 Ibid, para 17.
107 Ibid, para 26.
108 Ibid.

of Mr Seferi was his irregular status, rather than the nature of his prospective marriage.[109]

The conclusions reached in *Seferi & Anor* are very similar to the ones in *Molina*. In both cases, the High Court, first, erroneously placed the pre-marriage situations within the scope of the EEA Regulations, and second, expanded the definition of marriage of convenience to the one entered into with the primary purpose of obtaining an immigration advantage. It is remarkable that in *Seferi & Anor*, the Court did not refer to the 'sole purpose' definition found in the 1997 Resolution as it did in *Molina*, and only quoted provisions of the EEA Regulations instead. In *Seferi & Anor*, the Court saw no need at all to look for the relevant definition in EU law. This has led to a regrettable outcome where the High Court has explicitly allowed the executive and lower courts to employ a broader definition of marriages of convenience and thereby target an increasing number of couples leading a family life.

The erroneous 'predominant purpose' approach set out in *Sadovska* and *Molina* has meanwhile been followed in the subsequent UT case law. For example, in an Upper Tribunal decision in *Saeed* of 2022 the judge summarised their approach as follows:

> The terms 'sham marriage' and 'marriage of convenience' are not mutually exclusive. The absence of a genuine relationship at the time of the marriage being entered into would render the marriage one of convenience (and a 'sham'); however, if there is a genuine relationship at the time of the marriage, while it could not be categorised as a 'sham' marriage, it may still amount to a marriage of convenience (depending on the predominant purpose).[110]

Another problematic issue that needs to be considered in this context is the so-called 'marriage by deception'. As observed in Chapter 4, the Handbook refers to such marriages as falling within the concept of marriages of convenience. Yet, this interpretation hardly complies with the 'sole purpose' rule

109 Ibid, para 33.

110 *Saeed (Deception, knowledge, marriage of convenience)* [2022] UKUT 00018, § 29(ii). See also, *Raqueeb v SSHD* [2018] UKUT 01754 (IAC), para 24; *Khan v SSHD* [2019] UKUT 03191 (IAC), para 16; *Dhensa v SSHD* [2020] UKUT 01197 (IAC), paras 2,3; *Letitia* [*G*] (n 25), paras 11–14. The judgment in *Sadovska* was also quoted in *Gureckis, R (On the Application Of) v SSHD* [2017] EWHC 3298, [2017] WLR(D) 840, para 86 and *ZA* (*Reg 9. EEA Regs; abuse of rights*) *Afghanistan* [2019] UKUT 281 (IAC), para 63. Although these cases considered the issue of abuse in other contexts, it was stressed that a marriage is one of convenience if its predominant purpose is to obtain rights under EU law.

set out in the Citizenship Directive. The confusing approach endorsed by the Handbook, however, has been taken up by UK courts and thus become hard law. In *Sadovska*, the Supreme Court suggested that, in line with the Handbook, cases of deceit by the non-EU national were the only type of marriages of convenience where obtaining an immigration advantage for the TCN spouse was the purpose of only one of the parties.[111] In *Abouelhasaan*, both tribunals argued along the same lines. The FtT judge, in particular, considered that the Irish principal married a national of Egypt 'out of genuine love and affection' because she was only 18 years old, had not completed her education, and wanted to start a family of her own.[112] With respect to her TCN husband, the FtT stated that his position was 'substantially different', as he had no right to remain in the UK and, in the view of the judge, could do so only by marrying an EU citizen. Furthermore, the FtT placed weight on his failure to tell his wife that he entered the UK unlawfully, as well as the fact that he was nine years older than her and '[t]here was no basis for concluding that they had the interests in common'.[113] In the meantime, the judge placed significantly less weight on their cohabitation for 18 months than he would have done in the case of an older woman. In the view of the FtT, a more experienced woman would have been expected to observe the signs in her husband's behaviour, suggesting that his 'predominant purpose' was to secure the right to remain in the UK.[114]

The UT equally confirmed the Handbook did refer to 'marriages by deception' and quoted the relevant passage from it describing the concept.[115] However, the judge then went on to state that the FtT misdirected itself in law, since 'it was necessary to establish not only that the appellant's sole (or predominant) purpose in marrying was to secure an immigration advantage (…) but also that he did not have any genuine belief that it would be a genuine and lasting marital life'.[116] In the view of the UT, this was not met on the facts of the case, for the FtT judge found there was 'an element of genuineness' in the non-EU national's intentions towards the EU principal. For instance, it was noted that the applicant 'was of an age when he could be expected to be thinking of marriage' and that the sponsor was 'an attractive young woman'.[117]

111 *Sadovska and another* (n 9), para 29.
112 *Abouelhasaan v SSHD* [2019] UKUT 04931 (IAC), paras 14, 24.
113 Ibid, para 14.
114 Ibid, para 24.
115 Ibid, para 60.
116 Ibid, para 63.
117 Ibid, para 64.

Furthermore, the UT dismissed the FtT findings with regard to the cohabitation as a 'generalisation'.[118]

Irrespective of the fact that the appeal was ultimately allowed, the fundamental problem with this judgment is that (a) both tribunals regard 'marriages by deception' as a concept recognised in EU law and (b) wrongly refer to the 'primary purpose' instead of the 'sole purpose' rule. Likewise, in *Arshad,* the FtT judge rejected the Home Office finding that both parties intended the marriage to be one of convenience and concluded that the TCN appellant deceived the EU principal.[119] Similarly, as in the previous case, the judge stressed the age difference between the sponsor and the applicant who were 18 and 30, respectively. The FtT accordingly stated that the sponsor was an 'immature young woman' exploited by the applicant[120] – a highly speculative and paternalistic approach at best, provided that, in the author's view, the state should respect the partner choices of its adult residents. The finding that the marriage was one 'of deception' was also upheld by the UT.

4.1 *Literal Interpretation of the Definition*

Section 3 above has shown that judges frequently placed the main focus on the present state of the relationship, rather than the purpose of the marriage, disregarding the CJEU case law. On the other hand, as argued in Chapter 4, situations where a marriage, initially entered into to solely help a non-EU citizen obtain an immigration advantage, later transforms into a real relationship, should not be regarded as falling within the scope of marriages of convenience. In other words, the 'sole purpose' definition must not be interpreted literally but rather as covering cases having no other substance both before and after the wedding.

Yet, the courts did not seem to support this approach. Once they had established that the original purpose of the marriage had only been an immigration advantage, the current state of the relationship was considered irrelevant. The case law demonstrates how the literal interpretation of the definition provided in the EEA Regulations, in effect, divided established families of EU citizens. Such an outcome strikingly contrasted with the overarching aim of the family reunion provisions in EU law and was most likely unintended by the drafters of the Directive.

It was as early as 2008 when the then Asylum and Immigration Tribunal held that a marriage that was one of convenience at its inception shall be

118 Ibid, para 67.

119 *Arshad v SSHD* [2019] UKUT 04911 (IAC), para 5.

120 Ibid, paras 11–12.

regarded as such irrespective of the development of a real relationship after the wedding.[121] A similar position, albeit not as explicitly, was expressed in *Rosa,* where, by reference to the 2006 version of the EEA Regulations, Article 35 of the Citizenship Directive, and the 1997 Resolution, it was suggested:

> [T]he focus in relation to a marriage of convenience should be on the intention of the parties at the time the marriage was entered into, whereas the question of whether a marriage is 'subsisting' looks to whether the marital relationship is a continuing one.[122]

This view was further upheld in the later UT case law. In *Raqueeb,* the court similarly considered that '[e]vidence of subsequent cohabitation and/or devotion cannot assist the appellant since the question of a marriage of convenience is decided on the basis of the parties' intentions when the marriage was contracted'.[123]

Cases involving pregnancy or childbirth are particularly problematic in this respect. The judgment in *A U* concerned a national of Pakistan married to a Latvian national whose marriage was found to be one of convenience. In rejecting his application for a residence permit, the Home Office relied on their numerous conflicting responses during the interviews, which in its view, demonstrated that the spouses lacked basic knowledge about each other. On appeal, the FtT accepted that the parties lived together and were in an intimate relationship. It was undisputed that the wife had miscarried in the preceding year. However, looking back at the interview records dating from the time of the marriage, the FtT concluded that discrepancies were so fundamental that it could not be inferred that the couple was in a genuine relationship at that time. The FtT, therefore found that at its inception it was a marriage of convenience and the fact that it had later evolved into an actual relationship could not change that.[124] This finding was later supported by the UT, which confirmed that the interview records were sufficient to discharge the evidential burden upon the Home Office.[125] The tribunal also relied on *Rosa* to confirm that the FtT judge was right to draw a distinction between the state of affairs at the

---

121 *IS (marriages of convenience) Serbia* [2008] UKAIT 00031, para 26.

122 *Rosa* (n 17), para 41.

123 *Raqueeb* (n 110), para 23. See also, *Entry Clearance Officer v Yuliia* [*Z*] (n 84), paras 11–12; *Tariq v SSHD* [2020] UKUT 01252 (IAC), para 11; *K A W (Pakistan) v SSHD* [2021] UKUT 01859 (IAC), para 26; *Baro v SSHD* [2022] UKUT 03464 (IAC), paras 4, 22.

124 *A U v SSHD* [2017] UKUT 00052 (IAC), para 3.

125 Ibid para 8.

date of the appeal and the position at the time of marriage.[126] The appeal was consequently rejected.

Likewise, in *Abouelhasaan,* the FtT judge quoted the relevant passage in *Rosa* and stressed that the principal had become pregnant only after the date of marriage. Consequently, the judge did not find the birth of the child to be a substantial factor pointing against the marriage having been one of convenience,[127] a position that was later rejected by the UT. In *Woguia,* however, the UT essentially concluded that it was open to the FtT judge not to treat the pregnancy of the non-EU spouse several years after the wedding as a fact establishing that the marriage was genuine from the outset.[128] In *Al Hassan,* the UT confusingly suggested that '[a] marriage of convenience can become a genuine marriage (although such a marriage would still have been a marriage of convenience)'.[129] Yet, the judge was not persuaded that the relationship 'ever developed into a supportive marriage' despite the birth of two children and concluded that the marriage was one of convenience.[130]

A more recent ruling in *Nketia,* delivered in 2022 in the context of the EEA Regulations 2016, deserves special attention in this respect. Out of the judgments analysed, this is the only case where the FtT critically engaged with the approach set out in the preceding case law. In doing so, however, the judge did not focus on the EU-level legislation on marriages of convenience and the concept of abuse of free movement rights. Instead, the FtT relied on the proportionality test to determine whether a marriage of convenience which evolves into a genuine relationship shall continue to be treated as a marriage of convenience. In the particular case, the FtT argued that it would be disproportionate to do so, given that, at the time of the hearings, the parties were in a genuine relationship and had a son. These considerations, which also included the best interest of the child, let the judge conclude that the appellant should be treated as the EU citizen's spouse for the purposes of the 2016 Regulations. The FtT findings with respect to the general rule read as follows:

> Can a marriage of convenience cease to be a marriage of convenience? My view [as to] the answer to this question is that it is possible for a marriage

126 Ibid para 11.

127 *Abouelhasaan* (n 112), para 15.

128 *Woguia v SSHD* [2019] UKUT 12057 (IAC), para 25. See also, *Onwusakah v SSHD* [2016] UKUT 14926 (IAC), paras 13, 18.

129 *Al Hassan v SSHD* [2020] UKUT 07618 (IAC), para 37.

130 Ibid.

> of convenience to change and allow a party thereto to be treated as a family member under the regulations.[131]

The decision, however, was appealed by the Home Office, which ultimately resulted in an adverse outcome for the family concerned. In its judgment, the UT considered the reasoning employed by the FtT incorrect. By reference to *Sadovska* (and the provisions of the 2014 Handbook as interpreted in that case), the UT stressed that:

> The existence of a marriage of convenience is determined solely by reference to the intention of the parties to the marriage at the time it was contracted. Whether the relationship later evolves into a 'genuine and subsisting relationship' is nothing to the point. [..] The categorisation of a marriage as being one of convenience is not a dynamic concept, whereby marriage of convenience status falls away or re-attaches with the ebb and flow of the relationship. Once a marriage is one of convenience, it is always a marriage of convenience.[132]

The UT then went on to state that the refusal of a residence card would not automatically require the TCN party to leave the UK but simply place her 'into the same position she had been in for some time, namely as an overstayer of some vintage'.[133] Strikingly, the judge argued that such a decision would respect the best interests of her son, as the appellant would still be able to make a human rights claim. Finally, the UT suggested that the family could relocate to an alternative country, such as Belgium, the sponsor's home country, or another EU Member State.[134] Such reasoning demonstrates complete disregard for the overarching purpose of EU citizens' right to family reunion – namely, to enable them to live with their family members in the host Member State of their choice and remove any obstacles to free movement.

5 Cases Involving Pregnancy or Childbirth

The previous sections have shown that the judges frequently support the Home Office's approach in designating marriages involving pregnancy or children as

131 *SSHD v Nketia* [2022] UKUT 04841 (IAC), para 45.
132 Ibid, paras 39, 46.
133 Ibid, para 66.
134 Ibid.

ones of convenience. Out of the 193 UT judgments analysed, 15 involved marriages where the FtT did not accept these factors as evidence of their genuineness;[135] in five of them, the UT concurred with the FtT assessment.[136] In one case, discussed in Section 4.1 above, the UT overturned a FtT decision where it found that a marriage with a child should not be regarded as one of convenience.[137] This section offers a closer look at this group of cases which is particularly controversial – not least because (a) in the author's view, such situations *per se* must not be covered by the concept of marriages of convenience, and (b) the judges seem to give no consideration to the rights of the children involved. Below are outlined the main examples of the problematic approach employed by UK judiciary.

First, it has rightly been held in *Papajorgji* that a durable marriage with children and cohabitation is 'quite inconsistent' with the definition of marriage of convenience.[138] This is, however, one of the very rare cases where the judge drew explicit parallels between the fact of childbirth and the perceived genuineness of a marriage. As demonstrated in Section 4.1, in several judgments, the definition of 'marriages of convenience' was interpreted literally, which in effect, deprived families with children of their right to be together. In other cases involving children, the judges wrongly approached the issue of the burden of proof and applied an incorrect definition of marriages of convenience.

In *Rehman*, the FtT wrongly stated that there was an evidential burden on the claimant to address reasonable suspicions and also wrongly referred to the 'predominant purpose' test.[139] The judge then upheld the Home Office's finding that the marriage was one of convenience; in the view of the FtT, the fact of childbirth could not alter this conclusion, given the non-EU national spouse's 'continued dishonesty' (he was considered not truthful concerning his studies).[140] The UT considered this reasoning flawed. First, it established the correct burden of proof test with reference to *Papajorgji*. It then went on to note that the 2006 EEA Regulations in force at the time provided no definition

135 *Onwusakah* (n 128); *Rehman v SSHD* [2016] UKUT 16713 (IAC); *Adnan* (n 46); *Uddin v SSHD* [2017] UKUT 27273 (IAC); *Rajah [A]* (n 30); *Abouelhasaan* (n 112); *Woguia* (n 128); *Lulzime [C] and [RM]* [2019] UKUT 03329 (IAC); *Resul [M] v SSHD* [2019] UKUT 07602 (IAC); *Gjura v SSHD* [2019] UKUT 07856 (IAC); *Collins [E] v SSHD* [2019] UKUT 01818 (IAC); *Khan* (n 110); *Al Hassan* (n 129); *Wambui v SSHD* [2021] UKUT 06884 (IAC); *Mahmood v SSHD* [2023] UKUT 001447 (IAC); *Zubair v SSHD* [2023] UKUT 00918 (IAC).

136 *Onwusakah* (n 128); *Woguia* (n 128); *Resul [M]* (n 135); *Gjura* (n 135); *Al Hassan* (n 129).

137 *SSHD v Nketia* (n 131).

138 *Papajorgji* (n 8), para 30.

139 *Rehman* (n 135), para 6.

140 Ibid, para 4.

of marriage of convenience but that phrase 'has been construed in the context of the Immigration Rules as a marriage entered into without the intention of matrimonial cohabitation and for the primary reason of securing admission to the country'. In the view of the judge, even on this approach, 'intent to cohabit as man and wife is inconsistent with a marriage of convenience', and the FtT misapplied the law. In this particular case, there was clear evidence that the couple had cohabited in that they had a child. The appeal was subsequently allowed.

In *Virk*,[141] explored in Chapter 9, the Home Office concluded the marriage in question was one of convenience despite the pregnancy of the EU principal who was subjected to intimidating and intrusive questioning. The appeal was consequently dismissed by the FtT. The UT held that the FtT judge misapplied the burden of proof test set out in *Papajorgji* and *Rosa* by failing to address significant concerns by the couple as to the conduct of the interviewer and not giving weight to their explanations of the discrepancies. The decision was ultimately set aside.

In general, it is commendable that the UT has given appropriate consideration to the pregnancy of the EU spouse with respect to the conduct of the interviewer. At the same time, the court did not take the opportunity to explicitly consider whether and how pregnancy falls within the scope of the definition of a marriage of convenience. The issue was neither addressed in *Collins*[142] where the UT criticised the FtT for rejecting a significant body of evidence, including photographs and evidence of cohabitation, and failing to assess it as a whole. In particular, the FtT accepted that the couple had a child together but failed to give adequate weight to this fact. Instead, it expressed concerns about the credibility of the witnesses related to the principal's work history. Whilst the UT rightly concluded that the marriage was not of convenience, it did not state that the fact of having a child is incompatible with the concept.

In *Gjura*,[143] the FtT went as far as to suggest that the non-EU spouse fathered a child solely to obtain an immigration status. This finding seems even more disturbing, provided that the judge did accept that both parties were involved in the upbringing of the child. It nonetheless placed weight on other factors, such as 'scant evidence' of the couple living together, their perceived inability to easily communicate when they first met, and the fact that they gave different addresses to the registrar when recording the birth of their child. It is remarkable that the FtT findings were upheld by the UT, which considered that

141 *Virk v SSHD* [2018] UKUT 19843 (IAC).

142 *Collins* [*E*] (n 135). See also, *Adnan* (n 46); *Lulzime* [*C*] *and* [*RM*] (n 135).

143 *Gjura* (n 135).

the 'main' purpose of marriage was to obtain an immigration advantage. In a similar case of *Khan*, the FtT accepted that the non-EU national involved was a 'caring and loving parent' of his child, yet concluded that the marriage was one of convenience because of his 'dreadful' immigration history and several discrepancies identified in the marriage interviews.[144] The judge strikingly noted that the appellant had 'further sought to strengthen his position in the UK by conceiving a child with the sponsor' and expressed doubts that his intentions had been 'honourable or genuine'.[145] The UT rightly concluded that the FtT did not carry out a balanced assessment of all the evidence, focusing on the negative and failing to give due weight to the positive factors. The decision was, therefore set aside.[146]

Moreover, in a number of cases, the judges questioned the paternity of the child conceived during the marriage, contrary to the presumption in English family law. The judgment in *Uddin* involved a TCN spouse of a Romanian national whose application for a residence card was refused following a home visit by immigration officers. Although such a finding was unsupported by evidence and only based on speculations (i.e., sheets on the floor suggesting they were sleeping separately, see Chapter 9), it was upheld by the FtT. Moreover, the judge attached no weight to the fact that the wife had meanwhile given birth to her husband's child, despite the DNA evidence confirming his paternity. According to the judge, 'this would have been a cogent argument' if the DNA test provider was approved by the Home Office, which as the tribunal believed, was not the case.[147] Such reasoning was explicitly rejected by the Upper Tribunal, which found that the Home Office failed to discharge the burden of proof and the FtT erred in law in accepting their assertions as evidence. The UT judge went on to conclude that all this, together with the fact that the couple has a child together, was 'a strong indicator corroborative of a genuine relationship'.[148] The previous finding that the marriage was one of convenience was consequently rejected. It should be noted, however, that the applicant, in fact, was not even required to provide DNA evidence in order for his child to be treated as such.

The same approach has also been applied in other cases. In *Rajah*, the FtT judge attached little weight to the EU principal's miscarriage because he doubted that her TCN husband was the father of the unborn child.[149] In

144 *Khan* (n 110), paras 7, 8.
145 Ibid, para 7.
146 Ibid, paras 22–24.
147 *Uddin* (n 135), para 5.
148 Ibid para 24.
149 *Rajah* [*A*] (n 30). See also, *Woguia* (n 128).

another judgment, the fact that the non-EU citizen was named on the birth certificate as a father was not considered as proof of parentage, a position that was not challenged by the UT.[150] On the other hand, in *Resul,* both tribunals questioned the paternity of the child because she was given her EU mother's surname on the birth certificate, although the couple was married.[151]

Furthermore, a significant point of concern is that when examining cases involving children, the judges appear to make no reference whatsoever to the principle of the best interests of the child.[152] Since a finding that the marriage is one of convenience may result in the removal of one or both of the spouses, the Commission Handbook specifically provides that in such situations Member States must pay due regard to the UN Convention on the Rights of the Child[153] (see Chapter 4). The ignorance of judges is even more disturbing given that already in 2008, the UK lifted its reservation on the Convention with respect to children in migration situations, which was accordingly reflected in section 55 of the Borders, Citizenship and Immigration Act 2009. Since then, the principle of the best interests of the child has started to play a growing role in the domestic jurisprudence on Article 8 of the ECHR.[154]

The general guidance on the applicability of this approach in the UK was delivered, *inter alia*, in the landmark Supreme Court case of *ZH* (*Tanzania*), which concerned the removal to Tanzania, a mother and a primary carer of two UK national children. In its judgment, the Court emphasised that the principles set out in Article 3(1) of the CRC are relevant not only concerning how children are looked after in the UK whilst immigration decisions are being made, but also to the decisions themselves.[155] Consequently, whilst the strength of other considerations may ultimately outweigh the best interests of the child, they must be considered first when making the proportionality assessment under Article 8.[156]

Although Article 8 jurisprudence is a category distinct from the case law on marriages of convenience explored above, this should not act as a barrier for the application of the principles set out in the CRC to the latter group. At the international level, Article 3 of the CRC may operate independently of the

150 *Onwusakah* (n 128).

151 *Resul* [*M*] (n 135).

152 With *SSHD v Nketia* (n 131) being the only exception.

153 Convention on the Rights of the Child, 1577 UNTS 3 (20.11.1989).

154 For an analysis, see, Jason M Pobjoy, *The Child in International Refugee Law* (Cambridge University Press 2017) 209–13.

155 *ZH* (*Tanzania*) *v SSHD* [2011] UKSC 4, [2011] 2 AC 166, para 24.

156 Ibid para 33.

provisions of the ECHR, an approach that has also been acknowledged by UK courts. For instance, the Court of Appeal explicitly stated that the relevant statements expressed by the Supreme Court in *ZH* (*Tanzania*) could not be read as being confined to Article 8 considerations.[157]

Last but not least, in cases involving EU citizen children, a paradoxical finding that their parents' marriage is one of convenience may deprive them of the right to enjoy family life with their third-country national parent, which would otherwise be guaranteed by EU law. As explored in Chapter 1, under the Citizenship Directive (and under the Withdrawal Agreement), TCN parents of EU citizen children may retain a right of residence even in the event of the death or departure of the Union citizen, or where the marriage has ended by an annulment or divorce. Those accused of marrying for immigration purposes cannot avail themselves on these provisions. The only remaining routes for them under EU law would be to apply for derived rights of residence as a primary carer of an EU citizen child in line with the CJEU ruling in *Chen*,[158] or in exceptional cases, rely on the CJEU decision in *Zambrano*.[159] Yet, in light of the narrow scope of both options,[160] there may certainly be parents unable to benefit from such routes, and as a consequence, face separation from their children.

6 Conclusion

The case law analysis has shown that the decisions of British courts have frequently suffered from a lack of consistency and flawed interpretations of the issues related to the concept of marriages of convenience in EU law.

Regarding the application of EU free movement law in general, the situation is rather disappointing. Only a minority of judges have expressly referred to the relevant EU-level instruments or CJEU jurisprudence on the issue and correctly applied these. In the worst-case scenario, the judges have erroneously considered the cases in the context of UK domestic immigration law. In numerous rulings, the FtT wrongly placed the burden of proof on the applicant and/or required them to demonstrate that their marriage was 'genuine and subsisting', an obvious violation of EU law. In such situations, the UT typically allowed the

157 *DS* (*Afghanistan*) *v SSHD* [2011] EWCA Civ 305, [2011] INLR 389, para 22.

158 C-200/02 *Zhu* and *Chen* [2000] ECR I-09925. The ruling in *Chen* has been given effect in regulation 16 of the EEA Regulations 2016.

159 Case C-34/09 *Ruiz Zambrano* [2011] ECR I-01177.

160 See Chapter 1 for an analysis.

appeal by reiterating that the burden of proof rests with the Home Office and providing a reference to the relevant domestic case law. Furthermore, when examining the nature of marriages, judges tended to place excessive focus on cohabitation as the main evidence of its genuineness, rarely showing awareness of the CJEU rulings in *Diatta* and *Ogieriakhi*.

Explicit references to the Citizenship Directive in UK case law are hardly ever found. A number of judges, nonetheless, have relied on the relevant EU soft law instruments, thus incorporating their provisions into hard law. For instance, the UT referred to the 2009 Commission guidelines to state that the burden of proof rests with the Home Office. In another case, the UT considered both positive and negative indicative criteria of marriages of convenience listed in the document. In many cases, however, the FtT tended to follow the Home Office's approach of ignoring the evidence that the marriage was not one of convenience and placing the main focus on the alleged discrepancies instead. In doing so, the judges relied on their highly normative perceptions of how the 'genuine' marriage should look, as well as placed weight on cultural differences between the spouses and evaluated their language and communication skills. Whilst some UT judges condemned such practices as hopelessly subjective; others did not raise any objections. Further, when dealing with the problematic category of cases involving children, the principle of the best interests of the child, highlighted in the Handbook, has been ignored.

Yet, in some cases where the judges did make explicit reference to the Handbook, this has adversely impacted the position of the couples involved. In particular, the Supreme Court relied on the confusing passage in the Handbook stating that 'the notion of "sole purpose" should not be interpreted literally' but as the 'predominant purpose of the abusive conduct' to expand the definition of marriages of convenience provided in the Citizenship Directive. Another notable example illustrating this approach is the problematic concept of 'marriages by deception', which has been taken up by both the FtT and the UT, as well as the Supreme Court. As argued in Chapter 4, the interpretation suggested by the Commission contradicts the wording and spirit of the Citizenship Directive.

Similar issues arise due to the co-existence of different terms and definitions of marriages for residence purposes in UK domestic law. Due to the unclear terminology, both FtT and UT judges interpreted the EEA Regulations as covering cases where obtaining an immigration advantage is not the only but the primary or predominant purpose of the marriage. The definition of marriages of convenience provided in the EEA Regulations has then been juxtaposed with that of sham marriages found in the Immigration Act. In one Supreme Court and two High Court judgments, this has led to a paradoxical finding that a couple may enter into a marriage of convenience in a genuine relationship, an interpretation entirely inconsistent with EU law. Further, both the FtT and the UT tended to interpret the definition literally, i.e., as applicable *inter alia* to couples whose marriage did not have any content other than an immigration motive at its inception but later transformed into a real relationship. In the author's view, such situations are fully consistent with the overarching purpose of the family reunion provisions enshrined in EU law, which aim to facilitate the free movement of EU citizens and ensure their better integration into the society of the host Member State. Therefore, couples whose relationship developed only after the marriage should still be able to benefit from Treaty provisions, irrespective of their original intentions.

Overall, the endorsement of the Home Office practices by so many judges is deeply disturbing. The adverse decisions, most of which have been delivered in breach of EU law, created hardship for couples involving EU citizens and as a consequence, may have seriously hindered the latter in exercising their Treaty rights.

Conclusion

The present study has purported to answer two interrelated questions. First, it attempted to explore how the concept of marriages of convenience is reflected in EU free movement law and whether it is compatible with other relevant provisions in this area, particularly those of the Citizenship Directive.[1] Second, it sought to examine if, and to what extent, the UK domestic measures addressing the issue comply with EU law (and, more recently, the EU-UK Withdrawal Agreement)[2] in so far as it concerns the right of EU citizens to live in the UK with their family members.

As observed in Chapters 1 and 2, since the very inception of free movement, every beneficiary of Treaty rights was provided the ability to reside in the host Member State with their family members, irrespective of the latter's nationality. The central logic behind these rules is that the absence of this right would create obstacles to EU citizen's relocation to another Member State, as well as hinder their integration into the host society. Over the decades, the scope of family reunion rights has been continuously broadened by both Union legislation and the CJEU alongside the process of the general expansion of free movement rights. Although Article 35 of the Directive permits Member States to derogate from free movement rights in cases of abuse, such as marriages of convenience, this concept is defined narrowly, and the relevant provision is to be interpreted strictly.

When performing marriage checks, Member States must respect two key principles established by the CJEU. First, systematic checks are prohibited. Second, as long as the marriage is not officially terminated, the TCN spouse continues to benefit from the Citizenship Directive even where the couple does not cohabit or is no longer in a relationship (*Diatta*[3] and *Ogieriakhi*).[4] Further, in its landmark ruling in *Metock*,[5] delivered in 2008, the Court overturned

1 Directive 2004/38/EC of the European Parliament and of the Council of 29 April 2004 on the right of citizens of the Union and their family members to move and reside freely within the territory of the Member States amending Regulation (EEC) No 1612/68 and repealing Directives 64/221/EEC, 68/360/EEC, 72/194/EEC, 73/148/EEC, 75/34/EEC, 75/35/EEC, 90/364/EEC, 90/365/EEC and 93/96/EEC [2004] OJ L158/77 (Citizenship Directive).

2 Agreement on the withdrawal of the United Kingdom of Great Britain and Northern Ireland from the European Union and the European Atomic Energy Community [2019] OJ C384/1 (Withdrawal Agreement).

3 Case 267/83 *Diatta* [1985] ECR 00567.

4 Case C-244/13 *Ogieriakhi* ECLI:EU:C:2014:2068.

5 Case C-127/08 *Metock and Others* [2008] ECR I-06241.

 | DOI:10.1163/9789004499263_013

an infamous 'prior lawful residence' rule introduced in an earlier decision in *Akrich*.[6] This exceptional case was heavily criticised due to its unclear reasoning and inconsistency with the prior jurisprudence. In *Metock*, the CJEU explicitly held that, as long as the marriage is not one of convenience, the non-EU party qualifies under the Directive irrespective of their prior residence status in the Member State concerned, as well as of the place and time the marriage was entered into.

It is exactly after this judgment that the issue of marriages of convenience became the point of considerable friction between the EU and several Member States. As highlighted in Chapter 3, several factors seem to have contributed to this development. The first and principal one has been the growing dichotomy between the generous family reunion provisions under the Directive and restrictive national rules, a phenomenon called 'reverse discrimination'. In the mid-2000s, seeking to limit the number of TCN family migrants who could not be selected in the same way as foreign workforce, several Western European Member States significantly tightened up their family reunification rules, making the admission of family members of their own nationals subject to an extensive examination of their personal circumstances and several additional criteria.

Since these could not be applied to family members of mobile EU citizens, several governments, most notably the UK and Ireland, began to denounce the Citizenship Directive as a 'loophole' enabling otherwise undesirable non-EU nationals to regularise their status. This discourse was closely linked to the second factor, namely, that *Metock* was delivered at the time of increasing arrivals from EU-8 Member States after the UK and Ireland immediately opened their labour markets to their nationals. The British and Irish authorities now started expressing concerns about the increase in marriage pairing patterns which were considered 'highly unusual', most notably male migrants from West Africa and the Indian subcontinent marrying female nationals of EU-12 Member States. This trend, however, can easily be explained by the overall post-enlargement increase in intra-European mobility and the fact that many mobile EU citizens share work and study spaces with non-EU nationals, whereby similar social status and education play a significant role in their partner choice.

The governments, nevertheless, tended to excessively focus on the perceived 'large cultural differences' between the partners, strongly associating such combinations of nationalities with abuse. This paradigm was further reinforced by the third factor – proliferation of media and political narratives

6 Case C-109/01 *Akrich* [2003] ECR I-09607.

about marriages of convenience as a criminal enterprise where vulnerable Eastern European women are exploited by marriage 'fixers' and third-country national men.

Over the pre-Brexit years, the UK, intensely concerned over the perceived abuse of Treaty rights, stopped seeing the benefits in the delegation of its migration control powers to EU institutions. Along with 'poverty migration', 'welfare tourism', and perceived criminality, marriages of convenience allegedly contracted between mobile EU citizens and third-country nationals remained an important point of contention between the UK and the EU during this period. The UK has long been known for treating its own nationals significantly worse than mobile EU citizens with regards to their right to live with their TCN family members. The fear of migrants circumventing domestic immigration rules became an important public policy tool of the British government, used as a justification for attacking undesirable marriages and Treaty rights. As demonstrated in Chapter 3, from the very outset of the post-*Metock* debate on marriages of convenience, the British authorities have been very vocal about the issue. Together with a few other Member States, the UK has continuously attempted to persuade EU institutions to narrow down family reunion rights. The first two such initiatives were rejected by the Commission and the rest of the Council, not least due to the inability of the British authorities to provide statistical evidence of the 'widespread abuse' they were referring to.

The Commission nonetheless responded to the pressure of Member States by adopting two soft law instruments aimed at providing them with guidance on how to approach the issue. The principal document issued in this context is the 2014 Handbook on addressing alleged marriages of convenience between mobile EU citizens and third-country nationals.[7] The Handbook provides a detailed overview of the general principles Member States must pay attention to when exercising marriage controls – for instance, it reiterates that checks may only be performed on a case-by-case basis and that the burden of proof rests with the national authorities.

The Commission, however, did not limit itself merely to underlining the relevant safeguards. In response to Member State demands to specify what steps they can take to tackle perceived marriages of convenience, the Handbook provides its own interpretation of the concept, including a lengthy list of normative indicators aimed to distinguish 'genuine' marriages from those of convenience. As argued in Chapter 4, some of the proposed measures are highly

7 Commission, 'Staff Working Document – Handbook on addressing the issue of alleged marriages of convenience between EU citizens and non-EU nationals in the context of EU law on free movement of EU citizens' SWD(2014) 284 final.

contradictory and go well beyond what is permitted under the Citizenship Directive; if applied at the national level, this may have serious repercussions for the families of mobile EU citizens concerned.

Notwithstanding the criticism, it must be admitted that at that particular point, the Commission still remained committed to its role as the guardian of the Treaties, refusing to initiate changes in EU secondary law and upholding EU citizens' right to family reunion. It is, therefore, all the more striking that only two years later, the Union institutions entirely reversed their position in order to accommodate the same concerns voiced by the UK. As part of the EU-UK deal, concluded in early 2016 in order to dissuade the UK from leaving the EU, the Commission essentially came up with a pledge to act against the long-standing CJEU jurisprudence by adopting a proposal to amend the Citizenship Directive. The latter sought to significantly broaden the definition of marriages of convenience, as well as exclude from its scope third-country nationals who had no prior lawful residence status in a Member State before marrying an EU citizen or where the marriage took place only after their relocation to the host Member State.

Although following the outcome of the Brexit referendum, the arrangement never entered into force, its significance should not be underestimated. Following the poorly justified demands of the British government, the EU appeared ready to – for the first time in its history – effectively stagger the whole idea of European integration by considerably narrowing down free movement, including family reunion rights. This is an unprecedented sacrifice which gives cause for serious concern. As argued in Chapter 3, there is a danger that other Member States may equally interpret this step as a possibility to negotiate the exclusion of unwanted categories of persons from the scope of the Treaty rights, should they wish to do so in future.

Chapters 6–10 examined the regulation of the issue of marriages of convenience in UK domestic law and the extent to which it complied with the relevant EU-level rules. During the years preceding the Brexit referendum, the growing anxieties about the perceived abuse of EU free movement law via this route have prompted the UK authorities to adopt several legislative measures addressing the phenomenon. Marriage controls in the UK are exercised on two basic levels – before and after the marriage is entered into. In contrast to the post-marriage stage when Member States are bound by EU law restraints in performing checks, pre-marriage controls escape the ambit of the Directive. The reason for this is that the latter continues to pursue a conservative approach by regarding marriage as a proxy for a serious long-term commitment and privileging spouses (and registered partners) over unmarried couples. Hence, whilst spouses of EU citizens automatically become beneficiaries of the Directive without any additional conditions, admission of the so-called 'durable partners' entirely depends on the national laws of the Member State concerned. In the UK, unmarried partners of mobile EU citizens could qualify for residence rights under the Directive only where the couple could provide extensive evidence of living together in a relationship 'akin to marriage' for at least two years. For those who had not yet reached this threshold, marriage often represented the only opportunity to stay together, particularly where the non-EU party had an unstable or irregular residence status.

The process of entry into marriage, however, is equally determined by the national laws of Member States. The only constraints the national authorities are bound by when exercising pre-marriage checks are those found in international human rights law. Yet, although the right to marry and the right to respect for private and family life are guaranteed by both the ECHR[8] and the EUCFR,[9] these instruments provide (either married or unmarried) couples much weaker protection than that reserved for spouses under the Citizenship Directive. The relevant legal framework is described in Chapter 5. First, according to the ECtHR, the Convention does not guarantee a foreign national the right to choose the country of their matrimonial residence. Likewise, the recognition of the existence of family life protects an individual from removal only in very limited circumstances. With regards to measures targeting perceived marriages of convenience, the Strasbourg court precluded the contracting states from imposing blanket prohibitions to marry for foreigners with a short-term or irregular status. Notwithstanding that, the ECtHR case law expressly permits governments to prevent marriages of convenience aimed to secure an immigration advantage for the foreign party. Moreover, national authorities are granted a very wide margin of discretion with regard to defining and identifying such marriages. In contrast to the Citizenship Directive, human rights law does not prohibit systematic checks. The only constraint the states must observe in this regard is the prohibition of highly intrusive and degrading questions that violate the right to respect for human dignity.

As shown in Chapter 7, the British government used the legal lacuna to carry out systematic checks on yet unmarried couples who had already met in the UK. In 2015, as part of its then 'hostile environment' policy targeting irregular migrants, the UK government introduced the so-called 'referral and investigation scheme', which continues to operate after Brexit; the respective rules aim to act as a deterrent against marriages for residence purposes, referred

8 European Convention for the Protection of Human Rights and Fundamental Freedoms, CETS No.005 (04.11.1950) (ECHR).

9 Charter of Fundamental Rights of the European Union [2000] OJ C364/01 (EUCFR).

to as 'sham marriages' in the particular legal setting. Under the scheme, civil registrars are required to refer to the Home Office all intended marriages involving non-EU nationals without indefinite leave or a valid marriage visitor or fiancé(e) visa. The authorities would then consider if there are grounds to suspect that the marriage is a 'sham'. If that is the case, the marriage notice period can be extended to 70 days, during which the couple may be required to undergo an investigation. Formally, as long as the parties comply with the investigation, their marriage is allowed to proceed even if it is found to be a sham. During the pre-Brexit period, however, the Home Office would refuse any subsequent applications under the Citizenship Directive made by the third-country national party on these grounds.

In reality, however, the scheme goes much further than targeting couples who do not intend to lead a family life. As noted above, the right to marry is granted only to those who comply with the investigation; yet, the couple can be considered non-compliant purely for bureaucratic reasons unrelated to the nature of their marriage, such as failure to provide a tenancy agreement or bank statements. As noted in Chapter 7, such practices arguably constitute an unjustified restriction of the fundamental right to marry and violate the ECHR. Further, irrespective of whether or not the couple has complied with the investigation and if it has even been started in the first place, non-EU nationals with an irregular status can be removed from the UK at any point before the marriage is registered. For such individuals, giving a marriage notice would automatically mean coming to the attention of the Home Office. Before Brexit, couples involving third-country nationals with a precarious residence status could thus find themselves trapped between the inability to regularise their situation via alternative routes, on the one hand, and the inability to get married without the risk of being separated, on the other.

By contrast, at the post-marriage stage, UK measures targeting perceived marriages of convenience needed to comply with the relevant safeguards guaranteed to EU citizens under EU law. However, the situation in this area was rather disappointing. As demonstrated in Chapter 9, the UK legislator and the executive frequently disregarded EU law when dealing with the issue. In addition, Chapter 10 has shown that the UK courts have frequently endorsed the hostile and erroneous practices conducted by the Home Office. Only a minority of judges have relied on and correctly applied the EU legislation and CJEU case law on the subject; direct references to the Citizenship Directive are remarkably rare. Yet in some cases where judges have explicitly referred to the Commission Handbook on marriages of convenience, this has produced adverse legal effects for the couples involved – largely due to the legally questionable and inconsistent interpretation of the concept by the relevant guidance. This serves as a clear illustration of how an erroneous approach pursued by the EU soft law instrument, adopted by the Commission without the scrutiny of the European Parliament and the Council, found its way into domestic hard law.

One of the most problematic aspects in this respect is the definition of marriages of convenience. The crucial constraint on the concept, which is imposed by both the Citizenship Directive and the CJEU, is the narrow 'sole purpose' test; it implies that the acquisition of a residence status must be the only aim of the marriage rather than one among many. Such an approach is reasonable, given that the Directive privileges marital relationships over non-marital ones and many couples may wish to get married to be able to live together in the respective country.

The Handbook further reiterates that marriages of convenience are characterised by 'the absence of intention to create a family as a married couple and to lead a genuine marital life'.[10] Yet, in a subsequent passage, it claims that the notion of the 'sole purpose' should not be understood as being the exclusive but rather the predominant purpose. As underlined in Chapter 4, this interpretation seems to suggest that the Commission seeks to arbitrarily expand the definition provided by the Citizenship Directive, a step that arguably constitutes its breach.

The confusion is further exacerbated by the fact that there were two different terms and definitions of marriages for residence purposes in UK law, none of which accurately reflected the wording of the Citizenship Directive. As pointed out above, for the purposes of pre-marriage controls, the government uses the term 'sham marriage', defined as a marriage contracted with the aim to obtain an immigration advantage where there is no 'genuine relationship' between the parties. The EEA Regulations implementing the Citizenship Directive,[11] on the other hand, employed the term 'marriage of convenience'; the respective definition equally referred to the marriage purpose but did not include the 'genuine relationship' clause. The word 'sole', meanwhile, was absent from both definitions. The co-existence of several definitions of the same concept is not a satisfactory state of affairs. Such an approach significantly undermines clarity and legal certainty, which is best evident in the findings of several UK judges interpreting the concept. Having juxtaposed the definitions of 'sham marriages' and 'marriages of convenience' in UK domestic law, as well as referred to the problematic passage of the Handbook, the judges

10 SWD(2014) 284 final, 8.

11 Immigration (European Economic Area) Regulations 2016, SI 2016/1052 (EEA Regulations 2016).

ultimately concluded that a marriage of convenience might be entered into by a couple in a genuine relationship, a paradoxical interpretation that obviously contradicts the Directive.

Aside from the definition of the concept, a number of other UK measures targeting perceived marriages of convenience were equally problematic in terms of compliance with the Directive and CJEU case law. First, although the Directive prohibits systematic checks and only asks TCN spouses to present a valid marriage certificate, the Home Office required those seeking to benefit from the Treaty rights to provide extensive details of their relationship. Second, both the executive and the courts tended to place an excessive focus on cohabitation and the quality of the present relationship between the spouses, rarely showing awareness of the CJEU rulings in *Diatta* and *Ogieriakhi*. The criteria used to determine whether the marriage is one of convenience largely reflect those provided in the Handbook. This is unsurprising, given that the drafting process was significantly influenced by the UK officials who appeared ready to share their practices. The hints are normative in nature and typically reflect highly stereotypical perceptions of the authorities of how a 'real' marriage should look like.

Yet, although the Handbook advises Member States to first look for evidence suggesting that there is no abuse, the UK authorities and judges instead focused on the alleged discrepancies and other perceived signs of marriages of convenience. In the worst-case scenario, FtT judges entirely disregarded EU law by erroneously placing the burden of proof on the applicant and requiring their marriage to be 'genuine and subsisting' in line with domestic immigration rules. In addition, some of the investigation methods were particularly hostile and intrusive and arguably breached the ECHR and the EUCFR. Another important contradiction is that the terms 'sham marriage' and 'marriages of convenience' are only employed in the domains of immigration and free movement[12] law. Consequently, a marriage disqualified for the purposes of the EEA Regulations continued to be valid in family law, with all the rights and obligations emanating from this status.

When it comes to residence rights, however, a finding that a marriage is one of convenience had serious repercussions for both non-EU national and EU citizen parties. The former would not be allowed to enjoy Treaty rights on the basis of marriage and would typically be liable for removal. Moreover, under the EEA Regulations, an EU citizen allegedly involved in a marriage of convenience could equally be removed from the UK on public policy grounds, an

12 And, more recently, in the context of the Withdrawal Agreement.

approach which raises serious concerns with regards to its compatibility with the Citizenship Directive.

Against this background, it must be borne in mind that the overarching purpose of the family reunion rights granted under the Directive is to enable mobile EU citizens to enjoy family life in the host Member State. Whilst the Directive has enhanced the protection of TCN family members by granting them an autonomous status in certain situations, the right to family reunion, in essence, remains derivative in nature. The principal focus of the Directive, accordingly, is placed on the need to protect the right of mobile EU citizens to live with their close ones, which in turn would make it easier for the former to exercise their Treaty rights. This, however, does not seem to be a perspective endorsed by the British government when exercising marriage controls. Rather than attempting to reduce the risk of an erroneous decision and state intrusion into the lives of EU citizens, the British executive and courts concentrated all their efforts on preventing non-EU nationals with a short-term or irregular status from regularising their situation via marriage. The relevant measures, many of which violated EU law, disproportionately targeted couples whose situation does not easily fit into the narrow 'sole purpose' definition of marriages of convenience. As demonstrated in the present study, this frequently resulted in particularly disturbing outcomes, such as cases where marriages involving pregnancies and children were designated as ones of convenience.

Further, instead of protecting the family life of mobile EU citizens by providing their prospective spouses guarantees against pre-wedding removal, the UK authorities pursued the opposite approach. They sought to identify and remove non-EU nationals with an irregular status before the marriage takes place. All this created significant hardship for the couples involved and could effectively result in their separation or prompt them to live in legal limbo or relocate to another country. The book argues that this outcome was hardly compatible with the objective of eliminating all possible obstacles to the free movement of EU citizens.

Last but not least, the profiles of couples most frequently subjected to scrutiny suggest that the Home Office measures disproportionately targeted men from the Indian subcontinent, West Africa, or Albania and female nationals of EU-12 Member States, as well as EU citizens with a migrant descent whose (prospective) spouses come from the countries of their ancestors. Although the Home Office does not officially sanction profiling by nationality, evidence of this occurring gives rise to concerns that there has been disguised discrimination based on nationality, which has been used as a proxy to justify discrimination based on race and religion.

All in all, assessing the purpose of a marriage is an extremely complex and controversial task which unavoidably entails significant interference in the private and family life of the EU citizens concerned. Further, given the great variety of global relationship patterns, there is a serious risk of targeting a broad range of couples who do lead a family life (or intend to do so) but whose behaviour does not conform to the normative assumptions of how 'genuine' marriages should appear.

As to the UK government's concerns about the perceived exploitation of Eastern European women, typically associated with organised crime, such evidence is largely anecdotal and lacks a solid statistical basis. Accordingly, this study argues that such cases can effectively be addressed by instruments other than marriage controls, such as laws on human trafficking or domestic violence. Moreover, evidence suggests that the fact of involvement of intermediaries does not necessarily exclude the intention of the couple to found a family; indeed, there may be cases where a marriage, initially contracted only to help the non-EU national obtain residence rights, later transforms into an intimate relationship.

In this light, given the importance of the fundamental EU rights at stake, this study argues that governments should attempt to take every precaution to minimise the possibility of disrupting families involving mobile EU citizens. In line with this aim, the author advocates for a more narrow approach than the one permitted under the Directive and the Handbook. In the author's view, it would be more reasonable to define marriages of convenience as those that do not have, and never had, any other content apart from the immigration motive. Accordingly, a marriage should not be regarded as one of convenience in the absence of any reliable evidence that it has been a purely artificial arrangement and/or in the presence of *any* elements suggesting there is (or used to be) a relationship between the parties.[13]

Further, it should be stressed that the UK authorities did not collect aggregated statistics on identified marriages of convenience amongst those applying for EEA family permits or residence cards, whilst the number of prospective marriages determined to be 'sham' under the 'referral and investigation scheme' has consistently remained below 5%. Moreover, the book argues that even in the absence of *any* measures addressing marriages of convenience, the number of purely artificial arrangements is likely to remain low, not least because marriage is a serious commitment entailing a set of obligations and, under the Citizenship Directive, the couple need to stay married for at

13 Emphasis added.

least three years before the TCN party can qualify for independent status.[14] Against this background, the need for legal and practical tools aiming to curb the phenomenon appears strongly doubtful.

The post-Brexit developments in the UK give little reason for optimism. In essence, the British government has ultimately succeeded in its endeavours to deprive EU citizens of the generous family reunion rights guaranteed to them under EU law, making them instead subject to the restrictive national family reunification provisions. As demonstrated in Chapter 8, the end of the transition period on 31 December 2020 has effectively created two groups of EU citizens who are now covered by separate sets of rights. From then on, those who move to the UK after this date fall into the scope of British immigration law, including domestic family reunification rules. By contrast, those who have relocated to the country by 31 December 2020 are covered by the EU-UK Withdrawal Agreement, incorporated into British law by the Withdrawal Agreement Act.[15] Under the provisions of the Withdrawal Agreement, its beneficiaries continue to enjoy residence rights in the UK on the same terms as under the Citizenship Directive. All EU citizens resident in the UK by the cut-off date were asked to register under the so-called EU Settlement Scheme and correspondingly obtain either a settled or a pre-settled status depending on the length of their residence in the UK.

When it comes to the right to live in the UK with their family members, settled or pre-settled status holders are divided into two groups. The first, and the most privileged group, is comprised of those whose relationship was formed (i.e., marriage registered) by 31 December 2020. In these cases, their spouses have a right to live in the UK on the same conditions as under the Citizenship Directive, including EU law safeguards the states must respect when targeting perceived marriages of convenience. Regrettably, however, the UK Immigration Rules applicable to this group have introduced yet another definition of marriages of convenience. The latter largely resembles the definition previously provided by the EEA Regulations and is arguably broader than the 'sole purpose' one found in the Citizenship Directive. As noted above, two different terms ('marriage of convenience' and 'sham marriage') and several definitions of the same concept ((1) in the Citizenship Directive, reiterated in the Commission Handbook, (2) the Immigration Act 1999, (3) the EEA

14 Emphasis added.

15 European Union (Withdrawal) Act 2018 (WA 2018) as amended by European Union (Withdrawal Agreement) Act 2020.

Regulations, and (4) Appendix EU to the Immigration Rules) are highly confusing and undermine legal certainty.[16]

UK-resident EU citizens whose marriage was registered after the cut-off date, however, find themselves in a much more disadvantaged position. Couples belonging to this category need to comply with highly restrictive British domestic family reunification provisions, such as the minimum income requirement, the 'no-switching rule', and the requirement to show that their marriage is 'genuine and subsisting'. In this respect, this group has been placed in the same position as EU citizens who move to the UK after the deadline. Moreover, after 31 December 2020, the new rules also apply to family members who are EU citizens themselves. In other words, if, after the cut-off date, a German citizen with settled status in the UK marries another German citizen who is based in Germany, the couple will equally need to satisfy the UK domestic family reunification requirements to be able to live together in the UK.[17]

Limiting the application of the Withdrawal Agreement only to couples who registered their marriage before the cut-off date is a substantial departure from the approach established by the CJEU in *Metock*. In the latter case, the Court explicitly held that the TCN spouse of a mobile EU citizen should be able to benefit from generous EU family reunion provisions irrespective of when and where their marriage took place.[18] In the Court's view, the opposite approach could encourage EU citizens to relocate to another country where they could lead a family life and thus put obstacles to free movement.[19] Indeed, it can be anticipated that a UK-based German citizen would prefer to relocate to another EU Member State to be able to live with their spouse rather than attempt to comply with British family reunification rules. It can be agreed that, from a political perspective, the UK authorities would find it difficult to justify the continuous preferential treatment of EU citizens who have their marriage registered after the cut-off date. From a legal perspective, however, excluding this group from the scope of EU family reunion rights undermines legal certainty. It also comes into tension with the overarching principle of the Withdrawal Agreement, according to which EU citizens resident in the UK by the cut-off date retain their right to live in the country on the same terms as under the Treaties and the Citizenship Directive.

16 For a concise overview of how different types of pre- and post-marriage situations are covered by each definition, see Annex 2.

17 Unless the Germany-based spouse manages to obtain another type of leave.

18 *Metock and Others* (n 5), para 99.

19 Ibid paras 67, 68, 89.

Although marriage to a UK-based EU citizen no longer enables the foreign spouse to automatically obtain residence rights in the UK under EU law, the British government continues to exercise pre-marriage controls via the 'referral and investigation' scheme. Moreover, its scope has been extended to include family members who are EU citizens without an EUSS status. The low figures of detected sham marriages mentioned above raise serious doubts about the justification for existing measures, not only from a legal but also public policy perspective, particularly because their deterrent effect is questionable. Given that the couples would still need to comply with restrictive UK family reunification provisions, the number of foreigners who would wish to contract a sham marriage but are deterred from doing so by the 'referral and investigation' scheme is likely to be very low. By contrast, the scheme may still target many couples in a close relationship who may avoid getting married out of fear of separation.

After Brexit, a finding that a marriage is not genuine continues to have serious repercussions for couples involving UK-resident EU citizens – irrespective of whether the marriage was registered before or after the cut-off date. Foreign spouses of EU citizens accused of being involved in a sham marriage (or a marriage of convenience) risk curtailment or revocation of existing leave to remain (if any) and administrative removal. Moreover, in certain situations, EU citizens accused of such involvement may lose their EUSS status in the UK and face either deportation on public policy grounds or administrative removal.

Overall, this book has shown that British marriage control practices have frequently violated EU law and targeted a much broader group of couples than those whose circumstances fit the definition of a marriage of convenience under the Citizenship Directive. The book concludes that such measures could lead to the disruption of families and hinder EU citizens from exercising their Treaty rights, a situation that has further deteriorated after the post-Brexit transition period.

Having examined the regulation of the issue in UK law and its compliance with EU law, this research may serve as an example for future case studies in the field. Apart from the UK, the situation in Ireland clearly deserves closer inspection due to measures targeting marriages of convenience, which the country has enacted in recent years. As the first case study in this particular legal setting, this book provides an innovative set of tools and arguments for examining the issue from various angles, all of which are crucial for developing a comprehensive understanding of the subject. It is, hence, much hoped that this will simplify the difficult task of other scholars who may wish to approach the concept of marriages of convenience from a comparative perspective.

Annexes

ANNEX 1

Critical Analysis of the Home Office Methodology Used to Calculate the Estimated Numbers of Perceived Sham Marriages

Whilst advocating for the introduction of the 'referral and investigation scheme', the Home Office claimed that 4,000 to 10,000 applications a year to stay in the UK could be made on the basis of sham marriages.[1] However, a closer inspection of the methodology used to obtain these figures reveals serious flaws and deficiencies that severely undermine the credibility of the government findings.

The relevant methodology was described in detail in a Home Office document providing background information on the proposed rules,[2] as well as in an Impact Assessment for the scheme.[3] To obtain the lower figure, the Home Office simply applied the estimated percentage of foreigner-involved marriages that generated section 24 reports in England and Wales (8%) to the combined number of applications to stay in the UK on the basis of marriage and civil partnership (50,000).[4]

First, it is unclear why only England and Wales were selected since for the UK as a whole, the share of 'suspicious' marriages is different – namely, 5%.[5] Applying this estimate to the total number of applications gives us only 2,500, not 4,000 suspicious applications, as claimed earlier. Second, section

1 Home Office, 'Sham Marriages and Civil Partnerships: Background Information and Proposed Referral and Investigation Scheme' (November 2013), 43; Home Office, 'Tackling Sham Marriage: Impact Assessment' (HO0090, 11.09.2013), 3.

2 Home Office, 'Sham Marriages and Civil Partnerships' (n 1).

3 Home Office, 'Tackling Sham Marriage: Impact Assessment' (n 1).

4 Ibid, 3. Data from 2011.

5 To arrive at this figure, the author used the methodology employed by the Home Office and divided the total number of section 24 reports (1,741 in 2011) by the entire number of marriages and civil partnerships involving non-EU nationals who could potentially benefit from the union in immigration terms (35,000 in 2011). It should be noted that the latter figure also includes nationals with settled or permanent status in the UK. Therefore, the real number of those potentially able to gain from a marriage an immigration advantage was lower. Furthermore, the estimate of 35,000 should be approached with caution, since the Home Office did not collect statistics on non-EU nationals marrying in England and Wales and borrowed the respective figures from Scotland, adjusting them accordingly. See Home Office, 'Sham Marriages and Civil Partnerships' (n 1), 43–44.

 | DOI:10.1163/9789004499263_014

24 reports only reflected the suspicions of registrars; it is unknown how many of the reports actually involved prospective marriages falling within the definition of a 'sham marriage' as provided under the Immigration and Asylum Act 1999.

Furthermore, the percentage of 'suspicious' marriages reported by registrars could not simply be applied to the number of applications to stay in the UK. First, not all intended marriages that generated section 24 reports were allowed to go forward and later serve as a basis for an application for leave to remain: a number of prospective weddings were disrupted by immigration officers, frequently leading to the arrest and/or removal of TCN parties.[6]

Next, it was stated that the total number of applications included both leave to remain and EEA residence card applications.[7] Yet, it should be remembered that TCN partners of British nationals or settled persons were subject to a 'non-switching' rule which required them to leave the UK and apply from abroad before they could reunify with their family members. Prior to admission, such couples were subject to close scrutiny and required to satisfy the minimum income requirement.

Further, the criteria used by marriage registrars to identify 'suspicious' couples might not have applied to those TCN partners of British nationals or settled persons who sought admission in the UK either on the basis of an already existing marriage or a fiancé(e) visa. These groups were equally subject to close scrutiny that acted as a significant deterrent for couples who did not satisfy the restrictive criteria, such as those involving third-country nationals with adverse immigration history or insufficient knowledge of their UK-based partner. It, therefore follows, that the estimate of 4,000 announced by the Home Office lacked any reliable statistical foundation and appeared exaggerated.

The above considerations also apply to the higher estimate of 10,000 applications a year made on the basis of a sham marriage or civil partnership. To arrive at this figure, the Home Office asked senior immigration caseworkers to estimate the proportion of applications to stay in the UK under the EEA Regulations[8] that were based on marriages of convenience, which they considered was around 20 per cent.[9] This number was then applied to the total number of applications made under both the Immigration Rules and the EEA Regulations, resulting in 10,000.[10] First, it should be stressed that the estimate

6 See for instance, HC Deb 13 February 2014, col 764W.

7 Home Office, 'Sham Marriages and Civil Partnerships' (n 1), 44.

8 Immigration (European Economic Area) Regulations 2016, SI 2016/1052 (EEA Regulations 2016).

9 Home Office, 'Sham Marriages and Civil Partnerships' (n 1), 44.

10 Ibid.

provided by the caseworkers was purely speculative and only reflected their perception of the abuse, particularly in light of their admission that the higher estimate 'applied to high risk nationalities only'.[11] Second, assuming that not all of the respective applicants had their marriages registered in the UK, 'suspicious' applications on the basis of marriages that took place outside the UK could hardly serve as an argument for intensifying pre-marriage controls within the country.

11 Home Office, 'Tackling Sham Marriage: Impact Assessment' (n 1), 3.

ANNEX 2

The Scope of the Existing Definitions of 'Sham Marriages'/'Marriages of Convenience'

Applicable to Couples Consisting of Mobile EU Citizens and Non-EU Nationals

 | DOI:10.1163/9789004499263_015

1	2	3	4	5
Citizenship Directive 'Marriage of convenience' – a marriage contracted for the sole purpose of enjoying the right of free movement and residence.	*Commission Handbook* 'Marriage of convenience'- a marriage contracted for the sole purpose of conferring a right of free movement and residence under EU law on free movement of EU citizens to a spouse who would otherwise not have such a right.	*Immigration Act 1999* 'Sham marriage' – a marriage where (1) either, or both, of the parties is not a British or Irish national, or an EEA national beneficiary of the Withdrawal Agreement Act,	EEA *Regulations 2016* 'Marriage of convenience' – a marriage entered into for the purpose of using these Regulations, or any other right conferred by the EU Treaties, as a means to circumvent –	*EU Settlement Scheme* 'Marriage of convenience' – a marriage entered into as a means to circumvent any criterion the party would otherwise have to meet in order to enjoy a right to enter or reside in the UK under EU law.
	The notion of 'sole purpose' should not be interpreted literally (as being the unique or exclusive purpose) but rather as meaning that the objective to obtain the right of entry and residence must be the predominant purpose of the abusive conduct.	(2) there is no genuine relationship between the parties and (3) either, or both, of the parties enter into the marriage to avoid the effect of UK immigration law and/or obtain a right to reside in the UK.	(a) immigration rules applying to non-EEA nationals or; (b) any other criteria that the party to the marriage of convenience would otherwise have to meet in order to enjoy a right to reside under these Regulations or the EU Treaties.	

	1	2	3	4	5
Pre-marriage stage					
Marriage to be contracted for the only purpose of enabling the TCN to enjoy a right to reside, with no relationship between the parties.	N/A	N/A	✔	N/A	N/A
Parties in an existing relationship but wish to contract a marriage for the predominant purpose of enabling the TCN to enjoy a right to reside.	N/A	N/A	X	N/A	N/A
Arranged marriage: intention to create a family but no relationship at the pre-marriage stage.	N/A	N/A	X	N/A	N/A

	1	2	3	4	5
Post-marriage stage					
Marriage contracted for the only purpose of enabling the TCN to enjoy a right to reside, with no relationship between the parties neither before, nor after marriage.	✔	✔	N/A	✔	✔
Marriage contracted for the only purpose of enabling the TCN to enjoy a right to reside, but the couple start a relationship after the marriage.	✔	✔	N/A	✔	✔
Parties in an existing relationship but contracted a marriage for the predominant purpose of enabling the TCN to enjoy a right to reside.	X	✔	N/A	✔ *If interpreted literally	✔ *If interpreted literally

✔ The situation is covered by the definition.
X The situation is not covered by the definition.
N/A Not applicable.

ANNEX 3

Upper Tribunal Decisions

In Cases Involving TCN Spouses of EU Citizens Whose Marriages Were Previously Found to Be Ones of Convenience (July 2016–December 2023) (Full List)

 | DOI:10.1163/9789004499263_016

N	Case number	Promulgation date	Nationality of the non-EU national spouse	Gender of the non-EU national spouse	Nationality of the EU citizen spouse	Gender of the EU citizen spouse	Stage	Appellant	Outcome	Children
1.	E. C. and Others v SSHD [2016] UKUT 10919 (IAC)	5 July 2016	India	M	Slovakia	F	Removal (Regs 19(3) and 21B(2) of the EEA Regulations 2006)	TCN	Appeal dismissed	
2.	SSHD v Kashif [2016] UKUT 19663 (IAC)	12 July 2016	Pakistan	M	Not available	F	EEA RC (APP)	SSHD	No error of law on MC, but appeal allowed on other grounds	
3.	SSHD v Chami [2016] UKUT 12375 (IAC)	20 July 2016	Algeria	M	Hungary	F	EEA RC (APP)	SSHD	Appeal dismissed	
4.	Igwe v SSHD [2016] UKUT 27335 (IAC)	26 July 2016	Not available	F	Not available	M	EEA RC (APP)	TCN	Set aside, remitted for rehearing	
5.	Onwusakah v SSHD [2016] UKUT 14926 (IAC)	26 July 2016	Nigeria	M	Bulgaria	F	EEA RC (APP)	TCN	Appeal dismissed	1
6.	SSHD v Okofor [2016] UKUT 42725 (IAC)	3 August 2016	Nigeria	F	Not available	M	EEA RC (APP)	SSHD	Set aside, save for the positive findings that marriage was not one of convenience	

N	Case number	Promulgation date	Nationality of the non-EU national spouse	Gender of the non-EU national spouse	Nationality of the EU citizen spouse	Gender of the EU citizen spouse	Stage	Appellant	Outcome	Children
7.	Rehman v SSHD [2016] UKUT 16713 (IAC)	8 August 2016	Pakistan	M	Slovakia	F	EEA RC (APP)	TCN	Appeal allowed	1
8.	Iqbal v SSHD [2016] UKUT 09279 (IAC)	22 August 2016	Pakistan	M	Not available	F	EEA RC (REV)	TCN	Appeal dismissed	
9.	SSHD v Okpegwa [2016] UKUT 47227 (IAC)	2 September 2016	Nigeria	M	Portugal	F	EEA RC (APP)	SSHD	Set aside, remitted for rehearing	
10.	Singh Cheema v SSHD [2016] UKUT 06785 (IAC)	13 September 2016	Not available	M	Romania	F	EEA RC (APP)	TCN	Appeal dismissed	
11.	Grace [A] v SSHD [2016] UKUT 04646 (IAC)	22 September 2016	Nigeria	F	Germany	M	EEA RC (REV)	SSHD	Appeal dismissed	
12.	SSHD v Saleem [2016] UKUT 19636 (IAC)	22 September 2016	Pakistan	M	Portugal	F	EEA RC (APP)	SSHD	Appeal dismissed	
13.	Bonyface and Magilrajah v SSHD [2016] UKUT 08051 (IAC)	27 September 2016	Sri Lanka	M	Germany	F	Other type of leave (REV)	TCN	Appeal allowed (other grounds)	
14.	Kaur Butter v SSHD [2016] UKUT 27370 (IAC)	3 October 2016	India	F	Czech Republic	M	EEA RC (APP)	SSHD	Set aside, remitted to SSHD	

N	Case number	Promulgation date	Nationality of the non-EU national spouse	Gender of the non-EU national spouse	Nationality of the EU citizen spouse	Gender of the EU citizen spouse	Stage	Appellant	Outcome	Children
15.	SSHD v Susana [L] [2016] UKUT 47733 (IAC)	4 October 2016	Not available	M	Portugal	F	Removal (Regs 19(3) and 21B(2) of the EEA Regulations 2006)	SSHD	Appeal allowed	
16.	Gadaev v SSHD [2016] UKUT 29481 (IAC)	13 October 2016	Uzbekistan	M	Lithuania	F	EEA RC (REV)	TCN	Appeal dismissed	
17.	Jallow v SSHD [2016] UKUT 48840 (IAC)	19 October 2016	Gambia	F	Netherlands	M	EEA RC (APP)	TCN	Appeal dismissed	
18.	Bismark [B] v SSHD [2016] UKUT 50715 (IAC)	24 October 2016	Not available	M	Netherlands (and Ghana)	F	EEA RC (APP)	TCN	Set aside, remitted for rehearing	
19.	Aslam v SSHD [2016] UKUT 14470 (IAC)	4 November 2016	Pakistan	M	Lithuania	F	EEA RC (APP)	TCN	Set aside, remitted for rehearing	
20.	Osorio Leiva v Entry Clearance Officer, Bogota [2017] UKUT 01651 (IAC)	2 May 2017	Colombia	F	Spain	M	EEA FP (APP)	TCN	Set aside, remitted for rehearing	

N	Case number	Promulgation date	Nationality of the non-EU national spouse	Gender of the non-EU national spouse	Nationality of the EU citizen spouse	Gender of the EU citizen spouse	Stage	Appellant	Outcome	Children
21.	Sonde v SSHD [2017] UKUT 32338 (IAC)	3 May 2017	Nigeria	F	Poland	M	EEA RC (APP)	TCN	Appeal dismissed	
22.	Mazhar v SSHD [2017] UKUT 14102 (IAC)	11 May 2017	Not available	M	Not available	F	EEA RC (APP)	TCN	Set aside, remitted for rehearing	
23.	Uddin v SSHD [2017] UKUT 27273 (IAC)	24 May 2017	Not available	M	Romania	F	EEA RC (APP)	TCN	Appeal dismissed on other grounds, marriage found to be genuine	1
24.	De Vera v SSHD [2017] UKUT 07000 (IAC)	6 June 2017	Philippines	F	Poland	M	EEA RC (APP)	TCN	Appeal allowed	
25.	SSHD v Yeboah [2017] UKUT 22118 (IAC)	15 June 2017	Ghana	F	Netherlands	M	EEA RC (APP)	SSHD	Appeal allowed	
26.	Saeed v SSHD [2017] UKUT 09715 (IAC)	15 June 2017	Pakistan	M	Lithuania	F	EEA RC (APP)	TCN	Appeal dismissed	
27.	Kalu v SSHD [2017] UKUT 28763 (IAC)	16 June 2017	Nigeria	M	Not available	F	EEA PRC (APP)	TCN	Appeal dismissed	

N	Case number	Promulgation date	Nationality of the non-EU national spouse	Gender of the non-EU national spouse	Nationality of the EU citizen spouse	Gender of the EU citizen spouse	Stage	Appellant	Outcome	Children
28.	Bello v SSHD [2017] UKUT 09346 (IAC)	16 June 2017	Nigeria	M	Poland	F	EEA RC (APP)	TCN	Appeal dismissed	
29.	[B S] v SSHD [2017] UKUT 16879 (IAC)	21 June 2017	Sri Lanka	M	Not available	F	EEA RC (APP)	TCN	Set aside, remitted for rehearing	
30.	SSHD v Bilal [2017] UKUT 24492 (IAC)	23 June 2017	Pakistan	M	Not available	F	EEA RC (APP)	SSHD	Appeal dismissed on other grounds	
31.	K v SSHD [2017] UKUT 29770 (IAC)	26 June 2017	India	F	Poland	M	EEA RC (APP)	TCN	Appeal dismissed	
32.	Mubashar v SSHD [2017] UKUT 00171 (IAC)	6 July 2017	Pakistan	M	Not available	F	EEA RC (REV)	TCN	Set aside, remitted for rehearing	
33.	Faisal v SSHD [2017] UKUT 00817 (IAC)	11 July 2017	Pakistan	M	Poland	F	EEA RC (REV)	TCN	Appeal allowed	
34	Ngoka v SSHD [2017] UKUT 30554 (IAC)	20 July 2017	Nigeria	M	Portugal	F	EEA PRC (APP)	TCN	Appeal allowed	
35.	Zehri v SSHD [2017] UKUT 23934 (IAC)	28 July 2017	Algeria	M	Greece	F	EEA RC (APP)	TCN	Set aside, remitted for rehearing	

N	Case number	Promulgation date	Nationality of the non-EU national spouse	Gender of the non-EU national spouse	Nationality of the EU citizen spouse	Gender of the EU citizen spouse	Stage	Appellant	Outcome	Children
36.	SSHD v Aitjilal [2017] UKUT 00830 (IAC)	17 August 2017	Morocco	M	Portugal	F	EEA RC (REV)	SSHD	Set aside, remitted for rehearing	
37.	Mohammed and Lacmidas v SSHD [2017] UKUT 05863 (IAC)	18 August 2017	Not available	M	Not available	F	EEA RC (APP)	TCN	Set aside, remitted for rehearing	
38.	Ogbewi v SSHD [2017] UKUT 03381 (IAC)	30 August 2017	Nigeria	F	Spain	M	EEA RC (APP)	TCN	Appeal dismissed	
39.	Hussain v SSHD [2017] UKUT 19104 (IAC)	19 September 2017	Pakistan	M	Bulgaria	F	EEA RC (APP)	TCN	Appeal dismissed	
40.	Thomas v SSHD [2017] UKUT 05926 (IAC)	27 September 2017	Nigeria	F	Not available	M	EEA RC (RETD)	TCN	Set aside, remitted for rehearing	
41.	A U v SSHD [2017] UKUT 00052 (IAC)	28 September 2017	Pakistan	M	Latvia	F	EEA RC (APP)	TCN	Appeal dismissed	
42.	Singh Brar v SSHD [2017] UKUT 07611 (IAC)	5 October 2017	Not available	M	Hungary	F	EEA RC (APP)	TCN	Appeal dismissed	
43.	Jamil v SSHD [2017] UKUT 33121 (IAC)	11 October 2017	Pakistan	M	Lithuania	F	EEA PRC (APP)	TCN	Appeal dismissed	

N	Case number	Promulgation date	Nationality of the non-EU national spouse	Gender of the non-EU national spouse	Nationality of the EU citizen spouse	Gender of the EU citizen spouse	Stage	Appellant	Outcome	Children
44.	Aziz v SSHD [2017] UKUT 01427 (IAC)	12 October 2017	Pakistan	M	Not available	F	EEA RC (APP)	TCN	Set aside, remitted for rehearing	
45.	Sarkodie v SSHD [2017] UKUT 00736 (IAC)	16 October 2017	Ghana	M	Netherlands	F	EEA RC (APP)	TCN	Set aside, remitted for rehearing	
46.	Rovillos v SSHD [2017] UKUT 01821 (IAC)	31 October 2017	Philippines	F	Slovakia	M	EEA RC (APP)	TCN	Appeal allowed	
47.	Riaz v SSHD [2017] UKUT 04031 (IAC)	9 November 2017	Not available	M	Slovakia	F	EEA RC (APP)	TCN	Appeal dismissed	
48.	Anwar v SSHD [2017] UKUT 04104 (IAC)	27 November 2017	Pakistan	M	Not available	F	EEA RC (APP)	TCN	Appeal dismissed	
49.	Parmar v Entry Clearance Officer, New Delhi [2017] UKUT 09238 (IAC)	13 December 2017	India	M	Not available	F	EEA FP (APP)	TCN	Set aside, remitted for rehearing	
50.	Adnan v SSHD [2017] UKUT 25601 (IAC)	14 December 2017	Not available	M	Portugal	F	EEA RC (APP)	TCN	Set aside, remitted for rehearing	1
51.	Ugwunze v SSHD [2017] UKUT 04578 (IAC)	18 December 2017	Nigeria	M	Netherlands	F	EEA RC (APP)	TCN	Set aside, remitted for rehearing	

N	Case number	Promulgation date	Nationality of the non-EU national spouse	Gender of the non-EU national spouse	Nationality of the EU citizen spouse	Gender of the EU citizen spouse	Stage	Appellant	Outcome	Children
52.	Nasreen v SSHD [2018] UKUT 25249 (IAC)	8 January 2018	Bangladesh	F	Italy	M	EEA RC (APP)	TCN	Appeal allowed	
53.	Zwane v SSHD [2018] UKUT 00435 (IAC)	9 January 2018	Not available	F	Romania	M	EEA RC (APP)	TCN	Appeal dismissed	
54.	Virk v SSHD [2018] UKUT 19843 (IAC)	15 January 2018	Not available	M	Not available	F	EEA RC (APP)	TCN	Set aside, remitted for rehearing	
55.	Marquez v SSHD [2018] UKUT 00705 (IAC)	18 January 2018	Not available	F	Not available	M	EEA RC (APP)	TCN	Appeal dismissed	
56.	Daljit [S] and [S K] [2018] UKUT 04431 (IAC)	19 January 2018	Not available	M	Lithuania	F	EEA RC (RETD)	TCN	Appeal dismissed	
57.	Boadu v SSHD [2018] UKUT 11391 (IAC)	11 January 2018	Ghana	M	Netherlands	F	EEA RC (RETD)	TCN	Appeal dismissed	
58.	Khvedelidze v SSHD [2018] UKUT 08540 (IAC)	17 April 2018	Georgia	F	Not available	M	EEA RC (APP)	TCN	Set aside, remitted for rehearing	

N	Case number	Promulgation date	Nationality of the non-EU national spouse	Gender of the non-EU national spouse	Nationality of the EU citizen spouse	Gender of the EU citizen spouse	Stage	Appellant	Outcome	Children
59.	Ninsinghkhon v Entry Clearance Officer, Bangkok [2018] UKUT 08937 (IAC)	17 April 2018	Thailand	F	Romania	M	EEA FP (APP)	TCN	Set aside, remitted for rehearing	
60.	Sabbah v SSHD [2018] UKUT 10124 (IAC)	17 April 2018	Palestinian Authority	M	Hungary	F	EEA PRC (APP)	TCN	Set aside, remitted for rehearing	
61.	SSHD v Baffour-Agyekum [2018] UKUT 04274 (IAC)	18 April 2018	Ghana	M	Not available	F	EEA RC (APP)	SSHD	Set aside, but the TCN's appeal allowed	
62.	Akuoku v SSHD [2018] UKUT 09006 (IAC)	20 April 2018	Ghana	M	Not available	F	EEA RC (APP)	TCN	Set aside, but appeal dismissed on other grounds	
63.	Habib v SSHD [2018] UKUT 06534 (IAC)	20 April 2018	Pakistan	M	Not available	F	EEA PRC (APP)	TCN	Appeal dismissed	
64.	Rahman v SSHD [2018] UKUT 00894 (IAC)	30 April 2018	Bangladesh	M	Not available	F	EEA RC (REV)	TCN	Set aside, remitted for rehearing	
65.	Raja v SSHD [2018] UKUT 35032 (IAC)	1 May 2018	Pakistan	M	Not available	F	EEA RC (APP)	TCN	Set aside, remitted for rehearing	

N	Case number	Promulgation date	Nationality of the non-EU national spouse	Gender of the non-EU national spouse	Nationality of the EU citizen spouse	Gender of the EU citizen spouse	Stage	Appellant	Outcome	Children
66.	SSHD v Holmes [2018] UKUT 07786 (IAC)	4 May 2018	US	M	Not available	F	EEA RC (APP)	SSHD	Set aside, remitted for rehearing	
67.	Fadojutimi v SSHD [2018] UKUT 02223 (IAC)	14 May 2018	Nigeria	M	Not available	F	EEA PRC (APP)	TCN	Set aside, remitted for rehearing	
68.	Rajah [A] v SSHD [2018] UKUT 08581 (IAC)	15 October 2018	Pakistan	M	Not available	F	EEA PRC (APP)	TCN	Appeal allowed	2
69.	Mahmood v SSHD [2018] UKUT 02903 (IAC)	17 October 2018	Not available	M	Not available	F	EEA RC (APP)	TCN	Set aside, remitted for rehearing	
70.	Shaaban Aly v SSHD [2018] UKUT 07311 (IAC)	6 November 2018	Egypt	M	Slovakia	F	EEA RC (RETD)	TCN	Appeal dismissed	
71.	Yeya v SSHD [2018] UKUT 00515 (IAC)	7 November 2018	Niger	F	Not available	M	EEA RC (APP)	TCN	Set aside, remitted for rehearing	
72.	Sanyang v SSHD [2018] UKUT 07041 (IAC)	14 November 2018	Not available	F	Not available	M	EEA RC (APP)	TCN	Set aside, remitted for rehearing	

N	Case number	Promulgation date	Nationality of the non-EU national spouse	Gender of the non-EU national spouse	Nationality of the EU citizen spouse	Gender of the EU citizen spouse	Stage	Appellant	Outcome	Children
73.	SSHD v Michael [O] [2018] UKUT 02107 (IAC)	16 November 2018	Not available	M	Germany	F	EEA PRC (REV)	SSHD	Appeal dismissed	
74.	Alex [A] v SSHD [2018] UKUT 04343 (IAC)	20 November 2018	Ghana	M	Netherlands	F	EEA PRC (APP)	TCN	Appeal allowed	
75.	[A Z] and [R Z] v SSHD [2018] UKUT 06790 (IAC)	20 November 2018	Pakistan	M	Czech Republic	F	EEA RC (REV)	SSHD	Set aside, remitted for rehearing	
76.	Saquib v SSHD [2018] UKUT 13167 (IAC)	23 November 2018	Pakistan	M	Poland	F	EEA RC (APP)	TCN	Appeal dismissed	
77.	Elkhouly v SSHD [2018] UKUT 09234 (IAC)	27 November 2018	Not available	M	Not available	F	EEA RC (APP)	TCN	Set aside, remitted for rehearing	
78.	Raqeeb v SSHD [2018] UKUT 01754 (IAC)	3 December 2018	Pakistan	M	Poland	F	EEA RC (APP)	TCN	Appeal dismissed	
79.	Shahzad v SSHD [2018] UKUT 07380 (IAC)	4 December 2018	Pakistan	M	Romania	F	EEA RC (APP)	TCN	Appeal dismissed	
80.	Adi v SSHD [2019] UKUT 09432 (IAC)	25 January 2019	Not available	M	Not available	F	EEA PRC (APP)	TCN	Set aside, remitted for rehearing	

N	Case number	Promulgation date	Nationality of the non-EU national spouse	Gender of the non-EU national spouse	Nationality of the EU citizen spouse	Gender of the EU citizen spouse	Stage	Appellant	Outcome	Children
81.	Khan v SSHD [2019] UKUT 03191 (IAC)	8 February 2019	Pakistan	M	Lithuania	F	EEA RC (APP)	TCN	Set aside, remitted for rehearing	1
82.	Sokoya v SSHD [2019] UKUT 07559 (IAC)	15 February 2019	Nigeria	M	Portugal	F	EEA RC (APP)	TCN	Appeal dismissed	
83.	Collins [E] v SSHD [2019] UKUT 01818 (IAC)	18 February 2019	Not available	Not available	Not available	Not available	EEA RC (APP)	TCN	Appeal allowed	1
84.	Uddin v SSHD [2019] UKUT 01755 (IAC)	4 March 2019	Not available	M	Not available	F	EEA RC (APP)	TCN	Set aside, remitted for rehearing	
85.	Kouao v SSHD [2019] UKUT 09255 (IAC)	6 March 2019	Cote d'Ivoire	F	France	M	EEA PRC (REV)	TCN	Appeal dismissed	
86.	Waheed v SSHD [2019] UKUT 02885 (IAC)	7 March 2019	Not available	M	Poland	F	EEA RC (APP)	TCN	Appeal dismissed	
87.	Alhanouti v SSHD [2019] UKUT 02582 (IAC)	3 April 2019	Jordan	M	Latvia	F	EEA PRC (APP)	TCN	Set aside, remitted for rehearing	
88.	Gjura v SSHD [2019] UKUT 07856 (IAC)	15 April 2019	Albania	M	Slovakia	F	EEA RC (APP)	TCN	Appeal dismissed	1

N	Case number	Promulgation date	Nationality of the non-EU national spouse	Gender of the non-EU national spouse	Nationality of the EU citizen spouse	Gender of the EU citizen spouse	Stage	Appellant	Outcome	Children
89.	Muhammad [M] v SSHD [2019] UKUT 07160 (IAC)	2 May 2019	Pakistan	M	Not available	F	EEA RC (APP)	TCN	Set aside, remitted for rehearing	
90.	SSHD v Massod [2019] UKUT 04589 (IAC)	10 May 2019	Not available	M	Hungary	F	EEA RC (RETD)	SSHD	Appeal dismissed	
91.	Ahmed v SSHD [2019] UKUT 01401 (IAC)	15 May 2019	Not available	M	Not available	F	EEA PRC (APP)	TCN	Set aside, remitted for rehearing	
92.	SSHD v Lekeate [2019] UKUT 08363 (IAC)	16 May 2019	Cameroon	M	Not available	F	EEA RC (APP)	SSHD	Appeal dismissed	
93.	Tandel v SSHD [2019] UKUT 05031 (IAC)	16 May 2019	India	M	Portugal	F	Removal (Regs 23(6)(a) and 32(2) of the EEA Regulations 2016)	TCN	Appeal allowed (on different grounds)	
94.	De Zoysa Siriwardana Nanediri v SSHD [2019] UKUT 04892 (IAC)	13 June 2019	Not available	M	Not available	F	EEA RC (APP)	TCN	Set aside, remitted for rehearing	

N	Case number	Promulgation date	Nationality of the non-EU national spouse	Gender of the non-EU national spouse	Nationality of the EU citizen spouse	Gender of the EU citizen spouse	Stage	Appellant	Outcome	Children
95.	Gjana v SSHD [2019] UKUT 07850 (IAC)	20 June 2019	Albania	M	Czech Republic	F	EEA RC (APP)	TCN	Appeal dismissed	
96.	Andrushkiv v SSHD [2019] UKUT 07859 (IAC)	24 June 2019	Ukraine	F	Lithuania	M	EEA RC (APP)	TCN	Appeal dismissed	
97.	Resul [M] v SSHD [2019] UKUT 07602 (IAC)	26 June 2019	Albania	M	Romania	F	EEA RC (APP)	TCN	Appeal dismissed	1
98.	SSHD v Roman [O] [2019] UKUT 05234 (IAC)	27 June 2019	Not available	M	Not available	F	EEA RC (APP)	SSHD	Set aside, remitted for rehearing	
99.	Arshad v SSHD [2019] UKUT 04911 (IAC)	2 July 2019	Pakistan	M	Lithuania	F	EEA PRC (APP)	TCN	Appeal dismissed	
100.	Asghar v SSHD [2019] UKUT 07181 (IAC)	4 July 2019	Pakistan	M	Bulgaria	F	EEA RC (APP)	TCN	Appeal dismissed	
101.	Lulzime [C] and [RM] [2019] UKUT 03329 (IAC)	8 July 2019	Albania	F	Latvia	M	EEA RC (APP)	TCN	Appeal allowed	1
102.	Raza v SSHD [2019] UKUT 03566 (IAC)	10 July 2019	Pakistan	M	Romania	F	EEA RC (APP)	TCN	Appeal dismissed	

N	Case number	Promulgation date	Nationality of the non-EU national spouse	Gender of the non-EU national spouse	Nationality of the EU citizen spouse	Gender of the EU citizen spouse	Stage	Appellant	Outcome	Children
103.	Woguia v SSHD [2019] UKUT 12057 (IAC)	15 July 2019	Cameroon	F	France	M	EEA RC (APP)	TCN	Appeal dismissed	1
104.	Abouelhasaan v SSHD [2019] UKUT 04931 (IAC)	24 July 2019	Egypt	M	Ireland	F	EEA RC (APP)	TCN	Appeal allowed	1
105.	Akhtar v SSHD [2019] UKUT 04915 (IAC)	24 July 2019	Pakistan	M	Poland	F	EEA RC (APP)	TCN	Appeal dismissed	
106.	Arif v SSHD [2019] UKUT 06176 (IAC)	25 July 2019	Not available	M	Lithuania	F	EEA PRC (APP) EEA RC (REV)	TCN	Appeal dismissed	
107.	Ussenbai v Entry Clearance Officer [2019] UKUT 00472 (IAC)	25 July 2019	India	F	Portugal (and India)	M	EEA FP (APP)	TCN	Appeal dismissed	
108.	Azam v SSHD [2019] UKUT 04634 (IAC)	25 July 2019	Not available	M	Not available	F	EEA RC (APP)	TCN	Appeal dismissed	
109.	Kola v SSHD [2019] UKUT 05962 (IAC)	1 August 2019	Albania	M	Bulgaria (and Albania)	F	EEA RC (APP)	TCN	Remitted for rehearing	-
110.	Martinez Perez v SSHD [2019] UKUT 07668 (IAC)	7 August 2019	Bolivia	F	Spain (of Ecuadorian origin)	M	EEA RC (APP)	TCN	Appeal dismissed	

N	Case number	Promulgation date	Nationality of the non-EU national spouse	Gender of the non-EU national spouse	Nationality of the EU citizen spouse	Gender of the EU citizen spouse	Stage	Appellant	Outcome	Children
111.	Isufaj (PTA decisions/reasons; EEA reg. 37 appeals) [2019] UKUT 00283 (IAC)	12 August 2019	Albania	M	Lithuania	F	ENT (REF)	TCN	Set aside, remitted for rehearing	
112.	Entry Clearance Officer v Yuliia [Z] [2019] UKUT 01734	13 August 2019	Ukraine	F	Bulgaria	M	EEA FP (APP)	ECO (SSHD)	Decision remade, TCN's appeal allowed again	1, P
113.	Pujols Paulino v SSHD [2019] UKUT 05769 (IAC)	13 August 2019	Dominican Republic	F	Spain	M	EEA RC (APP)	TCN	Appeal dismissed	
114.	SSHD v O [2019] UKUT 03172 (IAC)	14 August 2019	Nigeria	M	Not available	F	EEA RC (RETD)	SSHD	Appeal dismissed	
115.	Gill v SSHD [2019] UKUT 07335 (IAC).	15 August 2019	Pakistan	M	Hungary	F	EEA RC (RETD)	TCN	Set aside, appeal allowed	
116.	Laizane v SSHD [2019] UKUT 17910 (IAC)	20 August 2019	Ukraine	F	Latvia	M	EEA FP (APP)	TCN	Appeal dismissed	
117.	Josephine [O] v SSHD [2019] UKUT 05252 (IAC)	20 August 2019	Nigeria	F	Not available	M	Not available	TCN	Set aside, remitted for rehearing	

N	Case number	Promulgation date	Nationality of the non-EU national spouse	Gender of the non-EU national spouse	Nationality of the EU citizen spouse	Gender of the EU citizen spouse	Stage	Appellant	Outcome	Children
118.	Sidhu v SSHD [2019] UKUT 07915 (IAC)	5 September 2019	Pakistan	M	Czech Republic	F	EEA RC (APP)	TCN	Appeal allowed	
119	Sanibal v SSHD [2019] UKUT 06516 (IAC)	10 September 2019	Morocco	M	Poland	F	EEA PRC (APP)	TCN	Appeal dismissed	
120.	Waseem v SSHD [2020] UKUT 07454 (IAC)	10 October 2019	Not available	Not available	Not available	M	EEA RC (APP)	TCN	Set aside, remitted for rehearing	
121.	Al Hassan v SSHD [2020] UKUT 07618 (IAC)	15 October 2019	Not available	M	Netherlands (of Ghanaian origin), proxy marriage	F	EEA RC (APP)	TCN	Set aside for error in law but appeal still dismissed	2
122	Fazal v SSHD [2020] UKUT 04047 (IAC)	15 October 2019	Pakistan	M	Norway	F	EEA RC (APP)	TCN	Appeal dismissed	
123.	Wang v SSHD [2020] UKUT 00107 (IAC)	17 October 2019	China	M	Belgium (of Chinese origin)	F	EEA RC (APP)	TCN	Appeal on MC grounds dismissed	
124.	Dashaj v SSHD [2020] UKUT 06081 (IAC)	15 November 2019	Not available	M	Not available	F	EEA RC (APP)	TCN	Set aside, remitted for rehearing	

N	Case number	Promulgation date	Nationality of the non-EU national spouse	Gender of the non-EU national spouse	Nationality of the EU citizen spouse	Gender of the EU citizen spouse	Stage	Appellant	Outcome	Children
125.	Cunningham v SSHD [2020] UKUT 06579 (IAC)	21 November 2019	Jamaica	F	Spain	M	EEA PRC (APP)	TCN	Set aside, remitted for rehearing	
126.	SSHD v Awais [2020] 01902 (IAC)	26 November 2019	Not available	M	Not available	F	EEA RC (REV)	SSHD	Appeal dismissed	
127.	Tariq v SSHD [2020] UKUT 01252 (IAC)	13 January 2020	Not available	M	Hungary	F	EEA RC (APP)	TCN	Appeal dismissed	
128.	Dhensa v SSHD [2020] UKUT 01197 (IAC)	15 January 2020	Pakistan	M	Poland	F	EEA RC (APP)	TCN	Appeal allowed	
129.	Andrushkiv v SSHD [2020] UKUT 07859 (IAC)	3 February 2020	Ukraine	F	Lithuania	M	EEA RC (APP)	TCN	Set aside, remitted for rehearing	
130.	Nimo (appeals: duty of disclosure) [2020] UKUT 00088 (IAC)	27 February 2020	Ghana	M	Netherlands	F	EEA RC (APP)	TCN	Appeal dismissed	
131.	Mirush [K] v SSHD [2020] UKUT 07293 (IAC)	5 March 2020	Not available	M	Greece	F	EEA RC (APP)	TCN	Set aside, remitted for rehearing	
132.	Letitia [G] v SSHD [2020] UKUT 00458 (IAC)	26 June 2020	Sierra Leone	F	Lithuania	M	EEA RC (APP)	TCN	Appeal dismissed	

N	Case number	Promulgation date	Nationality of the non-EU national spouse	Gender of the non-EU national spouse	Nationality of the EU citizen spouse	Gender of the EU citizen spouse	Stage	Appellant	Outcome	Children
133.	Singh v SSHD [2020] UKUT 01102 (IAC)	3 August 2020	India	M	Not available	Not available	EEA RC (APP)	TCN	Appeal dismissed	
134.	Raza v SSHD [2020] UKUT 00542 (IAC)	19 August 2020	Pakistan	M	Romania	F	EEA RC (APP)	TCN	Appeal dismissed	
135.	Ali & Dirie [2020] UKUT 00916 & 00918 (IAC)	22 September 2020	Somalia	F	Norway (of Somali origin)	M	EEA FP (APP)	TCN	Set aside, remitted for rehearing	
136.	Pellumb [M] v SSHD [2020] 00037 (IAC)	28 September 2020	Albania	M	France	F	EEA RC (APP)	TCN	Set aside, remitted for rehearing	
137.	Entry Clearance Officer v Ngalemo-Tchokotchieu [2020] 01257 (IAC)	1 October 2020	Cameroon	M	Romania	F	EEA FP (APP)	SSHD	Appeal allowed	
138.	Ulyana [I] v SSHD [2020] 05814 (IAC)	13 October 2020	Ukraine	F	Not available	M	Not available	TCN	Set aside, remitted for rehearing	
139.	Ikponmwen v SSHD [2020] 05940 (IAC)	2 November 2020	Nigeria	M	Not available	Not available	EEA RC (APP)	TCN	Appeal dismissed	
140.	Shaukat v SSHD [2020] 04896 (IAC)	17 November 2020	Pakistan	M	Latvia	F	EEA PRC (APP)	TCN	Set aside, remitted for rehearing	

N	Case number	Promulgation date	Nationality of the non-EU national spouse	Gender of the non-EU national spouse	Nationality of the EU citizen spouse	Gender of the EU citizen spouse	Stage	Appellant	Outcome	Children
141.	Azam v SSHD [2021] 04215 (IAC)	11 January 2021	Pakistan	M	Switzerland	F	EEA RC (APP)	TCN	Appeal dismissed	
142.	Wambui v SSHD [2021] UKUT 06884 (IAC)	4 February 2021	Kenya	M	Italy	F	EEA RC (APP)	TCN	Set aside, appeal allowed	1
143.	K A W (Pakistan) v SSHD [2021] UKUT 01859 (IAC)	14 April 2021	Pakistan	M	Czech Republic	F	EEA RC (APP)	TCN	Appeal dismissed	
144.	Hajdari v SSHD [2021] UKUT 03750 (IAC)	17 May 2021	Albania	M	Romania	F	EEA RC (APP)	TCN	Set aside, remitted for rehearing	
145.	Nakanwagi v Entry Clearance Officer, Pretoria [2021] UKUT 01779 (IAC)	4 August 2021	Uganda	F	Sweden	M	EEA FP (APP)	TCN	Set aside due to error of law but appeal dismissed	
146.	Usiobaifo v SSHD [2021] UKUT 02875 (IAC)	15 September 2021	Nigeria	F	Spain (of Nigerian origin)	M	EEA PRC (APP)	TCN	Appeal dismissed	
147.	Saeed (Deception, knowledge, marriage of convenience) [2022] UKUT 00018 (IAC)	6 December 2021	Pakistan	M	Lithuania	F	ILR (APP) but previously refused an EEA RC	TCN	Appeal dismissed	

N	Case number	Promulgation date	Nationality of the non-EU national spouse	Gender of the non-EU national spouse	Nationality of the EU citizen spouse	Gender of the EU citizen spouse	Stage	Appellant	Outcome	Children
148.	Zguri v SSHD [2021] UKUT 01803 (IAC)	9 December 2021	Albania	M	Romania	F	EEA RC (APP)	TCN	Appeal dismissed	
149.	Aroyehun v SSHD [2022] UKUT 05977 (IAC)	20 December 2021	Nigeria	M	Not available	F	ILR after having been granted an EEA RC	TCN	Appeal dismissed	
150.	Hima v SSHD [2022] UKUT 00495 (IAC)	27 January 2022	Albania	M	Romania	F	EEA RC (APP)	TCN	Appeal dismissed	
151.	Phiri v SSHD [2022] UKUT 06704 (IAC)	9 February 2022	Not available	F	Not available	M	EEA RC (APP)	TCN	Appeal dismissed	
152.	Hajdari v SSHD [2022] UKUT 03750 (IAC)	27 April 2022	Albania	M	Romania	F	EEA RC (APP)	TCN	Appeal dismissed	
153.	Gjymenga v SSHD [2022] UKUT 07120 (IAC)	10 May 2022	Albania	M	Greece	F	EUSS FP (APP)	TCN	Appeal dismissed	
154.	Baro v SSHD [2022] UKUT 03464 (IAC)	31 May 2022	Albania	M	Poland	F	EEA RC (APP)	TCN	Appeal allowed	
155.	Javed v SSHD [2022] UKUT 00470 (IAC)	7 June 2022	Pakistan	M	Bulgaria	F	EEA RC (APP)	TCN	Appeal dismissed	

N	Case number	Promulgation date	Nationality of the non-EU national spouse	Gender of the non-EU national spouse	Nationality of the EU citizen spouse	Gender of the EU citizen spouse	Stage	Appellant	Outcome	Children
156.	SSHD v Asonye [2022] UKUT 09049 (IAC)	14 July 2022	Not available	F	France	M	EUSS status (APP)	SSHD	Appeal dismissed	
157.	SSHD v Nketia [2022] UKUT 04841 (IAC)	27 July 2022	Ghana	F	Belgium	M	EEA RC (APP)	SSHD	Appeal allowed	1
158.	Jahaj v SSHD [2022] UKUT 09461 (IAC)	7 September 2022	Albania	M	Romania	F	EEA RC (APP)	TCN	Set aside, remitted for rehearing	
159.	Singh v SSHD [2022] UKUT 00091 (IAC)	7 September 2022	India	F	Portugal	F	EEA PRC (APP)	TCN	Appeal dismissed	
160.	Mohamud v SSHD [2022] UKUT 03758 (IAC)	5 October 2022	Not available	M	Not available	F	EUSS FP (APP)	TCN	Appeal allowed	
161.	Shakeel v SSHD [2022] UKUT 13405 (IAC)	27 October 2022	Pakistan	M	Lithuania	F	EUSS status (APP)	TCN	Set aside, remitted for rehearing	
162.	Khan v SSHD [2022] UKUT 06826 (IAC)	27 November 2022	Pakistan	M	Spain	F	EEA RC (RETD)	TCN	Appeal dismissed (on other grounds, marriage accepted as genuine)	P

N	Case number	Promulgation date	Nationality of the non-EU national spouse	Gender of the non-EU national spouse	Nationality of the EU citizen spouse	Gender of the EU citizen spouse	Stage	Appellant	Outcome	Children
163.	Latif v SSHD [2022] UKUT 01981 (IAC)	30 November 2022	Not available	Not available	Not available	Not available	EEA RC (APP)	TCN	Set aside, remitted for rehearing	
164.	SSHD v Mir [2022] UKUT 05762 (IAC)	1 December 2022	Algeria	M	Not available	F	EUSS status (RETD)	SSHD	Set aside, remitted for rehearing	
165.	Adu v SSHD [2023] UKUT 01926 (IAC)	27 March 2023	Ghana	M	Not available	F	EUSS FP (APP)	TCN	Appeal dismissed	
166.	Adeeko v SSHD [2023] UKUT 01285 (IAC)	27 March 2023	Nigeria	F	Not available	M	EUSS status (APP)	TCN	Appeal dismissed	
167.	Singh v SSHD [2023] UKUT 00087 (IAC)	28 March 2023	Not available	M	Not available	F	EEA RC (APP)	TCN	Set aside, remitted for rehearing	
168.	Osigwe v SSHD [2023] UKUT 11840 (IAC)	25 April 2023	Nigeria	M	Not available	F	EUSS status (RETD)	TCN	Set aside, remitted for rehearing	
169.	SSHD v Zaydulaev [2023] UKUT 01581 (IAC)	28 April 2023	Uzbekistan	M	Latvia	F	EUSS status (RETD)	SSHD	Appeal dismissed	
170.	Ashiru v SSHD [2023] UKUT 00248 (IAC)	28 April 2023	Nigeria	M	Not available	F	EUSS status (APP)	TCN	Appeal dismissed	

N	Case number	Promulgation date	Nationality of the non-EU national spouse	Gender of the non-EU national spouse	Nationality of the EU citizen spouse	Gender of the EU citizen spouse	Stage	Appellant	Outcome	Children
171.	Khan v SSHD [2023] UKUT 11835 (IAC)	30 April 2023	Not available	M	Not available	F	EUSS status (APP)	TCN	Set aside, remitted for rehearing	
172.	Villegas Garcia v SSHD [2023] UKUT 01690 (IAC)	17 May 2023	Peru	F	Not available	M	EUSS FP (APP)	TCN	Appeal dismissed	
173.	Babani v SSHD [2023] UKUT 02619 (IAC)	17 May 2023	Albania	M	Romania	F	EUSS status (APP)	TCN	Appeal dismissed	
174.	Aderinola v Entry Clearance Officer, Liverpool [2023] UKUT 15176 (IAC)	18 May 2023	Nigeria	F	Spain	M	EUSS FP (APP)	TCN	Set aside, remitted for rehearing	
175.	Palushi v Entry Clearance Officer [2023] UKUT 11206 (IAC)	28 May 2023	Albania	M	Bulgaria	F	EUSS FP (APP)	TCN	Set aside due to error of law but appeal dismissed	
176.	Abdelmotaleb v SSHD [2023] UKUT 01177 (IAC)	28 May 2023	Egypt	M	Not available	F	EEA RC (APP)	TCN	Appeal dismissed	
177.	Plaku v SSHD [2023] UKUT 10997 (IAC)	29 May 2023	Albania	M	Not available	F	EEA RC (APP)	TCN	Set aside, remitted for rehearing	

N	Case number	Promulgation date	Nationality of the non-EU national spouse	Gender of the non-EU national spouse	Nationality of the EU citizen spouse	Gender of the EU citizen spouse	Stage	Appellant	Outcome	Children
178.	Sofola v SSHD [2023] UKUT 000866 (IAC)	13 June 2023	Nigeria	M	Ireland	F	EUSS status (APP)	TCN	Appeal dismissed	
179.	SSHD v Ponari [2023] UKUT 002303 (IAC)	19 June 2023	Albania	M	Romania	F	EUSS status (APP)	SSHD	Appeal dismissed	
180.	SSHD v Abdeaziz [2023] UKUT 006527 (IAC)	28 June 2023	Egypt	M	Romania	F	EUSS status (APP)	SSHD	Set aside, remitted for rehearing	
181.	Zubair v SSHD [2023] UKUT 00918 (IAC)	6 July 2023	Pakistan	M	Romania	F	EUSS status (APP)	TCN	Set aside, remitted for rehearing	Misc
182.	Mahmood v SSHD [2023] UKUT 001447 (IAC)	27 July 2023	Pakistan	M	Not available	F	EUSS status (RETD)	TCN	Appeal allowed	Misc
183.	Velaj v Entry Clearance Officer [2023] UKUT 003050 (IAC)	18 September 2023	Albania	M	Romania	F	EUSS FP (APP)	TCN	Appeal dismissed	
184.	Elezi v SSHD [2023] UKUT 002330 (IAC)	3 October 2023	Albania	M	Not available	F	EUSS status (APP)	TCN	Appeal dismissed	

N	Case number	Promulgation date	Nationality of the non-EU national spouse	Gender of the non-EU national spouse	Nationality of the EU citizen spouse	Gender of the EU citizen spouse	Stage	Appellant	Outcome	Children
185.	Border Force Officer, Heathrow Airport v Appoh [2023] UKUT 003395 (IAC)	10 October 2023	Ghana	F	Netherlands	M	EUSS Pre-settled status cancellation	SSHD	Appeal dismissed	
186.	Zizinekpe v SSHD [2023] UKUT 003319 (IAC)	20 October 2023	Ghana	Not available	Not available	Not available	EUSS status (APP)	TCN	Appeal dismissed	
187.	Khan v SSHD [2023] UKUT 001516 (IAC)	2 November 2023	Bangladesh	M	Italy	F	EUSS status (RETD)	TCN	Set aside, remitted for rehearing	
188.	Kesmy v SSHD [2023] UKUT 006179 (IAC)	3 November 2023	Morocco	M	Belgium	F	EEA RC (APP)	TCN	Appeal dismissed	
189.	Oguntayo v SSHD [2023] UKUT 003183 (IAC)	7 November 2023	Nigeria	F	Czech Republic	M	EUSS status (APP)	TCN	Appeal dismissed	
190.	SSHD v Ahmed [2023] UKUT 004644 (IAC)	9 November 2023	Not available	M	Not available	F	Not available	SSHD	Set aside, remitted for rehearing	
191.	SSHD v Dedolli [2023] UKUT 003852 (IAC)	4 December 2023	Albania	M	Romania	F	EUSS status (APP)	SSHD	Appeal dismissed	

N	Case number	Promulgation date	Nationality of the non-EU national spouse	Gender of the non-EU national spouse	Nationality of the EU citizen spouse	Gender of the EU citizen spouse	Stage	Appellant	Outcome	Children
192.	Bamgbopa v SSHD [2023] UKUT 003260 (IAC)	6 December 2023	Nigeria	M	Slovakia	F	EUSS status (RETD)	TCN	Appeal allowed	
193.	Diallo v SSHD [2024] UKUT 002819 (IAC)	23 December 2023	Not available	F	Not available	M	Not available	TCN	Appeal dismissed	

F Female
M Male
P Pregnancy
Misc Miscarriage
MC Marriage of Convenience
EEA RC EEA Residence Card
APP Application
REV Revocation
EEA FP EEA Family Permit
EEA PRC EEA Permanent Residence Card
RETD Retained Following Divorce
ENT (REF) Entry Refusal
ECO Entry Clearance Officer
ILR Indefinite Leave to Remain
EUSS FP EU Settlement Scheme Family Permit

Bibliography

Legislation and Policy Documents

International Conventions, Treaties, Declarations

European Convention for the Protection of Human Rights and Fundamental Freedoms, CETS No.005 (04.11.1950).

International Covenant on Civil and Political Rights, 999 UNTS 171 (16.12.1966).

Treaty Establishing the European Coal and Steel Community, 261 UNTS 140 (18.04.1951).

Treaty Establishing the European Economic Community, 298 UNTS 11 (25.03.1957).

UN Convention on the Rights of the Child, 1577 UNTS 3 (20.11.1989).

European Convention on Nationality ETS No.166 (06.11.1997).

Universal Declaration of Human Rights, GA Res. 217 A (III) (10.12.1948).

Brexit-Related Instruments

Agreement between the United Kingdom of Great Britain and Northern Ireland and the Swiss Confederation on citizens' rights following the withdrawal of the United Kingdom from the European Union and the free movement of persons agreement [CS Switzerland No.5/2019].

Agreement on arrangements between Iceland, the Principality of Liechtenstein, the Kingdom of Norway and the United Kingdom of Great Britain and Northern Ireland following the withdrawal of the United Kingdom from the European Union, the EEA Agreement and other agreements applicable between the United Kingdom and the EEA EFTA States by virtue of the United Kingdom's membership of the European Union [MS No.1/2020].

Agreement on the withdrawal of the United Kingdom of Great Britain and Northern Ireland from the European Union and the European Atomic Energy Community [2019] *OJ C384/1*.

Draft text of the Agreement on the New Partnership with the United Kingdom *UKTF (2020)* 4 (18.03.2020).

Political Declaration setting out the framework for the future relationship between the European Union and the United Kingdom (TF50 (2019) 65 – Commission to EU 27).

EU

Primary Legislation

Charter of Fundamental Rights of the European Union [2000] OJ C364/01 (EUCFR).

Consolidated versions of the Treaty on European Union and the Treaty on the Functioning of the European Union [2016] OJ C202/1 (TFEU).

Treaty on European Union [1992] OJ C191/1.

Directives

Directive 2002/21/EC of the European Parliament and of the Council of 7 March 2002 on a common regulatory framework for electronic communications networks and services (Framework Directive) [2002] *OJ L108/33.*

Directive 2004/38/EC of the European Parliament and of the Council of 29 April 2004 on the right of citizens of the Union and their family members to move and reside freely within the territory of the Member States amending Regulation (EEC) No 1612/68 and repealing Directives 64/221/EEC, 68/360/EEC, 72/194/EEC, 73/148/EEC, 75/34/EEC, 75/35/EEC, 90/364/EEC, 90/365/EEC and 93/96/EEC [2004] *OJ L158/77.*

Directive 2011/36/EU of the European Parliament and of the Council of 5 April 2011 on preventing and combating trafficking in human beings and protecting its victims, and replacing Council Framework Decision 2002/629/JHA [2011] *OJ L101/1.*

Council Directive 64/221/EEC of 25 February 1964 on the co-ordination of special measures concerning the movement and residence of foreign nationals which are justified on grounds of public policy, public security or public health [1964] *OJ 56/850.*

Council Directive 68/360/EEC of 15 October 1968 on the abolition of restrictions on movement and residence within the Community for workers of Member States and their families [1968] *OJ L257/13.*

Council Directive 73/148/EEC of 21 May 1973 on the abolition of restrictions on movement and residence within the Community for nationals of Member States with regard to establishment and the provision of services [1973] *OJ L172/14.*

Council Directive 75/34/EEC of 17 December 1974 concerning the right of nationals of a Member State to remain in the territory of another Member State after having pursued therein an activity in a self-employed capacity [1970] *OJ L14/10.*

Council Directive 90/364/EEC of 28 June 1990 on the right of residence [1990] *OJ L180/26.*

Council Directive 90/365/EEC of 28 June 1990 on the right of residence for employees and self-employed persons who have ceased their occupational activity [1990] *OJ L180/28.*

Council Directive 93/96/EEC of 29 October 1993 on the right of residence for students [1993] *OJ L317/59.*

Council Directive 2003/86/EC of 22 September 2003 on the right to family reunification [2003] *OJ L251/12.*

Council Directive 2003/109/EC of 25 November 2003 concerning the status of third-country nationals who are long-term residents [2004] *OJ L16/44.*

Regulations

Regulation (EEC) No 1251/70 of the Commission of 29 June 1970 on the right of workers to remain in the territory of a Member State after having been employed in that State [1970] *OJ L142/24.*

Regulation (EEC) No 1612/68 of the Council of 15 October 1968 on freedom of movement for workers within the Community [1968] *OJ L257/2*.
Regulation 15/61 [1961] *JO 1073/61*.
Regulation 38/64 [1964] *JO 965/64*.

Commission Documents

Commission, 'Amended proposal for a Directive of the European Parliament and of the Council on the right of citizens of the Union and their family members to move and reside freely within the territory of the Member States' COM(2003) 199 final.
Commission, 'Communication from the Commission to the European Parliament and the Council on guidance for better transposition and application of Directive 2004/38/EC on the right of citizens of the Union and their family members to move and reside freely within the territory of the Member States', COM(2009) 313 final.
Commission, 'Draft minutes of the Meeting of the Group of Experts from Member States on Problems of Practical Application of Directive 2004/38/EC' (Meeting held on 22.09.2008).
Commission, 'Draft Minutes of the Sixteenth Meeting of Experts on the Right to Free Movement of Persons (Directive 2004/38/EC)' (Meeting held on 25.03.2013).
Commission, 'Employment and Social Developments in Europe 2011' (DG EMPL 2012).
Commission, 'Final minutes of the fifteenth meeting of experts on the right to free movement of persons (Directive 2004/38/EC)' (Meeting held on 05.02.2013).
Commission, 'Free movement of EU citizens and their families: Five actions to make a difference' (Communication) COM(2013) 837 final.
Commission, 'Meeting of the expert group FREEMO on the right to free movement of persons (Directive 2004/38 EC)' (Meeting held on 21.10.2016).
Commission, 'Minutes. Hybrid Meeting of the expert group on the right to free movement of persons (FREEMO) (Directive 2004/38/EC)' (Meeting held on 13.12. 2023).
Commission, 'Minutes. Virtual Meeting of the expert group on the right to free movement of persons (FREEMO) (Directive 2004/38/EC)'. Free movement and implementation of the Citizens' Rights Part of the Withdrawal Agreement' (Meeting held on 24.11.2021).
Commission, 'Proposal for a Council Directive on the right to family reunification' COM (1999) 638.
Commission, 'Proposal for a European Parliament and Council Directive on the right of citizens of the Union and their family members to move and reside freely within the territory of the Member States' COM (2001) 257 final.
Commission, 'Report from the Commission to the European Parliament and the Council on the application of Directive 2004/38/EC on the right of citizens of the Union and their family members to move and reside freely within the territory of the Member States' COM(2008) 840 final.

Commission, 'Second report on the progress made in the fight against trafficking in human beings (2018) as required under Article 20 of Directive 2011/36/EU on preventing and combating trafficking in human beings and protecting its victims', COM(2018) 777 final.

Commission, 'Staff Working Document – Handbook on addressing the issue of alleged marriages of convenience between EU citizens and non-EU nationals in the context of EU law on free movement of EU citizens' SWD(2014) 284 final.

Council Documents

Council, Document 12923/08 (Presse 250, 25.09.1986).

Council Resolution of 4 December 1997 on measures to be adopted on the combating of marriages of convenience [1997] *OJ C382/1*.

Council, 'Common Position (EC) No 6/2004 of 5 December 2003 adopted by the Council, acting in accordance with the procedure referred to in Article 251 of the Treaty establishing the European Community, with a view to adopting a directive of the European Parliament and of the Council on the right of citizens of the Union and their family members to move and reside freely within the territory of the Member States amending Regulation (EEC) No 1612/68 and repealing Directives 64/221/EEC, 68/360/EEC, 72/194/EEC, 73/148/EEC, 75/34/EEC, 75/35/EEC, 90/364/EEC, 90/365/EEC and 93/96/EEC' [2004] *OJ C54E/12*.

Council, Document 16325/1/08 REV 1 (Presse 344, 27–28.11.2008).

Council, Document 9650/12 (10.05.2012).

Council, Document 10316/13 (31.05.2013).

Council, Document 17395/13 (04.12.2013).

Council, Document 17342/13 (Presse 534, 05.-06.12.2013).

Council, Document EUCO 4/16 (02.02.2016).

Council, Document EUCO 1/16 (19.02.2016).

Council, Document 381/16 (24.06.2016).

Parliament Documents

Parliament, 'Free Movement of Persons in the European Union: Specific Issues' (Working document, 05–1999) (PE 167.028, 1999).

Parliament, 'Working Document on institutional and legal implications of the use of 'soft law' instruments' (PE 384.581v02-00, 14.02.2007).

Parliament, 'Obstacles to the right of free movement and residence for EU citizens and their families: Country report for the United Kingdom' (PE 556.967, 2016).

Parliament, 'Resolution of 4 September 2007 on institutional and legal implications of the use of 'soft law' instruments (2007/2028(INI))' [2008] *OJ C187 E/75*.

Parliament, 'Resolution of 2 April 2009 on the application of Directive 2004/38/EC on the right of citizens of the Union and their family members to move and reside freely within the territory of the Member States (2008/2184(INI))' [2010] *OJ C137 E/02*.

Other EU Documents

Europol, 'Marriages of Convenience: A link between facilitation of illegal migration and THB' (Early Warning Notification 2014/8, March 2014).
Explanations relating to the Charter of Fundamental Rights [2007] *OJ C303/17*.
Letter from David Cameron to Donald Tusk (10.11.2015) <https://assets.publishing.service.gov.uk/government/uploads/system/uploads/attachment_data/file/475679/Donald_Tusk_letter.pdf> accessed 9 April 2024.
Letter from the Ministers of the Interior of Austria, Germany, the Netherlands and the UK to the Irish Presidency (April 2013) <http://docs.dpaq.de/3604-130415_letter_to_presidency_final_1_2.pdf> accessed 9 April 2024.

UK

Primary Legislation

Anti-Social Behaviour, Crime and Policing Act 2014.
Asylum and Immigration (Treatment of Claimants, etc.) Act 2004.
Borders, Citizenship and Immigration Act 2009.
British Nationality Act 1948.
Child Support Act 1991.
Children (Northern Ireland) Order 1995, N.I.2 1995/755.
Commonwealth Immigrants Act 1962.
Criminal Law Act 1977.
European Union (Withdrawal Agreement) Act 2020.
European Union (Withdrawal) Act 2018.
Human Rights Act 1998.
Immigration Act 1971.
Immigration Act 2014 and Explanatory Notes.
Immigration Act 2016.
Immigration and Asylum Act 1999.
Income Tax Act 2007.
Inheritance (Provision for Family and Dependants) Act 1975.
Law Reform (Parent and Child) (Scotland) Act 1986.
Marriage (Northern Ireland) Order 2003.
Marriage (Scotland) Act 1977.
Marriage Act 1949.
Matrimonial Causes (Northern Ireland) Order 1978.
Matrimonial Causes Act 1973.
Modern Slavery Act 2015.

Nationality, Immigration and Asylum Act 2002.

Other Legal Instruments

Asylum and Immigration (Treatment of Claimants, etc.) Act 2004 (Remedial) Order 201, SI 2011/1158.
Citizens' Rights (Restrictions of Rights of Entry and Residence) (EU Exit) Regulations 2020, SI 2020/1210.
Home Office, 'Criminal Investigations: Sham Marriage' (Version 2.0, 12 November 2019).
Home Office, 'EEA Decisions on Grounds of Public Policy and Public Security' (Version 3.0, 14 December 2017).
Home Office, 'EEA Family Permits: Guidance for Entry Clearance Officers' (Version 2.0, 12 March 2017).
Home Office, 'Enforcement Visits' (Version 3.0, 22 December 2020).
Home Office, 'EU Settlement Scheme Appeals: Certification in National Security and Deportation Cases' (Version 2.0, 17 August 2022).
Home Office, 'EU Settlement Scheme: EU, Other EEA and Swiss Citizens and Their Family Members' (Version 23.0, 4 April 2024).
Home Office, 'Free Movement Rights: Direct Family Members of European Economic Area (EEA) Nationals' (Version 9.0, 21 February 2020).
Home Office, 'Free Movement Rights: Extended Family Members of EEA Nationals' (Version 7.0, 27 March 2019).
Home Office, 'Judicial Reviews and Injunctions' (Version 20.0, 10 October 2019).
Home Office, 'Marriage and Civil Partnership Referral and Investigation Scheme: Statutory Guidance for Home Office Staff' (March 2015).
Home Office, 'Marriage and Civil Partnership Referral and Investigation Scheme: Statutory Guidance for Home Office Staff' (Version 3.0, 23 June 2023).
Home Office, 'Marriage Investigations' (Version 3.0, 13 February 2019).
Home Office, 'Marriage Investigations' (Version 8.0, 22 June 2023).
Home Office, 'Marriage/Civil Partnership' (Detention Services Order 06/2015, Version 1.1, April 2016).
Home Office, 'MRAU Guidance' (Version 1.1).
Home Office, 'Prevention and Detection of Offences', (16.01.2017).
Home Office, 'Processes and Procedures for EEA Documentation Applications' (Version 8.0, 14 February 2019).
Home Office, 'Rights of Appeal,' (Version 8.0, 31 January 2020).
Home Office, 'Suitability: Sham Marriage or Civil Partnership' (Version 2.0, 10 November 2021).
Immigration (Citizens' Rights Appeals) (EU Exit) Regulations 2020, SI 2020/61.
Immigration (European Economic Area) Order 1994, SI 1994/1895.
Immigration (European Economic Area) Regulations 2006, SI 2006/1003.

Immigration (European Economic Area) Regulations 2016, SI 2016/1052.
Immigration (Procedure for Marriage) Regulations 2005, SI 2005/15.
Immigration and Nationality (Requirements for Naturalisation and Fees) (Amendment) Regulations 2018, SI 2018/618.
Immigration and Social Security Co-ordination (EU Withdrawal) Act 2020 (Consequential, Saving, Transitional and Transitory Provisions) (EU Exit) Regulations 2020, SI 2020/1309.
Immigration Directorate Instructions (February 2005).
Immigration Directorate Instructions (July 2012).
Immigration Rules (11.04.2024).
Immigration Rules (25.02.2016).
Proposed Marriages and Civil Partnerships (Conduct of Investigations, etc.) Regulations 2015 (Proposed Marriages Regulations), SI 2015/397.
Proposed Marriages and Civil Partnerships (Meaning of Exempt Persons and Notice) Regulations 2015, SI 2015/122.
Reporting of Suspicious Marriages and Registration of Marriages (Miscellaneous Amendments) Regulations 2000, SI 2000/3164.
Statement of Changes to the Immigration Rules HC 1496 (17 July 2023).
Statement of Changes to the Immigration Rules HC 194 (June 2012).
Statement of Changes to the Immigration Rules HC 538 (March 2003).

Policy Documents

'Asylum Statistics' (House of Commons Library Briefing Paper SN01403, 01.03.2024) <https://commonslibrary.parliament.uk/research-briefings/sn01403/> accessed 9 April 2024.
Explanatory Memorandum to the Immigration (Procedure for Marriage) Regulations 2005.
Home Affairs Committee, 'Immigration Control' (HC 2005–06, 775–I).
Home Office, 'Borders Immigration Citizenship Systems: Equality Impact Assessment'. Available at <https://www.whatdotheyknow.com/request/sham_marriages_8/response/1693677/attach/3/61422%20Maxwell%20Annex%20C%20Redacted.pdf?cookie_passthrough=1> accessed 15 April 2024.
Home Office, 'Control of Immigration: Statistics. United Kingdom 2009' (Home Office Statistical Bulletin 15/10, August 2010) <https://assets.publishing.service.gov.uk/government/uploads/system/uploads/attachment_data/file/116016/hosb1510.pdf> accessed 11 April 2024.
Home Office, 'Net Migration Measures – Further Detail' (Factsheet on net Migration Measures, 21.12.2023) <https://www.gov.uk/government/news/fact-sheet-on-net-migration-measures-further-detail> accessed 13 April 2024.

Home Office, 'Overarching Equality Impact Assessment of the Compliant Environment' (09.02.2023), <https://assets.publishing.service.gov.uk/media/63e5311ed3bf7f05bdd3091a/FINAL_Overarching_CE_EIA_.pdf> accessed 12 April 2024.

Home Office, 'Overarching Impact Assessment – Immigration Bill' (HO0097, 14.10.2013).

Home Office, 'Secure Borders, Safe Haven: Integration with Diversity in Modern Britain' (Cm 5387, 2002).

Home Office, 'Sham Marriages and Civil Partnerships: Background Information and Proposed Referral and Investigation Scheme' (November 2013).

Home Office, 'Tackling Sham Marriage: Impact Assessment' (HO0090, 11.09.2013).

Home Office, 'Why do People Come to the UK? (4) For Family Reasons' (Immigration Statistics, year ending December 2018, 28.02.2019) <https://www.gov.uk/government/publications/immigration-statistics-year-ending-december-2018/why-do-people-come-to-the-uk-4-for-family-reasons> accessed 12 April 2024.

Home Office, 'Why do People Come to the UK? (4) For Family Reasons' (Immigration Statistics, year ending December 2021, 24.02.2022) <https://www.gov.uk/government/statistics/immigration-statistics-year-ending-december-2021/why-do-people-come-to-the-uk-for-family-reasons> accessed 12 April 2024.

Letter from UK Minister for Immigration Damian Green to the Chair of the Human Rights Joint Committee (21.12.2010) <https://publications.parliament.uk/pa/jt201011/jtselect/jtrights/111/11110.htm> accessed 11 April 2024.

McKinney CJ, Gower M and Sturge G, 'The UK's New Points-Based Immigration System' (House of Commons Library Research Briefing CBP-8911, 27.09.2022) <https://researchbriefings.files.parliament.uk/documents/CBP-8911/CBP-8911.pdf> accessed 13 April 2024.

Select Committee on European Scrutiny, Thirty-first Report of Session 2013–14 (2013–14, HC 83-XXVIII).

Select Committee on European Scrutiny, Thirty-fourth Report of Session 2007–08 (2007–08, HC 16-XXX).

'Windrush Generation' (House of Commons Library Debate Pack CDP-2018-0111, 01.05.2018) <https://researchbriefings.files.parliament.uk/documents/CDP-2018-0111/CDP-2018-0111.pdf> accessed 12 April 2024.

Hansard

HC Deb 12 July 2004, vol 423, col 1225.

HC Deb 13 May 2004, vol 421, cols 563–64.

HL Deb 6 July 2004, vol 663, col 725.

HC Deb 13 February 2014, col 764W.

Denmark

Ægteskabsloven (Formation and Dissolution of Marriage Act).

Ireland

Civil Registration (Amendment) Act 2014.
Civil Registration Act 2004.
Criminal Law (Human Trafficking) Act 2008.
Domestic Violence Act 2018.

Latvia

Civilstāvokļa aktu reģistrācijas likums (Law On Registration of Civil Status Documents).
Krimināllikums (Criminal Law).

The Netherlands

Burgerlijk Wetboek (Civil Code).

Books, Articles, Reports, Opinions

Abrams K, 'Immigration Law and the Regulation of Marriage' (2007) 91 *Minnesota Law Review* 1625.

Abrams K, 'Marriage Fraud' (2012) 100 *California Law Review* 1.

Ancite-Jepifánova A (published under Jolkina A), 'CJEU, Judgment of 25 July 2008, *Metock*: Subsequent Developments in Denmark, Ireland, and the UK' [2021] (6–7) *Asiel & Migrantenrecht* 338.

Andone C and Greco S, 'Evading the Burden of Proof in European Union Soft Law Instruments: The Case of Commission Recommendations' (2018) 31 *International Journal for the Semiotics of Law* 79.

Andrikopoulos A, 'Love, Money and Papers in the Affective Circuits of Cross-Border Marriages: Beyond the "Sham"/"Genuine" Dichotomy' (2019) *Journal of Ethnic and Migration Studies.*

Arnull A, 'What is a General Principle of EU Law?' in Rita de la Feria and Stefan Vogenauer (eds), *Prohibition of Abuse of Law: A New General Principle of EU Law?* (Hart 2011).

Bade K, *Migration in European History* (Blackwell 2003).

Barrett G, 'Family Matters: European Community Law and Third-Country Family Members' (2003) 40 *Common Market Law Review* 369.

Berneri C, 'Marriages of Convenience: The Limitations of the UK legislation' (2015) 29 *Journal of Immigration, Asylum and Nationality Law* 372.

Berneri C, 'Protection of Families Composed by EU citizens and Third-Country Nationals: Some Suggestions to Tackle Reverse Discrimination' (2014) 16 *European Journal of Migration and Law* 249.

Berneri C, *Family Reunification in the EU* (Hart 2017).

Block L, 'Regulating Membership: Explaining Restriction and Stratification of Family Migration in Europe' (2015) 36 *Journal of Family Issues* 1433.

Block L, *Policy Frames on Spousal Migration in Germany* (Springer 2016).

Bonjour S and Block L, 'Ethnicizing Citizenship, Questioning Membership. Explaining the Decreasing Family Migration Rights of Citizens in Europe' (2016) 20 *Citizenship Studies* 779.

Bonjour S and de Hart B, 'A Proper Wife, a Proper Marriage: Constructions of "Us" and "Them" in Dutch Family Migration Policy' (2013) 20 *European Journal of Women's Studies* 61.

Carl N, Dennison J and Evans G, 'European but not European enough: An Explanation for Brexit' (2019) 20 *European Union Politics* 282.

Carlier J-Y, 'Case C-200/02, *Kunqian Catherine Zhu, Man Lavette Chen v. Secretary of State for the Home Department*' (2005) 42 *Common Market Law Review* 1121.

Carver N, '"For her Protection and Benefit": The Regulation of Marriage-Related Migration to the UK' (2016) 39 *Ethnic and Racial Studies* 2758.

Carver N, 'Displaying Genuineness: Cultural Translation in the Drafting of Marriage Narratives for Immigration Applications and Appeals' (2014) 3 *Families, Relationships and Societies* 271.

Charsley K and Benson M, 'Marriages of Convenience and Inconvenient Marriages: Regulating Spousal Migration to Britain' (2012) 26 *Journal of Immigration, Asylum and Nationality Law* 10.

Charsley K and Wray H, 'Kept Apart: Routine Family Separation in the UK Family Immigration System as Times of Crises' (2023) 11 *Migration Studies* 380.

Choudhry S, 'Article 9 – Right to Marry and Right to Found a Family' in Steve Peers and others (eds), *The EU Charter of Fundamental Rights: A Commentary* (Hart/Beck 2014).

Costello C, 'Citizenship of the Union: Above Abuse?' in Rita de la Feria and Stefan Vogenauer (eds), *Prohibition of Abuse of Law: A New General Principle of EU Law?* (Hart 2011).

Coutts S, 'Expulsion and Article 20 TFEU: Some Practical and Conceptual Issues' (2021) 23 *European Journal of Migration and Law* 29.

Cuibus M, 'EU Migration to and from the UK' (*Migration Observatory: COMPAS, University of Oxford* 20.11.2023) <https://migrationobservatory.ox.ac.uk/wp-content/uploads/2020/10/MigObs-Briefing-EU-migration-to-and-from-the-UK.pdf> accessed 13 April 2024.

D'Aoust A-M, 'A Moral Economy of Suspicion: Love and Marriage Migration Management Practices in the United Kingdom' (2018) 36 *Environment and Planning D: Society and Space* 40.

D'Aoust A-M, 'In the Name of Love: Marriage Migration, Governmentality, and Technologies of Love' (2013) 7 *International Political Sociology* 258.

de Hart B, 'Introduction: The Marriage of Convenience in European Immigration Law' (2006) 8 *European Journal of Migration and Law* 251.

de Hart B, 'The Europeanization of Love. The Marriage of Convenience in European Migration Law' (2017) 19 *European Journal of Migration and Law* 281.

De la Feria R, 'Introducing the Principle of Prohibition of Abuse of Law' in Rita de la Feria and Stefan Vogenauer (eds), *Prohibition of Abuse of Law: A New General Principle of EU Law?* (Hart 2011).

De la Feria R, 'Prohibition of Abuse of (Community) Law: The Creation of a New General Principle of EC Law through Tax' (2008) 45 *Common Market Law Review* 395.

Demetriou D, 'Discourse on Immigration in the UK: Representations and Evaluations of Romanians and Bulgarians as "Benefit Tourists"' (Dphil Thesis, Canterbury Christ Church University 2018).

Desmond A, 'The Private Life of Family Matters: Curtailing Human Rights Protection for Migrants under Article 8 of the ECHR?' (2018) 29 *European Journal of International Law* 261.

Di Filippo M, 'Can EU Free Movement Rights be Abused? Critical Remarks on the "Marriages of Convenience Clause"' in Antonio Marcello Calamia (ed) *L'Abuso del Diritto* (G. Giappichelli Editore, 2017).

Digruber D and Messinger I, 'Marriage of Residence in Austria' (2006) 8 *European Journal of Migration and Law* 281.

Dougan M, 'Some Comments on the Idea of a General Principle of Union Law Prohibiting Abuses of Law in the Field of Free Movement for Union Citizens' in Rita de la Feria and Stefan Vogenauer (eds), *Prohibition of Abuse of Law: A New General Principle of EU Law?* (Hart 2011).

Dummett A and Nicol A, *Subjects, Citizens, Aliens and Others* (Wiedenfeld and Nicholson 1990).

Duvell F, Cherti M and Lapshyna I, 'Does Immigration Enforcement Matter? Irregular Migration and Control Policies in the UK' (Final Report, Centre on Migration, Policy and Society, University of Oxford, October 2018).

Eggebø H, 'A Real Marriage? Applying for Marriage Migration to Norway' (2013) 39 *Journal of Ethnic and Migration Studies* 773.

Eliantonio M and Stefan O, 'Soft Law Before the European Courts: Discovering a "Common Pattern"?' (2018) 37 *Yearbook of European Law* 457.

EMN, 'Family Reunification with Third-Country National Sponsors in Belgium' (July 2017), 12 <https://emnbelgium.be/sites/default/files/publications/Final%20BE%20report%20on%20family%20reunification%20of%20TCN_%20July%202017.pdf> accessed 8 April 2024.

Eurojust, 'Report on National Legislation and Eurojust Casework Analysis on Sham Marriages' (January 2024).

Europol, 'Trafficking in Human Beings in the EU' (Document No: 765175, February 2016).

Farmer P, 'Prohibition of Abuse of (European) Law: The Creation of a New General Principle of EU Law through Tax: A Response' in Rita de la Feria and Stefan Vogenauer (eds), *Prohibition of Abuse of Law: A New General Principle of EU Law?* (Hart 2011).

Fernhout R, Groenendijk K and Minderhoud P, 'Report on the Free Movement of Workers in the Netherlands in 2006' (Nijmegen: Centre for Migration Law, 2007).

Fihel A and others, 'Free Movement of Workers and Transitional Arrangements: Lessons from the 2004 and 2007 Enlargements' (Centre of Migration Research, University of Warsaw 2015).

Foblets M-C and Vanheule D, 'Marriages of Convenience in Belgium: The Punitive Approach Gains Ground in Migration Law' (2006) 8 *European Journal of Migration and Law* 263.

Griffiths M, '"My Passport is Just My Way Out of Here". Mixed-Immigration Status Families, Immigration Enforcement and the Citizenship Implications' (2019) *Identities*.

Groenendijk K, 'Beschränkung der Freizügigkeit von Unionsbürgern?' in Klaus Barwig, Stephan Beichel-Benedetti and Gisbert Brinkmann (eds), *Freiheit* (Schriften zum Migrationsrecht 15, Nomos 2014) 56.

Groenendijk K, 'Brexit: Free movement of Union citizens and the Rights of Third-Country Nationals under Threat?' in Carolus Grütters, Sandra Mantu and Paul Minderhoud (eds), *Migration on the Move* (Brill 2017).

Groenendijk K, 'Lessen van Metock in Nederland en elders in de EU' [2021] (6–7) *Asiel & Migrantenrecht* 344.

Groenendijk K, 'Recent Developments in EU Law on Migration: The Legislative Patchwork and the Court's Approach' (2014) 16 *European Journal of Migration and Law* 313.

Groenendijk K, 'Reverse Discrimination, Family Reunification and Union Citizens of Immigrant Origin' in Elspeth Guild, Cristina Gortázar Rotaeche and Dora Kostakopoulou (eds) *The Reconceptualization of European Union Citizenship* (Brill 2014).

Groenendijk K, and Fernhout R and others, 'Draft Report on the Free Movement of Workers in The Netherlands in 2005' (Nijmegen: Centre for Migration Law, 2006).

Groenendijk K, and Fernhout R, 'Vrij Verkeer, Europa-Route en Omgekeerde Discriminatie: Wie Houdt Wie voor de Gek?' [2010] (1) *Asiel & Migrantenrecht* 4.

Guild E, 'EU Citizens, Foreign Family Members and European Union Law' (2019) 21 *European Journal of Migration and Law* 358.

Guild E, 'Free Movement of EU Citizens and Their Family Members' (2016) 7 *New Journal of European Criminal Law* 231.

Guild E, *Brexit and its Consequences for UK and EU Citizenship or Monstrous Citizenship* (Brill 2016).

Guild E, Peers S and Tomkin J, *The EU Citizenship Directive: A Commentary* (2nd edn, Oxford University Press 2019).

Hansen R, *Citizenship and Immigration in Postwar Britain: The Institutional Origins of a Multicultural Nation* (Oxford University Press 2000).

Hobolt S B, 'The Brexit Vote: a Divided Nation, a Divided Continent' (2016) 23 *Journal of European Public Policy* 1259.

ICIBI, 'A Short Notice Inspection of a Sham Marriage Enforcement Operation: 14–24 October 2013' (January 2014).

ICIBI, 'The Implementation of the 2014 "Hostile Environment" Provisions for Tackling Sham Marriage. August to September 2016' (December 2016).

ICIBI, 'The Rights of European Citizens and their Spouses to Come to the UK: Inspecting the Application Process and the Tackling of Abuse. October 2013 – January 2014' (June 2014).

Infantino F, 'Bordering "Fake" Marriages? The Everyday Practices of Control at the Consulates of Belgium, France and Italy in Casablanca' (2014) 1 *Etnografia e ricerca qualitativa* 27.

Joyce C, *Misuse of the Right to Family Reunification: Ireland. EMN Focussed Study 1* (The Economic and Social Research Institute 2012).

Kalmijn M, 'Intermarriage and Homogamy: Causes, Patterns, Trends' (1998) 24 *Annual Review of Sociology* 395.

Kjellgren A, 'On the Border of Abuse – The Jurisprudence of the European Court of Justice on Circumvention, Fraud and Other Misuses of Community Law' (2000) 11 *European Business Law Review* 179.

Klaassen M, 'Between Facts and Norms: Testing Compliance with Article 8 ECHR in Immigration Cases' (2019) 37 *Netherlands Quarterly of Human Rights* 157.

Kochenov D and Plender R, 'EU Citizenship: From an Incipient Form to an Incipient Substance? The Discovery of the Treaty Text' (2012) 37 *European Law Review* 369.

Kochenov D, 'A Real European Citizenship: A New Jurisdiction Test: A Novel Chapter in the Development of the Union in Europe' (2011) 18 *Columbia Journal of European Law* 56.

Kochenov D, 'Ius Tractum of Many Faces: European Citizenship and the Difficult Relationship between Status and Rights' (2009) 15 *Columbia Journal of European Law* 169.

Kochenov D, 'The Essence of EU Citizenship Emerging from the Last Ten Years of Academic Debate: Beyond the Cherry Blossoms and the Moon?' (2013) 62 *International and Comparative Law Quarterly* 97.

Kofman E, 'Family-Related Migration: A Critical Review of European Studies' (2004) 30 *Journal of Ethnic and Migration Studies* 243.

Korkea-aho E, 'National Courts and European Soft Law: Is *Grimaldi* Still Good Law?' (2018) 37 *Yearbook of European Law* 470.

Kostakopoulou D, 'Nested "Old" and "New" Citizenships in the European Union: Bringing out the Complexity' (1999) 5 *Columbia Journal of European Law* 389.

Kostakopoulou D, 'When EU Citizens Become Foreigners' (2014) 20 *European Law Journal* 447.

Kostakopoulou D, *Citizenship, Identity and Immigration in the European Union* (Manchester University Press 2001).

Kraler A, 'Civic Stratification, Gender and Family Migration Policies in Europe' (International Centre for Migration and Policy Development 2010).

Kroeze H and Van Elsuwege P, 'Revisiting Ruiz Zambrano: A Never Ending Story?' (2021) 23 *European Journal of Migration and Law* 1.

Lafleur J-M and Mescoli E, 'Creating Undocumented EU Migrants through Welfare: A Conceptualization of Undeserving and Precarious Citizenship' (2018) 52 *Sociology* 480.

Lansbergen A, 'Testing the Limits of European Citizenship' (The Federal Trust for Education and Research, *European Policy Brief*, May 2009).

Lyal R, '*Cadbury Schweppes* and Abuse: Comments' in Rita de la Feria and Stefan Vogenauer (eds), *Prohibition of Abuse of Law: A New General Principle of EU Law?* (Hart 2011).

MacDonald I, and Toal R, *Macdonald's Immigration Law and Practice* (9th edn, Butterworth 2014).

MacDonald I, *Immigration Law and Practice in the United Kingdom* (1st edn, Butterworth 1983).

MacDonald I, *Immigration Law and Practice in the United Kingdom* (2nd edn, Butterworth 1987).

Mantu S, 'Alternative Views on EU Citizenship' in Carolus Grütters, Sandra Mantu and Paul Minderhoud (eds), *Migration on the Move* (Brill 2017).

Marrington D, 'Legal Decisions Affecting Ethnic Minorities and Discrimination – No.24' (1985) 12 *New Community* 536.

Maskens M, 'Bordering Intimacy: The Fight against Marriages of Convenience in Brussels' (2015) 33(2) *The Cambridge Journal of Anthropology* 42.

McGlynn C, *Families and the European Union* (Cambridge University Press 2006).

Messinger I, 'There is Something about Marrying … The Case of Human Rights vs. Migration Regimes using the Example of Austria' (2013) 2 *Laws*, 376 <https://ideas.repec.org/a/gam/jlawss/v2y2013i4p376-391d29258.html> accessed 2 April 2024.

Messinger I, *Schein oder nicht Schein*: *Konstruktion und Kriminalisierung von 'Scheinehen' in Geschichte und Gegenwart* (Mandelbaum 2012).

Mühleisen W, Røthing Å and Svendsen S H B, 'Norwegian Sexualities: Assimilation and Exclusion in Norwegian Immigration Policy' (2012) 15 *Sexualities* 139.

Nehring D and Sealey C, 'Intimate Citizenship and the Tightening of Migration Controls in the United Kingdom' (2020) 54 *Social Policy & Administration* 427.

Neveu Kringelbach H, '"Mixed Marriage", Citizenship and the Policing of Intimacy in Contemporary France' (2013) University of Oxford: International Migration Institute Working Paper No 77 <www.migrationinstitute.org/publications/wp-77-13> accessed 29 July 2020.

Oosterom-Staples H, 'The Triangular Relationship Between Nationality, EU Citizenship and Migration in EU Law: A Tale of Competing Competences' (2018) 65 *Netherlands International Law Review* 431.

Oosterom-Staples H, 'To What Extent Has Reverse Discrimination Been Reversed?' (2012) 14 *European Journal of Migration and Law* 151.

Partos R and Bale T, 'Immigration and Asylum Policy under Cameron's Conservatives' (2015) 10 *British Politics* 169.

Peers S, 'Free Movement, Immigration Control and Constitutional Conflict' (2009) 5 *European Constitutional Law Review* 173.

Pellander S, '"An Acceptable Marriage": Marriage Migration and Moral Gatekeeping in Finland' (2015) 36 *Journal of Family Issues* 1472.

Pellander S, 'Buy Me Love: Entanglements of Citizenship, Income and Emotions in Regulating Marriage Migration' (2019) *Journal of Ethnic and Migration Studies*.

Pendry E and Dowling S (eds), *Misuse of the Right to Family Reunification: Marriages of Convenience and False Declarations of Parenthood* (Home Office 2012).

Perkins R and Neumayer E, 'Do Membership Benefits Buy Regulatory Compliance? An Empirical Analysis of EU Directives 1978–99' (2007) 8 *European Union Politics* 180.

Pilgram L, 'Tackling "Sham Marriages": The Rationale, Impact and Limitations of the Home Office's "Certificate of Approval" Scheme' (2009) 23 *Journal of Immigration, Asylum and Nationality Law* 24.

Pine L, *Nazi Family Policy 1933–1945* (Berg Publishers 1997).

Pobjoy J M, *The Child in International Refugee Law* (Cambridge University Press 2017).

Poiares Maduro M, 'The scope of European Remedies: The Case of Purely Internal Situations and Reverse Discrimination' in Claire Kilpatrick, Tonia Novitz and Paul Skidmore (eds), *The Future of Remedies in Europe* (Hart 2000).

Probert R and Pywell S, 'Love in the Time of Covid-19: A Case-Study of the Complex Laws Governing Weddings' (2021) 41 *Legal Studies* 676.

Sachdeva S, *The Primary Purpose Rule in British Immigration Law* (Trentham Books Ltd 1993).

Schlitz C, 'Akrich: A Clear Delimitation without Limits' (2005) 12 *Maastricht Journal of European and Comparative Law* 241.

Scott J, 'In Legal Limbo: Post-Legislative Guidance as a Challenge for European Administrative Law' (2011) 48 *Common Market Law Review* 329.

Senden L, 'Soft Post-Legislative Rulemaking: A Time for More Stringent Control' (2013) 19 *European Law Journal* 57.

Senden L, *Soft Law in European Community Law* (Hart 2004).

Shaw J, 'EU Citizenship: Still a Fundamental Status?' in Rainer Bauböck (ed) *Debating EU Citizenship* (Springer 2019).

Shuibhne N N, 'Free Movement of Persons and the Wholly Internal Rule: Time to Move On?' (2002) 39 *Common Market Law Review* 731.

Smith E, 'From the Aliens Act to the "Hostile Environment": The Making of the British Border Control System' in Kahina Le Louvier and Karen Latricia Hough (eds), *UK Borderscapes: Sites of Enforcement and Resistance* (Routledge 2024).

Snyder F, 'The Effectiveness of European Community Law: Institutions, Processes, Tools and Techniques' (1993) 56 *The Modern Law Review* 19.

Solanke I, 'Using the Citizen to Bring the Refugee In: *Gerardo Ruiz Zambrano v Office national de l'emploi* (ONEM)' (2012) 75 *The Modern Law Review* 101.

Solano G and Huddleston T, 'Migrant Integration Policy Index 2020' (CIDOB and MPG).

Sørensen K E, 'Abuse of Rights in Community Law: A Principle of Substance or Merely Rhetoric?' (2006) 43 *Common Market Law Review* 423.

Sørensen K E, 'What is a General Principle of EU Law? A Response' in Rita de la Feria and Stefan Vogenauer (eds), *Prohibition of Abuse of Law: A New General Principle of EU Law?* (Hart 2011).

Sparke M, 'Everywhere But Always Somewhere: Critical Geographies of the Global South' (2007) 1 *The Global South* 117.

Spaventa E, 'Case C-109/01, Secretary of State for the Home Department v. H. Akrich.' (2005) 42 *Common Market Law Review* 225.

Spaventa E, 'Comments on Abuse of Law and the Free Movement of Workers' in Rita de la Feria and Stefan Vogenauer (eds), *Prohibition of Abuse of Law: A New General Principle of EU Law?* (Hart 2011).

Spaventa E, 'Family Rights for Circular Migrants and Frontier Workers: O and B, and S and G.' (2015) 52 *Common Market Law Review* 753.

Staver AB and Eggebø H, 'Everything but the Marriage Certificate: Unmarried Partners in Norwegian Immigration Regulation' (2023) 30 *Social Politics: International Studies in Gender, State & Society* 1018.

Stefan O and others, 'EU Soft Law in the EU Legal Order: A Literature Review' (2019) King's College London Law School Research Paper (forthcoming), 5–8. <https://papers.ssrn.com/sol3/papers.cfm?abstract_id=3346629> accessed 8 August 2020.

Stefan O, 'European Competition Soft Law in European Courts: A Matter of Hard Principles?' (2008) 14 *European Law Journal* 753.

Stefan O, 'European Union Soft Law: New Developments Concerning the Divide Between Legally Binding Force and Legal Effects' (2012) 75 *The Modern Law Review* 881.

Stefan O, 'Helping Loose Ends Meet? The Judicial Acknowledgment of Soft Law as a Tool of Multi-Level Governance' (2014) 21 *Maastricht Journal of European and Comparative Law* 359.

Stefan O, 'Hybridity before the Court: A Hard Look at Soft Law in the EU Competition and State Aid Case Law' (2012) 37 *European Law Review* 49.

Strydom H, 'The Theory of Citizenship: A Reappraisal' (1985) 18 *The Comparative and International Law Journal of Southern Africa* 103.

Šūpule I, 'Human Trafficking and Sham Marriages in Latvia' in Minna Viuhko and others (eds), *Exploitative Sham Marriages: Exploring the Links Between Human Trafficking and Sham Marriages in Estonia, Ireland, Latvia, Lithuania and Slovakia* (Publication Series No. 82, HEUNI 2016).

Terpan F, 'Soft Law in the European Union – The Changing Nature of EU Law' (2015) 21 *European Law Journal* 68.

Toner H, *Partnership Rights, Free Movement, and EU Law* (Hart 2014).

Tryfonidou A, 'Mary Carpenter v Secretary of State for the Home Department: The Beginning of a New Era in the European Union?' (2003) 14 *King's Law Journal* 81.

Tryfonidou A, *Reverse Discrimination in EC law* (Kluwer 2009).

van den Brink M, 'Is It Time to Abolish the Substance of EU Citizenship Rights Test?' (2021) 23 *European Journal of Migration and Law* 13.

Van der Sloot B, 'Between Fact and Fiction: An Analysis of the Case-Law on Article 12 of the European Convention on Human Rights' (2014) 26 *Child and Family Law* 397.

van Eijken H, 'Connecting the Dots Backwards, What Did Ruiz Zambrano Mean for EU Citizenship and Fundamental Rights in EU Law?' (2021) 23 *European Journal of Migration and Law* 48.

Vandenbroucke M, 'Legal-Discursive Constructions of Genuine Cross-Border Love in Belgian Marriage Fraud Investigations' (2020) 17 *Critical Discourse Studies* 175.

Viuhko M, Lietonen A and Jokinen A, 'Happily Ever After? From Sham Marriages to Human Trafficking' in Minna Viuhko and others (eds), *Exploitative Sham Marriages: Exploring the Links Between Human Trafficking and Sham Marriages in Estonia, Ireland, Latvia, Lithuania and Slovakia* (Publication Series No. 82, HEUNI 2016).

Von Bogdandy A, Felix Arndt and Jürgen Bast, 'Legal Instruments in European Union Law and their Reform: a Systematic Approach on an Empirical Basis' (2004) 23 *Yearbook of European Law* 91.

Walter A, *Reverse Discrimination and Family Reunification* (Wolf Legal Publishers 2008).

Weber D, 'Abuse of Law –European Court of Justice, 14 December 2000 – Case C-110/99, *Emsland-Stärke*' (2004) *Legal Issues of Economic Integration* 43.

Wemyss G, Yuval-Davis N and Cassidy K, 'Beauty and the Beast': Everyday Bordering and "Sham Marriage" Discourse' (2018) 66 *Political Geography* 151.

Wollenschläger F, 'New Fundamental Freedom Beyond Market Integration: Union Citizenship and its Dynamics for Shifting the Economic Paradigm of European Integration' (2011) 17 *European Law Journal* 1.

Wray H, '"A Thing Apart": Controlling Male Family Migration to the UK' (2015) 18 *Men and Masculinities* 424.

Wray H, 'An Ideal Husband? Marriages of Convenience, Moral Gate-keeping and Immigration to the UK' (2006) 8 *European Journal of Migration and Law* 303.

Wray H, 'Regulating Spousal Migration in Denmark' (2013) 27 *Journal of Immigration, Asylum and Nationality Law* 139.

Wray H, 'The "Pure" Relationship, Sham Marriages and Immigration Control' in Joanna Miles, Perveez Mody and Rebecca Probert (eds) *Marriage Rites and Rights* (Hart 2015).

Wray H, Agoston A and Hutton J, 'A Family Resemblance? The Regulation of Marriage Migration in Europe' (2013) 16 *European Journal of Migration and Law* 209.

Wray H, Agoston A, Hutton J, Kofman E and Simic A, 'Subversive Citizens: Using EU Free Movement Law to Bypass the UK's Rules on Marriage Migration' (2019) *Journal of Ethnic and Migration Studies*.

Wray H, *Article 8 ECHR, Family Reunification and the UK's Supreme Court* (Hart 2023).

Wray H, *Regulating Marriage Migration into the UK: A Stranger in the Home* (Ashgate 2011).

Ziegler K S, '"Abuse of Law" in the Context of the Free Movement of Workers' in Rita de la Feria and Stefan Vogenauer (eds), *Prohibition of Abuse of Law: A New General Principle of EU Law?* (Hart 2011).

Jurisprudence

CJEU

115/78 *Knoors* [1979] ECR 00399.

149/73 *Witt* [1973] ECR 01587.

186/87 *Cowan* [1989] ECR 00195

267/83 *Diatta* [1985] ECR 00567.

286/82 and 26/83 *Luisi and Carbone* [1984] ECR 00377.

293/83 *Gravier* [1985] ECR 00593.

30–77 *Bouchereau* [1977] ECR 01999.

33–74 *Van Binsbergen* [1974] ECR 01299.

35/82 and 36/82 *Morson and Jhanjan* [1982] ECR 03723.

36–75 *Rutili* [1975] ECR 01219.

41–74 *Van Duyn* [1974] ECR 01337.

53/81 *Levin* [1982] ECR 01035.

59/85 *Reed* [1986] ECR 01283.

C-109/01 *Akrich* [2003] ECR I-09607.

C-110/99 *Emsland-Stärke* [2000] ECR I-11569.

C-127/08 *Metock and Others* [2008] ECR I-06241.
C-145/09 *Tsakouridis* [2010] ECR I-11979.
C-148/02 *Garcia Avello* [2003] ECR I-11613.
C-148/13 to C-150/13 *A, B and C* ECLI:EU:C:2014:2406.
C-148/91 Veronica [1993] ECR I-00487.
C-16/16 *Belgium v Commission* ECLI:EU:C:2018:794.
C-192/99 *Kaur* [2001] ECR I-01237.
C-193/16 E ECLI:EU:C:2017:542.
C-196/04 *Cadbury Schweppes* [2006] ECR I-07995.
C-200/02 *Zhu* and *Chen* [2004] ECR I-09925.
C-202/13 *McCarthy* ECLI:EU:C:2014:2450.
C-212/97 *Centros* [1999] ECR I-1459.
C-226/94 *Grand Garage Albigeois* [1996] ECR I-00651.
C-23/93 *TV10* [1994] ECR I-4795.
C-244/13 *Ogieriakhi* ECLI:EU:C:2014:2068.
C-255/02 *Halifax* [2006] ECR I-01609.
C-256/11 *Dereci and Others* [2011] ECR I-11315.
C-258/14 *Florescu and Others* ECLI:EU:C:2017:448.
C-28/15 *Koninklijke* ECLI:EU:C:2016:692.
C-285/95 *Kol* [1997] ECR I-03069
C-291/05 *Eind* [2007] ECR I-10719.
C-304/14 *CS* ECLI:EU:C:2016:674.
C-308/11 *Chemische Fabrik Kreussler* (*CFK*) ECLI:EU:C:2012:548.
C-321/05 *Kofoed* [2007] ECR I-05795.
C-322/88 *Grimaldi* [1989] ECR 04407.
C-326/11 *J.J. Komen en Zonen Beheer Heerhugowaard* ECLI:EU:C:2012:461.
C-331/16 and C-366/16 K and HF ECLI:EU:C:2018:296.
C-34/09 *Ruiz Zambrano* [2011] ECR I-01177.
C-348/09 *P.I* ECLI:EU:C:2012:300.
C-356/11 and C-357/11 *O and S* ECLI:EU:C:2012:776.
C-356/15, *Commission v Belgium* ECLI:EU:C:2018:555.
C-359/16 *Altun and Others* ECLI:EU:C:2018:63.
C-360/09 *Pfleiderer* [2011] ECR I-05161.
C-362/88 *GB-INNO-BM* [1990] ECR I-00667.
C-364/10 *Hungary v Slovakia* ECLI:EU:C:2012:630.
C-369/90 *Micheletti and Others* [1992] ECR I-04239.
C-370/90 *Surinder Singh* [1992] ECR I-04265.
C-38/02 *Collins* [2004] ECR I-02703.
C-40/11 *Iida* ECLI:EU:C:2012:691.
C-400/10 *PPU* [2010] ECR I-08965.

C-410/13, *'Baltlanta' UAB* ECLI:EU:C:2014:2134.
C-45/12 *Hadj Ahmed* ECLI:EU:C:2013:390.
C-451/19 and C-532/19 *Subdelegación del Gobierno en Toledo* ECLI:EU:C:2022:354.
C-456/12 *O and B* ECLI:EU:C:2014:135.
C-457/12 *S and G* ECLI:EU:C:2014:136.
C-459/99 *MRAX* [2002] ECR I-06591.
C-46/12 *L. N.* ECLI:EU:C:2016:674.
C-473/16, *F* ECLI:EU:C:2018:36.
C-490/20 *V.M.A. v Stolichna obshtina, rayon 'Pancharevo'* ECLI:EU:C:2021:1008.
C-50/06 *Commission* v *Netherlands* [2007] ECR I-04383.
C-504/10 *Tanoarch* [2011] ECR I-10853.
C-557/17 *Y.Z. and Others* ECLI:EU:C:2019:203.
C-578/08 *Chakroun* [2010] ECR I-01839.
C-60/00 *Carpenter* [2002] ECR I-06279.
C-61/89 Bouchoucha [1990] ECR I-03551.
C-63/99 *Gloszczuk* [2001] ECR I-06369.
C-64/96 and C-65/96 *Uecker and Jacquet* [1997] ECR I-03171.
C-653/11 *HMRC v Paul Newey* ECLI:EU:C:2013:409.
C-82/16 *K.A. and Others* ECLI:EU:C:2018:308.
C-83/11 *Rahman and Others* [2012] ECLI:EU:C:2012:519.
C-836/18 *Subdelegación del Gobierno en Ciudad Real* ECLI:EU:C:2020:119.
C-86/12 *Alokpa* ECLI:EU:C:2013:645.
C-87/12 *Ymeraga* ECLI:EU:C:2013:291.
C-92/09 and C-93/09 *Volker und Markus Schecke GbR and Hartmut Eifert* [2010] ECR I-11063.

ECtHR

A v United Kingdom (1982) 5 EHRR 296 (Commission Decision).
Abdulaziz, Cabales and Balkandali v United Kingdom (1985) 7 EHRR 471.
Al-Nashif v Bulgaria (2003) 36 EHRR 37.
App No 10914/84 v Netherlands (1986) 8 EHRR 308 (Commission Decision).
Benes v Austria App no 18643/91 (Commission Decision, 06.01.1992).
Berrehab v Netherlands (1988) 11 EHRR 322.
Boujlifa v France (2000) 30 EHRR 419.
Frasik v Poland App No 22933/02 (ECtHR, 5 January 2010).
Gül v Switzerland (1996) 22 EHRR 93.
Jaremowicz v Poland App no 24023/03 (ECtHR, 5 January 2010).
Jeunesse v Netherlands (2014) 60 EHRR 17.
Keegan v Ireland (1994) 18 EHRR 342.
Klip & Krüger v Netherlands (1997) 91 A-DR 66.

Kroon and Others v Netherlands (1995) 19 EHRR 263.
Marckx v Belgium (1979) 2 EHRR 330.
Moustaquim v Belgium (1991) 13 EHRR 802.
Nunez v. Norway (2011) 58 EHRR 17.
Nylund v. Finland App no 27110/95 (ECtHR, 29.06.1999).
O'Donoghue and Others v United Kingdom (2011) 53 EHRR 1.
Rodrigues da Silva v Netherlands (2007) 44 EHRR 34.
Sanders v France (1996) 87 B-DR 160.
Schembri v Malta App no 66297/13 (ECtHR, 19.09.2017).
Sisojeva v Latvia (*2006*) 43 EHRR 33.
Slivenko v Latvia (2004) 39 EHRR 24.
Vallianatos and Others v. Greece (2014) 59 EHRR 12.

UK Courts

A U v SSHD [2017] UKUT 00052 (IAC).
Abdelmotaleb v SSHD [2023] UKUT 01177 (IAC).
Abouelhasaan v SSHD [2019] UKUT 04931 (IAC).
Adi v SSHD [2019] UKUT 09432 (IAC).
Adnan v SSHD [2017] UKUT 25601 (IAC).
Agho v SSHD [2015] EWCA Civ 1198, [2016] INLR 411.
Ahmed v SSHD [2019] UKUT 01401 (IAC).
Ahmed, R (On the Application Of) v SSHD [2016] EWCA Civ 303, [2016] Imm AR 869.
Ahmed, R (On the Application Of) v SSHD IJR [2015] UKUT 436 (IAC).
Ait-Rabah, R (on the application of) v SSHD [2016] EWHC 1099 (Admin).
Alex [A] v SSHD [2018] UKUT 04343 (IAC).
Andrushkiv v SSHD [2020] UKUT 07859 (IAC).
Aroyehun v SSHD [2022] UKUT 05977 (IAC).
Arshad v SSHD [2019] UKUT 04911 (IAC).
Asghar v SSHD [2019] UKUT 07181 (IAC).
Awuku v SSHD [2017] EWCA Civ 178.
Azam v SSHD [2019] UKUT 04634 (IAC).
Aziz v SSHD [2017] UKUT 01427 (IAC).
Baiai and Others, R (On the Application Of) v SSHD [2006] EWHC 823 (Admin).
Baiai and Others, R (On the Application Of) v SSHD [2008] UKHL 53.
Baro v SSHD [2022] UKUT 03464 (IAC).
[B S] v SSHD [2017] UKUT 16879 (IAC).
Celik (EU exit; marriage; human rights) [2022] UKUT 00220 (IAC).
Collins [E] v SSHD [2019] UKUT 01818 (IAC).
Cunningham v SSHD [2020] UKUT 06579 (IAC).
Dauti v SSHD [2023] UKUT 11747(IAC).

De Vera v SSHD [2017] UKUT 07000 (IAC).
De Zoysa Siriwardana Nanediri v SSHD [2019] UKUT 04892 (IAC).
Dhensa v SSHD [2020] UKUT 01197 (IAC).
DS (Afghanistan) v SSHD [2011] EWCA Civ 305, [2011] INLR 389.
Entry Clearance Officer v Yuliia [Z] [2019] UKUT 01734.
Faisal v SSHD [2017] UKUT 00817 (IAC).
Gjana v SSHD [2019] UKUT 07850 (IAC).
Gjura v SSHD [2019] UKUT 07856 (IAC).
Gureckis, R (On the Application Of) v SSHD [2017] EWHC 3298, [2017] WLR(D) 840.
Habib v SSHD [2018] UKUT 06534 (IAC).
Hajdari v SSHD [2022] UKUT 03750 (IAC).
Igwe v SSHD [2016] UKUT 27335 (IAC).
Iqbal v SSHD [2016] UKUT 09279 (IAC).
IS (marriages of convenience) Serbia [2008] UKAIT 00031.
Isufaj (PTA decisions/reasons; EEA reg. 37 appeals) [2019] UKUT 00283 (IAC).
Jamil v SSHD [2017] UKUT 33121 (IAC).
Joint Council for the Welfare of Immigrants, R (On the Application Of) v SSHD [2019] EWHC 452 (Admin), [2019] 4 All ER 527.
Josephine [O] v SSHD [2019] UKUT 05252 (IAC).
K A W (Pakistan) v SSHD [2021] UKUT 01859 (IAC).
K v SSHD [2017] UKUT 29770 (IAC).
Khan v SSHD [2019] UKUT 03191 (IAC).
Khan v SSHD [2022] UKUT 06826 (IAC).
Khan v SSHD [2023] UKUT 001516 (IAC).
Khan v SSHD [2023] UKUT 11835 (IAC).
Laizane v SSHD [2019] UKUT 17910 (IAC).
Letitia [G] v SSHD [2020] UKUT 00458 (IAC).
Lulzime [C] and [RM] [2019] UKUT 03329 (IAC).
Mahmood v SSHD [2018] UKUT 02903 (IAC).
Mahmood v SSHD [2023] UKUT 001447 (IAC).
Marquez v SSHD [2018] UKUT 00705 (IAC).
Mazhar v SSHD [2017] UKUT 14102 (IAC).
Miah v SSHD [2016] UKUT 21503 (IAC).
Mirush [K] v SSHD [2020] UKUT 07293 (IAC).
Mohamud v SSHD [2022] UKUT 03758 (IAC).
Molina, R (On the Application Of) v SSHD [2017] EWHC 1730 (Admin).
Mubashar v SSHD [2017] UKUT 00171 (IAC).
Muhammad [M] v SSHD [2019] UKUT 07160 (IAC).
Nakanwagi v Entry Clearance Officer, Pretoria [2021] UKUT 01779 (IAC).
Nasreen v SSHD [2018] UKUT 25249 (IAC).

Ninsinghkhon v Entry Clearance Officer, Bangkok [2018] UKUT 08937 (IAC).
NS v MI [2006] EWHC 1646 (Fam), [2006] Fam Law 839.
Ogbewi v SSHD [2017] UKUT 03381 (IAC).
Onwusakah v SSHD [2016] UKUT 14926 (IAC).
Papajorgji (*EEA spouse – marriage of convenience*) *Greece* [2012] UKUT 38 (IAC).
Public Law Project v The Information Commissioner [2023] UKFTT 102 (GRC).
Qevani v SSHD [2023] UKUT 15774 (IAC).
Radwan v Radwan (*No 2*) [1973] Fam 35, [1972] 3 All ER 1026.
Raja v SSHD [2018] UKUT 35032 (IAC).
Rajah [*A*] *v SSHD* [2018] UKUT 08581 (IAC).
Raqueeb v SSHD [2018] UKUT 01754 (IAC).
Raqueeb v SSHD [2018] UKUT 01754 (IAC).
Raza v SSHD [2019] UKUT 03566 (IAC).
Raza v SSHD [2020] UKUT 00542 (IAC).
Rehman v SSHD [2016] UKUT 16713 (IAC).
Resul [*M*] *v SSHD* [2019] UKUT 07602 (IAC).
Rosa v SSHD [2016] EWCA Civ 14, [2016] WLR(D) 6.
Rovillos v SSHD [2017] UKUT 01821 (IAC).
Sadovska and another v SSHD [2017] UKSC 54, [2017] WLR(D) 556.
Saeed v SSHD [2017] UKUT 09715 (IAC).
Seferi & Anor, R (*On the Application Of*) *v SSHD* [2018] EWHC 287 (Admin).
Shakeel v SSHD [2022] UKUT 13405 (IAC).
Sidhu v SSHD [2019] UKUT 07915 (IAC).
Sokoya v SSHD [2019] UKUT 07559 (IAC).
Sonde v SSHD [2017] UKUT 32338 (IAC).
SSHD v Abdeaziz [2023] UKUT 006527 (IAC).
SSHD v Baiai & Others [2007] EWCA Civ 478.
SSHD v Beshiri [2023] UKUT 15942 (IAC).
SSHD v Consolacion [2023] UKUT 13871 (IAC).
SSHD v Gjini [2023] UKUT 11846 (IAC).
SSHD v Gjoni [2023] UKUT 13239 (IAC).
SSHD v Hasmuca [2023] UKUT 14985 (IAC).
SSHD v Hysenaj [2022] UKUT 13962 (IAC).
SSHD v Kashif [2016] UKUT 19663 (IAC).
SSHD v Lekeate [2019] UKUT 08363 (IAC).
SSHD v Meta [2022] UKUT 12192 (IAC).
SSHD v Michael [*O*] [2018] UKUT 02107 (IAC).
SSHD v Nketia [2022] UKUT 04841 (IAC).
SSHD v Okofor [2016] UKUT 42725 (IAC).
SSHD v Sam [2022] UKUT 10691 (IAC).
Tandel v SSHD [2019] UKUT 05031 (IAC).

Tariq v SSHD [2020] UKUT 01252 (IAC).
Uddin v SSHD [2017] UKUT 27273 (IAC).
Ul Abidin v Entry Clearance Officer, Islamabad [2022] UKUT 12501 (IAC).
Usiobaifo v SSHD [2021] UKUT 02875 (IAC).
Ussenbai v Entry Clearance Officer [2019] UKUT 00472 (IAC).
Vervaeke v Smith [1983] 1 AC 145 (HL).
Virk v SSHD [2018] UKUT 19843 (IAC).
Wambui v SSHD [2021] UKUT 06884 (IAC).
Waseem v SSHD [2020] UKUT 07454 (IAC).
Woguia v SSHD [2019] UKUT 12057 (IAC).
Yeya v SSHD [2018] UKUT 00515 (IAC).
ZA *(Reg 9. EEA Regs; abuse of rights) Afghanistan* [2019] UKUT 281 (IAC).
ZH *(Afghanistan) v SSHD* [2009] EWCA Civ 1060.
ZH *(Tanzania) v SSHD* [2011] UKSC 4, [2011] 2 AC 166.
Zubair v SSHD [2023] UKUT 00918 (IAC).

Online Material

Blog Posts

Cambien N, 'Cases C-456/12 O. and B. and C-457/12 S. and G.: Clarifying the Inter-State Requirement for EU Citizens?' (*European Law Blog*, 11.04.2014) <https://europeanlawblog.eu/2014/04/11/cases-c-45612-o-and-b-and-c-45712-s-and-g-clarifying-the-inter-state-requirement-for-eu-citizens/> accessed 8 April 2024.

Elgot J, 'Warning Home Office Could Be Raiding Genuine Weddings in Sham Marriage Panic' (*Huffington Post*, 24.07.2014) <https://www.huffingtonpost.co.uk/2014/07/23/sham-marriage-home-office_n_5614057.html> accessed 11 April 2024.

Gbikpi N, 'Who Qualifies as a "Durable Partner" under the EU Settlement Scheme?' (*Free Movement*, 18.08.2023) <https://freemovement.org.uk/who-qualifies-as-a-durable-partner-under-the-eu-settlement-scheme/> accessed 13 April 2024.

Guild E, 'Reflecting EU Law Faithfully? R (Bilal Ahmed) v SSHD IJR [2015] UKUT 00436 (IAC)' (*Free Movement*, 14.09.2015) <https://www.freemovement.org.uk/reflecting-eu-law-faithfully-r-bilal-ahmed-v-sshd-ijr-2015-ukut-00436-iac/> accessed 12 April 2024.

Kazim T, 'Home Office Refuses to Explain Secret Sham Marriage Algorithm' (*Free Movement*, 21.07.2021) <https://freemovement.org.uk/home-office-refuses-to-disclose-inner-workings-of-sham-marriage-algorithm/> accessed 15 April 2024.

Peers S, 'The Withdrawal Agreement Act: Implementing the Brexit Withdrawal Agreement in the UK' (*EU Law Analysis*, 17.02.2020) <http://eulawanalysis.blogspot.com/2020/02/the-withdrawal-agreement-act.html> accessed 13 April 2024.

Yeo C, 'Minister Misleads on Sham Marriage Numbers' (*Free Movement*, 16.12.2014) <https://www.freemovement.org.uk/minister-misleads-sham-marriages-numbers-statistics-1300/> accessed 12 April 2024.

Websites, Press, Press Releases and Political Statements

Barton J, 'Thousands of Couples Face "Humiliating" Home Office Sham Marriage Checks' (openDemocracy, 12.07.2023) <https://www.opendemocracy.net/en/home-office-immigration-sham-marriage-hostile-environment/> accessed 15 April 2024.

'David Cameron's EU Speech – Full Text' (*Guardian*, 23.01.2013) <https://www.theguardian.com/politics/2013/jan/23/david-cameron-eu-speech-referendum> accessed 9 April 2024.

Duncan C, 'Man Refused UK Visa to Visit Newborn Grandson Because He Did Not Send Photo of 1975 Wedding' (*The Independent*, 14.09.2018) <https://www.independent.co.uk/news/uk/home-news/uk-visa-wedding-photo-russian-grandson-refused-home-office-marriage-eea-family-permit-a8537946.html> accessed 12 April 2024.

Eurostat, 'GDP Per Capita in the EU in 2013: Seven Capital Regions Among the Ten Most Prosperous' (News release 90/2015, 21.05.2015) <https://ec.europa.eu/eurostat/documents/2995521/6839731/1-21052015-AP-EN.pdf/c3f5f43b-397c-40fd-a0a4-7e68e3bea8cd> accessed 9 April 2024.

Gardham D, 'Tough Rules Expose Scale of Bogus Marriages' (*The Telegraph*, 16.05.2005) <https://www.telegraph.co.uk/news/uknews/1490071/Tough-rules-expose-scale-of-bogus-marriages.html> accessed 11 April 2024.

'Government Announces Major Changes to Legal Immigration, Raising Minimum Skilled Worker Salary and Income Requirement for Spouse Visa to Over £38K' (*EIN*, 04.12.2023) <https://www.ein.org.uk/news/government-announces-major-changes-work-related-immigration-raising-minimum-skilled-worker> accessed 13 April 2024.

'How Many British Citizens Live in the EU?' (*UK in a Changing Europe*, 21.09.2020) <https://ukandeu.ac.uk/the-facts/how-many-british-citizens-live-in-the-eu/> accessed 13 April 2024.

'Initial Evidence Indicates a Sharp Drop in the Number of Marriages After New Rules Came into Force Last February' (*Migration News Sheet*, June 2005).

'Invitation to Join the Government of Britain: The Conservative Manifesto 2010' <https://conservativehome.blogs.com/files/conservative-manifesto-2010.pdf> accessed 11 April 2024.

'Ireland Addresses Sham Marriages – Significant Amendments to the Civil Registration Act of Ireland' (*Cilvektirdzniecibа.lv*, 15.04.2016) <http://www.cilvektirdzniecibа.lv/en/ireland-addresses-sham-marriages-%E2%80%93-significant-amendments-to-the-civil-registration-act-of-ireland> accessed 9 April 2024.

Kuci L, 'Scapegoating: UK Immigration Policy Rests on Villifying Albanians' (*BIRN*, 15.02.2023) <https://balkaninsight.com/2023/02/15/scapegoating-uk-immigration-policy-rests-on-villifying-albanians/> accessed 15 April 2024.

Leonard M, 'Shaping Europe's Present and Future' (*European Council of Foreign Relations*, 11.01.2019) <www.ecfr.eu/article/commentary_shaping_europes_present_and_future> accessed 2 April 2024.

'MiCLU: Hostile Environment Towards Albanian Asylum Seekers Poses Alarming Risk to Their Mental Health and Wellbeing' (*EIN*, 04.01.2024) <https://www.ein.org.uk/news/miclu-hostile-environment-towards-albanian-asylum-seekers-poses-alarming-risk-their-mental> accessed 15 April 2024.

'New Guidelines on "Sham Marriages" Introduced' (*TheJournal.ie*, 09.10.2010) <https://www.thejournal.ie/new-guidelines-on-sham-marriages-introduced-32919-Oct2010/> accessed 9 April 2024.

'"One in Five Marriages is Bogus"' (*BBC*, 10.06.2004) <http://news.bbc.co.uk/2/hi/uk_news/england/london/3794379.stm> accessed 11 April 2024.

Oakeshott I, 'One in Five Weddings May be Migrant Fraud' (*Evening Standard*, 10.06.2004). <https://www.standard.co.uk/news/one-in-five-weddings-may-be-migrant-fraud-6983676.html> accessed 11 April 2024.

Poole S, '"Compliant Environment": Is This Really What the Windrush Generation Needs?' (*The Guardian*, 03.05.2018) <https://www.theguardian.com/books/2018/may/03/compliant-environment-is-this-really-what-the-windrush-generation-needs> accessed 12 April 2024.

'Sham Marriages Leading to Abuses of EU Freedom of Movement Rights' (*Inis*, 09.06.2011) <https://merrionstreet.ie/en/category-index/sham-marriages-leading-to-abuses-of-eu-freedom-of-movement-rights.39421.shortcut.html> accessed 9 April 2024.

'Strong Leadership. A Clear Economic Plan. A Brighter, More Secure Future. The Conservative Party Manifesto 2015' <http://ucrel.lancs.ac.uk/wmatrix/ukmanifestos2015/localpdf/Conservatives.pdf> accessed 11 April 2024.

Taylor D and Perraudin F, 'Couples Face "Insulting" Checks in Sham Marriage Crackdown' (*The Guardian*, 14.04.2019) <https://www.theguardian.com/uk-news/2019/apr/14/couples-sham-marriage-crackdown-hostile-environment> accessed 12 April 2024.

UKVI, 'Application for a document certifying permanent residence or permanent residence card under the EEA Regulations' (EEA(PR), Version 03/2019).

UKVI, 'Application for a registration certificate or residence card as the family member of a European Economic Area (EEA) or Swiss national' (EEA(FM), Version 03/2019).

UKVI, 'EEA(FM): Guidance Notes' (Version 4.0, February 2020).

United Nations, 'End of Mission Statement of the Special Rapporteur on Contemporary Forms of Racism, Racial Discrimination, Xenophobia and Related Intolerance at the

Conclusion of Her Mission to the United Kingdom of Great Britain and Northern Ireland' (07.10.2019) <https://www.ohchr.org/EN/NewsEvents/Pages/DisplayNews.aspx?NewsID=23073&LangID=E> accessed 12 April 2024.

'Windrush: Corbyn Says PM Ignored Immigration Policy Warnings' (*BBC*, 22.04.2018) <http://www.bbc.co.uk/news/uk-politics-43857089> accessed 12 April 2024.

Wright R, 'Crackdown on Sham Marriages Leaves Migrants in Limbo' (*Financial Times*, 09.09.2018) <https://www.ft.com/content/3a724c10-ac47-11e8-94bd-cba20d67390c> accessed 12 April 2024.

Other Sources

Home Office response to a PLP FOI request (ref. 61422, 22.06.2021). Available at <https://www.whatdotheyknow.com/request/sham_marriages_8/response/1818059/attach/3/IR%2061422%20Jack%20Maxwell%20final%20response.pdf> accessed 15 April 2024.

ILPA, 'Comments for the Chief Inspector of Borders and Immigration. Review of Sham Marriages' (31.08.2016).

ILPA letter to Lord McIntosh (15.07.1994).

Latvian Embassy to Ireland, 'Fiktīvās Laulības – Cilvēktirdzniecības Forma' ('Fictitious Marriages as a Form of Human Trafficking') (Presentation to the Latvian Parliament, 12–13.06.2012).

Minutes of the ILPA European Group Meeting (15.09.1993).

'My Big Fat Fake Wedding' (BBC One, Panorama, 24.03.2011).

'Paul Connolly Investigates: Ireland's Sham Marriages' (TV3 Ireland, 2011).

Pro forma of a letter, sent by the Home Office to couples who are being referred for further investigation. Available at <https://www.whatdotheyknow.com/request/sham_marriage_triage_scheme/response/2143185/attach/4/71986%20Leslie%20Annex%20B.pdf> accessed 15 April 2024.

'The Sham Marriage Racket: How to Buy Your Way into Britain' (ITV, Exposure, 02.07.2015).

'The Sham Wedding Crashers' (Channel Five, 30.10.2014).

Index

Abuse of rights in EU law
  Doctrine of abuse of rights 36–39
  'U-turn' arrangements 36–37, 47–52
  in the area of free movement of
    persons 39, 49–56, 59–60, 62–64
  and marriages of convenience 35–36,
    62–64, 70–89, 97–123
African countries 73, 132, 155–156, 158, 161,
    224, 232, 235, 266, 273
Albania 169, 220–222, 224, 232, 235, 250–
    252, 273
Asylum seekers 54–55, 73, 137, 138, 148, 150,
    176, 220

Bogus marriage. *See* Marriage of convenience
Brexit
  European Union (Withdrawal Agreement)
    Act 10 198, 199, 201, 214, 234, 275
  EU Settlement Scheme (EUSS) 10, 197,
    199–209, 211–215, 234, 237, 275–277,
    285–287
  EUSS family permit 181, 202–203, 210,
    234, 240
  EU-UK Withdrawal Agreement 8, 10,
    14, 196, 198–209, 213–215, 233–234, 262,
    265, 272, 275–276
  Family members of EU citizens in the UK
    post-Brexit 201–206, 275–276
  Marriage controls post-Brexit 207–
    215, 277
  Pre-referendum EU-UK settlement 10,
    66, 86–90, 204–206, 207, 268
Bulgaria 83, 220, 225, 235

Central and Eastern Europe 2, 5, 75–83, 85,
    86, 89, 117, 156, 158, 224, 232, 235, 266–
    267, 274
Charter of Fundamental Rights of the
    European Union (EUCFR) 5, 9, 26,
    109, 124, 227, 269
Children
  Convention on the Rights of the Child
    (CRC) 110, 129, 213, 229, 261
  and marriages of convenience 80–81,
    109–110, 113–114, 119, 152, 157, 213–214,
    216, 222, 226, 228–232, 235, 241, 247,
    255–264, 273
  Principle of the best interests of the
    child 34, 110, 129, 213–214, 257, 261–263
Church of England 85, 146, 148, 152, 163
'Compliant environment' policy. *See* 'Hostile
    environment' policy

Denmark 44, 66–67, 71–74, 76

Eastern Europe. *See* Central and Eastern
    Europe
EEA family permit 173, 175, 177, 178, 180–184,
    187, 188, 196, 203, 227, 234, 274
EEA Regulations
  2006 149, 154, 191, 255, 258
  2016 149, 159, 165, 175, 177, 178–180, 182,
    186–189, 191–193, 200–201, 208–209,
    211, 213–215, 231, 234, 237, 246–247,
    249–252, 254–264, 271–272, 275–276,
    282, 285–287
EEA residence card 27, 54–56, 104, 156–157,
    171, 174–176, 177, 178, 184–190, 193, 196,
    201–203, 225, 227, 234, 245, 248, 257,
    260, 274, 282
European Convention on Human Rights
    (ECHR) 7, 9, 26, 74, 109, 152, 262,
    269–270, 272
  Article 8 (right to respect for private and
    family life) 5, 14, 57, 59, 109, 124–131,
    134, 137–138, 145, 174, 204, 261–262
  Article 12 (right to marry and to found a
    family) 5, 14, 109, 124–134, 151, 166,
    170, 196
  and immigration control 128–131
  and marriages of convenience 131–138
EU soft law
  Concept 92–95
  and marriages of convenience
    Commission Guidelines for the
      application of the Citizenship
      Directive 9, 38, 62, 75, 91, 97–98,
      105–106, 108, 111, 236, 238, 247, 263
    Commission Handbook addressing
      the issue of marriages of

EU soft law (*Cont.*)
convenience 10, 83, 85–86, 91, 97–123, 124, 129, 134, 136, 165–166, 208, 223, 227, 236–238, 246–248, 252–253, 257, 261, 263, 267, 270–272, 274, 275, 285–287
Legal effects 95–96

Family reunion under the Citizenship Directive
Akrich/'prior lawful residence rule' 26, 49–51, 53–54, 58–59, 62, 71, 73, 75, 88, 90, 112–114, 154, 204, 266, 268
Definition of family members 29–30
Direct family members 29–30, 59, 104, 138, 177, 181, 183, 187
Family formation in the host Member State 53–55
Married couples 30–32
Metock
Case 23, 35, 45, 51, 53–55, 63, 65, 66, 75–76, 83, 88–90, 91, 112, 113, 137, 154, 204–205, 265–267, 276
Reactions to *Metock* 70–74
Origins 25–29
Primary carers 59–60
Returning Member State nationals/ *Surinder Singh* route 42, 47–52, 57, 62–64, 72, 73, 75, 76, 88, 89, 154–155, 205
Reverse discrimination 36, 42–46, 74, 141, 154, 266
Substance of marriage 46–47
Static EU citizens 60–61
Visas 55–56
Family reunification rules and policies (national)
General observations 42–44
UK
Certificate of Approval scheme 132–133, 141, 147–152, 153, 158, 161–162, 236
History 142–144
Marriage visitor or fiancé(e) visa 147, 158, 163, 270
Minimum income requirement 153–154, 158, 202, 204, 206, 215, 276, 282
'No-switching rule' 154, 206, 215, 276
'Primary purpose rule' 70, 141, 144–146, 158, 179
Forced marriage 43, 77–79, 85, 101, 117
Fraud 11, 35–36, 38–39, 49, 56, 83–85, 87–88, 97, 115–116, 207, 238, 249
FREEMO working group 9, 73, 76
Free movement of persons
Development 20–23
Residence rights 23–25
Derogations from free movement rights
Public policy, public security and public health 32–34
Abuse of rights 35–39

'Hostile environment' policy 14, 159–164, 168, 233, 269
Hungary 85, 156, 231, 235

Immigration and Asylum Act 1999 146, 165, 171, 179, 189, 206, 209, 210–212, 231, 234, 249, 250, 251, 275, 282, 285–287
Immigration Act 2014 159–164, 165, 173
India 47, 73, 155–156, 161, 201, 205, 224, 235
Indian Subcontinent 5, 42–43, 76, 79, 82, 142, 146, 156, 158, 224, 232, 266, 273
Ireland 2, 4, 49–50, 53–55, 59–60, 64, 66, 71–74, 76–80, 82–83, 106, 132, 253, 266, 277, 285

Latvia 73, 77–79, 81, 157, 255
Lithuania 77, 156, 235, 239

Marriage of convenience
Appeals procedure 160, 173, 188–190, 193, 196, 211–213
Burden of proof 108, 112, 121, 150, 154, 182, 187, 190, 193, 208, 230–232, 235–241, 242, 243, 258–264, 267, 272
Civil registrars 79, 146, 155, 156, 158, 162–163, 270
Cohabitation 31, 44, 46–47, 65, 105–106, 113, 119–120, 122, 128, 134, 157, 166, 168, 175, 181–182, 184, 185, 187, 208, 224–226, 229–231, 235, 239, 241–246, 247, 251, 253–255, 258–259, 263, 265, 272
Criminal offences 78–79, 85, 189, 191–193, 217

Marriage of convenience (*Cont.*)
Criteria/'risk profiles' 73, 83, 98, 111–123, 162, 216–224, 228, 231, 232, 238, 244, 261, 263, 272, 282
Definition 11, 70–71, 79–80, 88, 90, 91, 98–107, 110, 121, 123, 125, 136, 146, 149, 159, 165–167, 179–180, 187–188, 195–196, 197, 206–209, 214, 215, 228–229, 235, 246–259, 263–264, 265, 268–277, 282, 285–287
Deportation/removal 33, 40, 110, 129, 136, 156, 157, 160, 171–174, 176, 188, 189–192, 195–196, 209, 210–215, 222, 228, 231, 234, 248, 251, 252, 261, 269, 270, 272–273, 277, 282
Divorce 27–28, 46–47, 68, 103, 112, 116, 167, 177, 185, 194, 234, 245, 246, 262
EU citizens in a vulnerable position 75–82, 85, 101–102, 112, 116–117, 267
'Exploitative sham marriages' 77–81
and Family law 5, 7, 9, 79, 190, 193–195, 196, 229, 260, 272
Groups perceived as suspicious 4–5, 43, 73, 76, 79, 82, 145, 155, 156, 158, 162, 224, 233, 267, 274
Home visits 161, 229–231, 242, 245
and Human trafficking/organised crime 9, 77–80, 89, 101, 106, 112, 117–118, 148, 156, 164, 192, 239, 267, 274
Investigation of marriages
Human dignity 124, 134–135, 227, 231, 269
Investigation methods 134–135, 217–232, 272
Limitations and procedural safeguards 35, 98, 107–110
'Marriages by deception'. *See* 'Unilateral sham marriages
Marriage interview 105, 149, 162, 167, 169, 170, 172–173, 180, 182, 216, 222–223, 224–229, 243, 251, 255
and Media 2, 4–5, 77, 148, 266–267
Proportionality considerations 34, 108, 133, 192, 193, 213–214, 222, 256, 261
Public policy test 32–34, 40, 191–193, 209, 211, 212–215
'Referral and investigation scheme' 14, 158, 159–177, 203, 206–207, 210, 215, 216, 227, 232, 250, 269, 274, 277, 281
Separation 46–47, 57, 102, 106–107, 137, 171, 172, 175, 176, 195, 205, 210, 213, 223, 246–247, 262, 270, 273, 27
Statistics 73, 79, 80, 81, 85, 121, 151, 155, 156, 161–162, 222, 227, 267, 274, 281–282
Stereotypes 68, 81, 82, 120–122, 238–241, 263, 267, 272, 274
'Unilateral sham marriages' 78, 80–81, 101–103, 214, 252–254, 263

Nigeria 73, 132, 155–156, 161, 224, 235

Pakistan 73, 85, 155–156, 161, 189, 224, 230, 235, 241, 255
Poland 54, 85, 156
Proxy marriage 100–102, 145, 155–156, 176, 222, 224

Romania 83, 189, 220, 235, 260

Sham marriage. *See* Marriage of Convenience
Slovakia 77, 85–86, 235
Soft law. *See* EU soft law

Printed in the United States
by Baker & Taylor Publisher Services